MERTON & HESYCHASM

"This tradition forms and affects the whole person: intellect, memory, will, emotion, body, skills [arts], all must be under the sway of the Holy Spirit."

— Thomas Merton, from the Introduction to
Lectures on Ascetical and Mystical Theology

Merton &
Hesychasm

The Prayer of the Heart

The Eastern Church

EDITED BY

Bernadette Dieker

AND

Jonathan Montaldo

Jonathan Montaldo and Gray Henry, General Editors,
The Fons Vitae Thomas Merton Series

FONS VITAE

Fons Vitae
49 Mockingbird Valley Drive
Louisville, Kentucky 40207-1366
U.S.A.
www.fonsvitae.com · fonsvitaeky@aol.com

The Fons Vitae Thomas Merton Series:
Merton & Sufism: The Untold Story, 1999
Merton & Hesychasm: The Prayer of the Heart, 2003
Merton & Judaism: Holiness in Words, 2003

Future Thomas Merton Editions:
Merton & Buddhism · *Merton & Taoism* · *Merton & Art*

Permissions for published and unpublished material for this volume can be found starting on page 505.

Front and back covers: With thanks to the Abbey of Gethsemani for the photo of the icon given to Thomas Merton for his hermitage by Marco Pallis, and to the Monastery at Mount Athos, Greece, for the photograph used.

Library of Congress Control Number: 2002102668

ISBN 1-887752-45-5

Printed in Canada.

Typesetting and design by R.G. Renzi · Louisville, Kentucky · U.S.A.

TABLE OF CONTENTS

Dedicated to
furthering
mutual respect
among the world's
sacred traditions
by sharing matters of
spiritual sustenance.

THE FONS VITAE
THOMAS MERTON SERIES

Professional theologians and lay readers, scholars and spiritual seekers in a broad spectrum of religious practice regard the Cistercian monk Thomas Merton (1915 - 1968) as one of the most important spiritual writers of the last half of the twentieth century. The writing impelled by his monastic life's interests in the world's religious traditions are recognized as a seminal and continuing catalyst for inter-religious dialogue in the twenty-first century.

Ewert Cousins, a distinguished Professor of Religion and the General Editor of the World Spirituality Series, has called Merton an "axial figure" who bridges within his own experience and theological work the contemporary estrangements between religious and secular perspectives. Dr. Cousins has publicly shared his opinion that Thomas Merton means almost more today to many than he actually did in his lifetime. He is becoming an iconic figure who models inter-religious dialogue for those who are seeking a common ground of respect for the varied ways in which human beings realize the sacred in their lives. Merton's life and writing, especially when it focuses on the contemplative practices common to the world's major religions, have indeed become a forum, or a "bridge" in Cousins' term, upon which those engaged in inter-religious dialogue can meet and engage one another.

In his reaching out to living representatives of the world's various religious traditions by correspondence, and by his immersing himself in the study of religious traditions other than his own Roman Catholicism, Merton models the inclusivity of intellect and heart necessary for fruitful inter-religious dialogue. His personal journals for April 28, 1957 witness to his zeal for a unity of learning and living as a method of personal "inner work" for ensuring communication and respect among religious persons:

> "If I can unite *in myself*, in my own spiritual life, the thought of the East and the West, of the Greek and Latin Fathers, I will create in myself a reunion of the divided Church, and from that unity in myself can come the exterior and visible unity of the Church. For, if we want to

bring together East and West, we cannot do it by imposing one upon the other. We must contain both in ourselves and transcend them both in Christ."

The Fons Vitae publishing project for the study of world religions through the lens of Thomas Merton's life and writing brings
Merton's timeless vision of all persons united in a "hidden ground
of Love" to a contemporary audience. The first volume in this
multi-volume series, *Merton & Sufism: The Untold Story*, included
essays by world-renowned scholars and practitioners of Islam's
contemplative traditions. Merton's own writing about Sufism over
various genres — essays, poetry and transcriptions of his conferences to monastic novices — were collected to indicate the depth
and range of Merton's intellectual and affective encounter with
Islam. This first volume has received critical acclaim and, more
importantly for the project, has become another catalyst for the
study of Islam's contemplative religious practices.

This second volume in the series, *Merton & Hesychasm: The
Prayer of the Heart*, gathers the scholarship, to name only few, of
Bishop Kallistos Ware, A.M. Donald Allchin, James Cutsinger,
John Eudes Bamberger, M. Basil Pennington and the new
Archbishop of Canterbury, Rowan Williams. Merton's own
writing on the Christian East collected here will provide access
for studying the centrality and importance of his encounter with
Greek and Russian Orthodoxy for his own contemplative practice
and to his discovering the universal dimensions of his own
religious faith. To those who believe the legacy of meditation
practices and methods for progress in a spiritual life is confined
mainly to Buddhist, Taoist and Hindu sources, this volume will
hopefully point toward the riches of the Christian East's
contemplative practice.

Succeeding volumes in this series will include studies on
Merton and Judaism, Merton and Taoism, Merton and Buddhism, Merton and Protestantism, and Merton and Art. We
hope that the Fons Vitae Thomas Merton Series will find a place
in the libraries of those persons who promote the study and practice of contemplative religious traditions.

— Jonathan Montaldo and Gray Henry,
General Editors for the Fons Vitae Thomas Merton Series

FOREWORD

MERTON AND HESYCHASM

The Greeks say that interior silence is not perfect unless it is centered upon the name of Jesus. For they do not love silence for its own sake. Silence for its own sake is only death. Love silence for the sake of the Word. . . .
— Thomas Merton, *Entering the Silence*

Merton & Hesychasm: The Prayer of the Heart is presented in three sections. Part I, "Hesychasm: The Gift of Eastern Christianity to Spiritual Practice," is an introduction to *hesychasm* in the language and practice of the Eastern Orthodox Churches. Here the reader will find descriptions of the *hesychast* method of prayer, the "prayer of the heart." Among other topics developed are the practices that constitute an ascetic life of spiritual struggle, the functions of a monastery and a monk's cell, and the need for a spiritual teacher, called a *staretz* in the Russian Orthodox tradition. We are assured by Bishop Kallistos Ware, however, that *hesychasm* is not the sole province of monastics who have withdrawn from the world: "The prayer of inward silence is not world-denying but world-embracing. It enables the *hesychast* to look beyond the world toward the invisible Creator; and so it enables the *hesychast* to return back to the world and see it with new eyes. To travel, as it has been often said, is to return to our point of departure and to see our home afresh as though for the first time. This is true of the journey of prayer, as of other journeys. The *hesychast*, far more than the sensualist or the materialist, can appreciate the value of each thing, because he or she sees each in God and God in each. . . . The *hesychast* denies in order to reaffirm; the *hesychast* withdraws in order to return."

Professor James Cutsinger writes of the rigorous asceticism necessary to reach the "purity of heart" to which the *hesychast* aspires. "The spiritual life," he writes, "demands real work, real movement, real discipline, which proceeds methodically and incrementally. It is dangerous, says Plato, to go too quickly from the many to the One, and the *hesychast* tradition takes account of this fact in distrusting ecstasies and consolations not grounded in method. On the other hand, one must not forget that man's climbing is not only toward God; it is in and by God. Each of the rungs of the ladder is a gift or a grace, a real and efficacious presence of the Goal in the very midst of the way. True spirituality is not Pelagian, not a self-help technique. 'Work out your salvation with fear and trembling, for *God is at work within you.*' (*Philippeans* 2:12-13)."

Part II, "Thomas Merton and Eastern Christianity" collects essays by recognized scholars of Thomas Merton and his interests in Eastern Christianity. Canon A.M. Allchin, who in particular has reflected deeply upon Merton's encounter with the thought of modern Russian theologians such as Vladimir Lossky and Paul Evdokimov, also notes Merton's interests in the early "Eastern Fathers," particularly in St. Maximus the Confessor. Like Bishop Kallistos, Canon Allchin views Merton's interest in the contemplative practice of Eastern Christianity as pointing a way for him to have greater contact with the contemporary world: "The monastic vocation may indeed involve a radical separation from the world, but it cannot involve an abandonment of the world. It is a life lived for the sake of the world. Secondly, there is the vocation to a life of prayer, worship and contemplation itself. This too must always be seen in a cosmic context. It is lived on behalf of all creation."

The essays by Abbots John Eudes Bamberger and M. Basil Pennington were culled from the volume *One Yet Two* that presented papers from a meeting of western and eastern Christians. The essay by Archbishop Rowan Williams on Merton and Paul Evdokimov was likewise first featured in this volume, and it is noted with admiration that Dr. Williams was nineteen when he produced this learned paper.

Included in Part II is Merton's long prose poem "Hagia Sophia," his moving meditation on the "feminine energies" of God. Canadian poet and scholar, Dr. Susan McCaslin, explains the poem and the role of "the feminine" in Merton's life:

In "Hagia Sophia," Merton invokes the sophianic character of Eastern Orthodoxy, anticipating later feminist reconfigurations of the divine by embracing a sense of reciprocity and unity of male and female polarities in God, the world, and the self.

Of this poem Merton wrote that "This is a very ancient intuition of reality which goes back to the oldest Oriental thought. . . . For the 'masculine-feminine' relationship is basic in all reality — simply because all reality mirrors the reality of God."

Part III, "Hesychasm in the Writing of Thomas Merton," collects Merton's own writing and teaching about the *Hesychast* tradition. It also highlights how *hesychastic* practice became a dimension of Merton's own personal appropriation of a life of prayer. Merton writes of the value of the eastern tradition for western contemplative practice. He writes of a mystical life centered on the Jesus Prayer ("Lord Jesus Christ, Son of God, have mercy on me"). The diligence and the vigor with which monks of the Eastern Orthodox tradition surrendered their lives to God in prayer affected Merton's own prayer life. "It is not so much," he wrote, "that they were exceptionally austere men, or that they had acquired great learning, but that they had surrendered themselves completely to the demands of the Gospel and to evangelical charity, totally forgetting themselves in obedience to the Spirit of God so that they lived as perfect Christians, notable above all for their humility, their meekness, their openness to all men, their apparently inexhaustible capacity for patient and compassionate love. The purpose . . . is then not so much to make use of daily spiritual direction in order to inculcate a special method of prayer, but rather to keep the heart of the disciple open to love, to prevent it from hardening in self-centered concern (whether moral, spiritual or ascetical). All the worst sins are denials and rejections of love, refusals to love. The chief aim of the *staretz* is first to teach the disciple not to sin against love, then to encourage and assist growth in love until the disciple becomes a saint."

Included in this final section is Merton's correspondence with the Russian writer Boris Pasternak, whose novel *Doctor Zhivago* deeply affected Merton. Although their correspondence was limited, Merton felt a close kinship with Pasternak. Merton appreciated Pasternak's portrait of Zhivago for his innocent, loving spirit. When Merton describes Pasternak in an article included in this section, "The Pasternak Affair," we note that Merton reflects on qualities in Pasternak that readers can identify with Merton's own work and spirit. In describing Boris Pasternak Merton perhaps delineates for us the contours of his own mirroring "kindred spirit":

"Both as a writer and as a man, Pasternak stands out as a sign of contradiction in our age of materialism, collectivism and power politics. His spiritual genius is essentially and powerfully solitary. Yet his significance does not lie precisely in this. Rather it lies in the fact that his very solitude made him capable of extraordinarily intimate and understanding contacts with men all over the face of the earth. The thing that attracted people to Pasternak was not a social or political theory, it was not a formula for the unification of mankind, not a collectivist *panacea* for all the evils in the world: it was the man himself, the truth that was in him, his simplicity, his direct contact with life, and the fact that he was full of the only revolutionary force that is capable of producing anything new: he is full of love."

May our work in editing this volume be of benefit to its readers.

— Bernadette Dieker and Jonathan Montaldo
December 10, 2002

Constantinople, mid-sixth century.

PART I

HESYCHASM:
THE GIFT OF
EASTERN CHRISTIANITY
TO SPIRITUAL PRACTICE

St. John the Baptist. About 1100 C.E.*, Cyprus.*

1

HOW DO WE ENTER THE HEART, AND WHAT DO WE FIND WHEN WE ENTER?

Kallistos Ware, Bishop of Diokleia

Note: Kallistos Ware gave the following lecture at a conference on Hesychasm and Sufism entitled "Paths to the Heart," in October 2001, at the University of South Carolina.

The Russian Orthodox saint Seraphim of Sarov says, "Acquire inner peace, and thousands around you will find their salvation." And we might put his statement in a negative form: We shall never achieve peace in the world around us unless we possess some measure of peace in our own hearts. My second saying is from the one-time Secretary General of the United Nations, Dag Hammarskjöld: "Understand through the stillness. Act out of the stillness. Conquer in the stillness." That was said by someone who had an intensely active life with very heavy outward responsibilities. "Act out of the stillness." Unless by God's grace we possess in some measure stillness of heart, a quality designated in the Greek Orthodox mystical tradition by the word *hesychia*, our acts will prove superficial and ineffective. But if we act out of the stillness, our actions may effect healing and transfiguration far beyond anything we imagine possible. "Act out of the stillness." Contemplative action is the most powerful action of all.

In one of his letters, St. Barsanuphios of Gaza (sixth century) says in passing that, at the present time, there are three persons whose prayers protect this wicked and sinful generation from the wrath of God, and because of these three persons and their prayers, the world continues in being. And then he mentions their names. John, he says, is one of them; Elias is the second; and the third is a person in the province of Jerusalem. Now the third person, presumably, designates himself, living at Gaza. But the first two, John and Elias, are otherwise totally unknown to us. So here we have the word of a saint, gifted with insight, that the people who were preserving the world from destruction in his day were three persons, two of whom are entirely unknown to history and the third of whom was a hermit in the desert. The most important people in any generation are not necessarily those whose names are prominent in the history books. In Barsanuphios' time, we might think the most important people were the emperor Justinian and his general Belisarius. But, in fact, in every age the world is upheld by the prayers of hidden saints — Christian and, I believe, also non-Christian. So in discussing inner prayer at this conference we are not being evasive or escapist. We are seeking for a solution to the world's problems on the only level where, in the end, a true solution can be found. To pray in spirit and in truth is to be highly effective. Prayer has far-reaching political consequences.

Now I come to my theme tonight. In my life, and doubtless in the lives of all those present with me this evening, there have been certain texts, passages in poetry or prose, which once read have never been forgotten. Perhaps for the majority of us these decisive texts are few in number, but rare though they may be they have altered our lives, helping to make us what we are. One such text, so far as my own life's journey is concerned, is a paragraph from Thomas Merton's *Conjectures of a Guilty Bystander* — a paragraph on what he terms *le pointe vierge*, the virginal point:

"At the center of our being is a point of nothingness which is untouched by sin and by illusion, a point of pure truth, a point or spark which belongs entirely to God, which is never at our disposal, from which God disposes of our lives, which is inaccessible to the fantasies of our mind or the brutalities of our will. This little point of nothingness and of absolute poverty is the pure glory of God in us. It is, so to speak, His name written in us. As our poverty, as our indigence, as our dependence, as our son-ship, it is like a pure diamond blazing with the invisible light of heaven. It is in everybody. And if we could see it we would see these billions of points of light coming together in the face and blaze of a sun that would make all the darkness and cruelty of life vanish completely. I have no program for this seeing; it is only given. But the Gate of Heaven is everywhere."

In this passage, Merton does not actually use the word "heart," but surely he is referring, with insight and precision, to what the Christian East means in its ascetic and mystical theology when it refers to the *deep heart*. So his words form an appropriate epigraph to my address this evening, in which I shall be asking two questions: What do we mean by the heart, and what do we find when we enter the heart?

So let us turn to my first question: What is the heart? My spiritual father, a Russian priest of the emigration, Father George Sheremetiev, liked to quote to me the work by Antoine de Saint-Exupéry, *Le Petit Prince*, that is, *The Little Prince*, and he liked to quote in particular the farewell words of the fox: *"Goodbye," said the fox, "and now here is my secret. It is very simple. Only with the heart can one see rightly. What is essential is invisible to the eye."* Only with the heart can one see rightly. That exactly expresses the meaning of the heart in the spiritual traditions.

In modern usage, the heart is generally thought to designate the emotions and the affections, but if we turn to scripture, to the Old and New Testaments, we shall find that the heart is not understood in that way. In the symbolical anthropology of the Christian scriptures, the emotions and the affections do not dwell in the breast, but are located instead lower down in the guts and the entrails. The heart is not primarily the seat of the emotions and affections and feelings, though it is the seat of love. The heart is rather the spiritual center of the whole person, the ground of our being, the root and source of all our inner truth. The heart is that which gives us spiritual vision, as the fox rightly points out. And in the Bible, there is no head-heart contrast. We think with our heart. So heart designates the inwardness of our human personhood in its totality. For example, in *Ephesians* 3 the heart is equivalent to the inner man, *ho eso anthropos*, which is our inner self or inner being: "May God grant that you may be strengthened in your inner man, or inner being, with power through His spirit, and may Christ dwell in your hearts through faith." Here the inner being is equivalent to the heart, which is an all-embracing symbol, a symbol of wholeness.

Christ says, in the Sermon on the Mount, "Where your treasure is, there will your heart be also" (*Matthew* 6:21). The heart is the place where we formulate our primary hopes, where we express our sense of direction, our purpose in life. It is the moral center, the determinant of action. It is equivalent to what today we often mean by the conscience. Or take again another familiar text: "Mary kept all these things, pondering them in her heart" (*Luke* 2:19). Here the heart is the place where we ponder, the place of reflection, of self-awareness, the seat of memory. At the same time, however, because of our fallen state, because of our sinfulness, the heart is deeply ambivalent; it is a battlefield. As Christ says, "Out of the heart come evil thoughts." The heart is the place where we are brought face to face with the power of evil and sin within us. Yet the heart is also the place where we encounter God. It is the locus of Divine indwelling, as St. Paul says in a very important text: "God has sent the spirit of his Son into our hearts, crying 'Abba, Father!'" (*Galatians* 4:6). So here, you see, the heart is the dwelling-place of the Holy Spirit. The heart is the place of self-transcendence. The heart is the place where my prayer becomes, under the Divine Mercy, the prayer of Christ and the Holy Spirit within me. "Not I, but Christ in me" (*Galatians* 2:20). So in this way, the heart signifies the human person seen as a spiritual subject, the human person seen as created in the image and likeness of God.

The meaning of the heart is beautifully expressed by the French Benedictine Henri Lassaux. In his book on prayer he says, "The heart is the place of our origin in which the soul is, as it were, coming from the hands of God and waking up to itself." Another important text on the heart that I will mention, among so many others in scripture, is from

Psalm 64, a key text in Orthodox neptic theology: "The heart is deep." What this means is that the human person is a profound mystery. So, in scripture, the heart means both a physical reality and a psychic and spiritual center. When we speak of the heart in scriptural terms there is no head-heart dichotomy, no body-soul contrast. The heart signifies the human person seen as an undivided unity. The heart is a symbol of wholeness, of integration. The Biblical anthropology of the heart is a holistic anthropology.

What do we find when we turn to the Greek fathers? They vary in their approach. Some adopt a Platonist stance, contrasting head and heart and associating the heart with feelings, or else giving it no special meaning, but others retain the richness of meaning found in scripture. They give to the heart an inclusive, holistic sense. The heart is the center of the person, the seat of wisdom, the place of inner vision. Take, for example, the words of St. John Climacus, Abbot of Mount Sinai, in his work *The Ladder of Divine Ascent*,[1] which Orthodox monks are supposed to read every Lent. "I cried with my whole heart," says the Psalmist, "that is to say, with my body, my soul and my spirit." In this passage, "heart" indicates the totality of the human person; it includes the body, but is also a psychic and spiritual reality. One author who preserves to an outstanding degree the full Semitic scriptural sense of the heart is the author of the pseudo-Macarian *Homilies*, a late fourth century text written in Greek, traditionally associated with St. Macarius of Egypt, though in fact its background is Syrian rather than Coptic. "The heart," says the author of the *Homilies*, "governs and reigns over the whole bodily organism, and when grace possesses the pasturages of the heart, it rules over all the members and the thoughts, for there in the heart is the intellect." The Greek word here for the "intellect" is *nous*, which does not mean the reasoning brain, the power of discursive argumentation. It means instead the faculty of inner vision whereby we apprehend spiritual truth, not as part of a reasoned argument, but immediately.

There in the heart is the intellect, the *nous* and all its
thoughts, and when grace possesses the heart, it penetrates also
to all the members of the body. When we read these early texts
concerning the heart, we have to remember that their authors
did not think in terms of the circulation of the blood as we do;
they did not think of the heart as a pump, but as a container,
an empty vessel, full of space and air. Thus it is that Macarius
speaks of grace possessing the pasturages of the heart, or the
prairies of the heart. So when you enter into the heart it is
like going out to Edmundton, England and looking at the vast
plains stretching out around you. He says that the heart governs and reigns over the whole bodily organism, so the heart is
certainly a physical center, and when the heart stops beating, a
person dies. But the heart is also the place where the intellect,
the *nous* or spiritual understanding, dwells, and it is the place
where grace is experienced. So the heart is the meeting place
between the Divine and the human, between the spiritual and
the physical, between God's grace and our freedom.

Within the heart, Macarius' unfathomable depths correspond
in some ways to what we now call the unconscious, those aspects of ourselves that we do not yet know. "Within the heart,"
he writes, "there are unfathomable depths; there are reception
rooms and bedchambers within it, doors and porches and many
offices and passages. In it is the workshop of righteousness;
in it is the workshop of wickedness. In it is death, and in it
is life." So the heart is the place where both evil and good
dwell — the battleground, the moral center. "The heart is
Christ's palace: there is God, there are the angels, there are
life and the kingdom, there are light and the apostles, the heavenly cities and the treasures of grace; all things are there." So
see how the heart, for Macarius, is an all-inclusive symbol of
wholeness, and above all, it is the place of Divine indwelling.
It is the place where our human personhood becomes transparent to the Divine, where I experience myself as God-sourced,
God-enfolded, where God is at work within me. So the heart
is open, both below and above. It is open below, to the abyss
of the subconscious, and it is open above to the abyss of Divine grace.

A thousand years after Macarius, St. Gregory Palamas, the great spiritual master of fourteenth century Hesychasm, gives exactly the same rich sense to the heart. He calls it "the innermost body within the body," "the shrine of the intelligence" and "the chief intellectual organ of the body." We thus think with our heart. "It is the ruling organ," says Palamas, "that which gives to our human personhood purpose and meaning," and then he says, "It is the throne of grace." In any case, when the *Philokalia* uses the phrase "prayer of the heart," it does not mean affective prayer in the Western sense, prayer of the feelings and emotions. It means prayer of the total person, prayer in which the body participates as well as the soul and spirit. After all, "The body is the messenger of the soul," as St. Maximus the Confessor says, and we ought to use our physicality in the work of prayer.

So prayer of the heart is prayer of the total person, body, soul and spirit. But since the heart is the place of Divine indwelling, prayer of the heart is prayer in which it is not only I who speak, but it is the prayer which Christ and the Holy Spirit are saying within me. Those who attain prayer of the heart have the experience of being prayed in. "Descend into the heart" is a phrase you will often find in Orthodox Hesychast authors. "Discover the place of the heart." "Unite your *nous*," your intellect, within your heart. These phrases mean that we should strive for integration in Christ. Enter into relationship with your deep self. Discover the true dimensions of your personhood. Realize yourself as created in the Divine image. Find God in the profundity of yourself.

Now I come to my second question: If that is the meaning of the heart, how do we enter the heart? That great Victorian Thomas Carlisle one Sunday came back from the morning service in a bad temper, and said to his mother over lunch, "I cannot think why they preach such long sermons. If I were a minister, I would go up into the pulpit and say no more than this: 'Good people, you know what you ought to do; now go and do it.'" And his mother replied, "Yes, Thomas, and would you tell them how?"

So how are we to enter the heart? My answer from the Hesychast tradition is to say there is no single way of entering. The encounter with God is personal. Prayer is one person, myself, speaking to another person, God, or rather to a three-fold person, Father, Son and Holy Spirit. Prayer is personal, and it is therefore an expression of freedom; it is diverse because we are all different. So we each express ourselves in prayer in a unique way. You may remember the story told in Martin Buber's *Tales of the Hasidim* concerning Rabbi Zussia. Rabbi Zussia said, "At the Last Judgment, I shall not be asked, 'Why were you not Abraham? Why were you not Moses?' I shall be asked, 'Why were you not Zussia?'" God has a vision from all eternity of the personhood of each one of us. It is for us to realize God's vision, through the use of our own freedom, and at the Last Judgment, God will not ask me why I was not Moses or Abraham, why I was not St. John the Baptist or St. Seraphim of Sarov. God will ask me why I was not my own true self. That is our aim, to become truly ourselves, to realize the vision that God has of each one of us from eternity. We are each free, and we are therefore each unique. Buber records two other Jewish sayings: "God never does the same thing twice" and "the universe has need of every single person." If I were exactly the same as somebody else, there would be no reason for me to exist. In the Book of *Revelation*, it is said that in the age to come, God will give to each one of us a white stone, and on that white stone will be written a new name, and this new name will be known only to God and to the person who receives it. That is a way of expressing the uniqueness of each human person. There is within each one of us a mystery known only to God and to a very small extent at the moment by ourselves, but in the age to come, by God's mercy, we shall know more.

How then do we enter? There are many ways of entering, but the classic path within the Orthodox Church is the Jesus Prayer, the invocation of the holy Name of Jesus. I do not claim that it has any monopoly. We should certainly not identify the Jesus Prayer with Orthodox spirituality as such; we should not say it is the only way; we should not say it is the best way. All that I wish to say for the Jesus Prayer is that it has helped me, it has helped many others, and perhaps it might help you also.

Now in the Orthodox tradition, the Name of Jesus is usually invoked in the formula "Lord Jesus Christ, Son of God, have mercy on me." One may say at the end: "Have mercy on me, the sinner." You may bring in the Holy Mother of God, or the angels, or the saints. "Lord Jesus Christ, Son of God, at the prayers of the Theotokos, have mercy on me." Or again, "Lord Jesus Christ, Son of God, through the protection of my guardian angel, have mercy upon me." Or you can say, "Have mercy on us." Many people find the standard form, "Lord Jesus Christ, Son of God, have mercy on me," too long, and so they might prefer to use a shorter form, "Lord Jesus, have mercy." "My Jesus" was sometimes what the fourteenth century Hesychasts said. In the nineteenth century, St. Ambrose of Optima recommended saying the Name of Jesus simply on its own, which was probably what the Latin West normally did, though many Orthodox find that the name of Jesus on its own is almost too powerful, too overwhelming, and that it needs to be diluted, as it were, with other words. What all these forms have in common, however, is the Name "Jesus." So to me, the Jesus Prayer means any short invocation, frequently repeated, that contains the holy Name of Jesus. And we are to remember the sense of the Name of Jesus, which means "savior" or "salvation." "You shall call His name Jesus, for He shall save His people from their sins" (*Matthew* 1:21).

Now, the Jesus Prayer exists in a context. We Orthodox would take it for granted that persons saying the prayer are baptized members of the Church, that they are receiving the sacraments, Holy Communion and Confession, that they are observing the fasts and feasts of the Church calendar, that they are reading Holy Scripture, the Bible. The Jesus Prayer is not a substitute for these things but it is an enhancement.

There are two ways in which the Jesus Prayer may be recited. The first is a free way in all the passing moments of the day that might otherwise be wasted: on waking up, dressing, cleaning our room, walking from place to place. The purpose of free use is to find Christ everywhere. And then there is the fixed use, if we may call it so, where we say the Jesus Prayer as part of our prayer time, when we are not doing anything else, when we are trying to concentrate as fully and deeply as we can on the prayer to the exclusion of other thoughts. And here, we might say, the purpose of the Jesus Prayer is summed up in the phrase: "Create silence." If we wish to say the Jesus Prayer in this fixed way, it is highly desirable that we should find a spiritual guide, that we should not follow simply our own initiative. Also when we say the Jesus Prayer, in this fixed way, we may link it with the rhythm of the breathing so as to enable the body to take part in the prayer. As St. Gregory of Nazianzos says, "Remember God more often than you breathe." And we may also use a prayer rope, the Orthodox equivalent of a rosary. The primary purpose of the prayer rope is not to measure the number of times we say the Jesus Prayer, because quantity is not the most important point. The purpose is to let us have a regular, rhythmical repetition of the prayer. In Orthodox teaching we are taught that the Jesus Prayer should be like a gently flowing stream. Nevertheless it is a fact of experience that if we give our hands something to do as we pray, this will help to reduce our restlessness and to make us more gathered.

The Jesus Prayer is of course a Christ-centered prayer. It is not addressed simply to God; it is addressed to the Second Person of the Trinity, to Jesus, who was born in Bethlehem, who is the Son of God, who was crucified and who rose from the dead. So the Jesus Prayer is not just a rhythmic incantation to induce relaxation or concentration; it is a confession of faith. It is a confession of faith in Jesus Christ, the Son of God and Savior. It is also a Trinitarian prayer. People sometimes ask, "Is the Trinity present in the Jesus prayer?" My answer is yes, though implicitly rather than explicitly. We address Jesus as Son of God, but in speaking of him as Son, we point to the person of His Father. Moreover, the Spirit is also present, though He is not named. One of the key texts in the Jesus Prayer tradition is *I Corinthians* 12:3, which says that "no one can say

'Lord Jesus' except in the Holy Spirit." So the Holy Spirit is not openly named in the Jesus Prayer, but He is the atmosphere in which the name is invoked. Gerard Manley Hopkins, in one of his poems, compares the Blessed Virgin Mary to the air that we breathe: "Be thou, O Mother dear, our atmosphere." We could also say the Holy Spirit is our atmosphere. The Jesus Prayer is thus a Trinitarian prayer, and I am bound to say as a Christian that I cannot pray except in the Trinity. I cannot accept the suggestion that I might pass beyond the Trinity, transcend the Trinity, and enter into some higher level of Divine unity. I would not ask a person of another faith to transcend the Divine Unity and enter into the Trinity, but I, on the Christian side, have to say that I cannot go beyond the Trinity. This is fundamental to my prayer. For me the oneness and the threefoldness of God are equally ultimate.

Now what distinguishes the Jesus Prayer from other short prayers is the presence within it of the Holy Name. As it says in the second century text *The Shepherd of Hermas*, "The Name of the Son of God is great and boundless, and it upholds the whole world." The Jesus Prayer is not a magic talisman, and very little is achieved by a merely mechanical repetition. At the same time, names, all personal names, and above all the personal Name of God incarnate, while they are not magical, possess a sacramental value. A name is an effective and dynamic sign and is linked to presence. To name a person, to invoke his personal name with loving trust, is in a practical and potent fashion to render that person present to ourselves, and we shall not begin to understand the tradition of the Jesus Prayer until we appreciate that there is a vital, grace-giving connection between the Name and the One who is named.

The Jesus Prayer is a prayer in words, but because the words are exceedingly simple, because they are constantly repeated, it is a prayer that leads through the words into silence, enabling us to discover the dimension of silence hidden within the words. We speak in the Jesus Prayer, but at the same time we listen. It would be good for us to reflect, in the midst of these troubling times, on the value of silence. St. Ignatius of Antioch, early in the second century, in a pregnant phrase, calls Jesus Christ "the Word that came out of silence." Silence is one of the profound sources of our being. Without silence we are not truly human. As Friedrich von Hügel says, "As persons, we are what we do with our silence." But silence is not just negative, an absence of sound, a pause between words. Silence is positive — not an absence, but a presence; not an emptiness, a void, but a fullness; not isolation, but the awareness of another. In the Psalms it is said, not just "Be still" but "Be still and know that I am God" (*Psalm* 46). True silence — *hesychia*, stillness of the heart — is God-awareness.

How does the Jesus Prayer help us to attain this creative silence? It is not a prayer of the imagination, nor a form of discursive meditation; we are not to think of particular incidents in the life of Christ or specific sayings and parables. Our hope is to attain, in the prayer, simply a sense of total presence. The prayer is to be marked by a feeling of tender love and of fervent devotion, but unaccompanied, so far as possible, by any word, image, or concept. The reasoning brain, the *dianoia*, is suspended, but not the spiritual intellect. So the Jesus Prayer is a form of apophatic, non-iconic prayer. "Pray," say St. Kallistos and St. Ignatios Xanthopoulos: "Pray without images, shapes or forms, with an intellect, a *nous*, and a soul that are entirely pure. Always keep your intellect free from color, form, shape and configuration, and from any quality or quantity." What we seek in the Jesus Prayer, then, is not analysis but invocation, not abstract reflection, but personal encounter. We are to lay aside thoughts, in the discursive sense, but we are not to lay aside our loving awareness of the presence of Jesus in a non-discursive sense. As St. Gregory of Nyssa puts it, "The bridegroom is present, but he is not seen." So that is the aim of the Jesus Prayer, a simple sense of presence, a state of imageless gazing.

Now the Jesus prayer leads on to things of which I cannot speak tonight. It leads to a vision of light on two levels. First is the created light of the intellect, when we experience our human personhood as luminous. And then it leads on to the uncreated light of God, to a vision of the light which shone from Christ at the transfiguration on Mount Tabor. We Orthodox believe that this light of Tabor, seen by the three disciples on the mountain, seen by the saints in prayer, is not just a created light of the senses; it is the uncreated energies of God, though not the Divine Essence. Nevertheless the energies are God Himself, and therefore, in being united with the energies, the saints are meeting God face to face. It is also understood to be the light which will shine from Christ when He returns to earth at His Second Coming. It is the light of the age to come, and is thus eschatological, being a true foretaste of the beatific vision. In our tradition we believe that the saints do indeed enjoy, by Divine grace, the beatific vision in this life.

For Hesychasm, the heart is the center of the human person, the place of vision. For Hesychasm, the heart is the place of the Divine indwelling. It is the place of Divine union reached by remembrance and invocation through devotion to the Holy Name with emphasis on the need for spiritual guidance and disciplined repetition, and reinforced by control of the breathing and by the use of the prayer rope or rosary. In the Hesychast tradition, the invocation of the Holy Name leads us to the point where prayer becomes part of us, not just something we do, but something that we are, and it can lead us to the point where we are no longer conscious of the subject-object dichotomy, no longer conscious of ourselves praying to God, which leads us in turn to the point where God is all in all. As T.S. Eliot says, "You are the music, while the music lasts." And as St. John Cassian says, "Prayer is not perfect when the monk is conscious of himself or of the fact that he is actually praying."

Let me end with a story from the Desert Fathers which expresses surely our ultimate hope. It is a story told concerning Abba Joseph of Panephysis from the *Sayings of the Desert Fathers*. A monk came to see Abba Joseph and said to him, "Abba, I try my best. I say a few prayers each day, I make prostrations, I keep the fasts, I try not to lose my temper with my brothers. What more can I do?" And Abba Joseph rose to his feet, and he lifted his hands to heaven, and his hands became like ten blazing torches of fire. And he said to the monk, "If you will, you can become all fire." So may each of one us present here at this conference become, through the Divine mercy, a living flame of prayer.

NOTE

1. See "The Yoga of Hesychasm" by James Cutsinger, page 75.

The Transfiguration, Russia, fifteenth century.

2

SILENCE IN PRAYER
The Meaning of Hesychia[1]

Kallistos Ware, Bishop of Diokleia

Divine truth does not consist in talk but in silence,
in remaining within the heart by long suffering.
— *The Book of the Poor in Spirit*

. . . . Jesus Christ, the Word that came out of silence.
— *St. Ignatius of Antioch*

One of the stories in the *Sayings of the Desert Fathers* describes a visit by Theophilus, Archbishop of Alexandria, to the monks of Scetis. Anxious to impress their distinguished guest, the assembled brethren appealed to Abba Pambo: "Say something to the Archbishop that he may be edified." And the old man replied, "If he isn't edified by my silence, then he won't be edified by my words."[2] It is a story which indicates the extreme importance attached by the Desert tradition to *hesychia*, the quality of stillness or silence. "God has chosen *hesychia* above all other virtues," it is affirmed elsewhere in the *Sayings of the Desert Fathers.*[3] As St. Nilus of Ancyra insists, "It is impossible for muddy water to grow clear if it is constantly stirred up; and it is impossible to become a monk without *hesychia*."[4]

Hesychia means, however, far more than merely refraining from outward speech. It is a term that can be interpreted at many different levels. Let us try to distinguish the main senses, working from the more external to the more inward.

(1) *Hesychia and Solitude.* In the earliest sources, the term "hesychast" (ἡσυχαστής) and its related verb usually denote a monk living in solitude, a hermit as opposed to the member of a coenobium. This sense is found already in Evagrius of Pontus (fourth century)[5] and in Nilus and Palladius (early fifth century).[6] It occurs also in the *Sayings of the Desert*

Fathers,[7] Cyril of Scythopolis,[8] John Moschus,[9] Barsanuphius[10] and in the legislation of Justinian.[11] *Hesychia* continues to be used with this meaning in later authors such as St. Gregory of Sinai (1346).[12] On this level, the term refers primarily to a man's relationship in space with other men. This is the most external of the various senses.

(2) Hesychia, the Spirituality of the Cell. "Hesychia," says Abba Rufus in the *Sayings of the Desert Fathers*, "is to sit in your cell with fear and in the knowledge of God, abstaining entirely from rancour and vainglory. Such *hesychia* is the mother of all the virtues and guards the monk from the fiery arrows of the enemy." Rufus goes on to connect *hesychia* with the remembrance of death, and he concludes by saying: "Be vigilant (νῆφε) over your own soul."[13] *Hesychia* is thus associated with another key term in the Desert tradition, *nepsis*, spiritual sobriety or vigilance.

When *hesychia* is linked in this way with the cell, the term still refers to the external situation of the hesychast in space, but its meaning is at the same time more inward and spiritual. The hesychast, in the sense of one who remains with watchful vigilance in his cell, need not always be a solitary but can be equally a monk living in community.

The hesychast, then, is one who obeys the injunction of Abba Moses, "Go and sit in your cell and your cell will teach you everything."[14] He bears in mind the advice which Arsenius gave to a monk who wished to perform works of mercy. "Someone said to Arsenius, 'My thoughts trouble me, saying, You cannot fast or labor; at least go and visit the sick, for this also is a form of love.' The old man, recognizing the seeds sown by the demons, said to him: 'Go — eat and drink and sleep without doing any work; only do not leave your cell.' For he knew that to remain patiently in the cell brings a monk to the true fulfillment of his calling."[15]

The link between *hesychia* and the cell is clearly stated in a famous saying of St. Antony of Egypt: "Fishes die if they tarry on dry land; and in the same way monks, if they linger outside their cell or pass their time with men of the world, lose the pitch of their *hesychia*."[16] The monk who remains within his cell is like the string of a well-tuned instrument. *Hesychia* keeps him

in a state of alertness; if he lingers outside the cell, his soul grows limp and flabby.

The cell, understood as the outward framework of *hesychia*, is envisaged above all as a workshop of unceasing prayer. The monk's chief activity, while remaining still and silent within his cell, is the constant remembrance of God (μνήμη θεοῦ), accompanied by a sense of compunction and mourning (πένθος). "Sit in your cell," says Abba Ammonas to an old man who proposes to adopt some ostentatious form of asceticism. "Eat a little every day and have the words of the publican ever in your heart. Then you can be saved."[17] The words of the publican, "God, be merciful to me a sinner" (*Luke* 18:13), are closely parallel to the formula of the Jesus Prayer, as found from the sixth century onwards in Barsanuphius, the *Life of Abba Philemon* and other sources. We shall return in due course to the subject of *hesychia* and the Invocation of the Name. The enclosure of the monastic cell and the name of Jesus are explicitly linked in a statement by John of Gaza about his fellow hermit Barsanuphius: "The cell in which he is enclosed alive as in a tomb, for the sake of the Name of Jesus, is his place of repose; no demon enters there, not even the prince of demons, the devil. It is a sanctuary, for it contains the dwelling place of God."[18]

For the hesychast, then, the cell is a house of prayer, a sanctuary and place of meeting between man and God. All this is strikingly expressed in the saying, "The monk's cell is the furnace of Babylon, in which the three children found the Son of God; it is the pillar of cloud, from which God spoke to Moses."[19] This notion of the cell as a focus of the *shekinah* is reflected in the words of a contemporary Coptic hermit, Abuna Matta al-Maskin. When asked if he ever thought of going on pilgrimage to the Holy Places, he replied: "Jerusalem the Holy is right here, in and around these caves; for what else is my cave, but the place where my Savior Christ was born; what else is my cave, but the place where my Savior Christ was taken to rest; what else is my cave, but the place from where he most gloriously rose again from the dead. Jerusalem is here, right here, and all the spiritual riches of the Holy City are found in this *wadi*."[20]

In all this we are moving steadily from the external to the inward sense of *hesychia*. Interpreted in terms of the spirituality of the cell, the word signifies not only an outward and physical condition but a state of soul. It denotes the attitude of one who stands in his heart before God. "The principal thing," states Bishop Theophan the Recluse (1815 - 1894), "is to stand before God with the mind in the heart and to go on standing before him unceasingly day and night, until the end of life."[21] That is precisely what the stillness and silence of his cell signify to the hesychast.

(3) Hesychia and the "Return into Oneself." This more inward understanding of *hesychia* is plainly emphasized in the classic designation of the hesychast supplied by St. John Climacus († ca. 649): "The hesychast is one who strives to confine his incorporeal being within his bodily house, paradoxical though this may sound."[22] The hesychast, in the true sense of the word, is not someone who has journeyed outwardly into the desert, but someone who has embarked upon the journey inwards into his own heart; not someone who cuts himself off physically from others, shutting the door of his cell, but someone who "returns into himself," shutting the door of his mind. "He came to himself," it is said of the prodigal son (*Luke* 15:17); and this is what the hesychast also does. He responds to Christ's words, "The Kingdom of God is within you" (*Luke* 17:21), and seeks to "guard the heart with all watchfulness" (*Proverbs* 4:23). Reinterpreting our original definition of the hesychast as a solitary living in the desert, we may say that solitude is a state of soul, not a matter of geographical location, and that the real desert lies within the heart.

The "return into oneself" is finely described by St. Basil the Great († 379) and St. Isaac the Syrian (seventh century). "When the mind is no longer dissipated amidst external things," writes Basil, "nor dispersed across the world through the senses, it returns to itself; and by means of itself it ascends to the thought of God."[23] "Be at peace with your own soul," urges Isaac, "then heaven and earth will be at peace with you. Enter eagerly into the treasure house that is within you, and so you will see the things that are in heaven; for there is but one single entry to them both. The ladder that leads to the Kingdom is hidden within your soul. Flee from sin, dive into yourself, and in your soul you will discover the stairs by which to ascend."[24]

At this point in our argument it will be helpful to pause briefly and to distinguish with greater precision between the external and inward senses of the word *hesychia*.[25] Three levels are indicated in a famous *apophthegma* of Abba Arsenius. While still tutor to the imperial children in the palace, Arsenius prayed to God, "Show me how to be saved." And a voice came to him, "Arsenius, flee from men and you will be saved." He withdrew into the desert and became a solitary; and then he prayed again in the same words. This time the voice said: "Arsenius, flee, keep silent (σιώπα), be still (ἡούχαζε), for these are the roots of sinlessness."[26]

Flee from men, keep silent, be still: such are the three degrees of *hesychia*. The first is spatial, to "flee from men" externally and physically. The second is still external, to "keep silent," to desist from outward speech. Neither of these things can by itself make a man into a real hesychast; for he may be living in outward solitude and may keep his mouth closed, and yet inwardly he may be full of restlessness and agitation. To achieve true stillness it is necessary to pass from the second level to the third, from external to interior *hesychia*, from the mere absence of speech to what St. Ambrose of Milan terms *negotiosum silentium*,[27] active and creative silence. The same three levels are distinguished by St. John Climacus: "Close the door of your cell physically, the door of your tongue to speech, and the inward door to the evil spirits."[28]

This distinction between the levels of *hesychia* has important implications for the relationship of the hesychast to society. A man may accomplish the visible and geographic flight into the desert and in his heart still remain in the midst of the city; conversely, a man may continue physically in the city and yet be a true hesychast in his heart. What matters is not the Christian's spatial position but one's spiritual state.

It is true that some writers in the Christian East, most notably St. Isaac the Syrian, have come close to maintaining that inward *hesychia* cannot exist without external solitude. But such is far from being the universal view. There are stories in the *Say-*

ings of the Desert Fathers where laymen, fully committed to a life of active service in the world, are compared with hermits and solitaries; a doctor in Alexandria, for instance, is regarded as the spiritual equal of St. Antony the Great himself.[29] St. Gregory of Sinai refused to tonsure one of his disciples named Isidore, but sent him back from Mount Athos to Thessalonika, to act as exemplar and guide there to a circle of lay people.[30] Gregory could scarcely have done this had he regarded the vocation of an urban hesychast as impossible. St. Gregory Palamas insisted in the most unambiguous fashion that the command of St. Paul, "Pray without ceasing" (*I Thessalonians* 5:17), applies to all Christians without exception.[31]

In this connection it should be remembered that, when Greek ascetic writers such as Evagrius or St. Maximus the Confessor use the terms "active life" and "contemplative life," the "active life" signifies for them not the life of direct service to the world — preaching, teaching, social work and the like — but the inward struggle to subdue the passions and acquire the virtues. Using the phrase in this sense, it may be said that many hermits, and many religious living in strict enclosure, are still predominantly concerned with the "active life." By the same token, there are men and women fully devoted to a life of service in the world who yet possess prayer of the heart; and of them it may justly be said that they are living the "contemplative life." St. Symeon the New Theologian († 1022) insists that the fullness of the vision of God is possible "in the middle of cities" as well as "in mountains and cells." Married people, so he believed, with secular jobs and children, burdened with the anxieties of running a large household, may yet ascend to the heights of contemplation; St. Peter had a mother-in-law, yet the Lord called him to climb Tabor and behold the glory of the Transfiguration.[32] The criterion is not the external situation but the inward reality.

Just as it is possible to live in the city and yet to be a hesychast, so there are some whose duty it is to be constantly talking and who yet are silent inwardly. In the words of Abba Poemen, "One man appears to be keeping silent and yet condemns others in his heart: such a person is speaking all the time. Another man talks from morning till evening and yet keeps silent;

that is, he says nothing except what is helpful to others."[33] This applies exactly to the position of *startsi* such as St. Seraphim of Sarov and the spiritual fathers of Optino in nineteenth century Russia; compelled by their vocation to receive an unending stream of visitors — dozens and even hundreds in a single day — they did not thereby forfeit their inward *hesychia*. Indeed, it was precisely because of this inward *hesychia* that they were enabled to act as guides to others. The words that they spoke to each visitor were words of power because they were words that came out of silence.

In one of his answers, John of Gaza made a clear distinction between inward and outward silence. A brother living in community, who found his duties as monastic carpenter a cause of disturbance and distraction, asked whether he should become a hermit and "practice the silence of which the Fathers speak." John did not agree to this. "Like most people," he replied, "you do not understand what is meant by the silence of which the Fathers speak. Silence does not consist in keeping your mouth shut. A man may speak ten thousand useful words, and it is counted as silence; another speaks a single unnecessary word, and it is counted as a breach of the Lord's commandment: 'You shall give account in the day of judgment for every idle word that comes out of your mouth.' (*Matthew* 12:32)"[34]

(4) Hesychia and Spiritual Poverty. Inward stillness, when interpreted as a guarding of the heart and a return into oneself, implies a passage from multiplicity to unity, from diversity to simplicity and spiritual poverty. To use the terminology of Evagrius, the mind must become "naked." This aspect of *hesychia* is made explicit in another definition provided by St. John Climacus: "*Hesychia* is a laying aside of thoughts."[35] Here he is adapting an Evagrian phrase, "Prayer is a laying aside of thoughts."[36] *Hesychia* involves a progressive self-emptying, in which the mind is stripped of all visual images and man-made concepts, and so contemplates in purity the realm of God. The hesychast, from this point of view, is one who has advanced from *praxis* to *theoria*, from the active to the contemplative life. St. Gregory of Sinai contrasts the hesychast with the *praktikos*, and goes on to speak of " . . . the hesychasts who are content to pray to God alone

within their heart and to abstain from thoughts."[37] The hesychast, then, is not so much one who refrains from meeting and speaking with others, as one who in his life of prayer renounces all images, words and discursive reasoning, who is "lifted above the senses into pure silence."[38]

This "pure silence," although it is termed "spiritual poverty," is far from being a mere absence or privation. If the hesychast strips his mind of all man-made concepts, so far as this is possible, his aim in this "self-noughting" is altogether constructive — that he may be filled with an all-embracing sense of the Divine Indwelling. The point is well made by St. Gregory of Sinai: "Why speak at length? Prayer is God, who works all things in men."[39] *Prayer is God*; it is not primarily something which I do but something which God is doing in me — " . . . not I, but Christ in me" (*Galatians* 2:20). The hesychast program is exactly delineated in the words of the Baptist concerning the Messiah, "he must increase, but I must decrease" (*John* 3:30). The hesychast ceases from his own activity, not in order to be idle, but in order to enter into the activity of God. His silence is not vacant and negative — a blank pause between words, a short rest before resuming speech — but intensely positive: an attitude of alert attentiveness, of vigilance, and above all of *listening*.

The hesychast is *par excellence* the one who *listens*, who is open to the presence of Another: "Be still and know that I am God" (*Psalm* 45 [46]:11). In the words of St. John Climacus, "The hesychast is one who cries out plainly, 'O God, my heart is ready' (*Psalm* 56 [57]:8); the hesychast is one who says, 'I sleep, but my heart keeps vigil' (*Song of Solomon* 5:2)."[40] Returning into himself, the hesychast enters the secret chamber of his own heart in order that, standing there before God, he may listen to the wordless speech of his Creator. "When you pray," observes a contemporary Orthodox writer in Finland, "you yourself must be silent; let the prayer speak"[41] — more exactly, let God speak. "Man . . . should always remain silent and let God alone speak."[42] That is what the hesychast is aiming to achieve.

Hesychia therefore denotes the transition from "my" prayer to the prayer of God working in me — to use the terminology of Bishop Theophan, from "strenuous" or "laborious" prayer to the prayer that is "self-acting" or "self-impelled." True inner silence or *hesychia*, in the deepest sense, is identical with the unceasing prayer of the Holy Spirit within us. As St. Isaac the Syrian expresses it, "When the Spirit makes his dwelling-place in a man, he does not cease to pray, because the Spirit will constantly pray in him. Then, neither when he sleeps nor when he is awake, will prayer be cut off from his soul; but when he eats and when he drinks, when he lies down or when he does any work, even when he is immersed in sleep, the perfumes of prayer will breathe in his heart spontaneously."[43]

Elsewhere St. Isaac likens this entry into self-acting prayer to a man's passing through a door after the key has been turned in the lock, and to the silence of servants when the master arrives in their midst. "The movements of the tongue and heart during prayer are keys," he writes. "What comes afterwards is the entering into the treasury. At this point every mouth and tongue falls silent. The heart, the treasurer of the thoughts, the mind, the governor of the senses, and the daring spirit, that swift bird, together with all their resources and powers and persuasive intercessions — all these must now stand still: for the Master of the house has come."[44]

Understood in these terms, as an entering into the life and the activity of God, *hesychia* is something which during this present age men can achieve only to a limited and imperfect degree. It is an eschatological reality, reserved in its fullness for the Age to Come. In the words of St. Isaac, "Silence is a symbol of the future world."[45]

HESYCHIA AND THE JESUS PRAYER

In principle, *hesychia* is a general term for inward prayer, and embraces a variety of more specific ways of praying.[46] In practice, however, the majority of Orthodox writers in recent centuries use the word to designate one spiritual path in particular: the invocation of the Name of Jesus. Occasionally, although with less justification, the term "hesychasm" is employed in a yet more restricted sense to indicate the physical technique and breathing exercises which are sometimes used in conjunction with the Jesus Prayer.[47] The association of *hesychia* with the Name of Jesus —

and so it would seem, with the breathing – is found already in St. John Climacus: "*Hesychia* is to stand before God in unceasing worship. Let the remembrance of Jesus be united to your breathing, and then you will know the value of *hesychia*."[48] What is the relationship between the Jesus Prayer and *hesychia*? How does the invocation of the Name help in establishing the kind of inner silence that has just been described?

Prayer, it was said, is a "laying aside of thoughts," a return from multiplicity to unity. Now anyone who makes a serious effort to pray inwardly, standing before God with the mind in the heart, becomes immediately conscious of his inward disintegration – of his powerlessness to concentrate himself in the present moment, in the *Kairos*. Thoughts move restlessly through his head, like "the buzzing of flies" (Bishop Theophan) or "the capricious leaping of monkeys from branch to branch" (Ramakrishna).[49] This lack of concentration, this inability to be *here* and *now* with the whole of our being, is one of the most tragic consequences of the Fall.

What is to be done? The Eastern Orthodox ascetic tradition distinguishes two main methods of overcoming "thoughts." The first is direct, to "contradict" our *logismoi*, to meet them face to face, attempting to expel them by an effort of will. Such a method, however, may well prove counter-productive. When violently suppressed, our fantasies tend to return with increased force. Unless we are extremely sure of ourselves, it is safer to employ the second method, which is oblique. Instead of fighting our thoughts directly and seeking to drive them out by an effort of will, we can seek to turn our attention away from them and to look elsewhere. Our spiritual strategy in this way becomes positive instead of negative: our immediate objective is not to empty our mind of what is evil but rather to fill it with what is good. It is this second method that is recommended by Barsanuphius and John of Gaza. "Do not contradict the thoughts suggested by your enemies," they advise, "for that is exactly what they want and they will not desist. But turn to the Lord for help against them, laying before him your own helplessness; for he is able to expel them and to reduce them to nothing."[50]

It is surely evident to each one of us that we cannot halt the inward flow of images and thoughts by a crude exertion of will-power. It is of little or no value to say to ourselves, "Stop thinking"; we might as well say, "Stop breathing." "The rational mind cannot rest idle," insists St. Mark the Monk.[51] How then are we to achieve spiritual poverty and inner silence? Although we cannot make the never-idle intelligence desist altogether from its restlessness, what we can do is to simplify and unify its activity by continually repeating a short formula of prayer. The flow of images and thoughts will persist, but we shall be enabled gradually to detach ourselves from it. The repeated invocation will help us to "let go" the thought presented to us by our conscious or sub-conscious self. This "letting go" seems to correspond to what Evagrius had in view when he spoke of prayer as a "laying aside" of thoughts — not a savage conflict, not a ruthless campaign of furious aggression, but a gentle yet persistent act of detachment. Such is the ascetic psychology presupposed in the use of the Jesus Prayer. The Invocation of the Name helps to focus our disintegrated personality upon a single point. "Through the remembrance of Jesus Christ," writes Philotheos of Sinai (?ninth - tenth century), "gather together your scattered mind."[52] The Jesus Prayer is to be seen as an application of the second or oblique method of combating thoughts: instead of trying to obliterate our corrupt or trivial imaginings by a direct confrontation, we turn aside and look at the Lord Jesus; instead of relying on our own power, we take refuge in the power and grace that act through the Divine Name. The repeated invocation helps us to "let go" and to detach ourselves from the ceaseless chattering of our *logismoi*. We concentrate and unify an ever-active mind by feeding it with a single thought, by nourishing it on a spiritual diet that is at once rich yet exceedingly simple. "To stop the continual jostling of your thoughts," says Bishop Theophan, "you must bind the mind with one thought, or the thought of One only"[53] — the thought of the Lord Jesus. In the words of St. Diadochus of Photice (fifth century), "When we have blocked all the outlets of the mind by means of the remembrance of God, then it requires of us at all costs some task which will satisfy its need for activity. Let us give it then as its sole activity the prayer, 'Lord Jesus . . .'"[54]

Such in outline is the manner whereby the Jesus Prayer can be used to establish *hesychia* within the heart. Two important consequences follow. First, to achieve its purpose the invocation should be rhythmical and regular, and in the case of an experienced hesychast — though not of the beginner, who needs to proceed with caution — it should be as uninterrupted and continuous as possible. External aids, such as the use of a prayer-rope *(komvoschoinion, tchotki)* and the control of the breathing, have as their main purpose precisely the establishment of a regular rhythm.

In the second place, during the recitation of the Jesus Prayer the mind should be so far as possible empty of mental pictures. For this reason, it is best to practice the Prayer in a place where there are few if any outward sounds; it should be recited in darkness or with the eyes closed, rather than before an icon illuminated by candles or a votive lamp. Staretz Silouan of Mount Athos (1866 - 1938), when saying the Prayer, used to stow his clock away in the cupboard in order not to hear its ticking, and then pulled his thick woolen monastic cap over his eyes and ears.[55] While visual images will inevitably arise within us as we pray, they are not to be deliberately encouraged. The Jesus Prayer is not a form of discursive meditation on incidents in the life of Christ. Those who invoke the Lord Jesus should have in their hearts an intense and burning conviction that they stand in the immediate presence of the Saviour, that he is before them and within them, that he is listening to their invocation and replying in his turn. This consciousness of God's presence should not, however, be accompanied by any visual concept, but should be confined to a simple conviction or feeling. As St. Gregory of Nyssa (†395) puts it, "The Bridegroom is present but he is not seen."[56]

PRAYER AND ACTION

Hesychia, then, involves a separation from the world — a separation either external or inward, and sometimes both at once: external through flight into the desert; internal through the "re-

turn into oneself" and the "laying aside of thoughts." To quote
the *Sayings of the Desert Fathers,* "Unless a man says in his heart,
I alone and God are in the world, he will have no rest."[57] "Alone
to the Alone":[58] but is this not selfish, a rejection of the spiritual value of the material creation and an evasion of our responsibility towards our fellow men? When the hesychast shuts his
eyes and ears to the outside world, as Fr. Silouan did in his cell
on Mount Athos, what positive and practical service is he rendering to his neighbor?

Let us consider this problem under two main aspects. In the
first place, is hesychasm guilty of the same distortions as Quietism
in the seventeenth-century West? Hitherto we have deliberately
refrained from translating *hesychia* as "quiet," because of the
suspect sense attached to the term "quietist." Is the hesychast in
fact upholding the same standpoint as the quietist? In the second
place, what is the attitude of the hesychast to his environment,
whether physical or human? What practical use is he to others?

"The fundamental principle of Quietism," it has been said,
"is its condemnation of all human effort. According to the Qui-
etists, man, in order to be perfect, must attain complete passivity
and annihilation of will, abandoning himself to God to such an
extent that he cares neither for heaven nor hell, nor for his own
salvation . . . The soul consciously refuses not only all discursive meditation by any distinct act such as desire for virtue, love
of Christ or adoration of the Divine Persons, but simply rests in
the presence of God in pure faith . . . Once a man has attained
to [the height of perfection], sin is impossible."[59]

If this is Quietism, then the hesychast tradition is definitely
not quietist. *Hesychia* signifies not passivity but vigilance *(nepsis),*
"not the absence of struggle but the absence of uncertainty and
confusion."[60] Even though a hesychast may have advanced to
the level of *theoria* or contemplation, he is still required to struggle
at the level of *praxis* or action, striving with positive effort to acquire virtue and to reject vice. *Praxis* and *theoria,* the active and
the contemplative life in the sense defined earlier, should be envisaged not as alternatives, nor yet as two stages, chronologically
successive — the one ceasing when the other begins — but rather
as two interpenetrating levels of spiritual experience, present simul-

taneously in the life of prayer. Everyone is required to fight on the level of *praxis* to the end of his life.

This is the clear teaching of St. Antony of Egypt: "A man's chief task is to be mindful of his sins in God's sight, and to expect temptation until his last breath . . . He who sits in the desert as a hesychast has escaped from three wars: hearing, speaking, seeing; but against one thing he must continually struggle — the warfare in his own heart."[61]

It is true that the hesychast, like the quietist, does not use discursive meditation in his prayer. But although *hesychia* involves a "letting go" or "laying aside" of thoughts and images, this does not imply on the hesychast's part an attitude of "complete passivity" nor an absence of "any distinct act such as . . . love of Christ." The "letting go" of evil or trivial *logismoi* during the saying of the Jesus Prayer, and their replacement with the one thought of the Name, is not passivity but in itself a positive way of controlling our thoughts. The invocation of the Name is certainly a form of "resting in the presence of God in pure faith," but it is at the same time marked by an active love for the Savior and an acute longing to share ever more fully in the divine life. Readers of the *Philokalia* cannot but be struck by the warmth of devotion displayed by hesychast authors, by the sense of immediate and personal friendship for "my Jesus." This note of personal vividness is especially apparent in Hesychios of Vatos (?ninth - tenth century).

Unlike the quietist, the hesychast makes no claim to be sinless or impervious to temptation. The *apatheia* or "dispassion" of which Greek ascetic texts speak is not a state of passive indifference and insensibility, still less a condition in which sinning is impossible. "*Apatheia*," states St. Isaac the Syrian, "does not consist in no longer feeling the passions but in not accepting them."[62] As St. Antony insists, man must "expect temptation until his last breath," and with the temptation there goes always the genuine possibility of falling into sin. "The passions remain alive," states Abba Abraham, "but they are bound by the Saints."[63] When an old man claims, "I have died to the world," his neighbor gently rejoins, "Do not be so confident, brother, until you depart from the body. You may say, 'I have died,' but Satan has not died."[64]

In Greek writers from Evagrius onwards, *apatheia* is closely linked with love, which indicates the positive and dynamic content of the term "dispassion." In its basic essence, it is a state of spiritual freedom, in which man is able to reach out toward God with ardent longing. It is "no mere mortification of the physical passions of the body but its new and better energy";[65] "it is a state of soul in which a burning love for God and man leaves no room for selfish and animal passions."[66] To denote its dynamic character, St. Diadochus uses the expressive phrase "the fire of *apatheia*."[67] All this shows the gulf between hesychasm and quietism.

To come now to the second question: accepting that the hesychast way of prayer is not "quietist" in a suspect and heretical sense, how far is it negative in its view of the material world and anti-social in its attitude toward men? The difficulty may be illustrated from a story in the *Sayings of the Desert Fathers* about three friends who become monks. As his ascetic labor the first adopts the task of peace-maker, seeking to reconcile those who go to law against one another. The second cares for the sick, and the third goes into the desert to become a solitary. After a time the first two grow utterly weary and discouraged. However hard they struggle they are physically and spiritually incapable of meeting all the demands placed upon them. Close to despair, they go to the third monk, the hermit, and tell him about their troubles. At first he is silent. After a while he pours water into a bowl and says to the others, "Look." The water is murky and turbulent. They wait for some minutes. The hermit says, "Look again." The sediment has now sunk to the bottom and the water is entirely clear; they see their own faces as in a mirror. "That is what happens," says the hermit, "to someone who lives among men: because of the turbulence he does not see his own sins. But when he has learnt to be still, above all in the desert, he recognizes his own faults."[68]

So the story ends. We are not told how the first two monks applied the hermit's parable. Perhaps they both returned to the world, resuming their previous work but at the same time taking back with them something of the *hesychia* of the desert. In that case, they interpreted the words of the third monk to mean that social action by itself is not enough. Unless there is a still center in the middle of the storm, unless a man in the midst of all his activism preserves a secret room in his heart where he stands alone before God, then he will lose all sense of spiritual direction and be torn in pieces. Doubtless this is the moral which most readers in the twentieth century would be inclined to draw — that all of us must be, in some measure, hermits of the heart. But was this the original intention of the story? Probably not. It is far more likely that it was intended as propaganda for the eremitic life in the more literal and geographical sense. And this raises at once the whole question of the apparent selfishness and negativity of this type of contemplative prayer. What, then, is the true relationship of the hesychast to society?

It must be admitted at once that, alike in the hesychast movement of the fourteenth century, in the hesychast *renaissance* of the eighteenth century, and in contemporary Orthodoxy, the chief centers of hesychast prayer have been the small *sketes*, the hermitages housing only a handful of brethren, living as a small and closely integrated monastic family hidden from the world. Many hesychast authors express a definite preference for the *skete* over the fully organized *coenobium*: life in a large community is considered too distracting for the intense practice of inward prayer.

But, if the outward setting of the *skete* is considered ideal, few would go so far as to claim that it enjoys an exclusive monopoly. Always the criterion is not one's exterior condition but one's inward state. Certain external settings may prove more favorable than others for interior silence; but there is no situation whatever which renders interior silence altogether impossible. St. Gregory of Sinai, as we have seen, sent his disciple Isidore back into the world;[69] many of his closest companions on Mount Athos and in the desert of Paroria became patriarchs and bishops, leaders and administrators of the Church. St. Gregory Palamas, who taught that continual prayer is possible for every Christian, himself concluded his life as archbishop of the second largest city in the Byzantine Empire.

The layman Nicolas Cabasilas (14th century), a civil servant and courtier who was the friend of many leading hesychasts, maintains with great emphasis: "And everyone should keep their art or profession. The general should continue to command; the farmer to till the land; the artisan to practice his craft. And I will tell you why. It is not necessary to retire into the desert, to take unpalatable food, to alter one's dress, to compromise one's health, or to do anything unwise, because it is quite possible to remain in one's own home without giving up all one's possessions, and yet to practice continual meditation."[70] In the same spirit, St. Symeon the New Theologian insists that the "highest life" is the state to which God calls each one personally: "Many people canonize the eremitic life, others the life in a monastic community, or else that of government, instruction, education, or church administration . . . Yet I would not prefer any one of these to the rest, nor would I exalt one form and depreciate another. But in every situation and activity, it is the life for God and according to God which is truly blessed."[71]

The way of *hesychia*, then, lies open to all: the one thing needful is inner silence, not outer. And though this inner silence presupposes the "laying aside" of images in prayer, the final effect of this negation is to assert with fresh vividness the ultimate value of all things and all persons in God. The way of negation is at the same time the way of super-affirmation. This point emerges very plainly from *The Way of a Pilgrim*. The anonymous Russian peasant who is the hero of this tale finds that the constant repetition of the Jesus Prayer transfigures his relationship with the material creation around him, changing all things into a sacrament of God's presence and rendering them transparent. "When . . . I prayed with all my heart," he writes, "everything around me seemed delightful and marvelous. The trees, the grass, the birds, the earth, the air, the light seemed to be telling me that they existed for man's sake, that they witnessed to the love of God for man, that everything proved the love of God for man, that all things prayed to God and sang his praise. Thus it was that I came to understand what *The Philokalia* calls 'the knowledge of the speech of all creatures.' . . . I felt a burning love for Jesus Christ and for all God's creatures."[72]

Equally, the Invocation of the Name transforms the Pilgrim's relationship with his fellow men: "Again I started off on my wanderings. But now I did not walk along as before, filled with care. The Invocation of the Name of Jesus gladdened my way. Everybody was kind to me, it was as though everyone loved me . . . If anyone harms me I have only to think, 'How sweet is the Prayer of Jesus!' and the injury and anger pass away and I forget it all."[73]

Further evidence of the world-affirming nature of *hesychia* is to be found in the central position assigned by the hesychasts to the mystery of the Transfiguration. Metropolitan Anthony (Bloom) gives a striking description of two icons of the Transfiguration which he saw in Moscow, the one by Andrei Rublev and the other by Theophan the Greek. "The Rublev icon shows Christ in the brilliancy of his dazzling white robes which cast light on everything around. This light falls on the disciples, on the mountains and the stones, on every blade of grass. Within this light, which is . . . the divine glory, the divine light itself inseparable from God, all things acquire an intensity of being which they could not have otherwise; in it they attain to a fullness of reality which they can have only in God." In the other icon "the robes of Christ are silvery with blue shades, and the rays of light falling around are also white, silvery and blue. Everything gives an impression of much less intensity. Then we discover that all these rays of light falling from the Divine Presence . . . do not give relief but give transparency to things. One has the impression that these rays of divine light touch things and sink into them, penetrate them, touch something within them so that from the core of these things, of all things created, the same light reflects and shines back as though the divine life quickens the capabilities, the potentialities, of all things and makes all reach out towards itself. At that moment, the eschatological situation is realized and, in the words of St. Paul, 'God is all and in all.'"[74]

Such is the double effect of the Transfiguration glory: to make each thing and each person stand out in full distinctiveness, in its unique and unrepeatable essence; and at the same time to make each thing and each person transparent, to reveal the divine presence beyond and within them:

A man that looks on glasse
On it may stay his eye;

> Or if he pleaseth, through it passe,
> And then the heav'n espie.[75]

The same double effect is produced by *hesychia*. The prayer of inward silence is not world-denying but world-embracing. It enables the hesychast to look beyond the world toward the invisible Creator; and so it enables him to return back to the world and see it with new eyes. To travel, it has been often said, is to return to our point of departure and to see our home afresh as though for the first time. This is true of the journey of prayer, as of other journeys. The hesychast, far more than the sensualist or the materialist, can appreciate the value of each thing, because he sees each in God and God in each. It is no coincidence that, in the Palamite controversy of the fourteenth century, St. Gregory and his hesychast supporters were concerned to defend precisely the spiritual potentialities of the material creation and, in particular, of man's physical body.

Such, in brief, is the answer to those who see hesychasm as negative and dualist in its attitude to the world. The hesychast denies in order to reaffirm; he withdraws in order to return.

In a phrase which sums up the relationship between the hesychast and society, between inner prayer and outward action, Evagrius of Pontus remarks: "A monk is one who is separated from all and united to all."[76] The hesychast makes an act of separation — externally, by retiring into solitude; inwardly, by the "laying aside of thoughts" — yet the effect of this flight is to join him to them more closely than ever before, to make him more deeply sensitive to the needs of others, more sharply conscious of their hidden possibilities. This is seen most strikingly in the case of the great *startsi*. Men such as St. Antony of Egypt or St. Seraphim of Sarov lived for whole decades in all but total silence and physical isolation. Yet the ultimate effect of this isolation was to confer on them clarity of vision and an exceptional compassion. Precisely because they had learned to be alone, they could instinctively identify themselves with others. They were able to discern immediately the deep characteristics of each person, perhaps by speaking only two or three sentences; but those few words were the one thing that at that particular juncture that person needed to be told.

St. Isaac the Syrian says that it is better to acquire purity of heart than to convert whole nations of heathen from error.[77] Not that he despises the work of the apostolate; he means merely that unless and until one has gained some measure of inward silence, it is improbable that one will succeed in converting anybody to anything. The point is made less paradoxically by Ammonas, the disciple of Antony (fourth century): "Because they had first practiced profound *hesychia*, they possessed the power of God dwelling within them; and then God sent them into the midst of men."[78] And even if many solitaries are never in fact sent back into the world as apostles or *startsi*, but continue the practice of inner silence throughout their lives, totally unknown to others, that does not mean that their hidden contemplation is useless or their life wasted. They are serving society not by active works but by prayer, not by what they do but by what they are, not externally but existentially. They can say, in the words[79] of St. Macarius of Alexandria, "I am guarding the walls."

St. John's Monastery, Patmos

NOTES

1. Originally published in *Cistercian Studies Number 29, One Yet Two: Monastic Traditions East and West*. Cistercian Publications, 1976.

2. *Apophthegmata Patrum [AP]*. Theophilus 2; PG 65:197D.

3. *Peri logismon* 21, editor J.C. Guy, "Un dialogue monastique inédit," *Revue d'Ascetique et de Mystique* 33 (1957) 180; translated by J.C. Guy, *Les Apophtegmes des Pères du Désert*. Collection Spiritualité Orientale 1 (Begrolles: Abbaye de Bellefontaine, 1966) page 413.

4. *Institutio ad monachos*; PG 79:1236B.

5. *De oratione* 107, 111; PG 79:1192A,C, translated by J.E. Bamberger, *The Praktikos – Chapters on Prayer*, CS 4 (Spencer, Massachusetts: Cistercian Publications, 1970) pages 73-74.

6. Nilus. *Ep.* iv, 1 and 17; PG 79:541C and 557D; *De monachorum praestantia* 1; PG 79:1061A; Palladius, *Vita Chrysostomi* 8, edited by Coleman-Norton, page 50, 6.

7. *AP*, Antony 34, PG 65:85D: Elias 8; 185A: this is relatively late — probably from the 6th century — since it refers to a monk in the community of St. Sabas in Palestine; Poemen 90 344A.

8. *Vita Sabae* 21, edited by Schwartz, page 105, 19.

9. *Pratum* 52; PG 87:2908A.

10. *Quaest et resp.*, edited by Schoinas, 164; edited by Regnault and Lemaire, 68. Here we find the doublet ἔγκλειστοι καὶ ἡσυχασταί.

11. *Novella* 5, 3 (AD 535), edited by von Lingenthal, page 63. 17: this speaks of ἀναχωρητὰς καὶ ἡσυχαστάς. For the same usage of *hesychia* compare the Council in *Trullo* (AD 692), canon 41.

12. *Quomodo oporteat sedere* 5; PG 150:1333D.

13. *AP*, Rufus 01; PG 65:389BC.

14. *AP*, Moses 6; PG 65:284C.

15. *AP*, Arsenius 11; PG 65:89C. Compare *Heirax* 1; PG 65:232D.

16. *AP*, Antony 10; PG 65:77B. For the connection between *hesychia* and the cell, see also Evagrius, *Rerum monachalium rationes* 8; PG 40:1260C.

17. *AP*, Ammonas 4; PG 65:120C.

18. *Quaest et resp.*, editor Schoinas, 73; edited by Regnault and Lemaire, 142.

19. *AP*, anonymous collection, edited F. Nau 206, *Revue de l'Orient chrétien* 13 (1908) 279; translated by J.C. Guy, *Les Apophtegmes des Pères du Désert*. 74, page 350.

20. Otto Meinardus, "The Hermits of Wadi Rayan." *Studia Orientalia Christiana, Collectanea* 11 (Cairo, 1966) 308.

21. Cited in Igumen Chariton of Valamo, *The Art of Prayer: An Orthodox Anthology*, translated by E. Kadloubovsky and E. M. Palmer (London 1966) page 63.

22. *Scala* 27; PG 88:1097B.

23. *Ep.* 2; PG 32:228A.

24. *Mystic Treatises by Isaac of Nineveh*, translated from Bedjan's Syriac text by A.J. Wensinck (Amsterdam, 1923), page 8 (translation adapted).

25. In what follows, I am much indebted to the fundamental study of I. Hausherr, "L'hésychasme. Etude de spiritualité," *Orientalia Christiana Periodica* 22 (1956): 5-40, 247-85, especially pages 18ff. This essay is reprinted in the collected volume of

Fr. Hausherr's writings, *Hésychasme et Prière Orientalia Christiana Analecta* 176 (Rome, 1966) 163-237.

26. *AP*, Arsenius 1, 2; PG 65:88BC.

27. *De Officiis* 1, iii (9); PL 16:26B.

28. *Scala* 27; PG 88:1100A.

29. *AP*, Antony 24; PG 65:84B.

30. Patriarch Philotheos. *Vita Isidori* 22, edited by A. Papadopoulos-Keramevs. *Zapiski Istoriko - Filologicheskago Fakul'teka Imperatorskago S. Peterburgskago Universiteta*, 76 (St. Petersburg, 1905) 77, 21-26.

31. Patriarch Philotheos. *Encomium S. Gregorii Thessalonicensis*: PG 151: 573 B-574B.

32. *Catéchèses* V. 122-141; VI. 153-61, edited by Krivochéine, *Sources chrétiennes* 96: 3086-8; 104:26-28.

33. *AP*, Poemen 27; PG 65:329A

34. Barsanuphius and John. *Quaest. et resp.* 554 (in the numbering both of Schoinas and of Regnault and Lemaire).

35. *Scala* 27; PG 88:1112A. The phrase is repeated by St. Gregory of Sinai, *Quomodo oporteat sedere* 5; PG 150:1333B.

36. *De oratione* 70; PG 79:1181C; CS 4:66.

37. *Quomodo oporteat sedere* 5; PG 150:1333B.

38. *The Book of the Poor in Spirit*, II iii, 2; edited by C. F. Kelley (London, 1954) page 151.

39. *Capita* 113; PG 150:1280A.

40. *Scala* 27; PG 88:1100A.

41. Tito Colliander, *The Way of the Ascetics* (London, 1960) page 79.

42. *The Book of the Poor in Spirit*, II. iii, 2; edited by Kelley, page 151.

43. *Mystic Treatises.* translated by Wensinck, page 174.

44. *Ibid.*, page 112.

45. *Ibid.*, p. 315.

46. Compare, for example, the definition given by P. Adnès: "Hesychasm may be defined as a spiritual system, essentially contemplative in orientation, which regards man's perfection as consisting in union with God by means of prayer or perpetual prayerfulness." – article on "Hésychasme," DS 7 (Paris, 1969) 384. This is wide enough to include many things.

47. Palamas and the other hesychast masters regard the physical technique (control of the breathing, inward "exploration," etc.) as no

more than an accessory, serviceable to some but by no means obligatory or indispensable. The Jesus Prayer can be practiced in its fullness without any bodily exercises at all. It is thus a misnomer to refer to these exercises as *"the* hesychast method of prayer." This is a blunder of which the illustrious Fr. Hausherr, among others, has been guilty. On the physical technique, see T. (Kallistos) Ware, "Introduction," Igumen Chariton, *The Art of Prayer*, pages 34-36; 3. Gouillard, "A note on the Prayer of the Heart," in J.M. Déchanet, *Christian Yoga* (Perennial Library: New York, 1972) pages 217-30.

48. *Scala* 27; PG 88:1112C.

49. I take these two similes from the article of Dr. André Bloom (now Metropolitan Anthony of Surozh), "Contemplation et ascese: contribution orthodoxe," in *Technique et contemplation (Etudes Carmelitaines*, no. 28: Bruges, 1949) pages 49-67. This is an important discussion of the various physical centres in a man and their implications for the spiritual life.

50. *Quaest et resp.*, edited by Schoinas, 91; edited by Regnault and Lemaire, 166.

51. *De paen.* 11; PG 65:981B. I have emended the Greek text, which is given inaccurately in Migne.

52. *Capita* 27; *Philokalia*, vol. ii (Athens 1958) page 283.

53. *The Art of Prayer*, page 97.

54. *De perfect. spir.* 59; edited by des Places, page 119, 1-5.

55. Archimandrite Sophrony, *The Undistorted Image: Staretz Silouan* (London, 1958) pages 40-41. But St. Maximus of Kapsokalyvia (14th century) said the Jesus Prayer in front of an icon of the Mother of God: Theophanes, *Vita* 15; edited by E. Kourilas and F. Halkin. *Analecta Bollandiana* 54 (1936) 85, 9-17.

56. *Comm. in Cant* xi; PG 044:01001B; edited by Langerbeck, page 324. 8-9.

57. *AP,* Alonius 1; PG 65:133A.

58. Cf. Plotinus, *Enneads VI,* ix, 11; edited by Henry and Schwyzer, page 328, 51.

59. F. L. Cross, editor, *The Oxford Dictionary of the Christian Church* (London, 1963), page 1133. It is, of course, beyond the scope of this paper to discuss how far this is in fact a just description of the viewpoint of de Molinos, Mme. Guyon and Fénelon.

60. A. Bloom, "Contemplation et ascèse," *art. cit.*, page 54.

61. *AP,* Antony, 4 and 11; PG 65:77A,C.

62. *Mystic Treatises*, translated by Wensinck, page 345.

63. *AP,* Abraham 1; PG 65:132B.

64. *AP*, anonymous collection, edited by Nau, 266, *Revue de l'Orient chrétien* 14 (1909) 369-70; translated by Guy, 134, page 370.

65. Fr. (now Archbishop) Basil Krivosheine, *The Ascetic and Theological Teaching of Gregory Palamas,* reprint from *The Eastern Churches Quarterly* (London, 1954) page 5.

66. Archimandrite Lazarus Moore, in St. John Climacus, *The Ladder of Divine Ascent* (London, 1959) page 51, note 3.

67. *De perfect. spir.* 17; edited by des Places, page 94. 3.

68. *AP*, anonymous collection, edited by Nau, 134, *Révue de l'Orient chrétien* 13 (1908) 47; translated by Guy, 2, pages 319-20.

69. See pages 28-29 *supra.*

70. *De vita in Christo* vi; PG 150:657-9, quoted in J. M. Hussey, "Symeon the New Theologian and Nicolas Cabasilas: Similarities and Contrasts in Orthodox Spirituality." *Eastern Churches Review* 4 (1972) 139. Some have thought that, by "meditation," Nicolas means specifically the Jesus Prayer; Prof. Hussey prefers to give the phrase a wider application.

71. *Capita* iii, 65; edited by Darrouzès, page 100, 9-16.

72. *The Way of a Pilgrim,* translated by R.M. French (London, 1954) pages 31-32, 41.

73. *Ibid.,* pages 17-18.

74. "Body and Matter in Spiritual Life," in A.M. Allchin, editor. *Sacrament and Image: Essays in the Christian Understanding of Man* (The fellowship of St. Alban and St. Sergius: London, 1967) pages 40-41.

75. George Herbert, *The Elixir.*

76. *De oratione* 124, PG 79:1193C; CS 4;76.

77. *Mystic Treatises,* edited by Wensinck, page 32.

78. *Ep.* i; edited by F. Nau, *Patrologia Orientalis* 11 (1915) 433. 4-5.

79. Palladius, *Hist. Laus.* 18; edited by Butler, page 58, 11.

3

THE POWER OF THE NAME
The Jesus Prayer in Orthodox Spirituality*

Kallistos Ware, Bishop of Diokleia

My doctor is Jesus Christ,
my food is Jesus Christ,
and my fuel is Jesus Christ.
– Contemporary Coptic Monk

PRAYER AND SILENCE

"When you pray," it has been wisely said by an Orthodox writer in Finland, "you yourself must be silent. . . . You yourself must be silent; let the prayer speak."[1] To achieve silence: this is of all things the hardest and the most decisive in the art of prayer. Silence is not merely negative – a pause between words, a temporary cessation of speech – but, properly understood, it is highly positive: an attitude of attentive alertness, of vigilance, and above all of listening. The hesychast, the person who has attained *hesychia*, inner stillness or silence, is *par excellence* the one who listens. He listens to the voice of prayer in his own heart, and he understands that this voice is not his own but that of Another speaking within him.

The relationship between praying and keeping silent will become clearer if we consider four short definitions. The first is from *The Concise Oxford Dictionary*, which describes prayer as ". . . solemn request to God . . . formula used in praying." Prayer is here envisaged as something expressed in words, and more specifically as an act of asking God to confer some benefit. We are still on the level of external rather than inner prayer. Few of us can rest satisfied with such a definition.

---

* Published at the Convent of the Incarnation, Fairacres, Oxford. Copyright
© by The Sisters of the Love of God, 1974. 1999, sixth impression.

Our second definition, from a Russian *starets* of the last century, is far less exterior. In prayer, says Bishop Theophan the Recluse (1815-94), "the principal thing is to stand before God with the mind in the heart, and to go on standing before Him unceasingly day and night, until the end of life."[2] Praying, defined in this way, is no longer merely to ask for things, and can indeed exist without the employment of any words at all. It is not so much a momentary activity as a continuous state. To pray is to stand before God, to enter into an immediate and personal relationship with him; it is to know at every level of our being, from the instinctive to the intellectual, from the sub- to the supra-conscious, that we are in God and He is in us. To affirm and deepen our personal relationships with other human beings, it is not necessary to be continually presenting requests or using words; the better we come to know and love one another, the less need there is to express our mutual attitude verbally. It is the same in our personal relationship with God.

In these first two definitions, stress is laid primarily on what is done by the human person rather than by God. But in the relationship of prayer, it is the divine partner and not the human who takes the initiative and whose action is fundamental. This is brought out in our third definition, taken from St. Gregory of Sinai (†1346). In an elaborate passage, where he loads one epithet upon another in his effort to describe the true reality of inner prayer, he ends suddenly with unexpected simplicity: "Why speak at length? Prayer is God, who works all things in all men."[3] Prayer is God — it is not something that I initiate but something in which I share; it is not primarily something that I do but something that God is doing in me: in St. Paul's phrase, "not I, but Christ in me" (*Galatians* 2:20). The path of inner prayer is exactly indicated in St. John the Baptist's words about the Messiah: "He must increase, but I must decrease" (*John* 3:30). It is in this sense that to pray is to be silent. "You yourself must be silent; let the prayer speak" — more precisely, let God speak. True inner prayer is to stop talking and to listen to the wordless voice of God within our heart; it is to cease doing things on our own, and to enter into the action of God. At the beginning of the Byzantine Liturgy, when the preliminary preparations are completed and all is now ready for the start of the Eucharist itself, the deacon approaches the priest and says: "It is time for the Lord to act."[4] Such exactly is the attitude of the worshipper not only at the Eucharistic Liturgy but in all prayer, public or private.

Our fourth definition, taken once more from St. Gregory of Sinai, indicates more definitely the character of this action of the Lord within us. "Prayer", he says, "is the manifestation of Baptism."[5] The action of the Lord is not, of course, limited solely to the baptized; God is present and at work within all humankind, by virtue of the fact that each is created according to His divine image. But this image has been obscured and clouded over, although not totally obliterated, by our fall into sin. It is restored to its primal beauty and splendor through the sacrament of Baptism, whereby Christ and the Holy Spirit come to dwell in what the Fathers call "the innermost majority"; however, Baptism is something received in infancy, of which we have no conscious memory. Although the baptismal Christ and the indwelling Paraclete never cease for one moment to work within us, most of us — save on rare occasions — remain virtually unaware of this inner presence and activity. True prayer, then, signifies the rediscovery and "manifestation" of baptismal grace. To pray is to pass from the state where grace is present in our hearts secretly and unconsciously, to the point of full inner perception and conscious awareness when we experience and feel the activity of the Spirit directly and immediately. In the words of St. Kallistos and St. Ignatios Xanthopoulos (fourteenth century), "The aim of the Christian life is to return to the perfect grace of the Holy and Life-giving Spirit, which was conferred upon us at the beginning in divine Baptism."[6]

"In my beginning is my end." The purpose of prayer can be summarized in the phrase, "Become what you are." Become, consciously and actively, what you already are potentially and secretly, by virtue of your creation according to the divine image and your re-creation at Baptism. Become what you are: more exactly, return into yourself; discover Him who is yours already, listen to Him who never ceases to speak within you; possess Him who even now possesses you. Such is God's message to anyone who wants to pray: "You would not seek me unless you had already found me."

But how are we to start? How, after entering our room and closing the door, are we to begin to pray, not just by repeating words from books, but by offering inner prayer, the living prayer of creative stillness? How can we learn to stop talking and to start listening? Instead of simply speaking to God, how can we make our own the prayer in which God speaks to us? How shall we pass from prayer expressed in words to prayer of silence, from "strenuous" to "self-acting" prayer (to use Bishop Theophan's terminology), from "my" prayer to the prayer of Christ in me?

One way to embark on this journey inwards is through the Invocation of the Name, "Lord Jesus . . ."

It is not, of course, the only way. No authentic relationship between persons can exist without mutual freedom and spontaneity, and this is true in particular of inner prayer. There are no fixed and unvarying rules, necessarily imposed on all who to seek to pray; and equally there is no mechanical technique, whether physical or mental, which can compel God to manifest His presence. His grace is conferred always as a free gift, and cannot be gained automatically by any method or technique. The encounter between God and the person in the kingdom of the heart is therefore marked by an inexhaustible variety of patterns. There are spiritual masters in the Orthodox Church who say little or nothing about the Jesus Prayer.[7] But, even if it enjoys no exclusive monopoly in the field of inner prayer, the Jesus Prayer has become for innumerable Eastern Christians over the centuries the standard path, the royal highway. And not for Eastern Christians only:[8] in the meeting between Orthodoxy and the West which has occurred over the past seventy years, probably no element in the Orthodox heritage has aroused such intense interest as the Jesus Prayer, and no single book has exercised a wider appeal than *The Way of a Pilgrim*. This enigmatic work, virtually unknown in pre-revolutionary Russia, has had a startling success in the non-Orthodox world and since the 1920s has appeared in a wide range of languages.[9] Readers of J.D. Salinger will recall the impact of the "small pea-green cloth-bound book" on Franny.

Wherein, we ask, lies the distinctive appeal and effectiveness of the Jesus Prayer? Perhaps in four things above all: first, in its simplicity and flexibility; secondly, in its completeness; thirdly, in the power of the Name; and fourthly, in the spiritual discipline of persistent repetition. Let us take these points in order.

SIMPLICITY AND FLEXIBILITY

The Invocation of the Name is a prayer of the utmost simplicity, accessible to every Christian, but it leads at the same time to the deepest mysteries of contemplation. Anyone proposing to say the Jesus Prayer for lengthy periods of time each day — and, still more, anyone intending to use the breathing control and other physical exercises in conjunction with the Prayer — undoubtedly stands in need of a *starets*, of an experienced spiritual guide. Such guides are extremely rare in our day. But those who have no personal contact with a *starets* may still practice the Prayer without any fear, so long as they do so only for limited periods — initially, for no more than ten to fifteen minutes at a time — and so long as they make no attempt to interfere with the body's natural rhythms.

No specialized knowledge or training is required before commencing the Jesus Prayer. To the beginner it is sufficient to say: "Simply begin. In order to walk one must take a first step; in order to swim one must throw oneself into the water. It is the same with the Invocation of the Name. Begin to pronounce it with adoration and love. Cling to it. Repeat it. Do not think that you are invoking the Name; think only of Jesus himself. Say his Name slowly, softly and quietly."[10]

The outward form of the prayer is easily learnt. Basically it consists of the words "Lord Jesus Christ, Son of God, have mercy on me." There is, however, no strict uniformity. We can say ". . . have mercy on us," instead of "on me." The verbal formula can be shortened: "Lord Jesus Christ, have mercy on me," or "Lord Jesus," or even "Jesus" alone, although this last is less common. Alternatively, the form of words may be expanded by adding "a sinner" at the end, thus underlining the penitential aspect. We can say, recalling Peter's confession on the road to Caesarea Philippi, ". . . Son of the living God . . ." Sometimes an invocation of the Mother of God or the saints is inserted. The one essential and unvarying element is the inclusion of the divine Name "Jesus." Each is free to discover through personal experience the particular form of words which answers most closely to his or her needs. The precise formula employed can of course be varied from time to time, so long as this is not done too often: for, as St. Gregory of Sinai warns, "Trees which are repeatedly transplanted do not grow roots."[11]

There is a similar flexibility as regards the outward circumstances in which the Prayer is recited. Two ways of using the Prayer can be distinguished, the "free" and the "formal." By the "free" use is meant the recitation of the Prayer as we are engaged in our usual activities throughout the day. It may be said, once or many times, in the scattered moments which otherwise would be spiritually wasted: when occupied with some familiar and semi-automatic task, such as dressing, washing up, mending socks, or digging in the garden; when walking or driving, when waiting in a bus queue or a traffic jam; in a moment of quiet before some especially painful or difficult interview; when unable to sleep, or before we have gained full consciousness on waking. Part of the distinctive value of the Jesus Prayer lies precisely in the fact that, because of its radical simplicity, it can be prayed in conditions of distraction when more complex forms of prayer are impossible. It is especially helpful in moments of tension and grave anxiety.

This "free" use of the Jesus Prayer enables us to bridge the gap between our explicit "times of prayer" – whether at church services or alone in our own room – and the normal activities of daily life. "Pray without ceasing", St. Paul insists (*I Thessalonians* 5:17): but how is this possible, since we have many other things to do as well? Bishop Theophan indicates the method in his maxim, "The hands at work, the mind and heart with God."[12] The Jesus Prayer, becoming by frequent repetition almost habitual and unconscious, helps us to stand in the presence of God wherever we are – not only in the sanctuary or in solitude, but in the kitchen, on the factory floor, in the office. So we become like Brother Lawrence, who "was more united with God during his ordinary activities than in religious exercises." "It is a great delusion," he remarked, "to imagine that prayer-time should be different from any other, for we are equally bound to be united to God by work at work-time as by prayer at prayer-time."[13]

The "free" recitation of the Jesus Prayer is complemented and strengthened by the "formal" use. In this second case we concentrate our whole attention on the saying of the Prayer, to the exclusion of all external activity. The Invocation forms part of the specific "prayer time" that we set aside for God each day. Normally, along with the Jesus Prayer, we shall also use in our "set" time other forms of prayer taken from the liturgical books, together with Psalm and Scripture readings, intercession, and the like. A few may feel called to an almost exclusive concentration upon the Jesus Prayer, but this does not happen with most. Indeed, many prefer simply to employ the Prayer in the "free" manner without using it "formally" in their "set" time of prayer; and there is nothing disquieting or incorrect about this. The "free" use may certainly exist without the "formal."

In the "formal" usage, as in the "free," there are no rigid rules, but variety and flexibility. No particular posture is essential. In Orthodox practice the Prayer is most usually recited when seated, but it may also be said standing or kneeling — and even, in cases of bodily weakness and physical exhaustion, when lying down. It is normally recited in more or less complete darkness or with the eyes closed, not with open eyes before an icon illuminated by candles or a votive lamp. Starets Silouan of Mount Athos (1866 - 1938), when saying the Prayer, used to stow his clock away in a cupboard so as not to hear it ticking, and then would pull his thick woolen monastic cap over his eyes and ears.[14]

Darkness, however, can have a soporific effect! If we become drowsy as we sit or kneel reciting the Prayer, then we should stand up for a time, make the Sign of the Cross at the end of each Prayer, and then bend from the waist in a deep bow, touching the ground with the fingers of the right hand. We may even make a prostration each time, touching the ground with our forehead. When reciting the Prayer seated, we should ensure that the chair is not too restful or luxurious; preferably it should have no arms. In Orthodox monasteries a low stool is commonly used, without a back. The Prayer may also be recited standing with arms outstretched in the form of a cross.

A prayer-rope or rosary (*komvoschoinion, tchotki*), normally with a hundred knots, is often employed in conjunction with the Prayer, not primarily in order to count the number of times it is repeated, but rather as an aid to concentration and the establishment of a regular rhythm. It is a widespread fact of experience that, if we make some use of our hands as we pray, this will help to still our body and to gather us together into the act of prayer. But quantitative measurement, whether with a prayer-rope or in other ways, is on the whole not encouraged. It is true that, in the early part of *The Way of a Pilgrim*, great emphasis is laid by the *starets* on the precise number of times that the Prayer is to be said daily: 3,000 times, increasing to 6,000, and then to 12,000. The Pilgrim is commanded to say an exact number, neither more nor less. Such attention to quantity is altogether unusual. Possibly the point here is not the sheer quantity but the inner attitude of the Pilgrim: the starets wishes to test his obedience and readiness to fulfill an appointed task without deviation. More typical, however, is the advice of Bishop Theophan: "Do not trouble about the number of times you say the Prayer. Let this be your sole concern, that it should spring up in your heart with quickening power like a fountain of living water. Expel entirely from your mind all thoughts of quantity."[15]

The Prayer is sometimes recited in groups, but more commonly alone; the words may be said aloud or silently. In Orthodox usage, when recited aloud it is spoken rather than chanted. There should be nothing forced or laboured in the recitation. The words should not be formed with excessive emphasis or inner violence, but the Prayer should be allowed to establish its own rhythm and accentuation, so that in time it comes to "sing" within us by virtue of its intrinsic melody. Starets Parfenii of Kiev likened the flowing movement of the Prayer to a gently murmuring stream.[16]

From all this it can be seen that the Invocation of the Name is a prayer for all seasons. It can be used by everyone, in every place and at every time. It is suitable for the "beginner" as well as the more experienced; it can be offered in company with others or alone; it is equally appropriate in the desert or the city, in surroundings of recollected tranquillity or in the midst of the utmost noise and agitation. It is never out of place.

COMPLETENESS

Theologically, as the Russian Pilgrim rightly claims, the Jesus Prayer "holds in itself the whole gospel truth"; it is a "summary of the Gospels."[17] In one brief sentence it embodies the two chief mysteries of the Christian faith, the Incarnation and the Trinity. It speaks, first, of the two natures of Christ the God-man (*Theanthropos*): of his humanity, for he is invoked by the human name, "Jesus," which his Mother Mary gave to him after his birth in Bethlehem; of his eternal Godhead, for he is also styled "Lord" and "Son of God." In the second place, the Prayer speaks by implication, although not explicitly, of the three Persons of the Trinity. While addressed to the second Person, Jesus, it points also to the Father, for Jesus is called "Son of God"; and the Holy Spirit is equally present in the Prayer, for "no one can say 'Lord Jesus', except in the Holy Spirit" (*I Corinthians* 12:3). So the Jesus Prayer is both Christocentric and Trinitarian.

Devotionally, it is no less comprehensive. It embraces the two chief "moments" of Christian worship: the "moment" of adoration, of looking up to God's glory and reaching out to him in love; and the "moment" of penitence, the sense of unworthiness and sin. There is a circular movement within the Prayer, a sequence of ascent and return. In the first half of the Prayer we rise up to God: "Lord Jesus Christ, Son of God . . ."; and then in the second half we return to ourselves in compunction: ". . . on me a sinner." "Those who have tasted the gift of the Spirit," it is stated in the *Macarian Homilies*, "are conscious of two things at the same time: on the one hand, of joy and consolation; on the other, of trembling and fear and mourning."[18] Such is the inner dialectic of the Jesus Prayer.

These two "moments" — the vision of divine glory and the consciousness of human sin — are united and reconciled in a third "moment" as we pronounce the word "mercy." "Mercy" denotes the bridging of the gulf between God's righteousness and the fallen creation. He who says to God, "Have mercy," laments his own helplessness but voices at the same time a cry of hope. He speaks not only of sin but of its overcoming. He affirms that God in his glory accepts us though we are sinners, asking us in return to accept the fact that we are accepted. So the Jesus Prayer contains not only a call to repentance but an assurance of forgiveness and restoration. The heart of the Prayer — the actual name "Jesus" — bears precisely the sense of salvation: "Thou shalt call his name Jesus, for he shall save his people from their sins" (*Matthew* 1:21). While there is sorrow for sin in the Jesus Prayer, it is not a hopeless but a "joy-creating sorrow," in the phrase of St. John Climacus (✝ c. 649).

Such are among the riches, both theological and devotional, present in the Jesus Prayer; present, moreover, not merely in the abstract but in a vivifying and dynamic form. The special value of the Jesus Prayer lies in the fact that it makes these truths come alive, so that they are apprehended not just externally and theoretically but with all the fullness of our being. To understand why the Jesus Prayer possesses such efficacy, we must turn to two further aspects: the power of the Name and the discipline of repetition.

THE POWER OF THE NAME

"The Name of the Son of God is great and boundless, and upholds the entire universe." So it is affirmed in *The Shepherd of Hermas*,[19] nor shall we appreciate the role of the Jesus Prayer in Orthodox spirituality unless we feel some sense of the power and virtue of the divine Name. If the Jesus Prayer is more creative than other invocations, this is because it contains the Name of God.

In the Old Testament,[20] as in other ancient cultures, there is a close connection between someone's soul and his name. One's personality, with its peculiarities and its energy, is in some sense present in one's name. To know a person's name is to gain an insight into his nature, and thereby to acquire a relationship with him — even, perhaps, a certain control over him. That is why the mysterious messenger who wrestles with Jacob at the ford Jabbok refuses to disclose his name (*Genesis* 32:29). The same attitude is reflected in the reply of the angel to Manoah, "Why askest thou thus after my name, seeing it is secret?" (*Judges* 13:18). A change of name indicates a decisive change in a person's life, as when Abram becomes Abraham (*Genesis* 17:5), or Jacob becomes Israel *(Genesis* 32:28). In the same way, Saul after his conversion becomes Paul (*Acts* 13:9); and a monk at his profession is given a new name, usually not of his own choosing, to indicate the radical renewal which he undergoes.

In the Hebrew tradition, to do a thing in the name of another, or to invoke and call upon another's name, are acts of weight and potency. To invoke a person's name is to make that person effectively present. "One makes a name alive by mentioning it. The name immediately calls forth the soul it designates; therefore there is such deep significance in the very mention of a name."[21]

Everything that is true of human names is true to an incomparably higher degree of the divine Name. The power and glory of God are present and active in His Name. The Name of God is *numen praesens*, God with us, Emmanuel. Attentively and deliberately to invoke God's Name is to place oneself in His presence, to open oneself to His energy, to offer oneself as an instrument and a living sacrifice in His hands. So keen was the sense of the majesty of the divine Name in later Judaism that the *tetragrammaton* was not pronounced aloud in the worship of the synagogue: the Name of the Most High was considered too devastating to be spoken.[22]

The Hebraic understanding of the Name passes from the Old Testament into the New. Devils are cast out and men are healed through the Name of Jesus, for the Name is power. Once this potency of the Name is properly appreciated, many familiar passages acquire a fuller meaning and force: the clause in the Lord's Prayer, "Hallowed be thy Name"; Christ's promise at the Last Supper, "Whatever you shall ask the Father in my Name, he will give it you" (*John* 16:23); his final command to the apostles, "Go therefore, and teach all nations, baptizing them in the Name of the Father, and of the Son, and of the Holy Spirit" (*Matthew* 28:19); St. Peter's proclamation that there is salvation only in "the Name of Jesus Christ of Nazareth" (*Acts* 4:10-12); the words of St. Paul, "At the Name of Jesus every knee should bow" (*Philippeans* 2:10); the new and secret name written on the white stone which is given to us in the Age to Come (*Revelation* 2:17).

It is this biblical reverence for the Name that forms the basis and foundation of the Jesus Prayer. God's Name is intimately linked with His Person, and so the Invocation of the divine Name possesses a sacramental character, serving as an efficacious sign of His invisible presence and action. For the believing Christian today, as in apostolic times, the Name of Jesus is power. In the words of the two Elders of Gaza, St. Barsanuphius and St. John (sixth century), "The remembrance of the Name of God utterly destroys all that is evil."[23] "Flog your enemies with the Name of Jesus," urges St. John Climacus, "for there is no weapon more powerful in heaven or on earth . . . Let the remembrance of Jesus be united to your every breath, and then you will know the value of stillness."[24]

The Name is power, but a purely mechanical repetition will by itself achieve nothing. The Jesus Prayer is not a magic talisman. As in all sacramental operations, the human person is required to co-operate with God through active faith and ascetic effort. We are called to invoke the Name with recollection and inward vigilance, confining our minds within the words of the Prayer, conscious who it is that we are addressing and that responds to us in our heart. Such strenuous prayer is never easy in the initial stages, and is rightly described by the Fathers as a hidden martyrdom. St. Gregory of Sinai speaks repeatedly of the "constraint and labor" undertaken by those who follow the Way of the Name; a "continual effort" is needed; they will be tempted to give up "because of the insistent pain that comes from the inward invocation of the intellect." "Your shoulders will ache and you will often feel pain in your head," he warns, "but persevere persistently and with ardent longing, seeking the Lord in your heart."[25] Only through such patient faithfulness shall we discover the true power of the Name.

This faithful perseverance takes the form, above all, of attentive and frequent repetition. Christ told his disciples not to use "vain repetitions" (*Matthew* 6:7); but the repetition of the Jesus

Prayer, when performed with inward sincerity and concentration, is most emphatically not "vain." The act of repeatedly invoking the Name has a double effect: it makes our prayer more unified and at the same time more inward.

UNIFICATION

As soon as we make a serious attempt to pray in spirit and in truth, at once we become acutely conscious of our interior disintegration, of our lack of unity and wholeness. In spite of all our efforts to stand before God, thoughts continue to move restlessly and aimlessly through our head, like the buzzing of flies (Bishop Theophan) or the capricious leaping of monkeys from branch to branch (Ramakrishna). To contemplate means, first of all, to be present where one is – to be here and now. But usually we find ourselves unable to restrain our mind from wandering at random over time and space. We recall the past, we anticipate the future, we plan what to do next; people and places come before us in unending succession. We lack the power to gather ourselves into the one place where we should be – here, in the presence of God; we are unable to live fully in the only moment of time that truly exists – now, the immediate present. This interior disintegration is one of the tragic consequences of the Fall. The people who get things done, it has been justly observed, are the people who do one thing at a time. But to do one thing at a time is no mean achievement. While difficult enough in external work, it is harder still in the work of inner prayer.

What is to be done? How shall we learn to live in the present, in the eternal Now? How can we seize the *kairos*, the decisive moment, the moment of opportunity? It is precisely at this point that the Jesus Prayer can help. The repeated Invocation of the Name can bring us, by God's grace, from dividedness to unity, from dispersion and multiplicity to singleness. "To stop the continual jostling of your thoughts," says Bishop Theophan, "you must bind the mind with one thought, or the thought of One only."[26]

The ascetic Fathers, in particular Barsanuphius and John, distinguish two ways of combatting thoughts. The first method is for the "strong" or the "perfect." These can "contradict" their thoughts, that is, confront them face to face and repel them in direct battle. But for most of us such a method is too difficult and may, indeed, lead to actual harm. Direct confrontation, the attempt to uproot and expel thoughts by an effort of will, often serves merely to give greater strength to our imagination. Violently suppressed, our fantasies tend to return with increased force. Instead of fighting our thoughts directly and trying to eliminate them by an effort of will, it is wiser to turn aside and fix our attention elsewhere. Rather than gazing downwards into our turbulent imagination and concentrating on how to oppose our thoughts, we should look upwards to the Lord Jesus and entrust ourselves into His hands by invoking His Name; and the grace that acts through His Name will overcome the thoughts which we cannot obliterate by our own strength. Our spiritual strategy should be positive and not negative: instead of trying to empty our mind of what is evil, we should fill it with the thought of what is good. "Do not contradict the thoughts suggested by your enemies," advise Barsanuphius and John, "for that is exactly what they want and they will not cease from troubling you. But turn to the Lord for help against them, laying before him your own powerlessness; for he is able to expel them and to reduce them to nothing."[27]

The Jesus Prayer, then, is a way of turning aside and looking elsewhere. Thoughts and images inevitably occur to us during prayer. We cannot stop them by a mere exertion of our will. We cannot simply turn off the internal television set. It is of little or no value to say to ourselves "Stop thinking"; we might as well say "Stop breathing." "The rational mind cannot rest idle," says St. Mark the Monk,[28] for thoughts keep filling it with ceaseless chatter. But while it lies beyond our power to make this chatter suddenly disappear, what we can do is to detach ourselves from it by "binding" our ever-active mind "with one thought, or the thought of One only" — the Name of Jesus. We cannot altogether halt the flow of thoughts, but through the Jesus Prayer we can disengage ourselves progressively from it, allowing it to recede into the background so that we become less and less aware of it.

According to Evagrius of Pontus (†399), "Prayer is a laying aside of thoughts."[29] A laying aside: not a savage conflict, not a furious repression, but a gentle yet persistent act of detachment. Through the repetition of the Name, we are helped to "lay aside," to "let go," our trivial or pernicious imaginings, and to replace them with the thought of Jesus. But, although the imagination and the discursive reasoning are not to be violently suppressed when saying the Jesus Prayer, they are certainly not to be actively encouraged. The Jesus Prayer is not a form of meditation upon specific incidents in the life of Christ, or upon some saying or parable in the Gospels; still less is it a way of reasoning and inwardly debating about some theological truth such as the meaning of *homoousios* or the Chalcedonian Definition. In this regard, the Jesus Prayer is to be distinguished from the methods of discursive meditation popular in the West since the Counter-Reformation (commended by Ignatius Loyola, François de Sales, Alphonsus Ligouri, and others).

As we invoke the Name, we should not deliberately shape in our minds any visual image of the Saviour. This is one of the reasons why we usually say the Prayer in darkness, rather than with our eyes open in front of an icon. "Keep your intellect free from colours, images and forms," urges St. Gregory of Sinai; beware of the imagination (*phantasia*) in prayer — otherwise you may find that you have become a *phantastes* instead of a *hesychastes*![30] "So as not to fall into illusion (*prelest*) while practising inner prayer," states St. Nil Sorskii (†1508), "do not permit yourself any concepts, images or visions."[31] "Hold no intermediate image between the intellect and the Lord when practising the Jesus Prayer," Bishop Theophan writes. ". . . The essential part is to dwell in God, and this walking before God means that you live with the conviction ever before your consciousness that God is in you, as he is in everything: you live in the firm assurance that he sees all that is within you, knowing you better than you know yourself. This awareness of the eye of God looking at your inner being must not be accompanied by any visual concept, but must be confined to a simple conviction or feeling."[32] Only when we invoke the Name in this way — not forming pictures of the Saviour but simply feeling His presence — shall we experience the full power of the Jesus Prayer to integrate and unify.

The Jesus Prayer is thus a prayer in words, but because the words are so simple, so few and unvarying, the Prayer reaches out beyond words into the living silence of the Eternal. It is a way of achieving, with God's assistance, the kind of non-discursive, non-iconic prayer in which we do not simply make statements to or about God, in which we do not just form pictures of Christ in our imagination, but are "oned" with him in an all-embracing, unmediated encounter. Through the Invocation of the Name we feel his nearness with our spiritual senses, much as we feel the warmth with our bodily senses on entering a heated room. We know him, not through a series of successive images and concepts, but with the unified sensibility of the heart. So the Jesus Prayer concentrates us into the here and now, making us single-centred, one-pointed, drawing us from a multiplicity of thoughts to union with the one Christ. "Through the remembrance of Jesus Christ", says St. Philotheus of Sinai (ninth - tenth century), "gather together your scattered intellect"[33] — gather it together from the plurality of discursive thinking into the simplicity of love.

Many, on hearing that the Invocation of the Name is to be non-discursive and non-iconic, a means of transcending images and thoughts, may be tempted to conclude that any such manner of praying lies altogether beyond their capacities. To such it should be said: the Way of the Name is not reserved for a select few. It is within the reach of all. When you first embark on the Jesus Prayer, do not worry too much about expelling thoughts and mental pictures. As we have said already, let your strategy be positive, not negative. Call to mind, not what is to be excluded, but what is to be included. Do not think about your thoughts and how to shed them; think about Jesus. Concentrate your whole self, all your ardor and devotion, upon the person of the Saviour. Feel His presence. Speak to Him with love. If your attention wanders, as undoubtedly it will, do not be discouraged; gently, without exasperation or inner anger, bring it back. If it wanders again and again, then again and yet again bring it back. Return to the centre — to the living and personal center, Jesus Christ.

Look on the Invocation, not so much as prayer emptied of thoughts, but as prayer filled with the Beloved. Let it be, in the richest sense of the word, a prayer of affection — although not of self-induced emotional excitement. For while the Jesus Prayer is certainly far more than "affective" prayer in the technical Western sense, it is with our loving affection that we do right to begin. Our inner attitude, as we commence the Invocation, is that of St. Richard of Chichester:

> O my merciful Redeemer, Friend and Brother,
> May I see thee more clearly,
> love thee more dearly,
> and follow thee more nearly.

Without denying or diminishing the classic teaching of the Hesychast masters on the Jesus Prayer as a "shedding of thoughts," it has to be acknowledged that over the centuries most Eastern Christians have used the Prayer simply as an expression of their tender, loving trust in Jesus the Divine Companion. And there is surely no harm in that.

INWARDNESS

The repeated Invocation of the Name, by making our prayer more unified, makes it at the same time more inward, more a part of ourselves — not something that we do at particular moments, but something that we are all the time; not an occasional act but a continuing state. Such praying becomes truly prayer of the whole person, in which the words and meaning of the prayer are fully identified with the one who prays. All this is well expressed by Paul Evdokimov (1901 - 1970): "In the catacombs the image that recurs most frequently is the figure of a woman in prayer, the Orans. It represents the only true attitude of the human soul. It is not enough to possess prayer: we must become prayer — prayer Incarnate. It is not enough to have moments of praise; our whole life, every act and every gesture, even a smile, must become a hymn of adoration, an offering, a prayer. We must offer not what we have, but what we are."[34] That is what the world needs above all else; not people who say prayers with greater or less regularity, but people who are prayers.

The kind of prayer that Evdokimov is here describing may be defined more exactly as "prayer of the heart." In Orthodoxy, as in other traditions, prayer is commonly distinguished under three headings, which are to be regarded as interpenetrating levels rather than successive stages: prayer of the lips (oral prayer); prayer of the *nous*, the mind or intellect (mental prayer); prayer of the heart (or of the intellect in the heart). The Invocation of the Name begins, like any other prayer, as an oral prayer, in which words are spoken by the tongue through a deliberate effort of will. At the same time, once more by a deliberate effort, we concentrate our mind upon the meaning of what the tongue says. In course of time and with the help of God our prayer grows more inward. The participation of the mind becomes more intense and spontaneous, while the sounds uttered by the tongue become less important; perhaps for a time they cease altogether and the Name is invoked silently, without any movement of the lips, by the mind alone. When this occurs, we have passed by God's grace from the first level to the second. Not that vocal invocation ceases altogether, for there will be times when even the most "advanced" in inner prayer will wish to call upon the Lord Jesus aloud. (And who, indeed, can claim to be "advanced"? We are all of us "beginners" in the things of the Spirit.)

But the journey inwards is not yet complete. A person is far more than the conscious mind; besides the brain and reasoning faculties there are the emotions and affections, the aesthetic sensitivity, together with the deep instinctive layers of the personality. All these have a function to perform in prayer, for the whole person is called to share in the total act of worship. Like a drop of ink that falls on blotting paper, the act of prayer should spread steadily outwards from the conscious and reasoning centre of the brain, until it embraces every part of ourselves.

In more technical terms, this means that we are called to advance from the second level to the third: from "prayer of the intellect" to "prayer of the intellect in the heart." "Heart" in this context is to be understood in the Semitic and biblical rather than the modern Western sense, as signifying not just the emotions and affections but the totality of the human person. The heart is the primary organ of our identity, it is our innermost being, "the very deepest and truest self, not attained except through sacrifice, through death".[35] According to Boris Vysheslavtsev, it is, "the centre not only of consciousness but of the unconscious, not only of the soul but of the spirit, not only of the spirit but of the body, not only of the comprehensible but of the incomprehensible; in one word, it is the absolute center."[36] Interpreted in this way, the heart is far more than a material organ in the body; the physical heart is an outward symbol of the boundless spiritual potentialities of the human creature, made in the image of God, called to attain his likeness.

To accomplish the journey inwards and to attain true prayer, it is required of us to enter into this "absolute center," that is, to descend from the intellect into the heart. More exactly, we are called to descend not from but with the intellect. The aim is not just "prayer of the heart" but "prayer of the intellect in the heart," for our varied forms of understanding, including our reason, are a gift from God and are to be used in His service, not rejected. This "union of the intellect with the heart" signifies the reintegration of our fallen and fragmented nature, our restoration to original wholeness. Prayer of the heart is a return to Paradise, a reversal of the Fall, a recovery of the *status ante peccatum*. This means that it is an eschatological reality, a pledge and anticipation of the Age to Come — something which, in this present age, is never fully and entirely realized.

Those who, however imperfectly, have achieved some measure of "prayer of the heart," have begun to make the transition about which we spoke earlier — the transition from "strenuous" to "self-acting" prayer, from the prayer which I say to the prayer which "says itself" or, rather, which Christ says in me. For the heart has a double significance in the spiritual life: it is both the center of the human being and the point of meeting between the human being and God. It is both the place of self-knowledge, where we see ourselves as we truly are, and the place of self-transcendence, where we understand our nature as a temple of the Holy Trinity, where the image comes face to face with the Archetype. In the "inner sanctuary" of our own heart we find the ground of our being and so cross the mysterious frontier between the created and the Uncreated. "There are unfathomable depths within the heart," state the *Macarian Homilies*. ". . . God is there with angels, light and life are there, the kingdom and the apostles, the heavenly cities and the treasures of grace: all things are there."[37]

Prayer of the heart, then, designates the point where "my" action, "my" prayer, becomes explicitly identified with the continuous action of Another in me. It is no longer prayer to Jesus but the prayer of Jesus himself. This transition from "strenuous" to "self-acting" prayer is strikingly indicated in *The Way of a Pilgrim*: "Early one morning the Prayer woke me up as it were."[38] Hitherto the Pilgrim has been "saying the Prayer"; now he finds that the Prayer "says itself," even when he is asleep, for it has become united to the prayer of God within him. Yet even so he does not consider that he has as yet attained prayer of the heart in its fullness.

Readers of *The Way of a Pilgrim* may gain the impression that this passage from oral prayer to prayer of the heart is easily achieved, almost in a mechanical and automatic fashion. The Pilgrim, so it seems, attains self-acting prayer in a matter of a few weeks. It needs to be emphasized that his experience, while not unique,[39] is altogether exceptional. More usually prayer of the heart comes, if at all, only after a lifetime of ascetic striving. There is a real danger that, in the early stages of the Jesus Prayer, we may too readily assume that we are passing from oral prayer to prayer of the heart. We may perhaps be tempted to imagine that we have already attained wordless prayer of silence, when in fact we are not really praying at all but have merely lapsed into vacant drowsiness or waking sleep. To guard against this, our teachers in the Hesychast tradition insist upon the need for strenuous effort when first embarking on the Jesus Prayer. They emphasize how important it is to concentrate full attention upon the recitation of the actual words, rather than to form high ambitions about prayer of the heart. Here, for example, is the advice given by a noted spiritual father of Mount

Athos, Geron Joseph of New Skete (died 1959): "The work of inner prayer consists in forcing yourself to say the prayer with your mouth continually, without ceasing . . . . Attend only to the words 'Lord Jesus Christ, have mercy on me'. . . . Just say the Prayer aloud, without interruption . . . . All your effort must be centred on the tongue, until you start to grow accustomed to the Prayer."[40]

The significance attached here to the power of the spoken word is indeed striking. As St. John Climacus tells us, "Struggle to lift up, or rather, to enclose your thought within the words of your prayer."[41] But of course we never think exclusively about the words on their own: always we are conscious also of the person of Jesus whom our words invoke.

Prayer of the heart, when and if it is granted, comes as the free gift of God, which he bestows as he wills. It is not the inevitable effect of some technique. St. Isaac the Syrian (seventh century) underlines the extreme rarity of the gift when he says that "scarcely one in ten thousand" is counted worthy of the gift of pure prayer, and he adds: "As for the mystery that lies beyond pure prayer, there is scarcely to be found a single person in each generation who has drawn near to this knowledge of God's grace."[42] One in ten thousand, one in a generation: while sobered by this warning, we should not be unduly discouraged. The path to the inner kingdom lies open before all, and all alike may travel some way along it. In the present age, few experience with any fullness the deeper mysteries of the heart, but very many receive in a more humble and intermittent way true glimpses of what is signified by spiritual prayer.

BREATHING EXERCISES

It is time to consider a controversial topic, where the teaching of the Byzantine Hesychasts is often misinterpreted — the role of the body in prayer.

The heart, it has been said, is the primary organ of our be-ing, the point of convergence between mind and matter, the centre alike of our physical constitution and our psychic and spiritual structure. Since the heart has this twofold aspect, at once visible and invisible, prayer of the heart is prayer of body as well as soul: only if it includes the body can it be truly prayer of the whole person. A human being, in the biblical view, is a psychosomatic totality – not a soul imprisoned in a body and seeking to escape, but an integral unity of the two. The body is not just an obstacle to be overcome, a lump of matter to be ignored, but it has a positive part to play in the spiritual life and it is endowed with energies that can be harnessed for the work of prayer.

If this is true of prayer in general, it is true in a more specific way of the Jesus Prayer, since this is an invocation addressed precisely to God Incarnate, to the Word made flesh. Christ at his Incarnation took not only a human mind and will but a human body, and so he has made the flesh into an inexhaustible source of sanctification. How can this flesh, which the God-man has made Spirit-bearing, participate in the Invocation of the Name and in the prayer of the intellect in the heart?

To assist such participation, and as an aid to concentration, the Hesychasts evolved a "physical technique." Every psychic activity, they realized, has repercussions on the physical and bodily level; depending on our inner state we grow hot or cold, we breathe faster or more slowly, the rhythm of our heart-beats quickens or decelerates, and so on. Conversely, each alteration in our physical condition reacts adversely or positively on our psychic activity. If, then, we can learn to control and regulate certain of our physical processes, this can be used to strengthen our inner concentration in prayer. Such is the basic principle underlying the Hesychast "method." In detail, the physical technique has three main aspects:

i) *External posture.* St. Gregory of Sinai advises sitting on a low stool, about nine inches high; the head and shoulders should be bowed, and the eyes fixed on the place of the heart. He recognizes that this will prove exceedingly uncomfortable after a time. Some writers recommend a yet more exacting posture, with the head held between the knees, following the example of Elijah on Mount Carmel.[43]

ii) *Control of the breathing.* The breathing is to be made slower and at the same time co-ordinated with the rhythm of the Prayer. Often the first part, "Lord Jesus Christ, Son of God," is said while drawing in the breath, and the second part, "have mercy on me a sinner," while breathing out. Other methods are possible. The recitation of the Prayer may also be synchronized with the beating of the heart.

iii) Inward exploration. Just as the aspirant in Yoga is taught to concentrate his thought in specific parts of his body, so the Hesychast concentrates his thought in the cardiac center. While inhaling through his nose and propelling his breath down into his lungs, he makes his intellect "descend" with the breath and he "searches" inwardly for the place of the heart. Exact instructions concerning this exercise are not committed to writing for fear they should be misunderstood; the details of the process are so delicate that the personal guidance of an experienced master is indispensable. The beginner who, in the absence of such guidance, attempts to search for the cardiac center, is in danger of directing his thought unawares into the area which lies immediately below the heart — into the abdomen, that is, and the entrails. The effect on his prayer is disastrous, for this lower region is the source of the carnal thoughts and sensations which pollute the mind and the heart.[44]

For obvious reasons the utmost discretion is necessary when interfering with instinctive bodily activities such as the drawing of breath or the beating of the heart. Misuse of the physical technique can damage someone's health and disturb his mental equilibrium; hence the importance of a reliable master. If no such *starets* is available, it is best for the beginner to restrict himself simply to the actual recitation of the Jesus Prayer, without troubling at all about the rhythm of his breath or his heart-beats. More often than not he will find that, without any conscious effort on his part, the words of the Invocation adapt themselves spontaneously to the movement of his breathing. If this does not in fact happen, there is no cause for alarm; let him continue quietly with the work of mental invocation.

The physical techniques are in any case no more than an accessory, an aid which has proved helpful to some but which is in no sense obligatory upon all. The Jesus Prayer can be practiced in its fullness without any physical methods at all. St. Gregory Palamas (1296 - 1359), while regarding the use of physical techniques as theologically defensible, treated such methods as something secondary and suited mainly for beginners.[45] For him, as for all the Hesychast masters, the essential thing is not the external control of the breathing but the inner and secret Invocation of the Lord Jesus.

Orthodox writers in the last 150 years have in general laid little emphasis upon the physical techniques. The counsel given by Bishop Ignatii Brianchaninov (1807 - 1867) is typical: "We advise our beloved brethren not to try to establish this technique within them, if it does not reveal itself of its own accord. Many, wishing to learn it by experience, have damaged their lungs and gained nothing. The essence of the matter consists in the union of the mind with the heart during prayer, and this is achieved by the grace of God it its own time, determined by God. The breathing technique is fully replaced by the unhurried enunciation of the Prayer, by a short rest or pause at the end, each time it is said, by gentle and unhurried breathing, and by the enclosure of the mind in the words of the Prayer. By means of these aids we can easily attain to a certain degree of attention."[46]

As regards the speed of recitation, Bishop Ignatii suggests: "To say the Jesus Prayer a hundred times attentively and without haste, about half an hour is needed, but some ascetics require even longer. Do not say the prayers hurriedly, one immediately after another. Make a short pause after each prayer, and so help the mind to concentrate. Saying the Prayer without pauses distracts the mind. Breathe with care, gently and slowly."[47]

Beginners in the use of the Prayer will probably prefer a somewhat faster pace than is here proposed — perhaps twenty minutes for a hundred prayers. In the Greek tradition there are teachers who recommend a far brisker rhythm; the very rapidity of the Invocation, so they maintain, helps to hold the mind attentive.

Striking parallels exist between the physical techniques recommended by the Byzantine Hesychasts and those employed in Hindu Yoga and in Sufism.[48] How far are the similarities the result of mere coincidence, of an independent though analogous development in two separate traditions? If there is a direct relation between Hesychasm and Sufism — and some of the parallels are so close that mere coincidence seems excluded — which side has been borrowing from the other? Here is a fascinating field for research, although the evidence is perhaps too fragmentary to permit any definite conclusion. One point, however, should not be forgotten. Besides similarities, there are also differences. All pictures have frames, and all picture-frames have certain features in common; yet the pictures within the frames may be utterly different. What matters is the picture, not the frame. In the case of the Jesus Prayer, the physical techniques are as it were the frame, while the mental invocation of Christ is the picture within the frame. The "frame" of the Jesus Prayer certainly resembles various non-Christian "frames," but this should not make us insensitive to the uniqueness of the picture within, to the distinctively Christian content of the Prayer. The essential point in the Jesus Prayer is not the act of repetition in itself, not how we sit or breathe, but to whom we speak; and in this instance the words are addressed unambiguously to the Incarnate Savior Jesus Christ, Son of God and Son of Mary.

The existence of a physical technique in connection with the Jesus Prayer should not blind us as to the Prayer's true character. The Jesus Prayer is not just a device to help us concentrate or relax. It is not simply a piece of "Christian Yoga," a type of "Transcendental Meditation," or a "Christian mantra," even though some have tried to interpret it in this way. It is, on the contrary, an invocation specifically addressed to another person — to God made man, Jesus Christ, our personal Saviour and Redeemer. The Jesus Prayer, therefore, is far more than an isolated method or technique. It exists within a certain context, and if divorced from that context it loses its proper meaning.

The context of the Jesus Prayer is first of all one of faith. The Invocation of the Name presupposes that the one who says the Prayer believes in Jesus Christ as Son of God and Saviour. Behind the repetition of a form of words there must exist a living faith in the Lord Jesus — in who he is and in what he has done for me personally. Perhaps the faith in many of us is very uncertain and faltering; perhaps it coexists with doubt; perhaps we often find ourselves compelled to cry out in company with the father of the lunatic child, "Lord, I believe: help my unbelief" (*Mark* 9:24). But at least there should be some desire to believe; at least there should be, amidst all the uncertainty, a spark of love for the Jesus whom as yet we know so imperfectly.

Secondly, the context of the Jesus Prayer is one of community. We do not invoke the Name as separate individuals, relying solely upon our own inner resources, but as members of the community of the Church. Writers such as St. Barsanuphius, St. Gregory of Sinai or Bishop Theophan took it for granted that those to whom they commended the Jesus Prayer were baptized Christians, regularly participating in the Church's sacramental life through Confession and Holy Communion. Not for one moment did they envisage the Invocation of the Name as a substitute for the sacraments, but they assumed that anyone using it would be a practicing and communicant member of the Church.

Yet today, in this present epoch of restless curiosity and ecclesiastical disintegration, there are in fact many who use the Jesus Prayer without belonging to any Church, possibly without having a clear faith either in the Lord Jesus or in anything else. Are we to condemn them? Are we to forbid them the use of the Prayer? Surely not, so long as they are sincerely searching for the Fountain of Life. Jesus condemned no one except hypocrites. But, in all humility and acutely aware of our own faithlessness, we are bound to regard the situation of such people as anomalous, and to warn them of this fact.

THE JOURNEY'S END

The aim of the Jesus Prayer, as of all Christian prayer, is that our praying should become increasingly identified with the prayer offered by Jesus the High Priest within us, that our life should become one with his life, our breathing with the Divine Breath that sustains the universe. The final objective may aptly be described by the Patristic term *theosis*, "deification" or "divinization." In the words of Archpriest Sergei Bulgakov, "The Name of Jesus, present in the human heart, confers upon it the power of deification."[49] "The *Logos* became man," says St. Athanasius, "that we might become God."[50] He who is God by nature took our humanity, that we humans might share by grace in his divinity, becoming "partakers of the divine nature" (*II Peter* 1:4). The Jesus Prayer, addressed to the *Logos* Incarnate, is a means of realizing within ourselves this mystery of *theosis*, whereby human persons attain the true likeness of God.

The Jesus Prayer, by uniting us to Christ, helps us to share in the mutual indwelling or *perichoresis* of the three Persons of the Holy Trinity. The more the Prayer becomes a part of ourselves, the more we enter into the movement of love which passes unceasingly between Father, Son, and Holy Spirit. Of this love St. Isaac the Syrian has written with great beauty: "Love is the kingdom of which our Lord spoke symbolically when he promised his disciples that they would eat in his kingdom: 'You shall eat and drink at the table of my kingdom.' What should they eat, if not love?. . . When we have reached love, we have reached God and our way is ended: we have passed over to the island that lies beyond the world, where is the Father with the Son and the holy Spirit: to whom be glory and dominion."[51]

In the Hesychast tradition, the mystery of *theosis* has most often taken the outward form of a vision of light. This light which the saints behold in prayer is neither a symbolical light of the intellect, nor a physical and created light of the senses. It is nothing less than the divine and uncreated Light of the Godhead, which shone from Christ at his Transfiguration on Mount Tabor and which will illumine the whole world at his second coming on the Last Day. Here is a characteristic passage on the Divine Light taken from St. Gregory Palamas. He is describing the Apostle's vision when he was caught up into the third heaven (*II Corinthians* 12:2-4): "Paul saw a light without limits below or above or to the sides; he saw no limit whatever to the light that appeared to him and shone around him, but it was like a sun infinitely brighter and vaster than the universe; and in the midst of this sun he himself stood, having become nothing but eye."[52]

Such is the vision of glory to which we may approach through the Invocation of the Name.

The Jesus Prayer causes the brightness of the Transfiguration to penetrate into every corner of our life. Constant repetition has two effects upon the anonymous author of *The Way of a Pilgrim*. First, it transforms his relationship with the material creation around him, making all things transparent, changing them into a sacrament of God's presence. He writes: "When I prayed with my heart, everything around me seemed delightful and marvellous. The trees, the grass, the birds, the earth, the air, the light seemed to be telling me that they existed for man's sake, that they witnessed to the love of God for man, that everything proved the love of God for man, that all things prayed to God and sang his praise. Thus it was that I came to understand what the *Philokalia* calls 'the knowledge of the speech of all creatures' . . . I felt a burning love for Jesus and for all God's creatures."[53]

In the words of Father Bulgakov, "Shining through the heart, the light of the Name of Jesus illuminates all the universe."[54]

In the second place, the Prayer transfigures the Pilgrim's relation not only with the material creation but with other humans: "Again I started off on my wanderings. But now I did not walk along as before, filled with care. The Invocation of the Name of Jesus gladdened my way. Everybody was kind to me, it was as though everyone loved me . . . If anyone harms me I have only to think, 'How sweet is the Prayer of Jesus!' and the injury and the anger alike pass away and I forget it all."[55]

"Inasmuch as you have done it unto one of the least of these my brethren, you have done it unto me" (*Matthew* 25:40). The Jesus Prayer helps us to see Christ in each one, and each one in Christ.

The Invocation of the Name is in this way joyful rather than penitential, world-affirming rather than world-denying. To some, hearing about the Jesus Prayer for the first time, it may appear that to sit alone in the darkness with eyes closed, constantly repeating ". . . have mercy on me," is a gloomy and despondent way of praying. And they may also be tempted to regard it as self-centered and escapist, introverted, an evasion of responsibility to the human community at large. But this would be a grave misunderstanding. For those who have actually made the Way of the Name their own, it turns out to be not sombre and oppressive but a source of liberation and healing. The warmth and joyfulness of the Jesus Prayer is particularly evident in the writings of St. Hesychius of Sinai (eighth - ninth century): "Through persistence in the Jesus Prayer the intellect attains a state of sweetness and peace . . . . The more the rain falls on the earth, the softer it makes it; similarly, the more we call upon Christ's Holy Name, the greater the rejoicing and exultation it brings to the earth of our heart . . . . The sun rising over the earth creates the daylight; and the venerable and Holy Name of the Lord Jesus, shining continually in the mind, gives birth to countless thoughts radiant as the sun."[56]

Moreover, so far from turning our backs on others and repudiating God's creation when we say the Jesus Prayer, we are in fact affirming our commitment to our neighbour and our sense of the value of everyone and everything in God. "Acquire inner peace," said St. Seraphim of Sarov (1759 - 1833), "and thousands around you will find their salvation." By standing in Christ's presence even for no more than a few moments of each day, invoking his Name, we deepen and transform all the remaining moments of the day, rendering ourselves available to others, effective and creative, in a way that we could not otherwise be. And if we also use the Prayer in a "free" manner throughout the day, this enables us to "set the divine seal on the world," to adopt a phrase of Dr. Nadega Gorodetzky (1901 - 1985): "We can apply this Name to people, books, flowers, to all things we meet, see or think. The Name of Jesus may become a mystical key to the world, an instrument of the hidden offering of everything and everyone, setting the divine seal on the world. One might perhaps speak here of the priesthood of all believers. In union with our High Priest, we implore the Spirit: Make my prayer into a sacrament."[57]

"We can apply this Name to people . . . ." Here Dr. Gorodetzky suggests a possible answer to a question that is often raised: Can the Jesus Prayer be used as a form of intercession? The reply must be that, in the strict sense, it is distinct from intercessory prayer. As an expression of non-discursive, non-iconic "waiting upon God," it does not involve the explicit recalling and mention of particular names. We simply turn to Jesus. It is true, of course that in turning to Jesus we do not thereby turn away from our fellow humans. All those whom we love are already embraced in his heart, loved by him infinitely more than by us, and so in the end through the Jesus Prayer we find them all again in him; invoking the Name, we enter more and more fully into Christ's overflowing love for the entire world. But if we are following the traditional Hesychast pattern of the Jesus Prayer, we do not bring others before him specifically by name, or hold them deliberately in our mind, as we recite the Invocation.

All this, however, does not exclude the possibility of also giving to the Jesus Prayer an intercessory dimension. On occasion, alike in the "free" and the "formal" use, we may feel moved to "apply" the Name to one or more particular persons, invoking Jesus upon them as we say ". . . have mercy on us," or even including the actual name or names, ". . . have mercy on John." Even if this is not exactly what the Hesychast texts envisage, it is surely a legitimate and helpful extension to the practice of the Jesus Prayer. The Way of the Name has a wideness, a generosity, not to be confined within rigid and unvarying rules.

"Prayer is action; to pray is to be highly effective."[58] Of no prayer is this more true than of the Jesus Prayer. While it is singled out for particular mention in the office of monastic profession as a prayer for monks and nuns,[59] it is equally a prayer for laymen, for married couples, for doctors and psychiatrists, for social workers and bus conductors. The Invocation of the Name, practiced aright, involves each one more deeply in his or her appointed task, making each more efficient in actions, not cutting one off from others but linking to them, rendering one sensitive to fears and anxieties in a way that one never was before. The Jesus Prayer makes each into a "person for others," a living instrument of God's peace, a dynamic center of reconciliation.

NOTES

1. Tito Colliander, *The Way of the Ascetics* (London 1960), page 79.

2. Cited in Igumen Chariton of Valamo, *The Art of Prayer: An Orthodox Anthology*, translated by E. Kadloubovsky and E.M. Palmer (London 1966), page 63.

3. *Chapters*, 113 (PG 150:1280A). See Kallistos Ware, "The Jesus Prayer in St. Gregory of Sinai," *Eastern Churches Review* iv (1972), page 8.

4. A quotation from *Psalm* 118 [119]:126. In some English versions of the Liturgy this is translated, "It is time to do [sacrifice] unto the Lord," but the alternative rendering which we have used is richer in meaning and is preferred by many Orthodox commentators.

The original Greek uses the word *kairos*: "It is the *kairos* for the Lord to act." *Kairos* bears here the special meaning of the decisive moment, the moment of opportunity: he who prays seizes the *kairos*. This is a point to which we shall return.

5. Chapters, 113 (PG 150:1277D).

6. Century, 4 (PG 147:637D). The idea of prayer as the discovery of God's indwelling presence can be expounded equally in terms of the Eucharist.

7. The Jesus Prayer is nowhere mentioned, for example, in the authentic writings of St. Symeon the New Theologian or in the vast spiritual anthology of Evergetinos (both of the eleventh century).

8. There existed, of course, a warm devotion to the holy Name of Jesus in the medieval West, not least in England. While this displays certain points of difference from the Byzantine tradition of the Jesus Prayer, there are also obvious parallels. See Kallistos Ware, "The Holy Name of Jesus in East and West: the Hesychasts and Richard Rolle" *Sobornost* 4:2 (1982), pages 163-84.

9. It has even been translated into one of the major languages of the Indian sub-continent, Mahratti. The introduction to this translation has been written by a Hindu university professor who is a specialist in the spirituality of the Name: see E.R. Hambye SJ, in *Eastern Churches Review* v (1973), page 77.

10. "A Monk of the Eastern Church" [Lev Gillet], *On the Invocation of the Name of Jesus* (The Fellowship of St. Alban and St. Sergius, London 1950), pages 5-6.

11. On stillness and the two ways of prayer, 2 (PG 150, 1316B).

12. *The Art of Prayer*, page 92.

13. Brother Lawrence of the Resurrection (1611-91), *Barefooted Carmelite, The Practice of the Presence of God*, edited by D. Attwater (Paraclete Books, London 1962), pages 13, 16.

14. Archimandrite Sofrony, *The Undistorted Image: Staretz Silouan* (London 1958), pages 40-41.

15. Quoted in E. Behr-Sigel, "La Prière à Jésus ou le mystère de la spiritualité monastique orthodoxe," *Dieu Vivant* 8 (1947), page 81.

16. *The Art of Prayer*, page 110.

17. *The Way of a Pilgrim*, translated by R.M. French (London 1954), page 29.

18. H. Berthold, *Makarios/Symeon, Reden und Briefe, Logos* B33, 2, 1: vol. ii (Berlin 1973), page 29.

19. *Similitudes*, ix, 14.

20. See J. Pedersen, *Israel*, vol. i (London/Copenhagen 1926), pages 245-59; but compare J. Barr, "The Symbolism of Names in the Old Testament," *Bulletin of the John Rylands Library* 52, 1(1969), pages 11-29.

21. Pedersen, *op. cit.*, page 256.

22. For the veneration of the Name among medieval Jewish Kabbalists, see Gershom G. Scholem, *Major Trends in Jewish Mysticism* (3rd ed., London 1955), pages 132-3; and compare the treatment of this theme in the remarkable novel of Charles Williams, *All Hallows' Eve* (London 1945).

23. *Questions and Answers*, edited by Sotirios Schoinas (Volos 1960), paragraph 693; translated by L. Regnault and P. Lemaire (Solesmes 1972), paragraph 692.

24. *Ladder*, 21 and 27 (PG 88, 945C and 1112C).

25. See Kallistos Ware, "The Jesus Prayer in St. Gregory of Sinai" (article cited in note 3 above), pages 14-15.

26. *The Art of Prayer*, page 97.

27. *Questions and Answers*, edited by Schoinas, paragraph 91; translated by Regnault and Lemaire, paragraph 166.

28. *On Penitence*, 11 (PG 65, 981B). The Greek text in Migne requires emendation here.

29. *On Prayer*, 70 (PG 79, 1181C).

30. *How the Hesychast Should Persevere in Prayer*, 7 (PG 150, 1340D).

31. *The Art of Prayer*, page 101.

32. *The Art of Prayer*, page 100.

33. *Texts on Watchfulness*, 27: cf. G.E.H. Palmer, Philip Sherrard and Kallistos Ware (translators), *The Philokalia*, vol. iii (London 1984), page 27.

34. *Sacrement de l'amour. Le mystère conjugal à la lumière de la tradition orthodoxe* (Paris 1962), page 83.

35. Richard Kehoe OP, "The Scriptures as Word of God," *The Eastern Churches Quarterly* viii (1947), supplementary issue on "Tradition and Scripture," page 78.

37. Quoted in John B. Dunlop, *Staretz Amvrosy: Model for Dostoevsky's Staretz Zossima* (Belmont, Massachusetts, 1972), page 22.

37. *Hom.* xv, 32 and xliii, 7 (edited by Dörries/Klostermann/Kroeger [Berlin 1964], pages 146, 289).

38. *The Way of a Pilgrim*, page 14.

39. Starets Silouan of Mount Athos had only been practicing the Jesus Prayer for three weeks before it descended into his heart and became unceasing. His biographer, Archimandrite Sofrony, rightly points out that this was a 'sublime and rare gift'; not until later did Father Silouan come to appreciate how unusual it was (*The Undistorted Image*, page 24). For further discussion of this question, see Kallistos Ware, " 'Pray without Ceasing': The Ideal of Continual Prayer in Eastern Monasticism," *Eastern Churches Review* ii (1969), pages 259-61.

40. *Ekphrasis monastikis empeirias* (Monastery of Philotheou, Holy Mountain 1979), pages 25-28.

41. *Ladder*, 28 (PG 88, 1132C).

42. *Mystic Treatises by Isaac of Nineveh*, translated by A.J. Wensinck (Amsterdam 1923), page 113.

43. "Elijah climbed to the crest of Carmel. There he crouched to the ground with his face between his knees" (*I Kings* 18:42). For an illustration of a hesychast praying in this position, from a 12th century manuscript of John Climacus, *The Ladder of Divine Ascent*, see *The Study of Spirituality*, edited by Cheslyn Jones, Geoffrey Wainwright and Edward Yarnold SJ (SPCK, London 1986), plate 3, following page 194.

44. For further bibliography on the control of the breathing, see Kallistos Ware, "The Jesus Prayer in St. Gregory of Sinai" (cited above), page 14, note 55. On the various physical centers and their spiritual implications, see Father Anthony Bloom (now Metropolitan of Sourozh), *Asceticism (Somatopsychic Techniques)* (The Guild of Pastoral Psychology, Guild Lecture No. 95: London 1957).

45. *Triads in defence of the Holy Hesychasts*, I, ii, 7 (edited by J. Meyendorff [Louvain 1959], vol. i, page 97).

46. *The Arena: An Offering to Contemporary Monasticism*, translated by Archimandrite Lazarus (Madras 1970), page 84 (translation slightly altered).

47. *Op. cit.*, page 81.

48. See Louis Gardet, "Un problème de mystique comparée: la mention du nom divin (dhikr) dans la mystique musulmane", *Revue Thomiste*, lii (1952), pages 642-79; liii (1953), pages 197-216; reprinted in G.C. Anawati and L. Gardet, *Mystique musulmane: aspects et tendances – expdériences et techniques* (Paris 1961), pages 187-256.

49. *The Orthodox Church* (London 1935), page 170 (translation altered).

50. *On the Incarnation*, 54.

51. *Mystic Treatises*, translated by Wensinck, pages 211-12.

52. *Triads in Defence of the Holy Hesychasts*, I, iii, 21 (edited by Meyendorff, vol. i, page 157).

53. *The Way of a Pilgrim*, pages 31-2, 41.

54. *The Orthodox Church*, page 171.

55. *The Way of a Pilgrim*, pages 17-18.

56. On *Watchfulness and Holiness*, 7, 41, 196: cf. Palmer, Sherrard and Ware, *The Philokalia*, vol. i (London 1979), pages 163, 169, 197.

57. "The Prayer of Jesus," *Blackfriars* xxiii (1942), page 76.

58. Tito Colliander, *The Way of the Ascetics*, page 71.

59. At the clothing of a monk, in both the Greek and the Russian practice, it is the custom to give him a prayer-rope (*komvoschoinion*). In the Russian use the abbot says the following as it is handed over: "Take, brother, the sword of the Spirit, which is the Word of God, for continual prayer to Jesus; for you must always have the Name of the Lord Jesus in mind, in heart and on your lips, ever saying: Lord Jesus Christ, Son of God, have mercy on me a sinner." See N.F. Robinson SSJE, *Monasticism in the Orthodox Churches* (London/Milwaukee 1916), pages 159-60. Note the usual distinction between three levels of prayer: lips, mind, heart.

The Christic monogram from the Catacombs.

4

THE LADDER OF THE DIVINE ASCENT
The Yoga of Hesychasm[1]

James Cutsinger

I must begin with a few words of caution. This talk is meant to serve as a prelude to our discussing the short poem now before you, "The Ladder of Divine Graces" by Theophanis the Monk. We know very little about Theophanis, not even when he lived. All we are sure of is that he was a monastic of the Christian East. Here is where a first warning comes in. Nothing I shall be saying is going to make the slightest sense unless you understand at the outset that for Theophanis Christianity is a mystagogical path, a way toward what is. It is not a creed, it is not a rite, it is not an ethic, and it is not a series of historical events. Or rather, while it includes all these things on the surface, in its essence it is the means of our becoming Divine.

A second caveat has to do with the expectations one brings to this discussion. We need to be realistic. Into these seventy-one lines of verse are distilled over a thousand years of spiritual teaching and ascetic discipline. The poem is like an alchemical tincture, very concentrated and very potent. My hope is simply to open a door into a world which for many of you will be unfamiliar, the world of the monks of Mounts Athos and Sinai, whose quest towards *hesychia* or stillness has given rise to their designation as the hesychast fathers. There is no question of providing an exhaustive interpretation of their tradition. I wish only to highlight a few salient ideas, while underscoring the poet's own repeated stress on experience. Experience teaches one, he says, not words. Whatever else, Theophanis means to prick the conscience of anyone who supposes that doctrine can stand alone without method, theory without practice. We need the effectual means of liberation supplied by a genuine yoga. Reading great books is not enough.

I have mentioned how little is known of this author. This fact is a great blessing, of course. By providing the ready excuse of necessity, it permits us cheerfully to dispense with that whole apparatus of biographical and other horizontal details which so often intrudes between a text and its readers. My only concession to the usual academic procedure is to tell you that "The Ladder" can be found in the third volume of *The Philokalia*, a classic compilation of Christian mystical writings ranging from the fourth to the fifteenth centuries. Beyond that, I would ask that you think of "Theophanis" strictly as a symbol for certain acts of reflection, and of his poem as but a provocation for entering the Supreme Reality.

Allow me to begin by reading the poem aloud as you follow along:

The Ladder of Divine Graces
which experience has made known to those inspired by God

The first step is that of purest prayer.
From this there comes a warmth of heart,
And then a strange, a holy energy,
Then tears wrung from the heart, God-given.
Then peace from thoughts of every kind.
From this arises purging of the intellect,
And next the vision of heavenly mysteries.
Unheard-of light is born from this ineffably,
And thence, beyond all telling, the heart's illumination.
Last comes — a step that has no limit
Though compassed in a single line —
Perfection that is endless.
The ladder's lowest step
Prescribes pure prayer alone.
But prayer has many forms:
My discourse would be long
Were I now to speak of them:
And, friend, know that always
Experience teaches one, not words.
A ladder rising wondrously to heaven's vault:
Ten steps that strangely vivify the soul.
Ten steps that herald the soul's life.
A saint inspired by God has said:
Do not deceive yourself with idle hopes

That in the world to come you will find life
If you have not tried to find it in this present world.
Ten steps: a wisdom born of God.
Ten steps: fruit of all the books.
Ten steps that point towards perfection.
Ten steps that lead one up to heaven.
Ten steps through which a man knows God.
The ladder may seem short indeed,
But if your heart can inwardly experience it
You will find a wealth the world cannot contain,
A god-like fountain flowing with unheard-of life.
This ten-graced ladder is the best of masters,
Clearly teaching each to know its stages.

If when you behold it
You think you stand securely on it,
Ask yourself on which step you stand,
So that we, the indolent, may also profit.
My friend, if you want to learn about all this,
Detach yourself from everything,
From what is senseless, from what seems intelligent.
Without detachment nothing can be learnt.
Experience alone can teach these things, not talk.
Even if these words once said
By one of God's elect strike harshly,
I repeat them to remind you:
He who has no foothold on this ladder,
Who does not ponder always on these things,
When he comes to die will know
Terrible fear, terrible dread,
Will be full of boundless panic.
My lines end on a note of terror.
Yet it is good that this is so:
Those who are hard of heart — myself the first —
Are led to repentance, led to a holy life,
Less by the lure of blessings promised
Than by fearful warnings that inspire dread.
"He who has ears to hear, let him hear."
You who have written this, hear, then, and take note:

Void of all these graces,
How have you dared to write such things?
How do you not shudder to expound them?
Have you not heard what Uzzah suffered
When he tried to stop God's ark from falling?
Do not think that I speak as one who teaches:
I speak as one whose words condemn himself,
Knowing the rewards awaiting those who strive,
Knowing my utter fruitlessness.

Now as you may have noticed, the text falls naturally into several distinct parts. First, there is a labeling of the ten steps on the ladder; second, an emphasis on the special importance of the initial step, purity in prayer; third, a listing of the ladder's benefits; fourth, a request for assistance from persons further advanced than the author; fifth, stern counsel for those who are just beginning, together with a justification for this severity; and sixth, the author's concluding self-reproach and effacement. An entire lecture could be given under each of these headings. I believe that I can best serve our discussion by concentrating on the meaning of the ten steps themselves, adding then a few broader strokes concerning the rest of the poem.

First, though, just a word or two concerning the title. In a sense, the title of this poem says it all: *The Ladder of Divine Graces.* The man who seeks union with God must understand before he even begins his search that synergy or cooperation is the key to his movement, a cooperation between human effort and Divine mercy. A ladder must be climbed, and the climbing is accomplished one step at a time. The spiritual life demands real work, real movement, real discipline, which proceeds methodically and incrementally. It is dangerous, says Plato, to go too quickly from the many to the One, and the hesychast tradition takes account of this fact in distrusting ecstasies and consolations not grounded in method. On the other hand, one must not forget that man's climbing is not only toward God; it is in and by God. Each of the rungs of the ladder is a gift or a grace, a real and efficacious presence of the Goal in the very midst of the way. True spirituality is not Pelagian, not a self-help technique. "Work out your salvation with fear and trembling, for God is at work within you" (*Philippians* 2:12-13).

The subtitle confirms this synergy. The authority of the poem's teaching is at once human and Divine. On one level it is a matter of embodied truth. What we are about to be told is no rarified speculation, concocted by some spiritual dreamer whose claims are untestable. It comes instead rooted in the concrete, the practical, the immediate, and it leads beyond mere credulity or acceptance to certainty. Notice that experience has made the ladder known. But at the same time, the knowledge is thanks to God, who has mercifully condescended to those inspired by Him. We should be grateful. Authentic wisdom is never man's alone, an accomplishment or achievement for which he can take credit. The wisdom born of God is to know that God knows Himself in us.

* * *

Turning now to the poem itself, you will observe that each of the ten steps of the ladder can be distinguished by a single noun. The journey passes through the several stages of prayer, heart, energy, tears, peace, purging, vision, light, illumination and perfection. But the nouns in each case are to be specified by adjectives. It is not just any prayer, but purest prayer that counts; not just any heart, but a warm one. So also we note that the energy is holy, the tears are God-given, the peace is mental, the purging is intellective, the vision is mystical, the light is ineffable, the illumination is cardiac and the perfection is endless.

Theophanis is careful to stress that the prayer of step one is of a most particular kind. Prayer may include but is more than a collection of petitions and praises, whether private or public, spoken or silent, personal or canonical. In its purest form, it is an imageless attention to the Divine presence, ontologically rather than discursively linked to its object, and often supported by the repetition of a short invocatory formula like the Jesus Prayer. Please note that the attention of this opening step is itself a highly advanced spiritual state, presupposing a background not even hinted at in the poem. Our exposition of the text is obliging us to begin at a point far beyond what most of us are ready for. Quintessential prayer is the bottom rung of a ladder that must first be set on a living sacramental foundation, and its scaling assumes a deliberate and extensive propaedeutic under the guidance of a spiritual father. The Christian mystical tradition knows very well that individual initiatives and exploits are always ruinous in the contemplative life. Hence the author's deference, in the lines below, to his own elders and betters: to a saint inspired by God and to one of God's elect.

Were a man granted the grace of this first step — were those of us in this room really prepared to go further — it would soon be discovered that true prayer is a transformative power, which begins to work its magic within the tissues of the human body itself. This is noticed initially, the hesychasts teach, in that central part of the body, the heart, where pure consciousness dwells, and the most common signal of change is a sensation of warmth. Warmth, like the heart, is no metaphor. Something really begins to happen in the breast. One could say that it happens in and to the four-chambered beating muscle if the concern is to stress, as one must, the material actuality of the process. But at the same time, the warmth comes as proof that our true heart was always more than its concealment in matter, more than just a physical pump. In either case, the ladder brings the whole man into play. The body is not left behind in our approach to full union, but is lifted up and drawn into its Divine prototype. Heaven is more, not less, solid than earth.

And then a strange, a holy energy. What was true at first for the central organ alone gradually makes itself felt throughout the entire human organism. A centrifugal radiation of power begins now to course outward through the various envelopes of the self. Energy is a technical term in this context. Western philosophy is accustomed to a distinction between form and matter. Energy is the third that connects these two, the living and interior pulse through which essence communicates itself as a substance. If we picture what a thing is as a center and how it appears as a sphere, then the radii are an image of its energy. God too has His own kind of energy, the effective and salvific presence of the Transcendent in the domain of the immanent. Theophanis is certainly no pantheist: the Divine Essence remains like an asymptote forever beyond our aspiration as creatures. Nevertheless we may participate fully in the Divine Substance and come to share in God's powers through an assimilation of His holy energies. The nexus of this exchange is man's heart, an exchange which begins when our own center moves toward coincidence with the center of God.

Tears, the fourth step, are a mark of this concentrical shift. Not just any tears, however: only those that are God-given. It is very important that we not confuse the "gift of tears," as it is sometimes called, with ordinary sorrow or grief. Climbing the ladder means mastering the passions, including the self-pity, resentment and anger which sometimes express themselves in crying. We are to become objective toward our ego, no longer controlled by its sentimental involvement in the shifting play of the world. Detach yourself from everything, says Theophanis. For without detachment nothing can be learnt. The tears of the ladder are not tears of selfish regret or refusal. On the contrary, they are the natural result of the ego's liquefaction. As the radiant energy of God carries the heart's warmth forward through the rest of our nature, the many layers of ice begin melting. We become the warm, soft water of our tears. The warmth is our fervor and longing for God; the softness is our yielding to the Divine influx; the water is the power of our new-found passivity.

The next pair of steps may be usefully treated as one, for they are two sides of a single coin: peace from thoughts and purging of the intellect. Notice that the peace is from thoughts of every kind. This is no power of positive thinking, which would simply replace bad or debilitating conceptions with good ones. The hesychast follows a path leading beyond conception as such. By thoughts he means any product of discursive mentation, any recording of the impressions of sense and any abstraction therefrom or combination thereof. He knows that our waking life is dominated by the mental chatter that comes from the jostling and sorting of these impressions, images, ideas and feelings, and that our so-called waking is therefore truly a dreaming. We are never simply now in the present, so fully occupied is our mind by the memory of what was and the idle hopes of what will be.

Against all of this must be placed an altogether different quality of attention, superintended by what the Christian East calls the *nous* or intellect. Unlike discursive thinking, which proceeds sequentially with the information it has gleaned from the surface of things, the intellective or noetic faculty goes straight to their core, contemplating the inner *logoi* or essences of creatures by direct apprehension. Present in all of us but dormant in most, the intellect is first awakened and set into motion by the efforts of prayer and ascetic discipline. Once purged of the encrusting dross which surrounds it, the noetic faculty becomes in turn a purging or purifying force of its own. Cutting through the veils of forgetfulness and piercing to the world's very marrow, it there discovers by recollection its own inward content. "For, behold, the kingdom of God is within you" (*Luke* 17:21).

Theophanis has incorporated within his own ten-fold sequence a more common and better known distinction among three basic stages in the spiritual life: purification, illumination and union. The first of these has been the subject of the poem to this point, beginning with purest prayer in step one and culminating with the purging of the intellect in step six. His aim has been to describe the indispensable initial work of repentance, a negative movement away from illusion and death. Now we begin glimpsing the positive results of that work, for the next three steps are all concerned in some way with vision and light, and thus with the second fundamental stage of illumination. There is a vision of heavenly mysteries, next the perception of unheard-of light, and then the illumination of the heart itself.

Now please understand, the mysteries which Theophanis has in view are not secret facts or formulas, nor is the fruit of his path a knowledge of celestial statistics. If you are interested in dating the end of the world or in the number of ascended masters on Venus or in how many lives you might have lived before this one or in any of the other similar bits and pieces of occult information so often dangled before the curious seekers of our day, you shall have to go elsewhere. Theophanis has counseled detachment not only from what is senseless but from what seems intelligent, and this latter category doubtless includes much of what passes for spirituality in this so-called new age. He knows that a true mystery by definition exceeds the form of data, no matter how peculiar or enticing those data might be. The inner is always inner even in the midst of our seeing it, weekend workshops notwithstanding! Etymology is important here: the term "mystery" comes from the Greek verb *muo*, which refers to a closing or shutting of the eyes and mouth. The vision of mysteries remains a vision of mysteries, of realities which continue to elude ordinary empirical perception and which cannot be adequately conveyed by any language. I might add that the eastern Christian tradition regularly uses the term "mysteries" to refer to its sacraments, especially the eucharist. We are reminded that the spiritual ladder must be firmly positioned on a living faith before we even consider ascending it.

Whatever it is that one noetically sees, the hesychasts are unanimous about its being bathed in an extraordinary light. Indeed, the doctrine of the uncreated light is characteristic of their teaching. Once again we are using more than a metaphor. It is said that the light in question is objectively real, its model being the light of Christ's transfiguration on Mount Tabor, when "his face shone as the sun, and his raiment was white as the light" (*Matthew* 17:2). Being born from one's vision ineffably, this dazzling darkness eclipses all description. And yet it is truly there, suffusing creation with the radiance of God, a sort of visible band in the spectrum of His holy energy. Intimately tied to our transformed perception of this light all about us, there will come next a corresponding and complementary illumination within. Beyond all telling, this ninth step of the ladder admits man to a degree of Divine participation where he himself begins to shine with Christ's glory. True to the maxim that like can be known only by like, the hesychast strives by grace toward the moment when the body, now thoroughly steeped in God, bears witness in its own substance to the realities it has seen. The iconographical tradition of the halo or nimbus is no pious extravagance. Had we the eyes to see, we would realize that the true saint shines like the heaven he is.

And yet heaven is not enough. Heaven is a prison for the Sufi, say the mystics of Islam, for who wants the garden when there is also the Gardener? Theophanis agrees. There is more than illumination in the spiritual journey. We are not to rest satisfied with a contemplation of the splendor of God nor with an appreciative spectator's place, however joyful and permanent, in the Divine proximity. A tenth step remains: a coinherence or union with the Supreme Reality itself. For as the hesychast sees it, the only truly endless perfection is the perfection of what is intrinsically endless or infinite, namely, God. It is therefore into this Infinite that human nature will eventually be drawn at the very top of the ladder. Like God Himself, the top rung has no limit, even though its description may be compassed in a single line. The end of the way is in fact the beginning of an immeasurable advance into the Love that loves Love and in Love all things. Those of you who are familiar with eastern Christian theology will recognize this as the Orthodox doctrine of deification, classically summed up in the Patristic formula "God became man that man might become God." Salvation is not just the restoration of an Edenic status quo. It is an unprecedented and unheard-of life, no longer restricted by the qualities and conditions of created existence in this present world. A reversion has taken place along the path of creation, a voluntary return of what we are into God. Two distinct circles remain, the human and the Divine, but their center is now the same.

*   *   *

I turn now as promised to the remaining parts of the poem. The most important question we should be asking ourselves at this juncture is why there is a remainder at all. After scaling the summit of deification, the succeeding lines will seem to many of us tedious and anticlimactic. What is Theophanis's point in reserving by far the larger part of his text for what follows?

Why not stop, as he easily might have, with three highly charged quatrains leading up to perfection? The rest of the first page makes a certain amount of sense. As I observed in my opening sketch, the author now goes on to accentuate the crucial first step of the ladder and then offers some reflections on the beauties and benefits of the path, rekindling our wonder at the full glory of participation in God. But why the second page? Why all this imploration, admonition, and self-reproach?

To answer these questions, we need to consider a common feature of all hesychast writing, common in fact to the Christian East as a whole, and that is its preference for the mystical way of negation. It is often said that there are two distinct spiritual paths: the *cataphatic* way or way of affirmation and the *apophatic* way or way of negation. In the former, which is somewhat more typical of western theology, one approaches God by affirming His goodness in good things, His beauty in things that are beautiful, and His truth in all truths. God is the highest or greatest of beings, to whom creatures point through their positive qualities. In the negative way, by contrast, one approaches God by prescinding from all qualities or attributes, by denying that the Supreme Reality has anything whatsoever in common with this world. God is not created or finite, of course. Every theologian knows that. But neither is He even good with the goodness we know, nor wise in terms of earthly wisdom, nor indeed does He exist by our standards. He is not the highest or greatest of beings, but superessentially beyond even being itself.

We have seen evidence of this apophaticism in the opening section of "The Ladder." The vision is a vision of mysteries, the Divine light is unheard-of, and the heart's illumination is beyond all telling. In short, experience alone can teach these things, not talk. All language is reduced to stammering and silence when confronted by the experience of God. But of course the same thing is true of all our experiences. Which words are really sufficient for a rose or a friendship? Perception on every level of being is always more than the concepts describing it.

Theophanis is therefore obliged to go further, extending the range of negation and deepening its intensity. Do not

deceive yourself, he continues. The full force of his imper-
ative will not be felt unless we have first admitted that our
entire waking life is a web of delusion and vanity. Recall what
I said earlier on the subject of thoughts. Try to attend to one
thing alone, and you will soon discover that your days are but
daydreams. Whatever contact we may hope for with absolute
Truth will come only at the expense of all those idle hopes
aroused by our present, passion-laden experience. This does
not mean that we should despair of making any progress toward God, believing ourselves condemned to a sort of total depravity. The apophatic path is still a path, and the poet is quick
in counseling us to make every effort to find the Truth in this
present world. It should be understood, however, that this last
phrase is adverbial, not adjectival; it modifies man's endeavors
toward finding, not the Truth found. For the Supreme Reality
is beyond even more than our personal experience. It transcends the entire cosmic order. What we shall find when we
find it is a wealth the world cannot contain. The author means
what he says: if you wish to enter God, you must detach yourself from everything.

Understanding this stress on negation should help us
considerably when it comes to the second page of "The Ladder." If you are like me, the poet's vivid expressions of
unworthiness may at first seem excessive, rather like the protestations of the well-bred Confucian who always speaks of
himself as "this contemptible person." We are told that
Theophanis is indolent, hard of heart and void of all these
graces; that he is presumptuous in having dared to write on so
sublime a subject and is therefore deserving of the fate of the
Biblical Uzzah, who was killed for touching the ark of God (*II
Samuel* 6:6-7); and finally that he is worthy only of words that
condemn himself, an example of utter fruitlessness. Surely, one
feels, this very eloquent monk cannot have been quite such a
villain! And then, making matters perhaps even more indigest-
ible, there are the threats of boundless panic. A note of terror
is sounded by the author's fearful warnings, which he deliberately intends to strike us harshly and to inspire our dread. What
is going on here? Is this pious sentimentality? Is the author
following some ancient stylistic precedent? Is he just trying to

scare us?

Our answer in each case must be *No*. I admit that the poem could be read this way and that it is easy to be put off by its seeming platitudes and fire-and-brimstone exhortations. Such a reading, however, would be quite mistaken. Think about it. A man who understands so precisely the pure science of prayer, who is subtle enough to distinguish between illumination and light, and who from his own experience in wrestling with thoughts can speak so powerfully about the limits of language is surely aware of what we ourselves can see so clearly. We all know from our own not-so-subtle experience that terror and panic are emotions belonging to the hardened, not the liquefied, heart. They are measures of the ego's continuing eccentricity in relation to God, the result of its congenital complicity in a world which will finally disappoint every one of us. In hesychast terms, such passions are simply more thoughts, more psychic chatter. Theophanis cannot possibly be construed as encouraging them. Nor can he have failed to see that insofar as someone recognizes his fruitlessness, he cannot be utterly fruitless. The poet is aware, as we are, that the ego has a way of feeding even on abjection and self-condemnation, of being proud of its sin. When he refers to himself as the first among those who are hard of heart, it would therefore be absurd to imagine that he expects us to think we are his rightful superiors.

Only the negative way can make sense of these puzzling expressions; both the self-reproaches and the warnings require transposing into an apophatic key. It is helpful to recall the relative anonymity of the poet. The compilers of *The Philokalia* have recorded his name, of course, or at least his pen name, but that is all. This is most important. In reading "The Ladder," we are not listening to the voice of a particular individual whose actual biography might be used in checking the accuracy of his judgments. We are listening to a voice which the accidents of history have now rendered impersonal, according perhaps to its own design: the voice (if you will) of the search itself, the inward voice of every man's longing for God. I suggested in starting that the author's name should be seen as a symbol, and I can now be more precise about that symbol's significance. "Theophanis the Monk" is not such and such an ego. He is the ego as such.

With this in mind, his estimate of himself becomes perfectly intelligible. He is indeed void of all graces, not just in fact but in principle. For measured against the Supreme Reality at the top of the ladder, the ego is even less than unworthy; it is itself a virtual void. It is nothing but a centrifugal tendency toward the "outer darkness" (*Matthew* 8:12) of destruction, the root of blind and fruitless craving, and its mortification is essential to seeing that God's is the only true center. Competition with the Divine is never more than illusion.

The promises of terror and the fearful warnings can be interpreted along similar lines. I singled out the words terror and panic as signs of a purely emotional and egocentric attachment. But suppose we read them instead in conjunction with two other of Theophanis's terms: fear and dread. Fear is often just a passion itself, of course, a feeling of malaise, consternation or anxiety, and as such it too must be excluded from the soul of the man who is seeking peace from thoughts. But in an older and deeper sense, as you know, fear means awe. Rather than a subjective and blood-freezing fright, it points us toward an objective and liberating wonder. No mere reactive emotion, this kind of fear is a real organ for perception and participation in God. I do not wish to expunge the common sense meaning of the poet's words. Doubtless there will come a day of sheer panic for those who in this life did not ponder always on these things and did not by a serious spiritual effort grow accustomed to the daily death of desire. But for those who did, the holy fear of awe, the exquisite joy of dread, will be itself among the blessings promised. Far from something they might wish to escape, it is among the many rewards of their way, a delicious fruit of all the books. These seekers know from repeated experience that the negation of a negation is something wondrously positive. Theophanis is not trying to scare them or force their submission to a sectarian ideology. With a precise and carefully selected apophatic language, he is simply describing what it means to climb the ladder; the negations are nothing but the spaces between the rungs. We are being shown from the point of view of the ego what happens when the many layers of ambition and cowardice and resentment and greed and smugness and torpor are each in turn stripped away and the naked soul is ushered, beyond all possibility, into the heart of the living God.

NOTE

1. Lecture delivered at St. John's College, Santa Fe, New Mexico, 1 May 1996. Copyright © 2001 James S. Cutsinger.

Mount Sinai.

St. Seraphim of Sarov, by Monk Gregory Kroug.
Twentieth century, Montgeron, Paris.

5

A SUFIC PERSPECTIVE ON
SAINT SERAPHIM OF SAROV*

Gray Henry

Of Seraphim of Sarov, Thomas Merton wrote: "He is without a doubt the greatest mystic of the Russian Church, and the Hesychast tradition is evident in his mysticism of light."[1] As *Merton & Hesychasm* is the second in a series begun with *Merton & Sufism: The Untold Story*, it would seem appropriate to show some ways in which these two sources of Merton's inspiration have parallels. These two spiritual methodologies, or "Paths to the Heart," have much to offer the seeker.[2] This essay takes the aspect of light as one of many possible illuminating topics for comparison.

In Merton's view, "One of the best known (or least unknown) of the Russian mystics is St. Seraphim of Sarov who lived the life of a desert Father in the forests at the beginning of the nineteenth century. He affords a striking contrast to other post-medieval saints and ascetics who have tried to imitate the Desert Fathers . . . . Whether or not Seraphim had studied ancient monastic tradition, it is certain that he was a living and spontaneous exemplar of the most authentic monastic ideal. His solitary life in the forest was extremely austere and yet his spirituality was marked by pure joy. Though he gave himself unsparingly to each ascetic exploit (*podvig*), he remained simple, childlike, meek, astonishingly open to life and to other men, gentle, and profoundly compassionate."[3]

This morning I will very simply mention a number of the parallels to be found in these two methodologies for realization: the way of the Sufi, and that of the Hesychast. Then I propose to make a few further remarks on the subject of Light, particularly in regard to St. Seraphim of Sarov.

---

* *This lecture was given at the conference on Hesychasm and Sufism, entitled "Paths to the Heart," in October 2001 at the University of South Carolina.*

In *The Orthodox Way*[4], Bishop Kallistos Ware states, "We are on a journey through the inward space of our heart — a journey out of time into eternity." I emphasize the word *way* in the title of his book, for elsewhere he points out that one of the most ancient names for Christianity is the "Way." A Sufi order is called a *Tariqa*, which translates also as a Way. The aim of both ways is *theosis* or divinization of a person. We are asked to be who we already are — beings made in God's image. Neither way envisions this transmutation as a substitute for the rites or sacraments enjoined by Christianity and Islam. Central to each path is the invocation of a sacred name — Jesus or Allah. Whether the name is used on its own or contained within other formulations, in Hesychasm this strenuous prayer is called "The Hidden Martyrdom" and in Islam, "The Greater *Jihad*." The effort made against the soul's lower disruptive tendencies also is described by both traditions as a martyrdom, with Paradise as its reward.

A person wishing to undertake this most serious and noble of pursuits takes guidance from a master. The word *staretz* in Russian, *gerōn* in Greek, and *sheikh* in Arabic all refer to an elder capable of guiding an aspirant, someone who knows the Way and its pitfalls. In both traditions there have been women and men both as masters and disciples. One cannot help but be struck when reading *Early Sufi Women* by as-Sulami[5] — a record of the lives of Sufi women around the tenth century — that the austerities they sought to imitate were those practiced by the Virgin Mary herself.[6] For those who may not be familiar with Islam, Mary is considered the highest woman in all creation and is an example for both men and women to follow in regards to her piety and purity.

In both Hesychasm and Sufism, the master gives the disciple instructions according to the degree of his or her progress. Postures and breathing exercises which may accompany the Jesus Prayer are permitted in stages, as are the recitations or ritual participation in Sufism. In each methodology, there are the free and formal uses of the practices, used both when alone and in groups. Regular retreats and the rosary provide further support. Most Eastern Orthodox prayer rosaries have 100 woolen beads or knots and the Muslim prayer beads also number 100 — ninety-nine representing the divine attributes and a single longer bead called an *alif* or "A" which refers to God.[7]   There is also a parallel here, where the so-called Essence and the energies of the Eastern Church stand next to the Essence or *Dhat* (Allah) and the ninety-nine names.   In John Meyendorf's study of St. Gregory of Palamas[8] he says: "As God (Essence) is completely present in each of the divine energies, each serves as His name."   Palamas writes: "Manifesting the personal being of God, the divine energies reflect the unity of the Divine Essence — inseparable from the Essence, but not identical with it."   For both the Hesychast and the Sufi, the heart is the meeting place with God.   In Hesychasm and Sufism it is usual for the disciple to receive a second name, symbolic of this second birth upon entering the Way.

In his *Ways of Prayer and Contemplation*,[9] Bishop Kallistos Ware describes three stages of the spiritual journey: as follows:

1) *Praktike* — (repentance, *metanoia* — changed mind).   One's aim is to purify the heart.   In Arabic the term for this is *tawbah* or turning with the intention not just of asking forgiveness, but literally of turning completely around.   The Hesychast redirects his or her passions, rather than suppress or mortify them.   This is called *apatheia*.

2) *Physiké* — the second stage involves contemplation of both the natural world and then the angelic and other realms of immateriality.   "To see all things in God, and God in all things . . . treat each thing as a sacrament."[10]   According to Evagrius, someone came to the righteous St. Anthony asking how he could manage without the consolation of books.

St. Anthony replied, "My book is the nature of created things and it is at hand whenever I wish to read the words of God."[11]

For the Muslim too, natural forms are seen as the *ayat* or signs of God.   Quranic verses are also called *ayat*.

3) *Theoria* — represents knowledge beyond concepts.   According to Evagrius, "When you pray, do not shape within yourself any image of the Deity."[12]   The aim here is God's immediate presence.

*   *   *

In Gregory of Nyssa's symbolic interpretation of the first of the ten commandments prohibiting graven images, he says, "Every concept grasped by the mind becomes an obstacle. Our aim is to attain beyond all words and concepts a contained presence." Of this, Bishop Kallistos Ware comments, "This non-iconic, non-discursive consciousness of God's presence — often referred to in Greek as *Hesychia*, *i.e.* tranquility and inner stillness — is not an emptiness or a void but a Presence."[13]

The word for this presence in Arabic is *hadrat*. A Sufi gathering to invoke God's name is called a *hadrat*. When you politely speak to a person, you say "Your Presence" — "*Hadritik*," referring to the Divine presence within. St. Seraphim would say to a person seeking council from him, "Your Godliness." This is excellent — we should do it! Speak to that person who is truly before us!

It is the same with the Buddhist *Namaste* — "the light in me recognizes and honors the light in you."

Now this same idea in Hesychasm of quietude and presence appears in a Quranic verse recited at Sufi *hadrats*. The etymological root of the term *Sakina* has different levels of related meaning:

Sakan — dwelling;

Sakana — to be quiet;

Sukun — pause;

Sekinah — the indwelling distillation of grace and presence.

A Quranic verse recited at Sufi *hadrats* translates: "He it is Who has caused the Spirit of Peace (*Sakina*) to descend into the Heart of the believers — that they may increase in faith."

In this third stage where both the Hesychast and the Sufi aim at union or knowledge of God beyond all concepts, the Sufi apophatically recites upon his or her rosary, *la ilaha ilalah* — there is no divinity save The Divinity.

*   *   *

*"The Light Shines in the Darkness
but the darkness has not understood it."*
— John 1-5

"Lord have mercy upon us" is *Kyrie Eleison* in Greek. The word *Eleison* shares the same etymological root with the word for olive oil and the olive tree. Metropolitan Anthony Bloom has suggested that the dove returning to Noah bearing an olive branch conveys a healing mercy "that we should be able to live and become that which we are called to be."

In the Light verse of the *Quran*, we hear of this olive oil and tree, this Mercy:

"Allah is the Light of the heavens and the earth; the likeness of His Light is as a niche wherein is a lamp — the lamp is in a glass, the glass is as it were a brightly shining star kindled from a blessed Olive Tree that is neither of the East nor of the West, whose oil well-nigh would shine, though fire does not touch it; Light upon Light; Allah guides to His Light whom He wills."

This verse concludes: "God strikes similitudes for man and God is all knowing."

And a similitude He struck for me was this. I came down the hill from my home in Kentucky to our river and was walking along the banks of the Ohio — and ahead in the mud I saw something shining brightly like a star. I found it was an empty shell — whose emptiness exposed its pearl-like lustrous interior. As not a fleck of the former inhabitant remained — so it totally reflected the light — I saw it as a sign or *ayat* in Nature: the way I should be. Only in total emptiness, humility and the corresponding silence can I too shine forth.

And this reminds me of Saint Seraphim of Sarov — whose emptiness shone, and then on to a Sufic perspective bearing on his luminosity.

The Flame in the Snow[14] describes the life of Saint Seraphim (1759 - 1833) who entered a monastery in the Taiga Siberian Forest at nineteen, and after sixteen years in the community spent twenty-six years in seclusion sheltered by a hut in the forest. He endured great hardship as he fiercely wrestled with his soul. His feet became swollen from illness. He could speak with the animals. He carried stones on his back to remind himself of the burdens of those he could not relieve. Even he despaired of God. But he repeated the Jesus Prayer incessantly, and at last his carnal body was transfused with Light — a Light that would shine into the darkness and destroy it. At sixty-seven, he had attained a perfect blend of spirit and body.

Having withdrawn to the forest for purification, in 1815 he returned to society and received all who came, very like the father of Christian hermits, St. Anthony. After his austerities and night vigils, he was granted a vision of the Divine and Uncreated Light which also transformed him outwardly. One can envision him moving, laden down with stones, in the deep snow and gloom, glowing. A woman who came for consolation bent her head, unable to endure the brightness of his face.

When a certain man, Motovilov, asked Saint Seraphim how a man could be sure of Being in the Spirit of God, the following occurred:

Father Seraphim replied: "I have already told you, your Godliness, that it is very simple and I have related in detail how people come to be in the Spirit of God and how we can recognize His presence in us. So what do you want, my son?"

"I want to understand it well," I said.

Then Father Seraphim took me very firmly by the shoulders and said: "We are both in the Spirit of God now, my son. Why don't you look at me?"

I replied: "I cannot look, father, because your eyes are flashing like lightning. Your face has become brighter than the sun, and my eyes ache with pain."

Father Seraphim said: "Don't be alarmed, your Godliness! Now you yourself have become as bright as I am. You are now in the fullness of the Spirit of God yourself; otherwise you would not be able to see me as I am."

Then bending his head towards me, he whispered softly in my ear: "Thank the Lord God for His unutterable mercy to us! You saw that I did not even cross myself; and only in my heart I prayed mentally to the Lord and said within myself: 'Lord, grant him to see clearly with his bodily eyes that descent of Thy Spirit which Thou grantest to Thy servants when Thou art pleased to appear in the light of Thy majestic glory.'"

After these words I glanced at his face and there came over me an even greater sense of reverent awe. Imagine in the center of the sun, in the dazzling light of its midday rays, the face of a man talking to you. You see the movement of his lips and the changing expression of his eyes, you hear his voice, you feel someone holding your shoulders, yet you do not see his hands; you do not even see yourself or his figure, but only a blinding light spreading far around for several yards and illumining with its glaring sheen both the snow-blanket which covered the forest glade and the snow-flakes which besprinkled me and the great elder.[15]

According to Bishop Kallistos Ware, this passage is important for our understanding of the Orthodox doctrine of deification and union with God, which is the goal of the whole Eastern Orthodox Church. He says, "It shows how the Orthodox idea of sanctification includes the body: it is not Seraphim's or Motovilov's soul only — but the whole body which is transfigured by the Grace of God. We may note that neither Seraphim nor Motivilov is in a state of ecstasy — both can talk in a coherent way and are still conscious of the outside world — but both are filled with the Holy Spirit and surrounded by the Light of the Age to Come."

This recalls Moses, who shone with such extraordinary light people could not bear to behold him.

In his book *In the Image and Likeness of God*,[16] Vladimir Lossky quotes from St. Gregory's *Homily on the Transfiguration* in a chapter entitled "The Theology of Light in the Thought of St. Gregory Palamas": "The light of the Lord's transfiguration had no beginning and no end; it remained uncircumscribed and imperceptible to the senses although it was contemplated with corporeal eyes. By a transmutation of their senses the disciples of the Lord passed from the flesh to the Spirit."

Lossky explains, "In order to see the Divine Light with corporeal eyes, as the disciples did on Mount Tabor, one must participate in His Light, one must be transformed by it — to a greater or lesser degree."

In another homily, St. Gregory of Thessalonica says of the mystical experience, "He who participates in the divine energy, becomes himself, in a sense, Light."

Both Islam and Sufism are filled with references to light, but it is to the genre of Sufi writing called the School of Illumination that we turn for this moment, and to the writings of a thirteenth century poet, Fakhruddin Iraqi, whose central concern was the purification of the heart, elucidated in *Divine Flashes*[17] translated by William Chittick and P.L. Wilson. In his introduction, Professor Chittick describes how the various schools of Islamic thought employ a variety of terms when referring to Ultimate Reality:

— Theologians speak of God/Allah and explain his attributes in Quranic terms.

— The peripatetic philosophers spoke of the Necessary Being, "*wajib al wujud.*"

— The Illuminist philosophers referred to Ultimate Reality as Light or *Nur*.

In her *Mystical Dimension of Islam*[18] A.M. Schimmel states that "what is conceived metaphysically as existence (*wujud*) coincides with what is grasped in terms of root experience as Light. In this context existence is Light. Iraqi identifies Being with Light. Chittick explains that Being belongs to God and nonexistence is the inherent quality of the creatures.

When we refer to Being as Light, then a creature or entity whose nature is darkness can only be luminous when he or she participates in and reflects Diving Being. Darkness mixed with Light results in the "brightness or the dimming of the Light." Professor Chittick says, "By acting as a veil over sheer light, darkness allows the myriad colors to be perceived, that is, the possibilities and perfections of outward manifestation latent within the very nature of Light to be perceived. But what becomes outward and visible is never anything other than Light — for darkness has no positive reality and thus can never itself be seen. The nature of the varying degrees of "brightness" that are perceived is not determined by darkness but by the Essence of light itself" — like God's Grace to Saint Seraphim.

Being is none other than sheer light. Only humans have the capacity to attain a station where they can act as reflectors or transmitters for this Light.

Iraqi says: "One needs THY light to see Thee."

PART II

THOMAS MERTON
AND EASTERN CHRISTIANITY

Church of the Holy Cross, Aght'amar (present-day Turkey), 915 - 921 C.E.

1

THE WORSHIP OF THE WHOLE CREATION
Merton and the Eastern Fathers[1]

Canon A.M. Allchin

One of the things which Merton does for us is to establish friendships between us. He does this by sharing himself wholly with us, by giving that amazing sense that he is speaking directly to us, which I suppose we have all known in our initial meeting with his writings. Elizabeth Jennings speaks of the art of Thomas Traherne, perhaps Merton's favorite among the seventeenth century Anglicans, as the "Accessible Art." "The poetic prose of Traherne's *Centuries of Meditations*, is an example of the art of sharing, of participation. It is an art wholly accessible . . . . Traherne is, in the deepest sense, a man possessed. What possesses him is a sense of God and this he wishes to share, to distribute." He gives himself to us in such a way that his work "becomes our property, part of our life."[2] Surely this is the case with Merton, so I feel I can share with you at once the perplexity which has been mine in trying to prepare this lecture.

I suppose we have all known the problem of having to give a talk when we feel we have nothing to say. My problem today has been quite the reverse. I have far too much to say. The more I have thought about the topic I have been given, the more it has seemed to be a topic with immense implications which has as yet, with the exception of a fine article by Father Basil Pennington, been only a little explored. It is, moreover, a topic on which there is a vast quantity of material which has not yet been fully examined.

What I shall seek to do is to show:
a) How Merton's basic understanding of the nature of mysticism and theology was decisively influenced by Orthodox models;
b) How important was the influence on him of two of the outstanding theologians of the Byzantine period,

St. Maximus the Confessor (7th century) and St. Gregory Palamas (14th century);

c) His particular attraction for some of the Russian writers of the 19th and 20th centuries, among them St. Theophan the Recluse and Alexander Schmemann;

d) His continuing commitment to the study of the monastic tradition as a whole from its earliest period until today.

Through it all there is the thought of the worship of all creation, since it is a characteristic of Eastern Orthodoxy that it has never lost the early Christian sense of the unity of all creation in the praise of God.

This necessarily brief treatment of a very large subject will bring us to a conclusion which will centre on Merton's importance as a theologian and as a prophet of the renewal of Christian unity. Merton was that rare thing, a theologian who is also a poet, a poet who is also a theologian. If I wanted a motto for this lecture I would take the lines:

So all theology
Is a kind of birthday
A coming home to where we are
Epiphany and Eden.[3]

I. ORTHODOX INFLUENCE ON MERTON'S MYSTICISM

In *Conjectures of a Guilty Bystander* Merton wrote, "If I can unite in myself the thought and devotion of Eastern and Western Christendom, the Greek and the Latin Fathers, the Russian with the Spanish Mystics, I can prepare in myself the reunion of divided Christians . . . If we want to bring together what is divided we cannot do so by imposing one division upon another or absorbing one division into another. We must contain all the divided worlds in ourselves and transcend them in Christ."[4] This is precisely what Merton has done, containing the divisions within himself and transcending them in the unity which is in Christ. This is a unity which is cosmo-theandric. I dislike technical terms but this one has its uses. It brings together God, humankind and the world into a single focus. It speaks of the worship of the whole of creation, the huge chorus of living beings.

This cosmic dimension of Merton's thought cannot be separated from the two other dimensions, human and divine, which meet in Christ in whom God, humanity and all things created are reconciled. Merton's whole effort of mastering the tradition of Christian East and West, or rather of letting himself be mastered by it, was anything but antiquarian. It was motivated by an urgent desire to enter more deeply into the life and death and rising of Christ for the sake of the world today. In his introduction to the *Lectures on Ascetical and Mystical Theology* he writes, "the mystical tradition of the Church — a collective memory and experience of Christ living and present within her. This tradition forms and affects the whole man: intellect, memory, will, emotions, body, skills (arts), all must be under the sway of the Holy Spirit. Important human dimensions given by tradition — its incarnate character — Note especially the memory." And he goes on to say that, if we do not have a healthy and conscious grasp of tradition, we shall be a prey to "unhealthy and unconscious traditions — a kind of collective disposition to neurosis," a highly perceptive comment on some movements that call themselves traditionalist.[5]

I have spoken of the mystical tradition of the Church. But I must go on at once to make the point from which Merton begins his whole teaching on the subject. There is nothing esoteric or exclusive about this tradition. It is simply the handing on of the Gospel of Christ, the faith by which the people of God have lived for 2000 years, in its deepest and most authentic form.

One basic purpose of the *Lectures* is to show that "the mystical tradition cannot be separated from the dogmatic and moral tradition but forms one whole with it. Without mysticism there is no real theology and without theology there is no real mysticism" (*Lectures on Ascetical and Mystical Theology*, page 1). Merton makes this point at the beginning and he repeats it later on, spelling it out in words which he has adapted from one of the most creative writers of the Russian emigration, Vladimir Lossky. "By mysticism we can mean the personal experience of what is revealed to all and realised in all in the mystery of Christ. And by theology we mean the common revelation of the mystery which is to be lived by all. The two belong to-gether, there is no theology without mysticism (for it would have no relation to the real life to God in us) and there is no mysti-cism without theology (because it would be at the mercy of in-dividual and subjective fantasy)" (*Lectures on Ascetical and Mys-tical Theology,* page 26). Unless our mysticism is truly theo-logical, growing from God's revelation of himself in Christ and his gift of himself in the Spirit, then it becomes turned in on itself, "the experience of experience . . . the death of contem-plation" (*Lectures on Ascetical and Mystical Theology,* page 10).

For Merton, then, the heart of the matter lies in an appro-priation of the tradition which is at once mystical and theologi-cal, subjective and objective, experiential and yet more than ex-periential. He is aligning himself here quite consciously with a school of thought which was particularly active in continental Catholicism in the middle of this century, and whose outstand-ing representatives were men like Henri de Lubac, Hans Urs von Balthasar, Yves Congar, Louis Boyer and amongst monas-tic writers, Jean Leclercq. It was a movement which aimed to recover the theological vision of the first ten centuries, the cen-turies before the division between East and West, and before the rise of scholasticism in the West; and, while it involved a great deal of historical study and investigation, its aims were anything but antiquarian. As Merton remarks, this theological movement had been stimulated by the bitter experience of nazism and fascism and the Second World War, an experience which showed Christians in Europe something of the force of the powers of destruction at work in our age, and had made them realize the need to go to first principles in Christian the-ology, and in the whole life of the Church.

It was also a movement which was greatly stimulated by the presence in the West, for the first time for ten centuries, of a school of theologians who represented the Eastern half of the earlier common tradition. This centered on the group of Rus-sian theologians who worked in Paris in the 1930s and the 1940s. Merton was well aware of their writings and he quotes another of their outstanding representatives, Father George Florovsky, at another vital point in the introduction to his *Lec-tures.* Florovsky is for him not only a witness to the Eastern tradition of Christianity but also a spokesman for a Church which in 1917 had felt the full impact of 20th century secularization. It was a Church which was aware that we live in apocalyptic times, and that it is only in the power of Christ himself, only in the gift of the Holy Spirit, that the Christian faith can be maintained today:

It is precisely because we are thrown into the apocalyptic battle that we are called upon to do the job of theologians . . . Theology is called not to judge but to heal. We must penetrate into the world of doubt, of illusion and lies, to reply to doubts as well as to reproaches.

And Merton adds by way of qualification, "But not to reply with complacent and ambiguous platitudes. Must be the word of God lived in us." And as if to confirm his own intuition he quotes again Florovsky:

A theological system must not be a mere product of erudition . . . it needs the experience of prayer and spiritual concentration and pastoral concern . . . We must experience in ourselves by intimate suffering all the problems of the soul without faith who does not seek . . . The time has come when the refusal of theological knowledge has become a deadly sin: the mark of complacency and lack of love, of pusillanimity and malignity.

The call to the monk is nothing less than to become a theologian in this sense (*Lectures on Ascetical and Mystical Theology*, page 10).

How did Merton set out to present this tradition to his brethren? The *Lectures* open with a masterly resume of the dogmatic and mystical teaching of the Church centred around the twin doctrines of incarnation and deification, which are in fact two sides of the same mystery; God's coming to be with us where we are that we may come to be with him where he is; coming out of himself to us and our going out of ourselves to him. This doctrine Merton sees as firmly rooted in the New Testament, in St. John's Gospel which he looks at in some detail, and in St. Paul's Epistles which he treats much more briefly. It is expressed afresh in the writings of the martyrs — Ignatius of Antioch is central here — and of the Christian teachers of the second and third centuries, most notably Irenaeus and Clement of Alexandria. It is articulated in greater detail in the writings of the Cappadocians, above all in Gregory of Nyssa, and of the spiritual writers of that time, Evagrius, the Macarian homilies, and Denys the Areopagite. It is of course of great significance that Merton makes absolutely no break between the New Testament writers and the post-apostolic writers. Scripture and tradition form one whole.

The movement of Merton's exposition in his lecture notes, which so far has been rapid and confident, now seems to falter as he comes to what may seem at first sight a relatively secondary question, the question of the spiritual senses. He allows himself a long digression into a controversy between two French scholars of the earlier part of this century, Poulain and Olphe-Gaillard. This discussion is cut short with the help of the Fathers of the Church and an appeal to St. Gregory Palamas, the theologian of the Transfiguration and of our vision of the divine light. Merton comments, "the lesson of this is that the doctrine of the spiritual senses when it is expressed in scholastic or phenomenological terms is confusing and inconclusive. It is especially unfortunate that the doctrine gets lost in psychology" (*Lectures on Ascetical and Mystical Theology*, page 39).

*   *   *

I would pause for a moment to comment on the significance of this appeal to Palamas. Palamas flourished in the first half of the fourteenth century. Because of the fall of the Eastern empire in 1453 and the schism between East and West, his work was never properly known in the West and was largely forgotten in the East. Much of it was published for the first time only in the 1950s and 1960s. The recovery of the knowledge of his theology in Romania, in Greece, in the Russian emigration, and finally in Russia itself in the last half-century, has been of great importance for the survival of Orthodoxy through these difficult decades. Merton knew his thought through the work of John Meyendorff, at that stage still teaching in Paris, and he immediately sensed its importance. Here in Palamas was a theologian who gave himself to defend and expound the reality of the Christian experience of God and to see that experience as rooted in the body and in the bodily senses. Merton sums up the matter thus: "the spiritual senses are thus the senses themselves, but spiritualised under the sway of the Spirit, rather than new spiritual faculties." He refers to a number of vital passages from Palamas on this subject. "The spiritual joy that comes from the spirit into the body is not at all corrupted by communion with the body but transforms the body and makes it spiritual" (*Lectures on Ascetical and Mystical Theology*, page 40).

One only has to think of the way that Merton formulated his own deepest and intimate experience of things in such a superb passage as the "Prayer to God the Father on the Vigil of Pentecost" (*Conjectures*), to see how vital the insights of Palamas were for him. I am here, Merton writes, "to speak your name of Father just by being here as 'son' in the Spirit and the Light which you have given and which is no unearthly light but simply this plain June day, with its shining fields, its tulip tree, the pines, the woods, the clouds and the flowers everywhere" (*Conjectures of a Guilty Bystander*, page 175). Through the body and the senses we experience our solidarity with all creation; through the body and the senses we are able to perceive the light of God shining out in that creation, and thus we are able, through the body and the senses, to offer the praise of all creation to almighty God.

The climax of the first part of the *Lectures* comes in chapter 8, "Contemplation and the Cosmos," a chapter wholly given to the thought of Maximus the Confessor [presented in Part III of this volume]. Here Merton treats directly the East-West theme of our meeting today, wedding Byzantine mystical theology to the vision and the skill of the Shakers in nineteenth century America, and drawing together different elements in his own experience in ways which are both creative and healing. It is interesting to note that in his introduction to the *Lectures*, when he describes the subjects he intends to cover, he makes no mention of this chapter. It seems as though it grew under his hands as he was writing.

Merton begins by giving his estimate of Maximus (died 662) as one of the greatest and most authoritative of all the Greek Fathers. "He has the broadest and most balanced view of the Christian cosmos of all the Greek Fathers, and therefore of all the Fathers" (*Lectures on Ascetical and Mystical Theology*, page 58). Maximus is a great and complex thinker. Like Palamas he is a theologian who was very little known and studied in the West until the last twenty or thirty years. One of his most striking characteristics is his capacity to unite the mystic's concern with the One, the ultimate unity of all things, with the artist's ense of the value of each specific thing, of the infinite diversity of the creation.

> The love of Christ hides itself mysteriously in the *Logoi* of created things . . . In all that is varied lies He who is simple and without parts, in those which have a beginning. He who has no beginning, in all the visible He who is invisible. (*Lectures on Ascetical and Mystical Theology*, page 58).

Maximus teaches that if we are to come to look into the mysteries of God himself and his love for humankind, that is to say, *theologia*, we need first to look into the things which God has made, to exercise ourselves in *theoria physike*, natural contemplation which discerns the inner *logoi* in events and things, their God-given meaning, inscape, specificity and nature. The world is full of *logoi*, expressions of God's creative will and purpose. They meet together in the One who is the *Logos*, the Word, in whom and for whom all things were made. The *logos* within human persons, not just our reason but our whole capacity to see and know, to discern and understand, is created in order to respond to the *logoi* in the world around us, to praise and celebrate their goodness.

In a paragraph where Merton tells us not only what he thought but also what he lived, he writes "the vision of *theoria physike* is essentially Sophianic. Man by *theoria* is able to unite the hidden wisdom of God in things with the hidden light of wisdom in himself. The meeting and marriage of these two brings about a resplendent clarity within Man himself, and this clarity is the presence of Divine Wisdom fully recognized and active in him. Thus Man becomes a mirror of the divine glory and is resplendent with divine truth not only in his mind but in his life. He is filled with the light of wisdom which shines forth on him and thus God is glorified in him. At the same time he exercises a spiritualising influence in the world by the work of his hands which is in accord with the creative wisdom of God in things and in history" (*Lectures on Ascetical and Mystical Theology*, page 59). Something of this resplendence is to be seen in the faces of Merton and the Dalai Lama, in the photograph taken after their long and truly sophianic conversation in which something healing and creative had been given to both of them. We have also the words of a stranger who met Merton on the last stages of his Asian journey and who tells us of "that cleaner than clean, serenely open, quite halo-like face" as he perceived it in Merton waiting in the airport lounge for the flight to Calcutta.[6] It is a commentary on our times that the observer could interpret the phenomenon in terms of "psychedelic experience."

It would be tempting to expound at length Merton's understanding of *theoria physike* as he develops it under the guidance of Maximus. He sees it as an expression of Christian faith in the inherent goodness of things which remains despite all the ravages of sin, and in the power of the divine grace which is always at work to make up what is lacking and to heal what is wounded in the creation of God. He sees the relevance of all this not only to our contemplation of things, but to our use and transformation of them, and he comments on the dangers of our advanced technology when it is ruled by the desire to exploit and manipulate. He speaks about the role of the artist and of the way in which the artist of all people must be in touch with the *Logoi*.

> He [the artist] does not necessarily have to be fully respectable in a conventional sense. A kind of unconventionality may be in him a form of humility and folly for Christ . . . We must not forbid the artist a necessary element of paradox in his life . . . He must at all costs attain to an inner purity and honesty, and sincerity and integrity of spirit. He must be *holokleros*, one who understands the *Logoi* of things, and is attuned to the *tropoi* (*Lectures on Ascetical and Mystical Theology*, page 63).

But it is to the Shakers that I wish to come, and to the way in which Merton speaks about them here. It is important to remember that this was written thirty years ago, when books on the Shakers were few and interest in their work quite limited in extent.

> Shaker handicrafts and furniture. Deeply impregnated by the communal mystique of the Shaker community. The simplicity and austerity demanded by their way of life enabled an unconscious spiritual purity to manifest itself in full clarity. Shaker handicrafts are, then, a real epiphany of *Logoi*. Characterised by spiritual light.

> See also their buildings. Barns especially. Highly mystical quality; capaciousness, dignity, solidity, permanence. *Logos* of a barn? "But my wheat, gather ye into my barn." Note, it is never a question of a barn in the abstract and in no definite place; the Shaker farm building always fits right into its location, manifests the *logos* of the place where it is built, grasps and expresses the hidden *logos* of the valley of hillside which forms its site. *Logos* of the site. Important in Cistercian monestaries of the twelfth century (*Lectures on Ascetical and Mystical Theology*, page 64).

This last point is of the greatest significance. The *logos* of a thing is always specific. It is in some way universal, it is never abstract. It is in and through the particular qualities of place, a person, a time, an event, that the divine light shines out, transfiguring the limitations of what is given by nature. This can be seen even in the names of the places, whether twelfth century Cistercians or nineteenth century Shaker, Clara Vallis, Pleasant Hill, Sabbath Day Lake, Fountain Abbey, Logumkloster, Locus Dei.

II. THE WORKING NOTEBOOKS: CONTINUED DEVELOPMENT

We have been looking at Merton's *Lectures* from 1961. I want now to turn to the subsequent years, the last six or seven years of his life, and see something of how his mind grew and developed during that time. I am reliant here to a large extent on the *Working Notebooks* in the Archive at Bellarmine. From his early days in the monastery Merton seems to have been in the habit of making copious notes on books that he was reading. These he kept in large bound or looseleaf notebooks. Some of the material at Bellarmine goes back to the early 1950s; more of it dates from the 1960s. The last notebooks show his reading in the months and weeks before he set off on the Asian journey. I cannot pretend to have done more than scratch the surface of this material, but in two visits to the Archive it became clear that there is much of the greatest value to be found.

The notebooks give one a new impression of the width of Merton's interests and the seriousness with which he pursued them. They reveal an almost frightening intensity of purpose. In these last years Merton was exploring all the major religious traditions of humankind: Hinduism, Buddhism (Japanese and Tibetan), Taoism, Hasidism, and the world of Judaism. And then in the last years he made a determined raid on the treasures of Sufism. At the same time he was expanding his knowledge of twentieth century literature, the poets of Latin America, novelists in France and the United States. He was breaking into new areas, examining developments in the Third World particularly at the meeting point between primitive and developed cultures; not to mention his constant involvement with questions of justice, peace and non-violence.

It seems to me that during these years there was an explosion of activity going on in Merton's heart and mind. But it was a special kind of explosion, one which has no exact equivalent in the physical world. It was a non-disintegrating explosion, and hence effects were constructive and not destructive. The center did hold. He did not fall apart. Anyone less well integrated than he was might have done so. I am not surprised that *The Vow of Conversation* contains quite a number of references to physical ailments. Someone living at such an intensity of spiritual and intellectual activity might well find curious side effects in the physical part of their makeup, and might be so absorbed into these things as to neglect their physical condition.

When I say that the center held, I mean quite specifically that the *Notebooks* show how through these years Merton was continuing to maintain his interest in the central theological and spiritual tradition of Christendom, both in its patristic and in its modern versions. He was continuing to deepen and develop his already considerable knowledge of the monastic tradition of Christian East and West. More than one hundred pages of notes on Celtic Christianity and Celtic monasticism, for instance, in *Notebook* 48 dating from 1963 to 1965, show him still pursuing insights into the origins of the Christianity of our offshore islands.

The center held, too, in the sense that Merton's discipline of prayer, silence and meditation, so movingly described in the letters to Abdul Aziz provided the background to all this mental activity, the necessary foundation on which it could stand. An entry in his California diary, *Woods, Shore, Desert*, is extraordinarily illuminating in this regard. "Not to run from one thing to the next, says Theophane the Recluse, but to give each one time to settle in the heart. Attention: concentration of the spirit in the heart. Sobriety: concentration of the feeling in the heart."[7] It was this characteristically monastic centering of feeling, will and spirit in the heart, this constant search for the place of the heart in the disciplined use of the Jesus Prayer which kept Merton centered in himself and made the immense expansion of his interests during these years both possible and fruitful.

This quotation comes from the nineteenth century Russian writer who evidently attracted Merton greatly. Theophan the Recluse (George Govorov, 1815 - 1894) was the bishop who after seven years of pastoral activity resigned his see and lived the latter part of his life as a hermit. During these years he made a new Russian translation of the *Philokalia* and exerted a considerable influence as a spiritual director through his extensive correspondence. He is one of those who were canonized by the Orthodox Church at the Council in Moscow in 1988.[8] Merton had come to know his work partly through the writings of Serge Bolshakoff, but more particularly, through an anthology of texts on prayer published in England in 1966, called *The Art of Prayer*. The book has an excellent introduction by Father (now Bishop) Kallistos Ware. In some ways this is a very ordinary collection of texts about the way of prayer as practiced in Russian lay and monastic circles in the nineteenth and twentieth centuries. It is clear from the markings in Merton's copy of the book in the Archive at Bellarmine College that it was a work that he particularly appreciated. Constantly, it is the extracts from Theophan that are underlined and singled out[8] [see Merton's marginalia in the *Art of Prayer* with reference to Theophane the Recluse, presented later in Part II of this volume].

The notebooks give further evidence of Merton's interest in the spiritual and intellectual tradition of Russian Orthodoxy. In 1966 he published a review article in *Monastic Studies* on the first two of Alexander Schmemann's books to appear in English, *Sacraments and Orthodoxy* and *Ultimate Questions* [presented in Part III of this volume]. The first of these is a brilliant introduction to the Orthodox understanding of faith and worship, in which the writer introduces his reader to the vision of the world itself as the sacrament of God's wisdom and love. The second is an anthology of texts from some of the major Russian thinkers of the nineteenth and twentieth centuries. The published review reveals Merton's enthusiasm for both books, but the notes in *Notebook* 16 (August - November 1965) show the immediacy of his response, as he copies out passages that capture his attention and comments on them on the facing page. It is interesting to note that the same notebook contains twenty-four pages of notes on Bonhoeffer's *Ethics*, a book which he read with even greater interest and excitement.

Schmemann was a man who had something of Merton's own gift of making theological topics accessible to the general reader, and one feels in Merton a very special resonance to some of his positions. Throughout his writings Schmemann saw two dangers for the Church in the twentieth century, on the one side that of retreating into a little, tight, artificial world of religious concerns, on the other, that of going out to meet the world wholly on the world's terms. Merton applies this discernment to the position of the monk. I quote from the review:

> The true way of the monk is in fact not to be sought in devising some explicit or implicit answer to any special problems which the world may have formulated for itself. The monk is not a man of answers. He need not be concerned with either an optimistic or a pessimistic attitude towards these questions, however crucial they

may seem. His life is an expression of eschatological hope and joy, of the presence of the Lord in his creation which he has redeemed, and which by the power of the Spirit he will transform. When this is understood, the monastic life will be seen for what it is: complete openness to the Spirit, and hence openness to all that is blessed by God, whether in the world or out of it.

It is in this sense, that without proposing this or that answer to the problems of social injustice, war, racism, technology, automation, the monk will be all the more open, in compassion and love, to his brother in the world, because he is liberated by his vocation from the false answers dictated by the world itself. This openness is illusory unless it is explicitly paid for by obedience to the Spirit and to the word of the Cross.[9]

It is interesting to see here how Merton has become more resistant to the notion of the monk, or Christian, as one who provides "answers" in terms of the questions which the world poses. The monk, the Church, like Christ himself, is to witness "to the presence of the Lord in the creation which he has redeemed," to bear witness to the presence of the kingdom in our midst, to the power and wisdom of God hidden in the Logoi of all creation.

If the Notebooks give evidence of Merton's interest in the more recent manifestations of Eastern Orthodoxy, they also show his continuing concern for the earliest expressions of that same tradition. One text in particular, in Notebook 24, is very striking. It is dated explicitly "Pentecost 1967," and contains a résumé of the story of the meeting between St. Anthony and St. Paul of Egypt as told in St. Jerome's Life of St. Paul. This story is one which is well-known in early monastic history and Merton certainly knew it before 1967. It looks as though he took it on purpose for his reading and meditation on that feast and made it a kind of celebration of Pentecost for that year. In the story we hear how St. Anthony, generally recognized as the first of Christian monks and already an old man, was told by God to go and find another older, better monk, who had preceded him in the desert. Anthony goes off and is guided to the oasis where Paul has lived all these years a life of hidden prayer. They pass the day in conversation together, and receive their meal from the hand of God, a large loaf brought to them by a raven, which eventually they agree to break together so that one should not take precedence over the other. The story ends with the death of Paul and the arrival of two lions who come to bury him.

The text is an extraordinarily beautiful one, full of characteristic themes of early monastic literature. It is a story about the surprises of God. Anthony thinks he is the pioneer but finds there was another before him. He sets out to look for Paul, like Abraham, not knowing where he is going and he is guided to his destination in unexpected ways. The narrative contains a repeated note of thanksgiving, of eucharist, and a kind of gentle half-ironic humor which would have particularly attracted Merton. Animals, real and fabulous, play a large part in the story. There is a centaur and a satyr as well as a wolf which give Anthony directions on the way. There is a raven which brings the loaf. There are the lions which perform the last rites. All creation serves God; the animal creation seems to do rather better than the human race. Here in a text from one of the greatest Latin Fathers you have a celebration of the lives of the very monks of the Egyptian desert. It is a place where Latin West and Greek and Coptic East are entirely at one, in the grace of the Holy Spirit who unites the two solitaries in their day of eucharistic sharing.

Why did Merton choose to work on that text on Whitsunday 1967? A hint is provided by a note which, also unexpectedly, happens to be dated from a few days earlier. Merton had been reading about the great Anglo-Saxon poem *The Dream of the Rood*. Verses of that poem are inscribed on the Ruthwell Cross, the greatest stone monument from the Anglo-Saxon centuries in Britain. The cross dates from the beginning of the eighth century, and all the scenes carved on it come from the Gospel except this one scene of the meeting of St. Paul and St. Anthony of Egypt. This story from the beginnings of monastic life was of crucial significance to the early monastic communities of Britain and Ireland. The scene is to be found on some of the greatest standing crosses in Ireland. Reference to it is found in early Welsh religious verse. It is an element of the one tradition which is to be found at the roots of the Christian history of our two off-shore European islands. It is more than probable that it was the reading of these articles about the Ruthwell Cross which sent Merton down to the monastery library to collect volume 23 of the *Patrologia Latina* and make his Whitsun meditation on the description of the meeting of Paul and Anthony in the desert.

III. Merton: Mystical Theologian

To conclude, I would want to affirm that Merton is a great theologian, one of the great theologians of the twentieth century America. He is a theologian primarily in the sense that Evagrius uses that word, one whose prayer is true, one who sees deeply into the mysteries of God. But he is also a theologian in the sense that he is a great and gifted servant of the Word, with a gift for communicating that Word to others, one who allows the mystery of faith to be named and heard in a great many places where it is not usually named and heard. He was, to use the term which Albert Outler uses to describe John Wesley, a fold theologian, not a theologian's theologian. I should prefer to say a people's theologian, a theologian of the people of God. And what Outlet says of Wesley is surprisingly true of Merton. He had no academic base, no political base, and no intention of founding a new denomination, yet we don't have many mass evangelists/popular writers on religion with anything like Wesley's/Merton's immersion in classical culture, his eager openness to modern science and social change, his awareness of the entire Christian tradition as a living resource — and even fewer with his ecclesial vision of a sacramental community as the nurturing environment of Christian experience.[10]

Merton was a great mystical and experiential theologian, a great historical theologian, with a firm grasp of the main outlines of the development of Christian doctrine and a remarkably detailed knowledge of the development of monastic life and thought from the fourth century to the present day. Perhaps above all he was a great poetic theologian who in his writing gives voice to the praise and worship of the whole creation; that rare thing, a great poet, more in his prose than in his verse, who is also a great theologian.

In saying all this, I am not in any way wishing to minimize the importance and creativity of his work in promoting the dialogue of religions, his work at the point of meeting of theology and culture, or his work in the field of justice, non-violence and peace. He is important to us for a great variety of reasons and he excelled in a great variety of fields. But at the heart of it all there was his concern for the tradition of the church "the collective memory and experience of Christ living within her," and there was "his awareness of the entire Christian tradition as a living resource." By his gift of making accessible to us wisdom from distant periods and distant parts of that tradition, he challenges us to grow into a deeper awareness of the resources which are latent there. In particular, he challenges us Western Christians to rediscover the riches of the Christian East, maybe to learn Russian or Romanian or Greek and actually go to the countries of Eastern Europe which have been cut off from us for so long to learn firsthand from our brothers and sisters there what they have learnt of Christ in this twentieth century. It may well be that in the future, it will be Merton's intuitive and prophetic actions in the field of the relations between Christians and people to the life of the twenty-first century. But there is an immense amount still to be done by way of that inner recovery of Christian unity of which he spoke in *Conjectures of a Guilty Bystander*. This is in some ways a more prosaic task, nearer to us and less glamorous, but it is nonetheless necessary if we are to recover both depth and balance in our understanding and living of the Christian faith.

Perhaps it is in the end not an either/or but a both/and. The Merton who so impressed the Tibetan abbots and teachers on his visit to India did so in part because he had troubled to learn enough about Tibetan Buddhism to be able to enter into a real and intelligent conversation with them. But he impressed them still more because they at once recognized in him an authoritative and discerning representative of the Christian tradition as a whole, Catholic and Protestant, Eastern and Western. So let the last word be with the Dalai Lama: "This was the first time that I had been struck by such a feeling of spirituality in anyone who professed

Christianity . . . It was Merton who introduced me to the real meaning of the word 'Christian'."[11]

NOTES

1. This essay first appeared in *The Merton Annual: Volume 5.* AMS Press, Inc.: New York, 1992.

2. Elizabeth Jennings, *Every Changing Shape* (London: A. Deutsch. 1961), 83-84.

3. Thomas Merton, *Eighteen Poems* (New York: New Directions, 1985), no page number.

4. Thomas Merton, *Conjectures of a Guilty Bystander* (Garden City, New York: Doubleday and Company, 1966), page 20.

5. Thomas Merton, *Lectures on Ascetical and Mystical Theology*, page 9.

6. Michael Mott, *The Seven Mountains of Thomas Merton* (Boston: Houghton Mifflin, 1984), page 555.

7. Thomas Merton, *Woods, Shore, Desert, a Notebook, May 1968* (Sante Fe: Museum of New Mexico Press, 1982), page 16.

8. Theophan (George Govorov), Anthologized in *The Art of Prayer* (introduction by Bishop Kallistos Ware), (London: Faber & Faber, 1966).

9. *Monastic Studies* (Number 4, Advent 1966), page 115.

10. *The Place of Wesley in the Christian Tradition*, edited by Kenneth F. Rowe. (Metuchen, New Jersey: Scarecrow, 1976), page 13.

11. *Freedom in Exile: The Autobiography of the Dalai Lama* (New York: Harper Collins Publishers, 1990), page 189.

I should like to acknowledge the great help of Dr. Robert E. Daggy on my two visits to Bellarmine College.

2

OUR LIVES, A POWERFUL PENTECOST
Merton's Meeting with Russian Christianity[1]

Canon A.M. Allchin

Looking back on the three visits which I made to Gethsemani during Thomas Merton's lifetime, in 1963, 1967 and 1968, I have often wondered what it was that I could have brought to him. News from England, occasional small presents from friends of his I had encountered, a direct contact with Oxford and also with the Anglican tradition as a whole? But I also soon discovered that there was another world that Merton knew of only through books where I happened to have direct personal knowledge. This was the world of Russian Paris, or more specifically the Russian Orthodox theological community there. Since my student days I had had friends in that Russian world, very close friends, and I was able to give Merton personal information and anecdotes about people whom previously he had known only as writers of books.

Merton had for long been aware of the existence and the importance of this group of Russian theologians in Paris. They represented the first major intellectual presence of Eastern Orthodoxy in the Western Christian world since the schism nine centuries before. Already, in a letter to Jean Leclercq in 1950, Merton had shown his appreciation of Vladimir Lossky's pioneering study *The Mystical Theology of the Eastern Church*.[2] He already had seen how important it was for a proper understanding of the first Cistercians, Bernard and William of St. Thierry in particular, to understand the way in which they were indebted, not only to the theology of the Latin West but also to the teaching of the Greek Fathers. He writes in that letter, rather wistfully, "The thought of reunion with the Greeks is one that haunts me."[3]

It is clear from the opening section of the *Lectures on Ascetical and Mystical Theology*,[4] which Merton gave at the monastery in 1960, that the writings of Lossky and George Florovsky had helped him to shape his basic idea of the nature of mystical theology itself. I have already written in *The Merton Annual 5* about those lectures and the picture that they give us of Merton's understanding of the Greek Fathers and of Gregory of Nyssa and Maximus the Confessor in particular.[5] Now in the newly published volumes of the *Journals* it has become clear how much Russian theology Merton was reading in the years 1957-62. This discovery has brought back to me elements of our conversation during that first visit in 1963.

I.

I have told this story and come to this particular place, to the Russian theological world in Paris, because it brings me to the subject that I want to look at in this article. This is the influence of a number of those Orthodox theologians on Merton at a crucial point in the development of his life, the years from 1957 to 1961 when he began to see more clearly the way that was to lead him further and further into the universal mystery of God's love and knowledge, the journey he was to make during the last decade of his life. Reading the volumes of his journals as we now have them, I have been struck by the significance of these writers for Merton, and the part that they played in the development of his heart and mind at this crucial period [significant quotations in reference to these Russian writers in Merton's journals are presented in Part III of this volume].

What I intend to do in these pages, after a brief look at Merton's correspondence with Pasternak, is to examine something of the influence of two of the principal figures of the first generation of the emigration, Berdyaev and Bulgakov, as we see it already in the journal of 1957.

Then we shall look at Merton's response to the work of a younger Orthodox writer, Olivier Clement, a Frenchman who was converted to Christianity in its Orthodox form, a writer who, in the last thirty-five years has become an acknowledged spokesman for the Christian faith in France, his writings appreciated by Catholics, Protestants and Orthodox alike.

Finally, after a fleeting reference to Paul Evdokimov, we shall come to Vladimir Lossky, whose first book, as we have already seen, Merton had read in the 1940s, and whose study of Meister Eckhart he received with joy in the summer of 1961.

This subject of Merton's meeting with the Russian theologians has, so far as I know, not been much studied until now. It is not a subject that emerges at all clearly in Merton's own published writing, with the exception of a deceptively simple looking essay on the Russian Mystics in *Mystics and Zen Masters*,[6] an article which recent events have shown to be almost prophetic. [Presented in Part III of this volume.] But it is one element, and I believe a vital element, in the total picture of Merton's growth into maturity. I have been moved to tackle this subject by the fact that there is at present the beginnings of a Thomas Merton Society in Moscow and that the first translations of Merton's writings into Russian are now being made. We have prospects of collaboration and exchange between ourselves in the West and our friends in Russia which until recently would have been unthinkable. I believe, in the present Russian situation, Merton's viewpoint may be of particular importance and encouragement.

I have to say at the beginning that I do not intend to deal at length with the most moving and perhaps the most important of all Merton's Russian contacts, that is to say, his correspondence with Boris Pasternak and what that correspondence meant to him. This is one of the most beautiful of all Merton's friendships, a friendship which in a brief period had a profound and creative influence on his own vocation as a writer and as a friend of other writers. Surely Mgr. Shannon is right in saying, in *Silent Lamp*, that in this correspondence with Pasternak we have the root of Merton's sense of mission to the world of writers and intellectuals.[7] Out of his sense of a deep and spontaneous communion of heart and mind with Pasternak, a communion established across all the barriers and boundaries of his day, he gained a new confidence that God meant him to cultivate such contacts with men and women of letters, contacts which in the end spread across the continents. There was, he felt, some deep and healing mystery in these friendships. [The

Merton-Pasternak correspondence is presented in Part III of this volume.]

One of the things that moved and fascinated Merton most in that exchange with Pasternak was the sense that in their discovery of one another they had broken through the iron curtain, which at that time divided East and West; a barrier whose strength it is very difficult, for those who did not live through those years, to understand. In his contact with Russian Paris, of course, Merton was in touch with the Russian emigration. But he felt rightly that he was also in touch with Russia itself, for the writers whose work he was reading were Orthodox Christians, either directly under the jurisdiction of the Moscow Patriarchate, like Vladimir Lossky, or members of the diocese that had put itself under the jurisdiction of Constantinople, a Patriarchate which always remained in communion with Moscow.

None of them belonged to the third Russian jurisdiction existing at that time in the West, the Russian Church in Exile or the Russian Church outside Russia, as it now calls itself. This is a body which has long had its headquarters in New York, and has as its very reason for being its refusal of communion with the Patriarchate of Moscow. That church, which is "too Orthodox" to recognize its fellow Orthodox, not surprisingly has never wished for contacts with Christians from the non-Orthodox West, whether Catholic or Protestant.

Another thing that is clear in this connection is that Merton's fascination with Pasternak's writing predates the publication of *Dr. Zhivago* and that Merton's interest in Russian religious thought predates his first discovery of Pasternak. Indeed it was his knowledge of such nineteenth-century thinkers as Soloviev and Khomiakov that enabled him to read the Christian meaning of *Dr. Zhivago* with more depth and assurance than most Western commentators.

If we look at Volume 3 of the journals, one of the first and most striking of Merton's expressions of interest in the ideas of this Russian tradition of thought, theological and philosophical, is to be found in the entry for 25 April, 1957. In it Merton speaks of the two writers Sergei Bulgakov and N.A. Berdyaev, both of whom had been at the height of their powers in the Paris of the 1920s and 1930s.

Bulgakov and Berdyaev are writers of great, great attention. They are great men who will not admit the defeat of Christ who has conquered by his resurrection. In their pages . . . shines the light of the resurrection and theirs was a theology of triumph.

One wonders if our theological cautiousness is not after all the sign of a fatal coldness of heart, an awful sterility born of fear, or of despair. These two men have dared to make mistakes and were to be condemned by every church, in order to say something great and worthy of God in the midst of all their wrong statements. They have dared to accept the challenge of the sapiential books, the challenge of the image of *Proverbs* where Wisdom is "playing in the world" before the face of the creator. And the Church herself says this. Sophia was somehow, mysteriously to be revealed, and fulfilled, in the mother of God and in the Church.

Most important of all — man's creative vocation to prepare, consciously, the ultimate triumph of divine wisdom. Man, the microcosm, the heart of the universe is the one who is called to bring about the fusion of cosmic and historic process in the final invocation of God's wisdom and love. In the name of Christ and by his power, man has a work to accomplish — to offer the cosmos to the Father, by the power of the Spirit, in the glory of the Word. Our life is a powerful Pentecost in which the Holy Spirit, ever active in us, seeks to reach through our inspired hands and tongues into the very heart of the material world created to be spiritualised through the work of the Church, the mystical body of the incarnate word of God.[8]

This powerful conflation of ideas from Bulgakov and Berdyaev might suggest at first that Merton had not altogether realized how different the two men were. It is true that as a theologian Father Sergei Bulgakov was both daring and speculative, and that at a certain moment in the 1930s the Patriarchate of Moscow condemned his teaching about the divine wisdom, his sophiology. But in Paris, Bulgakov's position was assured; he belonged to that part of the Russian *diaspora* which was in communion with Constantinople so that the condemnation of Moscow did not touch him directly. At the St. Sergius Institute, as Professor of Dogmatic Theology, he taught with great authority. He was highly valued as a preacher, a confessor and a spiritual guide, as well as a theological writer; he was emphatically a man of the church.

Berdyaev on the other hand was an outstanding example of that line of free religious thinkers who have characterized Russian Orthodoxy in the last 150 years. They are writers who do not fit easily into our Western categories. They are too openly religious, indeed explicitly Christian, in the substance and inspiration of their thought to be considered genuine philosophers. On the other hand they are too free and speculative, too nonconformist and idiosyncratic in their approach to ultimate questions, to be thought of as real theologians.

Nevertheless, in putting together Bulgakov and Berdyaev in this way, despite their manifest differences, Merton was bearing witness to some of the thoughts that they shared, elements of their teaching that were to become more and more important to him in the development of his own thought in the years ahead. First there is the cosmic vocation of humankind. We are called to be at the center of creation. We cannot opt out. The monastic vocation may indeed involve a radical separation from the world, but it cannot involve an abandonment of the world. It is a life lived for the sake of the world. Secondly there is the vocation to a life of prayer, worship and contemplation itself. This too must always be seen in a cosmic context. It is lived on behalf of all creation. It must also be seen in its Trinitarian dimensions, a call to offer all things to the Father, through the life-giving death of the Son, in the transforming power of the Spirit. Thirdly, the Holy Spirit is to be at work through our hands and through our tongues, spiritualizing the material world. All this is to be done with power, in the freedom which the Spirit gives, as we become co-creators working with the Spirit who is the Creator of life.

Undoubtedly one of the elements in Berdyaev's thought, which was of most importance to Merton at this time in his life, was his idea of the ethics of creativity. Human beings grow towards maturity, begin to become the people God intends them to be, not by conforming to an externally fixed and static pattern of behaviour, but by discovering within themselves a potential for growth and transformation, an inner dynamic of change which enables them in the end to become free in God, and thus co-creators with the Creator. In such a view God is seen not only as continually holding creation in being but himself constantly working towards the realization of creative freedom on the part of his creatures. God himself withdraws from his creation so that his creation may begin to become free.

On 8 June, 1959, Merton writes:

Berdyaev's distinction between ethics of law and ethics of creativeness is a very good one for me now. So good, perhaps, that it is a temptation. In any case: the ethics of law says stay at Gethsemani and the ethics of creativity says go out and do something that has not been done. The ethics of law says – Who is this Berdyaev? What authority has he? He is a heretic. You are doing your own will. What is creativeness? An illusion, which would lead the whole place into madness if everyone followed the same principles! It's safer to accept what is established, even if it is not so good. God works in and through the community. The individual has to conform to the community in order to find God. And so on.[9]

And then there comes a very telling paragraph. Supposing he does just conform? What then? "If only it were a simple question! Supposing for instance there is really in me nothing creative . . . But what a question to ask! That is what one must start by believing and hoping, otherwise Christ died in vain."[10] Here we see the real urgency of his inner questioning. To deny his own power of creativity would be to deny God, to deny Christ, to deny Christ's death.

But the whole series of questions ends with a very interesting, if still quite uncertain conclusion, nevertheless a conclusion that points us towards the way which, in the end, Merton was to discover. "Meanwhile it is very important to get out of the dilemma. Either Gethsemani or not-Gethsemani. Both. Neither. There has to be a way of rising completely above the division and going above it."[11] It was this which, by God's grace, Merton in the end succeeded in doing.

II.

It is very typical of Merton that, during these years, he ranged widely over the literature which was available to him from the Russian community in Paris. In July 1960 we find him in correspondence with Olivier Clement, at that time a man in his thirties, teaching in a private college in Paris and just beginning to be known as a writer on Orthodox subjects. Merton comments about him as one who was "brought up by atheist parents in Languedoc, converted to Orthodoxy, writing for *Contacts*."[12] *Contacts* was an Orthodox quarterly which had printed an article of Merton's about Mount Athos [presented in Part III of this volume], and through *Contacts* Merton came into correspondence with Clement and through him with the Orthodox monastery in England founded by Father Sophrony.

We are not surprised to find Merton already busy reading Olivier Clement's first book, a small but very significant work called *The Transfiguration of Time*. He notes in his journal that "this book of Olivier Clement is really excellent. Only now that I am in the middle do I realise that I have missed much by not reading with very close attention. A book to read twice. Few books deserve two readings."[13]

Two days later he felt he was penetrating to the center of the work.

The heart of Clement's book — that "fallen time" has no present. Fallen time is simply that pure transience where the present is only a point with no content, between the abyss of the past and the abyss of the future, only emerging from the former to be swallowed up in the latter. It is only the expression of an absence — the absence of God, and thus the absence of man to himself and to others. Redeemed time is concentrated in a

"present moment" and born of the presence of God even
in our misery, insofar as our misery does not fall into
despair, but rather, as one might put it, falls into the divine love, becoming therefore an opening of humility onto
the new life in the risen Lord.[14]

"Keep your mind in hell and do not despair," said
Christ to the Staretz Silouan, "for," as Father Sophrony
comments on these words, "in condemning himself to
hell and thus destroying all passion, man liberates his
heart to receive the divine love." Merton adds with enthusiasm: "This is great reading for a Sunday, an Easter, a renewal in Christ! I praise the Lord Christ for his
great mercy."[15]

Clement points out that this understanding of the
fullness of the divine presence, revealed in the midst of
time, gathers up our longing for a return to the state of paradise and at the same time looks forward towards the end of all
things, anticipating here and now the fullness which shall
be in the end. Already in this fallen world the dynamic
power of the divine forgiveness and healing is at work within
us drawing us to the future. The divine future itself draws us
towards itself.

This liturgical repetition is not an impotent return to the origin of things but an ever new meeting with the one who does
not cease to come to meet us. Each Easter, each Sunday, since
Sunday is itself Easter, helps us to interiorize the sacramental
life, and thus make this meeting more intimate.

"When the water of tears is united, under the sand of the
passions, with the life-giving water of baptism . . . then the light
of the one and only feast, the one and only Sunday, the one
perpetual Easter, the light of the eighth day illumines every one
of our moments."[16] If, in his reading of Bulgakov, Merton had
found his life as a powerful Pentecost, here, in Clement, he finds
it as an Easter constantly renewed. In either case one has a
personal appropriation of a typically Orthodox understanding
of realized eschatology.

Two days later Merton applies this vision to his own situation and to his own particular vocation:

The importance of being able to rethink thoughts that were fundamental to men of other ages, or are fundamental to men in other countries. For me especially — contemporary Latin-America — Greek patristic period — Mount Athos — Confucian China — Tang dynasty — Pre-Socratic Greece. Despair of ever beginning truly to know and understand, to communicate with these pasts and these distances, yet a sense of obligation to do so, to live them and combine them in myself, to absorb, to digest, to "remember." *Memoria*. Have not yet begun. How will I ever begin to appreciate their problems, reformulate the questions they tried to answer? Is it even necessary? Is it sane? For me it is an expression of love for man and for God. An expression without which my contemplative life would be senseless. And to share this with my own contemporaries.[17]

Here we find Merton beginning to realize something of the catholicity, the universality of the human person, discovering his own vocation to become, through the power of the Holy Spirit, that truly universal catholic person whom we see at the end of his life. His vocation is to cross frontiers, to cross frontiers in time, searching back into the past, and to cross barriers in space, barriers of language and culture and political situation and deep historical prejudice. We see here his sense that he is called to unite in himself the vision, the experience, the understanding of many times and many places, to hold them together in one and to share them with his own contemporaries.

Merton has not only seen the value of Clement's book in itself, he has also seen it as a way through into an experience of the life and witness of Staretz Silouan, the Russian monk on Mount Athos who Father Sophrony had discovered as a spiritual father and guide in the 1920s and who died in 1938. Sophrony had felt it his duty and calling to make known his life and writings in the West. How that in fact has happened in the last forty or fifty years is a whole story in itself. It is the story of a Russian monk, a peasant by upbringing, a man with only two years' formal schooling, never ordained, never well known, becoming, in his own lifetime, through his life of prayer, repentance and devotion, a greatly valued *Staretz*, a spiritual guide and father to a handful of his monastic brethren. And now, in this last decade, Silouan has been recognized as a saint of the Orthodox Church, canonized by the Patriarch of Constantinople, a figure who becomes more widely known, his name more widely invoked. Already in 1960, privately at Gethsemani, Merton was beginning to keep his anniversary.

Today is the anniversary of the death of the holy Staretz Silouan, at St. Panteleimon on Mount Athos — September 11th, 1938 . . . .

Staretz Silouan did not want to die in the infirmary because they would put him in a room with a clock which would disturb his prayer.

Sitting at a table with other stewards he refused to join all the others in criticizing one of their number who had failed in some monastery business.

His combats and sorrows. The Lord said to him, "Keep your mind in hell and do not despair." This is to me one of the most enlightening and comforting of statements, lifting a weight from my heart, inexplicably. (Ten years ago it would have weighed me down with foreboding.)

In so far as hell means apparent rejection and darkness, some of us must elect it, as it is ours and Job's way to peace. The far end of nothing, the abyss, of our own absurdity, in order to be humble, to be found and saved by God. In a way this sounds idiotic and even heretical. Yet no — I am one who is saved from hell by God.

Or rather that is my vocation and destiny.

If I spend my time saying "I have been saved," then I may have to resist the awful fear of falling back, of saying I have not fallen back, of denying that I have fallen back when I have . . . etc. And never knowing at any time where I am. Foolish concern.

To have the flames of hell around you like Sylvan and to hope I shall be saved. Thus I am saved, but no need to insist on myself. Jesus, Saviour.[18]

So already, more than thirty-five years ago Merton had discovered the Staretz Silouan and the heart of his message. Already, at a time when Silouan was scarcely known to Western Christendom, he had been able to identify with him and to recognize in his monastic experience a monastic experience very close to his own.

How Merton would have rejoiced to read Sophrony's account based on his experience of Father Silouan, of the paradoxical way in which the true monk, having left all things for God, finds them again, mysteriously, in God:

> Having started by breaking with the world, through Christ he finds it again in himself, but now in an entirely different form, and becomes linked to it by the bonds of love for all eternity. Then, through prayer, he integrates everyone into his own eternal life, whatever the geographical distance or historical time between them. Then he discovers that his heart is not just a physical organ or centre of his psychic life, but something indefinable yet capable of being in contact with God, the source of all being. In his deep heart the Christian, after a certain fashion, lives the whole history of the world as his own history, and sees not only himself but all humanity, the whole complex of ideas and spiritual experiences, and then no-one is alien to him — he loves each and everyone as Christ commanded.[19]

This discovery of the Staretz Silouan was also something that brought Merton and myself together in an unexpected way, for on my first visit to Mount Athos in August 1955, landing at the Russian monastery, St. Panteleimon, with a friend, we were shown around the buildings by an elderly Russian layman who was staying with the community. Almost at once he took us to the charnel house, and one of the first things which our guide did was to pick up a numbered skull and say, "This is the skull of a monk who some of the Fathers thought was a saint" — it was Staretz Silouan.

III.

We have been looking at the influence on Merton of two writers of the older generation of the Russian emigration,

Bulgakov and Berdyaev, and one of the new generation, that of a convert to Orthodoxy, Olivier Clement.

But for any full account of Merton's meeting with this school of writers one would need to look at two major figures in the generation in between, the generation of those who were born in the first decade of the twentieth century and who left Russia after the Revolution, during their student years. Among them the two outstanding figures would be Vladimir Lossky and Paul Evdokimov.

This is not the place to look at both, so I have chosen to concentrate my attention on Vladimir Lossky. This is not because there is little material about Paul Evdokimov. Quite the reverse is the case. In Volume 3 of the journals there is ample reference to Evdokimov.[20] It would be a fascinating task to work through the quotations there in direct reference to Evdokimov's originals and see how it is that Merton responds to his characteristic positions. I will say only one thing about Evdokimov. Merton assumed that he was a priest. I was able to assure him that, like Vladimir Lossky, he was a married layman. It is interesting to note that much of the most vital Orthodox theology of this century in Russia, Romania and Greece has been written either by married lay-people or married clergy. Creative monastic theologians have been few. Here is another thing that makes Merton's work particularly precious for the Christian world of East as well as West.

The high point of Merton's involvement with Russian theology, judging by the journals, seems to have been in the years 1958-61. But although references to Russian writers become much less frequent in Volume 5, those that are to be found are highly significant.

This is particularly the case with the reference to Vladimir Lossky in the journal entry for 5 December, 1964. In the pages of this journal we can see that that December was a particularly fruitful and creative time in Merton's development. He was at last beginning to be able to experience directly both the challenge and the gifts of a more solitary way of life. It was a time in which he was continuing to work on some of his favourite authors, as well as beginning to initiate new explorations.

"Thank God I have been purged of Sartre by Ionesco. I don't think Ionesco is a great artist but he is healthy and alive and free. Sartre is not free . . . " Merton's preference for the Romanian playwright is very evident.[21]

But it is also a time in which he is drawn back by solitude onto the vital need for prayer, a prayer which is constantly confronting the reality of penitence and death. Like John Henry Newman in the Oratory at Birmingham, Thomas Merton too has the *Preces Privatae* of Lancelot Andrewes to hand.

> In the hermitage one must pray or go to seed. The pretence of prayer will not suffice. Just sitting will not suffice. It has to be real — yet what can one do? Solitude puts you with your back to the wall (or your face to it!) and that is good. One prays to pray. And the reality of death, Donne's poems and Lancelot Andrewes.[22]

The day before he had quoted Lancelot Andrewes: "Evening: the heart is deceitful above all things. The heart is deep and full of windings. The old man is covered up in a thousand wrappings."[23]

December 1964 was, however, not only a time of new beginnings for Merton himself. It was a time for new beginnings in the church and in the world. Sister Mary Luke Tobin, one of the very first women to be invited as an auditor to participate in the Second Vatican Council, came over to Gethsemani from Loretto to talk to a group of monks about the session that had just concluded and to tell them about its achievements and its frustrations.

It is in this context that Merton notes, on 22 December, "Am finally reading Vladimir Lossky's fine book, *La vision de Dieu*, which reminds me that the best thing that has come out of the Council is the Declaration on Ecumenism, particularly the part on oriental theology."[24] In its radical rethinking of the Roman Catholic attitude towards all the other families of Christendom, the Council had especially insisted on the importance on being open to receive the witness and tradition of Eastern Orthodoxy.

Let us pause for a moment at this point to ask who this writer Vladimir Lossky was. It so happens that as a student and a newly ordained priest I came to know him well; his family became almost a second family for me in Paris. His son and his two daughters, who all still teach in Paris, remain among my closest friends.

Vladimir Lossky belonged to the middle generation of the writers we have been considering. Thirty years younger than Berdyaev or Bulgakov, he was contemporary with Evdokimov and Florovsky. But unlike them he died in his fifties, in 1958, with only one major book published, *The Mystical Theology of the Eastern Church* — a book which, as we have seen, Merton already knew in French in 1950. After Lossky's death more of his books began to become available. There was a massive study of the theology of Meister Eckhart,[25] the first study in depth of a major figure in Western Christendom to come from the pen of an Eastern Orthodox writer (the second such study is the work of Lossky's son: Nicolas Lossky's study of Lancelot Andrewes[26]). This book on Eckhart was one which Merton received with special delight. Despite its highly technical nature, at least in certain parts, it spoke directly to him. In a letter to Etta Gullick on 25 July, 1961, he writes,

> [T]oday came the Lossky book on Eckhart. It is fabulously good, not only that but it is for me personally a book of immense and providential importance, because I can see right away in the first chapter that I am right in the middle of the most fundamental intuition of unknowing which was the first source of my faith and which ever since has been my whole life . . . I cannot thank you enough.[27]

It is very significant that this highly specialized work should have moved Merton so much. It was not only its contents that spoke directly to Merton but also something of its spirit. As I look back on Vladimir Lossky over forty years, I can see him as a man who had much in common with Merton. He was a man who lived every minute of his life to the full. One of his sons said, after his death, "He wouldn't have known what 'wasting time' meant." He was a man of great intelligence, and of strong aesthetic perceptions. Like Merton's, his life was uprooted; growing up in Russia, exiled first in Prague, then in Paris, knowing all the upheaval of World War II and the Ger-

man occupation of France. He was a man to whom the difference between sacred and secular simply did not exist, for he
lived his life and his faith with the whole of himself. If Merton
has showed us what a monk in the twentieth century may be,
people like Vladimir Lossky have shown us the real meaning
of the witness of a layman as a true man of the church, a Christian scholar and intellectual whose whole work is at the service
of the mystery of God revealed in Christ.

Lossky's book *The Vision of God*, published in 1963,[28]
is based on lectures given at the Sorbonne twenty years
earlier. It is a careful, lucid exposition of the Eastern Christian
tradition from the apostolic age to the culminating moment in
the fourteenth century, the last full century of the Eastern
Christian Empire. This was a time marked by the theology of
St. Gregory Palamas, a theology that was confirmed and
canonized in the Councils held in Constantinople in 1341,
1347 and 1351. It is a tradition of Christian faith and
understanding which down to the present has been too little
studied in the Christian West, whether Catholic or Protestant,
and which even today is considered by many to be of only
marginal importance.

But for Merton this tradition is anything but marginal. Reading Lossky's book seems to have released in him a kind of personal confession of faith which is at the same time an affirmation of the whole tradition which he has received and which
has become his life, in the years that have followed since that
moment of his conversion and reception into the Catholic
Church in his student days at Columbia. The tradition of the
centuries of East and West has become a life-giving experience
in him and for him, and through him it has become so for
many others. These are paragraphs of such a quality, both as
a personal testimony and as an exposition of the whole inheritance of Christian East and West, that I intend to quote them
at length and I intend that they will bring this essay towards
its conclusion.

> Here in the hermitage, returning necessarily to begin-
> nings, I know where my beginning was, hearing the Name
> and Godhead of Christ preached in Corpus Christi

Church. I heard and believed. And I believe that he has raised me freely, out of pure mercy, to his love and salvation, and that at the end (to which all is directed by Him) I shall see Him after I have put off my body in death and have risen together with Him, And that at the last day *"videbit omnis caro salutare Dei"* (all flesh shall see the salvation of God). What this means is that my faith is an eschatological faith, not merely a means of penetrating the mystery of the divine presence resting in Him now. Yet because my faith is eschatological it is also contemplative, for I am, even now, in the Kingdom and I can, even now, "see" something of the glory of the Kingdom and praise him who is king. I would be foolish then if I lived blindly, putting off all "seeing," until some imagined fulfilment (for my present seeing is the beginning of a real and unimaginable fulfilment!). Thus contemplation and eschatology are one, in Christian faith and in surrender to Christ. They complete each other and intensify each other. It is by contemplation and love that I can best prepare myself for the eschatological vision — and best help all the Church, and all men, to journey toward it.

The union of contemplation and eschatology is clear in the gift of the Holy Spirit. In Him we are awakened to know the Father because in Him we are refashioned in the likeness of the Son. And it is in this likeness that the Spirit will bring us at last to the clear vision of the invisible Father in the Son's glory, which will also be our glory. Meanwhile it is the Spirit who awakens in our heart the faith and hope in which we cry for the eschatological fulfilment and vision. And in this hope there is already a beginning, an *arrha* ["earnest"] of the fulfilment. This is our contemplation: the realization and "experience" of the life-giving Spirit in whom the Father is present to us through the Son, our way, truth and light. The realization that we are on our way, that because we are on our way we are in that Truth which is the end and by which we are already fully and eternally alive. Contemplation is the loving sense of this life and this presence and this eternity.[29]

IV.

In the article already alluded to I stated my conviction that in our proper admiration for Merton's contribution to the inter-faith dialogue we ought not to underestimate the value of his contribution to Christian ecumenism. The two elements in his thought are inextricably related to one another. It is not by chance that in *Mystics and Zen Masters* a large part of the book is taken up with the discussion of urgent but sometimes technical questions of inner Christian debate. Merton's capacities in this field too need to be fully appreciated for they were part of his total view. In the two paragraphs from the journal for 1964, which have just been quoted, paragraphs at once deeply trinitarian and incarnational, Merton has succeeded in giving us a summary of the tradition that is true to the perspectives both of Christian East and Christian West. He has done more; he has given us a way of reconciling two contrasting strands in the Christian tradition — the contemplative or mystical on the one side, and the prophetic or eschatological on the other; strands which it is still commonly assumed are inimical to one another and mutually exclusive. How much it would alter our whole perspective on what Christianity is, how much it would alter the relation between Catholic and Protestant in the Christian West, if this view of the complementarity of these two strands was generally accepted and understood.

We need Merton's teaching, and we need it today, not only for our dialogue with peoples of other faiths. We need it above all to overcome the present tendency towards polarization which we can see today in all the churches, Orthodox, Catholic and Protestant alike, the tendency towards a needless, and in the end sterile, controversy between people who call themselves progressive and people who call themselves traditionalist. What true progress can there be unless it is rooted in the eternal, given realities of the tradition? What true tradition can there be unless it is seen as something living, changing, adapting and improvising with the creative power of the one Holy life-creating Spirit? It is only in his coming that our life can become a powerful Pentecost, a transformation of creation, both inner and outer, a manifestation of the light and life of the Risen Christ, who by his death has destroyed death.

NOTES

1. This essay first appeared in *The Merton Annual: Studies in Culture, Spirituality and Social Concerns* Volume 11, 1998.

2. London: James Clark, 1957.

3. Thomas Merton, *The School of Charity: The Letters of Thomas Merton on Religious Renewal*. Edited by Patrick Hart (New York: Farrar, Straus & Giroux, 1990), pages 23-26.

4. "An Introduction to Christian Mysticism: From the Apostolic Fathers to the Council of Trent," lectures given at the Abbey of Gethsemani, 1961.

5. A.M. Allchin, "The Worship of the Whole Creation: Merton and the Eastern Fathers," *The Merton Annual 5* (1997), pages 189-204.

6. Thomas Merton, *Mystics and Zen Masters* (London: Sheldon Press, 1965), pages 178-187. In this essay on the Russian mystics Merton clearly delineates the conflicting tendencies to be found in the nineteenth-century Russian monastic renewal.

7. W.H. Shannon, *Silent Lamp: The Thomas Merton Story* (New York: Crossroad, 1992), page 186.

8. Thomas Merton, *A Search for Solitude* (Journals; edited by Lawrence S. Cunningham; San Francisco: HarperSanFrancisco, 1995), pages 85-86.

9. *A Search for Solitude*, page 288.

10. *A Search for Solitude*, page 288.

11. *A Search for Solitude*, page 289.

12. Thomas Merton, *Turning Toward the World* (Journals; edited by Victor A. Kramer; San Francisco: HarperSanFrancisco, 1996), page 23.

13. *Turning Toward the World*, page 39.

14. *Turning Toward the World*, page 42. I have added the lines that are in italics, translating from Olivier Clement's original *Transfigurer le temps* (Neauchatel: Delachaux & Niestle, 1964), page 166.

15. *Turning Toward the World*, page 42.

16. *Turning Toward the World*, page 42. I have supplemented Merton's quotation with two sentences from Clement, *Transfigurer le temps*, page 162.

17. *Turning Toward the World*, pages 42-43.

18. *Turning Toward the World*, page 44-45.

19. Archimandrite Sophrony (Sakharov), *Saint Silouan the Anthonite* (Maldon, Essex: The Stavropegic Monastery of St. John the Baptist, 1991), pages 233-34. Father Sophrony's first publication about Staretz Silouan, *The Undistorted Image*, which Merton had read, was published in 1958 (London: The Faith Press). This book is a very much fuller version of that work, with a great deal of new material.

20. It is unfortunate that Paul Evdokimov's name does not occur in the index of Volume 3. It should have the following references: pages 124, 152, 276, 330, 334. Many of the entries for Russian writers in the index are incomplete. In the case of Bulgakov, who is wrongly noted as Macarius instead of Sergei, the following references should be added: pages 104-106, 108, 109, 226, 237, 253. In the case of Berdyaev, pages 194, 211 and 284 should be added.

21. Thomas Merton, *Dancing in the Water of Life* (Journals, edited by Robert E. Daggy; New York: HarperCollins 1997), page 176.

22. *Dancing in the Water of Life*, page 173.

23. *Dancing in the Water of Life*, page 173.

24. *Dancing in the Water of Life*, page 181.

25. V. Lossky, *Theologie negative et connaissance de Dieu chez Maitre Eckhart* (Paris: Vrin, 1960).

26. N. Lossky, *Lancelot Andrewes the Preacher (1555 - 1626): The Origins of the Mystical Theology of the Church of England* (Oxford: Clarendon Press, 1991).

27. Thomas Merton, *The Hidden Ground of Love: Letters of Thomas Merton on Religious Experience and Social Concerns*. Edited by W.H. Shannon (New York: Farrar, Straus & Giroux, 1985).

28. London: Faith Press, 1963.

29. *Dancing in the Water of Life*, pages 181-82. The passage is included in Merton's posthumously published 1964-1965 journals, *A Vow of Conversation: Journals 1964-1965* (edited by Naomi Burton Stone; New York: Farrar, Straus & Giroux, 1988), pages 116-117.

3

THOMAS MERTON AND THE CHRISTIAN EAST[1]

Abbot John Eudes Bamberger, OCSO

When Thomas Merton died he had a small icon with him, carried about in the breviary he used for his daily office during the trip to the Far East. On the reverse side of this icon, which I have in my possession, he had written in his own hand a Greek text taken from the *Philokalia* which he wished to keep before his eyes. It reads as follows.

If we wish to please the true God and to be friends with the most blessed of friendships, let us present our spirit naked to God. Let us not draw into it anything of this present world — no art, no thought no reasoning, no self-justification — even though we should possess all the wisdom of this world.[2]

A great deal could be said about this text and its significance for Merton. For the present let it suffice to underline the fact that it represents one of the more characteristic elements of the spirituality of the *Philokalia* in its emphasis on the "spirit naked to God." This tradition goes back to Evagrius who taught the doctrine of pure prayer taking place beyond images in the highest part of man, his *nous*, as the means to perfect union with God. In focusing on this text Father Merton was at the center of the Eastern tradition, at the heart of the *Philokalia*. But also he was pursuing the same path that he had followed from his first readings on mysticism in the writings of the Spanish mystic of the sixteenth century, John of the Cross. Already as a layman, prior to his entry into Gethsemani, he read the books of the Spanish writer with careful attention. He found his teaching difficult to understand, for they referred also to a "naked" knowledge of God.

. . . these words I underlined, although they amazed and dazzled me with their import, were too simple for me to understand. They were too naked . . . however, I am glad that I was at least able to recognize them, obscurely, as worthy of the greatest respect.[3]

Thus we find in Merton's first contacts with mystical writings as well as in his last days a fascination with the "naked knowledge" of the God who is love. This "naked knowledge," spoken of by Eastern and Western mystics became increasingly important to him.

Some years before his death Father Merton became explicitly aware of the fact that his own spiritual life was rooted in the Eastern tradition as well as in the Western, and he came to understand his own identity and his vocation in terms of this fact.

> I am more and more convinced that my job is to clarify
> something of the tradition that lives in me and in which
> I live the tradition of wisdom and spirituality that is found
> not only in Western Christendom but in Orthodoxy.[4]

This conviction that Merton speaks of was not a sudden eruption of some quick enthusiasm. It was rather the ripe fruit of a seed that had been planted in the days of his first conversion to the spiritual life when as a young student he was visiting Rome. For Merton Rome was not only Latin and Western, but also Byzantine through its history and early monuments. He had come to Rome rather as a tourist and in search of a wider humanistic culture, but while there he visited the ancient churches where he found numerous, well preserved works of Christian art, many of them Byzantine. "I was fascinated by these Byzantine mosaics . . . and thus without knowing anything about it I became a pilgrim . . . [5] As he passed his days in the presence of these awesome images Merton felt himself drawn to leave aside the modern novels he had brought with him to read on his tour and he felt himself drawn increasingly to Christ, for the first time in his life. "I read more and more of the Gospels, and my love for the old churches and their mosaics grew from day to day."[6] As a consequence of this prolonged contact "for the first time in my whole life," he adds, "I really began to pray — praying not with my lips and with my intellect and my imagination but praying out of the very roots of my life and of my being, and praying to the God I had never known, to reach down toward me out of his darkness . . . "[7]

In later years he still felt the deep attraction of these images of God's holiness incarnated in the human form: "No art form stirs or moves me more deeply, perhaps, than Byzantine and Russian *ikons*."[8] It is significant that the experience of God he discovered under the influence of these *ikons* was an experience of God's light that reached "down toward me out of his darkness," which is related to the "naked spirit" prepared to receive the pure light of its creator that John Carpathios speaks of.

Once Fr. Louis had entered the monastery he began to acquaint himself with various early Christian writers. In his earlier years he was interested especially in St. Augustine and various other Latin Fathers, especially the early Cistercians of the twelfth century. His interest in John of the Cross with his doctrine of the dark ascent was also to continue unabated and indeed to prove life-long, for one of his last essays, as yet unpublished, treats of the Spanish Carmelite's teaching at length and contains some admirable pages, full of vitality.

But Merton also began to have some more direct contact with the Eastern tradition. The *Apophthegmata* at some early date in his monastic life became some of his preferred reading. He felt a great attraction to the wisdom condensed into these brief sayings, artfully revealing a world of intense and authentic experience. Later on, Fr. Louis translated some of these *Sayings of the Fathers*, and, since his death, this book has been used for readings at the Divine Office by some of our monks. I recall on one occasion in earlier years, in the course of a conference in the novitiate, his remark that "these men from the Egyptian desert have more reality for me than the people living in Louisville."

But it was through his study of the early Cistercians that Merton was to be led to further contact with some of the great Greek theologians and mystics. Very probably when reading Gilson's *The Mystical Theology of St. Bernard* he began to recognize the importance of the Greek tradition for the Cistercian Fathers and was led to a serious study of two of the more important Greek theologians. Gilson pointed out the primordial importance of the *Vitae Patrum* for the early Cistercians who consciously sought to appropriate their teaching and follow their example in many practices. When Gilson went on to speak of "the admirable doctrine of Gregory of Nyssa, which undoubtedly had its influence on St. Bernard through Maximus,"[9] Fr. Louis would have been led to both of these writers. When his book on the teachings of St. John of the Cross appeared in 1951 [*The Ascent to Truth*], he devoted the first chapter in good part to the mystical teaching of Gregory of Nyssa. Why so? Precisely because St. Gregory presented so forcefully the basic orientation of the kind of mystic that Merton was most attracted to: "And there are the great theologians of darkness: Saint Gregory of Nyssa, Pseudo-Dionysius, Saint John of the Cross."[10] Gregory presents, as few others have, the mystic view of the two ways — vision and illusion. Fr. Louis considered him to be "at one the most important and the most neglected of the early Christian mystical theologians." (This was written prior to the work of Werner Jaeger and the translations in *Sources chrétiennes*.) One of Gregory's teachings that held great appeal for Merton was the doctrine of *epektasis* that saw each advance of the spiritual life as satisfaction of some spiritual aspiration and, at the same time, an invitation to further movement into God. Though he does not refer to this view in any writing of this period, he spoke of it in a community discussion at Gethsemani with enthusiasm. Its vision of the life of union with God as a continuous movement and growth devoid of restlessness or desire was exciting to his imagination and corresponded to the modern dynamic psychology with which Merton was familiar. He also read *Maximus the Confessor* and found in him many of the elements that had stimulated St. Bernard and which were taken over by him. He became for a time one of his favorite authors. Gilson had pointed out that Maximus provided St. Bernard with a word that held so much importance for his mystical doctrine, *excessus*, ecstasy. Bernard made a very independent use of this word with its related themes of love, participation, and deification but he had discovered these concepts already brought together in the *Ambigua* of Maximus.[11] Having entered so deeply into the teaching of Bernard, when Merton found some of its origins in the writings of Maximus, he had a personal sense of discovery in reading the texts of this Byzantine theologian whose writings on the spiritual life proved so fertile in the history of Christian spirituality.

Doubtless, some of the conference materials that remain unpublished deal at length with the writings of this Confessor who stirred Merton's early enthusiasm so deeply, but it is curious to note that in his published works Merton refers explicitly to Maximus only in passing.

Once he had entered into the Greek tradition Merton would never get very far away from it, even while he continued his studies in the Western Fathers and later spiritual writers and enlarged the scope of his interest. Among the Eastern Fathers he found Clement of Alexandria particularly attractive and translated a portion of his writings into English. It was above all Clement's vast culture, his open spirit that was able to assimilate Greek values while deepening his Christian commitment that attracted him. He read Denis the Areopagite, Evagrius Ponticus and John Chrysostom and found in each of them a vision and an insight that enriched his own. We find him utilizing their teachings in his last book on monastic spirituality, showing their relation to St. John of the Cross. "The teaching of St. John of the Cross . . . is in the direct line of ancient monastic and patristic tradition, from Evagrius Ponticus, Cassian and Gregory of Nyssa on down through Gregory the Great and the followers of Psuedo-Dionysius in the West. St. John Chrysostom writes of the 'incomprehensibility of God'."[12]

Other writers too brought him into touch with one of the more important currents of Byzantine spirituality, the hesychastic tradition as presented by the *Philokalia* especially. Already in the 1950s Merton wrote a detailed and nuanced account of Mt. Athos and its traditions which had profound appeal for him. He discusses the spirituality of St. Gregory of Palamas with his doctrine of the "divine light" and the implications of it for the spiritual life, and in fact he sees the Light of Tabor as the meaning of Mt. Athos, for it is the mystery of Easter. This light is related to the "void" that is in man's heart and whose darkness can be illuminated only by its divine rays.[13]

The prayer of the heart, as he discovered it in the various Eastern writers, struck a very sympathetic cord in Merton's spirit. When he was writing his final work on monastic prayer he returned to this theme and developed it at some length, pointing out its significance for certain basic values which held great importance for him, such as authenticity, remaining "rooted in one's own inner truth."[14] Merton believed that the prayer of the heart is eminently suited to monks of our time when used intelligently and recommended it as an effective approach to interior prayer and so to spiritual growth, showing how it can lead to deepening purity of heart.[15]

It is instructive to note in this book on monastic prayer how Merton cites alternately various Eastern and Western authors. It was indeed true that his roots were deeply buried in both these traditions so that presenting the climate of monastic life meant interpreting for men of our time the teachings of Issac of Nineveh as well as Gregory the Great, and Macarius and Basil as well as Augustine and John of the Cross.

John Climacus was the subject of a special essay by Merton [presented in Part III of this volume] when a new English translation of his works appeared in 1959.[16] In addition to providing a detailed appreciation of his *Ladder of Divine Ascent* Merton pointed out how much his spirit had entered into the formation of the Russian character and how an understanding of it throws light on such writers as Dostoievsky, for example. *Crime and Punishment* has a lot to do with the spirituality of St. John Climacus, in a perverse and inverted sort of way. In fact all Russian literature and spirituality is tinged with the ferocity and paradox of Sinai.[17]

The Russian mystics had a particular place in the affections of Merton as did various Russian writers and modern theologians such as Dostoievsky and Berdyaev and especially Sololvyev, whose contemplative vision, with his emphasis on Sophia in the world, was congenial to Merton's own vision of the world. In addition to their profoundly contemplative and monastic spirit, the Russians display a tenderness and humanity that is evident in their iconography as well as in their spiritual writings. That commended their art and spirituality to Merton.

Above all others, St. Seraphim of Sarov was for Merton the most perfect example of that mysticism of light which is characteristic of the Orthodox Church: completely positive and yet compatible with, indeed based on, the *apophatic* (negative) theology of Pseudo-Dionysius and St. Maximus the Confessor. It is perhaps this which distinguished Russian mysticism in its pure state.[18]

In this article Fr. Louis points out that Russian mysticism takes its origin largely in the traditions brought from Mt. Athos and for centuries maintained a nourishing contact with the Holy Mountain. Through this channel the Prayer of Jesus became a prominent feature of Russian piety and reached its highest expression in the figure of St. Seraphim, who taught that the culmination of the ascetic life is the acquisition of the Holy Spirit. Even more than Staretz Silouan, for whom Merton felt "a great admiration,"[19] Seraphim stands at the center of this great spiritual tradition in which Merton found so much of what he felt to be most central to his own vision of life.

In his description of *starchestvo* Merton presents a positive and ardent picture of this form of holiness, which corresponds in large measure to his own ideal. It is characterized above all by a "total surrender to the power of love" and this "love was the sole basis of their spiritual authority." But few are capable of so exalted an ideal and rather prefer to conform to "law because in reality, law is less demanding than pure charity."[20]

Even in his literary criticism the Eastern Fathers continued to play a role, as one can see in Merton's fine discussion of Pasternak's novel *Doctor Zhivago*. He points out that Pasternak, whether he knows it or not, is plunged fully into midstream of the lost tradition of "natural contemplation" [*Theoria physica*] which flowed among the Greek Fathers after it had been set in motion by Origen.[21]

He points out, however, that Pasternak does not share the dogmatic and ascetic preoccupations of Origen and the Cap-

padocian Fathers. He is not the prophet of this regained Paradise, as were Origen and Gregory of Nyssa . . . Rather he is a
prophet of the original, cosmic revelation . . . . [22]

The ease with which Merton points out, convincingly, such
aspects of the Eastern tradition reveal to what extent familiarity
with the Greek Fathers had formed his awareness and judgment
and influenced his taste.

Fr. Louis had an intense nostalgia for the eremitical life.
The solitary aspect of monastic life had been so important
to him from the beginning of his conversion that he considered seriously, more than once, entering an order of hermits.
Though he decided to remain a monk of Gethsemani, he
did receive permission to live as a hermit, and the last
three years of his life [1965 - 1968] were dedicated to
the practices of the eremitical life. Yet he never ceased to
think of himself as having a function as spiritual guide
which he exercised above all by his writing and to a lesser
extent also by conferences he gave to the community every
week and by spiritual direction. From the time that Merton
was assigned the task of spiritual master to the young monks
at Gethsemani he gave himself generously to this work and
it became an important element in his personal development,
as he himself attested various times.[23] He dates his concern
with social and political matters to the years he spent as spiritual guide to the student-monks and, significantly, dedicated the
book he wrote during those first years, *No Man Is An Island*,
to his students.

The ideal spiritual Father then became a part of his own identity. And he occupied himself with the traditional teaching on
his role and qualities. In the interesting article he wrote on
"The Spiritual Father in the Desert Tradition," as well as what
we have already seen above in his treatment of *starchestvo*, he
portrayed in good part his idea of this office. He chose to study
it in the Eastern tradition in a particular way, though elsewhere
he also wrote of certain Western spiritual guides whom he admired and from whom he learned a great deal, Augustine Baker,
Eckhart, Newman and others.[24] The *Apophthegmata* is one of
the chief sources of his ideal. Other Eastern writers are cited

as well and contributed to his ideal of a spiritual guide, such as
Evagrius Ponticus and Pachomius and Barsanuphius and
Evergetinus and the *Philokalia*. He appreciated in the Desert
Fathers especially their flexibility, their judgments based on con-
crete circumstances. This approach to life was primary with
Merton who repeated the need for this Christian manner
of using rules and law constantly to his young students in
the monastery:

> The sayings of the Fathers are not to be taken as
> hard and fast rules which apply in the same way in
> every situation: they are applications of broad general
> principles . . . [25]

In the advice, so often given by the Desert Fathers, to
"guard the cell" Merton saw the expression of a whole
orientation in spirituality which he considered important enough
to merit a special essay [presented in Part III of this volume],
which was again based primarily on the *Sayings of the Fathers*.[26]
The spiritual Father, then, had to be a man who had experience
with the *ascesis* of the cell and solitude and who could use
it with mastery, along with other traditional practices that
in Merton's eyes remained useful and even necessary for
spiritual progress. Merton's view in all these respects accepts
and conforms to the tradition of these various Fathers and
in making use of them both in his own life and in guiding
others, Merton did more than learn from them. He became a
disciple and allowed himself to be formed by them, to enter
into their experience so as to be himself transformed by their
teaching. He became himself one with them. For a striking
instance of how such identification influenced Merton's
perception as well as his thought consider the following passage
that speaks of one of his favorite eastern Saints, the Hermit of
Lebanon, Charbel:

> Everywhere is beauty . . . Alive and dead I climb the
> glorious barn. The mud of my feet going up is the mud
> of my hands going down. I will go down more wretched
> than I went up because more glorious. This barn cannot
> be known. It is Mount Lebanon, where Father Charbel
> Makhlouf saw the sun and moon.[27]

If Fr. Louis wrote relatively little about dogmatic questions and formal theology for its own sake, it was not because he had no interest in it, nor because he thought it unimportant. He used to tell us that all of us future priests should seek to become theologians, and he sought to enter deeply into the heart of the best theologians of the Church. But he strove still more to penetrate into the dogmatic formulations and discover, in a personal way, their hidden truth and life. For him dogma was spirituality because it was to be contemplated, assimilated and lived. In short, he was in accord with Evagrius: "If you are a theologian, you truly pray. If you truly pray, you are a theologian."[28]

Merton's early and persistent and vast interest in ecumenism was the fruit rather of prayer than of theological reflection. In this he had the same approach as some of the spiritual Fathers on Mt. Athos with whom I discussed ecumenical and spiritual matters on the occasion of a recent visit. Merton was convinced that the way to union among the churches is not through argument or theological discussion, in the first place, but through encounter among men of the Spirit, men who have learned something of the mystery of Christ through contemplation and long ascetic practice. Once a meeting took place where one lives in the Presence of the Spirit of Christ, important dogmatic matters could then be fruitfully examined together. He understood his contribution as demanding above all this spiritual encounter. He was stimulated immensely by such meetings with men of the Spirit from the Eastern as well as from the Western Tradition and such meetings represented more for him than a search for broader understanding. They were a necessity of the Spirit, for he felt he had inherited many of the values of the Byzantine tradition "as a son inherits his father's estate."[29] He had a profound conviction that "the only source of the spiritual life is the Holy Spirit"[30] and that its purpose is to attain to possession of the Holy Spirit, by the free gift of God in Christ. He was convinced that, when we attain to this greatest of all gifts through ascetic preparation and through prayer of the heart, we would discover that in the Holy Spirit we are already united, already one, and in this realization we would receive the light and strength to give corporate expression to this unity so that, in the end, we would be fully united in the Whole Christ.

Abbey of the Genesee, Piffard, New York

NOTES

1. This essay first appeared in Cistercian Studies Number 29, *One Yet Two: Monastic Tradition East and West*, 1976.

2. John Carpathios, *Kephaliaia Paramythitika*, page 49.

3. Thomas Merton, *The Seven Storey Mountain* (New York: Harcourt, Brace, 1948) pages 238-39.

4. Thomas Merton, *Conjectures of a Guilty Bystander* (New York: Doubleday, 1966) page 176.

5. *The Seven Storey Mountain*, page 108.

6. *Ibid.*, page 110.

7. *Ibid.*, page 111.

8. *Conjectures of a Guilty Bystander*, page 280

9. (London-New York, 1940, 1955), page 17.

10. Thomas Merton, *The Ascent to Truth* (New York: Harcourt, Brace, 1951), page 25.

11. Gilson, *The Mystical Theology*, page 26, 27.

12. Thomas Merton, *The Climate of Monastic Prayer*, CS 1 (Spencer, Massachusetts: Cistercian Publications, 1969 page 110.

13. Cf. Thomas Merton, *Disputed Questions* (New York: Farrar, Straus and Cudahy, 1960) pages 68-82

14. *The Climate of Monastic Prayer*, page 34.

15. *Ibid.*, page 93.

16. Cf. *Disputed Questions*, pages 83-93.

17. *Ibid.*, page 88.

18. Thomas Merton, *Mystics and Zen Masters* (New York: Farrar, Straus and Giroux, 1967), page 182.

19. *Conjectures of a Guilty Bystander*, page 147.

20. *Mystics and Zen Masters*, page 186

21. *Disputed Questions*, page 17.

22. *Ibid.*

23. Thomas Merton, *The Sign of Jonas* (New York: Harcourt, Brace, 1953) pages 333-34.

24. See, for example, the index of *Mystics and Zen Masters*.

25. Thomas Merton, *Contemplation in a World of Action* (New York: Doubleday, 1965), page 280

26. *Ibid.*, pages 252-59.

27. *The Sign of Jonas*, page 326.

28. Evagrius Ponticus, *Chapters on Prayer*, 60 in *Evagrius Ponticus: Praktikos – Chapters on Prayer.* CS 4 (Spenser, Massachusetts: Cistercian Publications, 1972), page 65

29. *Conjectures of a Guilty Bystander*, page 176.

30. *Contemplation in a World of Action*, page 271.

Constantinople, mid-sixth century.

4

THOMAS MERTON
AND BYZANTINE SPIRITUALITY[1]

M. Basil Pennington

Thomas Merton has been without doubt the most influential
Catholic writer on the American scene in the twentieth century. His heart was indeed ecumenical. In fact it stretched beyond the bounds of ecumenism properly so-called to embrace all
that is good in the human spirit even if that be found among so-
called pagans or Marxists. I do not think it would be possible
to exaggerate the importance of the influence of Byzantine spirituality and especially that of the Fathers of Eastern Christendom
on the development of Merton's well-integrated spirituality. We
might say that Merton's Christian life, writings and spirit are
marked from their first serious awakening to their end by the
influence of the Christian East. When he went to Rome in 1933,
still very much a hedonist, it was the great Byzantine mosaics that
called him forth and changed the tourist into a pilgrim. In *Seven
Storey Mountain* he tells us:

> I was fascinated by these Byzantine mosaics. I began to
> haunt the churches where they were to be found. . . . And
> now for the first time in my life I began to find out
> something of Who this Person was that men called Christ.
> It was obscure, but it was a true knowledge of Him, in
> some sense, truer than I knew and truer than I would
> admit. . . . And now I think for the first time in my whole
> life I really began to pray — praying not with my lips and
> with my intellect and my imagination, but praying out of
> the very roots of my life and of my being, and praying to
> the God I had never known. . . . [2]

At the end of his journey in the last book which Merton prepared for publication, *The Climate of Monastic Prayer*,[3] Merton
moves from the *Fathers of the Desert* to share the kernel of the
teaching of the *Philokalia*. As we progress through the text, which

offers a clear and relatively concise history of contemplative spirituality and the teachings of the masters, we come upon such
names as Isaac of Nineveh, Saint Ammonas, Evagrius Ponticus,
Saint Basil, Saint Gregory of Nyssa, the Pseudo-Dionysius, Saint
Nilus, and others in the Byzantine tradition.

The influence of the great Fathers of the Eastern Church first
came to Merton mediated through the Cistercian Fathers whom
he read extensively in his early years in the monastery.[4] As his
studies moved forward he came, in part with the help of Gilson,[5]
to recognize and identify these Fathers' sources. But I think it
can also be said that it was the *Fathers of the Desert*, whose delightful pithy and profound sayings so attracted him, who opened
Merton to pursue the evolution of this strong, rich current of
spirituality. Keith Egan in his very interesting and informative
series of taped talks, *Solitude and Community, The Paradox of Life
and Prayer*, has said of Merton: "He began to read the literature
that came out of the desert, the Christian desert of the fourth
century. And one of the most important books he wrote is his
shortest and that is *The Wisdom of the Desert.* . . . The study that
lies behind the writing of this little book was transforming and
changed Merton's life forever."[6]

In 1960, when he published this short collection of the
Sayings, Merton wrote a very rich introduction of twenty-two
pages [presented in Part III of this volume]. He traced the spiritual path laid out by the Fathers in their sayings. It begins with
a "clean break" type of compunction, a lament over the madness of our attachments to unreal values. Through solitude and
labor, poverty and fasting, charity and prayer, the old superficial
self is purged away and the true secret self is permitted to emerge.
The monk moves toward purity of heart: a clean unobstructed
vision of the true state of affairs, an intuitive grasp of one's own
inner reality as anchored or rather lost in God through Christ.
This leads to *quies*, the sanity and praise of a being that no longer
has to look at itself because it is carried away by the perfection of
being that is in it. And carried where? Wherever Love itself of
the Divine Spirit sees fit to go. Rest, then, was a kind of simple
no-whereness and no-mindedness that had lost all preoccupation
with a false or limited "self."[7]

The terminology Merton uses here is not that of the *Desert Fathers*. By this time the *Fathers* had opened Merton to other even broader influences.[8] But first they opened him to their own immediate heirs. Merton went on to expand and deepen his vision through the developing theology of the Christian East, with the Cappodocians, especially Saint Gregory of Nyssa, and with Evagrius Ponticus, who really belongs to the desert tradition, and above all in Maximus the Confessor.

In his first full-length work on spirituality, a study of the teaching of Saint John of the Cross entitled *The Ascent to Truth*, Merton devotes many pages in the first and third chapters to those "great theologians of darkness: Saint Gregory of Nyssa, and Pseudo-Dionysius."[9] The former he hails as "the most important and the most neglected of the early Christian mystical theologians, the Father of Christian apophatic mysticism."[10] He also says of him: "There are pages in the works of Saint Gregory of Nyssa which might easily fit into a context of Zen Buddhism or Patanjali's Yoga."[11] He depends here largely on Gregory's scriptural commentaries, those on *Ecclesiastes*, *Psalms* and the *Song of Songs*. He traces out Gregory's journey from light to darkness with the Mosaic imagery of the burning bush, the pillar of cloud, and finally the darkness of Sinai and suggests a parallel with the three dark nights of Saint John of the Cross. On page twenty-seven he speaks of *theoria physike*, distinguishing the positive and negative aspects of it. But I do not think at this time this important element of Eastern Christian spiritual teaching had had the impact on him that later was to be, in my opinion, very significant. In the introduction to the *Sign of Jonas*, Merton himself clearly indicated the shortcomings of the very dry intellectual approach to this teaching which he presented in the Ascent.[12]

Some years later Merton had the opportunity to study these Fathers more fully and reflect more profoundly on them as he prepared and gave a course to his fellow monk-priests on Christian Mysticism. We have only the notes of these lectures,[13] but they are quite full and, while they lack his usual rich literary style they do have his candid clarity and forceful impact. It is here that he highlights the central place of Saint Gregory more in detail, indicating his influence on the Cistercian Fathers — on Saint Bernard through Origen, on William of St. Thierry through the Pseudo — Dionysius and John Scotus Erigena, and on all of them through Cassian through Evagrius — on the Syrians through Saint Marcarius, and on the Greeks in general through Maximus the Confessor.[14] Here he studies extensively and deeply the meaning of the "spiritual senses," disagreeing with the interpretations or understanding of previous Western writers such as Poulain and Olphe Gaillard. Merton adopts a more integrated view, seeing them closely allied with the bodily senses that have been freed and purified by mortification, virginity and passive purification, and elevated and spiritualized by grace and the operation of the Holy Spirit until they approach a full restoration of that state of paradise where God was enjoyed by the senses "deifying the body" (Saint Gregory Palamas).[15]

More important is the insight he attains into *theoria physike* under the tutelage of Evagrius Ponticus, whom he strongly defends,[16] and Maximus the Confessor. The spiritual life is seen to involve three stages: *bios praktikos* — *praxis* — the purification of the body, of the senses, of the passions — *apatheia* — the *puritas cordis* of John Cassian, something more than detachment, a positive openness to reality, to the Divine: *theoria physike* — a spiritualized knowledge of the created, a sort of natural contemplation, which does reach on to the divine *oikonomia*, God's plan for things, and the *logoi* of things, the Divine plan within things. At its higher levels it reaches to the contemplation of the spiritual: *theologia* — the contemplation of the Trinity without form or image.

I believe it was the understanding of *theoria physike* that enabled the zealous, ascetic, world-despising young monk who constantly fought with his own human gifts for poetry and literature to reintegrate his natural appreciation and love for the wonders of creation and all that the good God made and to go on to become the very full and integrated person he became. He himself said: "We can in fact say that the lack of *theoria physike* is one of the things that accounts for the stunting of spiritual growth among our monks today."[17]

He goes on to say:

It is by *theoria* that man helps Christ to redeem the logoi of things and restore them to Himself. . . . This *theoria* is inseparable from love and from a truly spiritual conduct of life. Man must not only see the inner meaning of things but he must regulate his entire life and his use of time and of created beings according to the mysterious norms hidden in things by the Creator, or rather by the Creator himself in the bosom of His creation.[18]

I would like to quote more extensively from Merton in this place because I think this matter is absolutely central to the understanding of his spiritual development and outlook.

Man by *theoria* is able to unite the hidden wisdom of God in things with the hidden light of wisdom in himself. The meeting and marriage of these two brings about a resplendent clarity within man himself, and this clarity is the presence of Divine Wisdom fully recognized and active in him. Thus man becomes a mirror of the divine glory and is resplendent with divine truth not only in his mind but in his life. He is filled with the light of wisdom which shines forth in him, and thus God is glorified in him. At the same time he exercises a spiritualizing influence in the world by the work of his hands which is in accord with the creative wisdom of God in things and in him.

No longer are we reduced to a purely negative attitude toward the world around us, toward history, toward the judgments of God. The world is no longer seen as purely material, hence as an obstacle to be grudgingly put up with. It is spirit there and then. But grace has to work with and through us to enable us to carry out this real transformation. Things are not fully spiritual in themselves, they have to be spiritualized by our knowledge and love in the use of them. Hence it is impossible for one who is not purified to "transfigure" material things. On the contrary, the *logoi* will remain hidden and he himself will be captivated by the sensible attraction of these things.[19]

In this last sentence we see the difference between these Greek Fathers, and Merton with them, and the currently popular "creation theology." The Fathers and Merton emphasize that it is impossible to enter into a true *theoria physike*, a true appreciation of the creation and the presence of God in creation, without first embracing the *bios praktikos*, that purification that produces *apatheia*, a true purity of heart that enables us to appreciate the overwhelming beauty transfiguring the creation without being ensnared by it. Otherwise we are in danger of resting in the creation and becoming attached to it and ourselves rather than finding all in God and God in all, being attached to him alone.

Also, the Fathers and Merton never stop at the *theoria physike*, the wonders of the creation, even transfigured by God, but are ever conscious of this as a stage on the way to true *theologia*, to finding our true place within the very life of the Trinity, we who have been made truly and most mysteriously one with the Son in baptism, we who have been "deified." In this context, and in this context alone does *theoria physike* or "creation theology" attain its full meaning. May I quote Merton again:

> The "will of God" is no longer a blind force plunging through our lives like a cosmic steamroller and demanding to be accepted willy nilly. On the contrary we are able to understand the hidden purpose of the creative wisdom and the divine mercy of God, and can cooperate with Him as sons with a loving Father. Not only that, but God himself hands over to man, when he is thus purified and enlightened, and united with the divine will, a certain creative initiative of his own, in political life, in art, in spiritual life, in worship: man is then endowed with a causality of his own.[20]

As I have said, I believe that Merton's "discovery" and full perception of *theoria physike* had a profound formative and liberating influence on him. Later in this paper I will return to further indications of this. Let us now continue to look at the influences of the Eastern Christian spiritual heritage on Merton and his writings.

At the same time as Merton was preparing and teaching this course he was preparing one of his more significant and weighty theological volumes, *The New Man*.[21] In this study he does depend heavily on Western Fathers and theologians: Saint Augustine and Saint Bernard, Aquinas and Ruysbroeck. But the names of Eastern Fathers keep cropping up: Clement of Alexandria and Gregory of Nyssa, Cyril of Jerusalem and others. But the influence is perhaps more profoundly marked by the extraordinary frequency with which he employs Greek works in this text. We find *pneuma, pneumatikos, metanoia, antitypos* and *parousia* all used more than once. More significant is the very extensive study of *parrhesia*, which Merton well defines as "free spiritual communication of being with Being."[22]

Also at this period Merton wrote a rather poor piece on Mount Athos[23] [presented in Part III of this volume], "the last important Christian survival of the typical ancient monastic colonies."[24] I do not think Merton can be blamed for the poverty and inaccuracies of this piece. He never had the opportunity to visit the Holy Mountain (something I am sure he would have loved to have done) and had to depend on the accounts of others of which he noted: "In such books one rarely receives any insight into the profound religious mystery of Athos."[25] He was enthusiastic about the idea of Athos and proposed a similar western monastic republic with a similar freedom of monastic expression. He was a bit pessimistic about the future of the Holy Mountain. I am sure he would be elated at its present vigorous revival, even to the inclusion of more monks from Holy Russia.[26]

In the same volume in which he published the Athos piece he added a study on "The Spirituality of Sinai" [presented in Part III of this volume], largely a commentary on Saint John Climacus' *Ladder*.[27] The piece is rather rough, filled with slang (*fanatical windbag, busting him in the teeth, Climacus was nuts*, etc.) and homely details (such as the brethren's reaction to reading the *Ladder* in the community refectory at Gethsemani).[28] The piece was occasioned by the publication of Archimandrite Lazarus Moore's translation, which Merton praises. He appreciates more the stream of spirituality that Climacus represents then this "tough, hard-hitting, merciless book,"[29] for "all Russian literature and spirituality is tinged with the ferocity and paradox of Sinai."[30] From Sinai, too, the practice of the Jesus Prayer came to Athos and to Russia: "Let the remembrance of Jesus be present with each breath, and then you will know the value of solitude," says Climacus.[31]

Russia had a special place in Merton's heart. The only Athonite monk to whom he seemed to get close as a living reality was the humble and saintly procurator of the Russian monastery of Saint Panteleimon, Father Siloan. Through the writings of Father Siloan's disciple, Father Sophrony, Merton was able to appreciate this simple and profoundly prayerful man who never lost his love for solitude even in the midst of serving a monastery of hundreds of monks.[32] In his preface to Sergius Bolshakoff's *Russian Mystics*[33] [presented in Part III of this volume], Merton gives evidence of an extensive knowledge of Russian monastic history. Saint Nilus, in his controversy with the institutional monasticism represented by Saint Joseph Volokolamsk, was of special interest, especially since much of Evagrius' teaching has come down to us under Saint Nilus' patronage. But for Merton Saint Seraphim of Sarov was "without doubt the greatest mystic of the Russian Church."[34] In him there was a balance between the ascetic tradition and austerity (*podvig*), repentance and tears and a humanism filled with joy, open to life, gentle, and profoundly compassionate. He had "evangelical and patristic purity, pure and traditional theology, ingenuous amazement of the divine light shining through the darkness."[35] Saint Seraphim's was a mysticism of light (albeit based on the apophaticism of PseudoDionysius and Maximus) which approached the Invisible as visible in a creation transfigured in Divine Light.

Merton's interest in the Russian writers ranged far beyond the monastic and even the so called religious. In the late fifties he even made an abortive attempt at learning Russian so that he could read them in their original language. *Conjectures* is sprinkled with names like Belinsky, Lenin and Berdyaev, along with the pages devoted to Evdokimov.[36] His next published journal includes a quote from Yelchaninov in the Prelude.[37]

This broadening is indicated in a curious way in an interesting piece that reflects Merton's first days in his hermitage. He had never moved very far from the *Desert Fathers*. In those days he wrote a very fine piece on the Spiritual Father in the desert tradition.[38] Dom John Eudes rightly notes that the ideal of the spiritual father had become part of his own identity.[39] Merton also wrote a piece on the cell drawing from the same sources.[40] But the biographical piece that opens *Raids on the Unspeakable*[41] is the piece to which I am referring. In "Rain and the Rhinoceros"[42] Merton tells us of sitting in his hermitage on the hill above the Abbey, reading by his Coleman lantern (he did not yet have electricity there). On this particular rainy night he was reading Philoxenos (a sixth-century Syrian Father), seeking to understand better the solitude he was so drawn to and finding more and more. On this night he read Philoxenos' ninth *memra* to dwellers in solitude. Merton heard again that 'there is no explanation and no justification for the solitary life, since it is without a law."[43] ". . . leave the rule of the world where he [Christ] has left the law, and go out with him to fight the power of error."[44] Merton concludes his passage on Philoxenos saying: "Today the insights of a Philoxenos are to be sought less in the tracts of theologians than in the meditations of the existentialists and in the Theater of the Absurd."[45]

Without a shadow of doubt Merton's favorite among the modern Russian writers is Boris Pasternak. He wrote three articles[46] on this poet and novelist ["The Pasternak Affair" is presented in Part III of this volume], whom he saw as "immensely more important that Sholokov."[47] He found Pasternak's witness "essentially Christian."[48] The Christianity Pasternak presented was "reduced to the barest and most elemental essentials: intense awareness of all cosmic and human reality as 'life in Christ', and the consequent plunge into love as the only dynamic and creative force which really honors this 'Life' by creating itself anew in Life's-Christ's-image."[49] Merton sensed a very deep oneness with Pasternak and expresses it powerfully and beautifully in the first letter he addressed to the Russian, some months prior to the explosion over the Nobel Prize awarded to Pasternak:

> I feel much more kinship with you, in your writing, than I do with most of the great modern writers in the West. That is to say that I feel that I can share your experience more deeply and with greater intimacy and sureness. . . . With other writers I can share ideas, but you seem to communicate something deeper. It is as if we meet on a deeper level of life on which individuals are not separate beings.

In a language familiar to me as Catholic monk, it is as if we were known to one another in God.[50]

I believe this is so because by this time Merton had fully integrated the outlook and experience of *theoria physike* and Pasternak comes out of the same living tradition; they experience the creation in the same basic way and express this in their poetry and writing. Merton actually points to this in his first article on Pasternak:

> Pasternak, whether he knows it or not, is plunged fully into midstream of the lost tradition of "natural contemplation" [Merton's English expression for *theoria physike*, as we have seen above] which flowed among the Greek Fathers after it had been set in motion by Origen. Of course the tradition has not been altogether lost and Pasternak has come upon it in the Orthodox Church. The fact is clear in any case: he reads the Scriptures with the avidity and the spiritual imagination of Origen and he looks on the world with the illuminated eyes of the Cappadocian Fathers. . . .[51]

Merton appreciated this "sophianic" view of the cosmos — a creation impregnated by Santa Sophia, Holy Wisdom, the Word and Love of God — in other Russian writers such as Soloviev and Berdyaev (Merton's articles on Pasternak bring out his extensive familiarity with the Russian authors) but he identified most strongly with Pasternak's spirit so akin to his own. It is a question of *sobornost*. This is perhaps why he shared with him in his second letter a secret he had shared with only three others. Because of its important bearing on a significant turning point in Merton's life and because it is relatively little known I would like to quote the passage from the letter in full:

> It is a simple enough story but obviously I do not tell it to people — you are the fourth who knows it, and there seems to be no point in a false discreteness that might restrain me from telling you since it is clear that we have so very much in common.
>
> One night I dreamt that I was sitting with a very young Jewish girl of fourteen or fifteen, and that she suddenly manifested a very deep and pure affection

for me and embraced me so that I was moved to the depths of my soul. I learned that her name was "Proverb," which I thought very simple and beautiful. And also I thought: "She is of the race of Saint Anne." I spoke to her of her name, and she did not seem to be proud of it, because it seemed that the other young girls mocked her for it. But I told her that it was a very beautiful name, and there the dream ended. A few days later when I happened to be in a nearby city, which is very rare for us, I was walking alone in the crowded street and suddenly saw that everybody was Proverb and that in all of them shone her extraordinary beauty and purity and shyness even though they did not know who they were and were perhaps ashamed of their names — because they were mocked on account of them. And they did not know their real identity as the Child so dear to God who, from before the beginning, was playing in His sight all days, playing in the world.[52]

Thus we have here a very intimate and, I think, a very important insight into the well-known experience on the streets of Louisville which Merton has reported elsewhere.[53] Not only was it impacted with the rich imagery of a dream but with the ever-deepening insight into *theoria phsyike* that Merton was integrating into his perceptions of reality. Merton was in many ways a very private person, even in his many published journals. We owe to the extraordinary openness of a very unusual friendship this beautiful and touching revelation that throws so much light on the integration of its writer.

In the last journal that Merton himself prepared for publication, the one flowing from his two-week trip to the west coast and New Mexico in May of 1968, Merton is still with his Russian friends. He returns to Theophane the Recluse with his salutary advice for prayer of the heart:

Not to run from one thought to the next. . . . but to give each one time to settle in the heart.

Attention. Concentration of the spirit in the heart.

Vigilance. Concentration of the will in the heart.

Sobriety. Concentration of the feeling in the heart.[54]

Here, too, in his constant quest for true freedom Merton writes: "I wonder about the definition of Orthodoxy as hostility to rules. . . ." [55] His reference is to a quote from Yelchaninov: "Orthodoxy is the principle of absolute freedom."[56]

But the most important thing about this journal, especially as it has been published with inclusion of some of the photographs that Merton took on the journey, is that it is a magnificent witness to the full flowering of *theoria physike* in its author. It conveys his cosmic and earthy contemplation in the way it can best be conveyed: through poetics and artistry. This severe critic of technology (and in his criticisms I think he was not wholly off) does not hesitate with the true freedom of the son of God to use a bit of technology — the camera — to produce some real art that powerfully highlights and shares his contemplative insight.

The Asian Journal,[57] his last, posthumously published book, is totally free from any mention of Russians or Eastern Christian Fathers. This may be due to the editors. In his notes for the talk he gave at the Spiritual Summit Conference of the Temple of Understanding in Calcutta he indicated his intention to speak on the Hesychast tradition, Mount Athos and Orthodox monasteries.[58] And though in actual fact Merton did not employ these notes and rather spoke extemporaneously, the spirit of this tradition was not missing from his presentation that day. In those same notes Merton speaks about the qualities needed for true dialogue between the different traditions: ". . . it must be reserved for those who have entered with full seriousness into their own monastic tradition and are in authentic contact with the past of their own religious community — besides being open to the tradition and to the heritage of experience belonging to other communities."[59] Speaking of such a person in another article published after his death he adds:

> Such a man is fully "Catholic" in the best sense of the word. He has a unified vision and experience of the one truth shining out in all its various manifestations, some clearer than others, some more definite and certain than others. He does not set these partial views up in opposition to each other but unifies them in a dialectic or insight of complementarity. With this view of life he is able

to bring perspective, liberty and spontaneity into the lives of others. The finally integrated man is a peace-maker.[60]

This certainly Merton was. He entered very deeply and lived deeply his own tradition. He also entered deeply into the traditions of others. In his introductory essay to *The Wisdom of the Desert* Merton says: "Love demands a complete inner transformation — for without this we cannot possibly come to identify ourselves with our brother. We have to become, in some sense, the person we love."[61] Merton did this. He loved and he identified. Finally, in *Conjectures* he says: "I am more convinced that my job is to clarify something of the tradition that lives in me and in which I live: the tradition of wisdom and spirituality that is found not only in Western Christendom but in Orthodoxy. . . ."[62] As Rowan Williams said in a comparative study of Evdokimov and Merton: "Merton's spirituality. . . would not be what it is without his devoted and careful study of Greek patristic thought and the Desert Fathers."[63] And, I would add, all that flowed out of them. And not only study but an assimilation and integration that produced a profound and profoundly beautiful lived synthesis.

Assumption Abbey, Ava, Missouri

NOTES

1. This essay first appeared in Cistercian Studies Number 103: *Toward an Integrated Humanity: Thomas Merton's Journey*. Cistercian Publications: Kalamazoo, Michigan, 1988.

2. Thomas Merton, *The Seven Storey Mountain* (New York: Harcourt, Brace, 1948) pages 108-111.

3. Thomas Merton, *The Climate of Monastic Prayer*, Cistercian Studies Series (hereafter CS) no. 1 (Cistercian Publications, 1969).

4. John Eudes Bamberger, OCSO, "Thomas Merton and the Christian East" in *One Yet Two, Monastic Tradition East and West*, M. Basil Pennington, OCSO, editor, CS 29 (Cistercian Publications, 1976) page 443.

5. Etienne Gilson, *The Mystical Theology of St. Bernard* (London: Sheed and Ward, 1955).

6. Keith Egan, *Solitude and Community, The Paradox of Life and Prayer* (Kansas City, Missouri: NCR Casettes, 1981), tape 3, "The Desert Place of Discovery."

7. Thomas Merton, *The Wisdom of the Desert* (London: Sheldon Press, 1960), page 8.

8. Merton goes on to say: "In many respects, therefore, these Desert Fathers had much in common with Indian Yogis and with Zen Buddhist monks of China and Japan." *Ibid.*, page 9.

9. Thomas Merton, *The Ascent to Truth* (New York: Harcourt, Brace, 1951) page 25.

10. *Ibid.*, page 319.

11. *Ibid.*, page 26. I do not know if this is a slip of the pen, a typo (I have not yet been able to see the original manuscript for this piece) or an indication of how little Merton knew at this time of the Eastern masters, but to speak of the "Zen Buddhism of Patanjali's Yoga" does not make much sense. In later English editions and in some of the translations the "of" is changed to "or," which makes perfect sense.

12. Thomas Merton, *The Sign of Jonas* (New York: Harcourt, Brace, 1953) page 9.

An Introduction to Christian Mysticism (From the Apostolic Fathers to the Council of Trent), Lectures given at the Abbey of Gethsemani, Manuscripts. At the end of the "Forward" we find the date: Vigil of the Assumption, 1961.

14. *Ibid.*, page 31.

15. *Ibid.*, pages 35-42.

16. "Evagrius of Pontus is one of the most important, the least known (until recently), most neglected and the most controversial of Christian mystics. He merits, with Gregory of Nyssa, the title of "Father of Christian Mystical Theology." *Ibid.*, pages 42f. Merton does later (page 56) say: "There remains a considerable danger of misunderstanding him. He is an interesting and important source, but in forming young monks and in preaching the contemplative life it would of course be wiser to find the same things said much better in great saints like Gregory of Nyssa, Maximus, etc."

17. *Ibid.*, page 56.

18. *Ibid.*, page 59.

19. *Ibid.*

20. *Ibid.* It is worthy of note that Merton includes here and in a primary place, "political life."

21. Thomas Merton, *The New Man* (New York: Farrar, Straus & Cuhady, 1961).

22. *Ibid.*, page 76.

23. Thomas Merton, "Mount Athos" in *Disputed Questions* (New York: Farrar, Straus & Giroux, 1960) pages 68-82.

24. *Ibid.*, page 70.

25. *Ibid.*, page 69.

26. For a detailed description of this renewal of Athos, see my *0 Holy Mountain* (Washington, D.C.: Michael Glazier, 1978).

27. *Disputed Questions*, pages 83-93.

28. According to Merton's secretary, Brother Patrick Hart, Merton used this style for this piece because it was written for *Jubilee*.

29. *Ibid.*, page 84.

30. *Ibid.*, page 88.

31. *Ibid.*, page 93.

32. Thomas Merton, *Conjectures of a Guilty Bystander* (Garden City, New York: Doubleday, 1966) page 147. Merton refers to Father Siloan as "Staretz Sylvan"; this is undoubtedly a slip of memory.

33. Sergius Bolshakoff, *Russian Mystics* CS 26 (Cistercian Publications, 1977) pages ix–xviii. This preface was also published in Thomas Merton, *Mystics and Zen Masters* (New York: Farrar, Straus & Giroux, 1967) pages 178-187.

34. *Russian Mystics*, page xii.

35. *Ibid.*, page xiii.

36. *Conjectures of a Guilty Bystander*, pages 308-310. Merton gives the title "Father" to Evdokimov, mistakingly thinking that this lay theologian was a priest.

37. Thomas Merton, *Woods, Shore, Desert, A Notebook*, May 1968 (Santa Fe: Museum of New Mexico Press, 1982) page 3.

38. Thomas Merton, "The Spiritual Father in the Desert Tradition" in *Contemplation in a World of Action* (Garden City, New York: Doubleday, 1971) pages 269-293.

39. Bamberger, page 449.

40. "The Cell" in *Contemplation in a World of Action*, pages 252-259.

42. Thomas Merton, *Raids on the Unspeakable* (New York: New Directions, 1966).

42. *Ibid.*, pages 9-26.

43. *Ibid.*, page 14.

44. *Ibid.*, page 19.

45. *Ibid.*

46. "The Pasternak Affair" in *Disputed Questions*, pages 3-67.

47. *Ibid.*, page 13.

48. *Ibid.*, page 12.

49. *Ibid.*

50. Boris Pasternak and Thomas Merton, *Six Letters* (Lexington, Kentucky: The King Library Press, 1973) pages 3-4.

51. *Disputed Questions*, page 17.

52. *Six Letters*, pages 11f. Merton then adds with delightful humor: "Thus you are initiated into the scandalous secret of a monk who is in love with a girl, and a Jew at that! One cannot expect much from monks these days. The heroic asceticism of the past is no more."

53. "In Louisville, at the corner of Fourth and Walnut, in the center of the shopping district, I was suddenly overwhelmed with the realization that I loved all those people, that they were mine and I theirs, that we could not be alien to one another even though we were total strangers. It was like waking from a dream of separateness, of spurious self-isolation in a special world, the world of renunciation and supposed holiness. The whole illusion of a separate holy existence is a dream. . . . I suppose my happiness could have taken form in the words: "Thank God, thank God that I am like other men, that I am only a man among others." To think that for sixteen or seventeen years I have been taking seriously this pure illusion that is implicit in so much of our monastic thinking." *Conjectures of a Guilty Bystander*, pages 156f.

54. *Woods, Shore and Desert*, page 16.

55. *Ibid.*, page 20.

56. *Ibid.*, page 3.

57. *The Asian Journal of Thomas Merton* (London: Sheldon, 1974).

58. *Ibid.*, page 311.

59. *Ibid.*, page 316.

60. *Contemplation in a World of Action*, page 212.

61. *Wisdom of the Desert*, page 18.

62. Conjectures of a Guilty Bystander, page 176.

63. Rowan Williams, "Bread in the Wilderness. The Monastic Ideal in Thomas Merton and Paul Evdokimov" in *One Yet Two*, pages 452f.

5

HESYCHASM[1]

Patrick F. O'Connell

The Hesychast movement of the Eastern church was associated particularly with the "Jesus Prayer" or "prayer of the heart." Thomas Merton first discusses it on his thirty-fifth birthday as "my latest discovery," focusing on its importance for understanding the desert fathers, its similarities to St. Bernard's devotion to the name of Jesus, and its integration of bodily, mental and spiritual dimensions in prayer (*Entering the Silence*, pages 404-5). He traces the origin of the term to the rest or tranquility (*hesychia* in Greek, *quies* in Latin) that was a principal goal of early desert spirituality (*Contemplation in a World of Action*, page 272). Rest in this context was not inactivity but a spiritual repose in God and in the divine will, a liberation from worldly anxieties and cares, from the demands of the ego and from the subsequent illusions intrinsic to such a self-centered life. It was the calmness of a heart not roiled by passionate upheavals (the *apatheia* of Evagrius Ponticus). Such a state was not achieved by ascetical austerity alone, but was the gift of God: "*quies* is not something in ourselves, it is God the Divine Spirit. Thus we do not 'possess' rest, but go out of ourselves into him who is our true rest" (page 275).

From early in the monastic tradition this rest was associated with recollection of the name of Jesus, "since the sacramental power of the Name of Jesus is believed to bring the Holy Spirit into the heart of the praying monk" (*Contemplative Prayer*, 23). The simple "repetitive invocation of the name of Jesus in the heart emptied of images and cares" (page 103), typically integrated with an echo of the words of the publican of the Gospel, "Lord Jesus Christ, Son of the Living God, have mercy on me a sinner" (see *Disputed Questions*, page 78), was considered the key to banishing distraction and temptation and to praying in the midst of other activities of the day. This prayer of the heart was preeminently "a way of keeping oneself in the presence of God and of reality, rooted in one's own inner truth" (*Contemplative Prayer*, page 24). It was prayer on a deeper level than the mind or the affections, an encounter with the presence of God in the very center of one's self (page 34), "the ground of our identity before God and in God" (page 87).

This emphasis on contemplative repose centered on the recollection and repetition of the name of Jesus underwent a revival in Greek monasticism of the Middle Ages, associated particularly with the figure of St. Gregory Palamas, a monk of Mount Athos who later became archbishop of Salonika, who taught that Hesychasts could experience in this life the "divine energies," the light manifested to the disciples in the transfigured Jesus (see *Mystics and Zen Masters*, pages 179-80; *Disputed Questions*, pages 77-78). Merton points out that this movement was controversial in its own time and aroused suspicion in Western Christian writers for centuries. He rejects what he calls the "outraged platitudes" of those who dismissed the Jesus Prayer as self-hypnosis (*Mystics and Zen Masters*, page 180) and defends Hesychasm as "an authentically Christian and deeply simple way of prayer" (*Disputed Questions*, page 78). In more recent times Hesychast prayer flourished in Russia, nourished by the translation of the *Philokalia*, the anthology of passages from Eastern monastic sources concerned with prayer, above all the prayer of the heart (*Contemplative Prayer*, pages 22-23). Of particular significance in Russia was the way in which this typically monastic form of prayer was adopted by the laity, particularly the poor peasantry, as described, for example, in *The Way of a Pilgrim*, which Merton calls "surely one of the great classics of the literature of prayer" (*Mystics and Zen Masters*, page 180).

While Merton is both an enthusiastic expositor and exponent of the authenticity of Hesychasm, he nonetheless is quite restrained when it comes to recommending this method of prayer for his contemporaries. He notes that it was not practiced in Russia except under the guidance of a *staretz*, or elder, and warns that it "is not safely to be followed by us in the West without professional direction" (page 180). Writing in 1963 to a fellow monk who had been reading *The Way of a Pilgrim*, he remarks that "it is all very well for a hard-headed nineteenth-century Russian moujik to do that all day and all night, but it is not going to work for Americans today" (*School of Charity*, page 176). He comments that "this repetition of the prayer is useful at certain times" and mentions that he uses it himself, especially when he finds himself distracted or too tired to pray in other ways, but recommends the Bible as "a much better source of light than the Jesus Prayer" (page 177). He is particularly wary of too much attention to the Jesus Prayer as technique, the concentration on breathing, as well as of too much expectation of psychophysical consequences, "the inner warmth around the heart, as a result of pushing the prayer" (page 177). In a later letter to another monk he summarizes his attitude: "I favor the Prayer of Jesus only in cases where it comes rather spontaneously and I do not think that our monks ought to make a deliberate project out of it with a great deal of concentrated introversion. This will do more harm than good. But the prayer is good on and off, when needed and when one feels it is helpful" (page 226). This corresponds to Merton's general teaching that methods of prayer must not become "projects," quasi-Pelagian techniques to reach God by human effort,[2] but should simply be used as ways of reminding oneself that God is always already present within and beyond oneself in gracious love.

See also HEART.

NOTES

1. William H. Shannon, Patrick F. O'Connell and Christine M. Bochen, *The Thomas Merton Encyclopedia*. (New York: Crossroads Publishing Company, 2002).

2. See, for example, his comment on Western and, particularly, Benedictine indifference to techniques in comparison with Eastern and Orthodox mysticism in *Entering the Silence*, page 402.

Icon, Monastery of Saint Catherine, Mount Sinai, Egypt. Eleventh century.

6

HEART[1]

Patrick F. O'Connell

The heart, as Thomas Merton points out, traditionally is used to symbolize the inner-most self, though because of its associations in other contexts there is always a danger of a more superficial interpretation that does not go beyond the level of the emotions and associates the heart with the sentimental or the erotic ("Inner Experience," 2:129). But for the Christian contemplative tradition, as well as analogous traditions such as Sufism, the heart is "a traditional and technical term" (*Birds of Appetite*, page 72). The heart is "the root and source of all one's own inner truth" (*Contemplative Prayer*, page 22); it is used to refer to "the deepest psychological ground of one's personality," where one encounters not merely one's inner self but the "Abyss of the unknown yet present," who can be described in Augustine's terms as the one "more intimate to us than we are to ourselves" (page 38). To find one's heart, then, is to recover an awareness of one's deepest identity as grounded in the divine (page 87). In biblical terms this self-discovery entailing a death to the superficial self is the essence of *metanoia*, conversion, a change of heart profound enough "to transform our spirit and make us 'new men' in Christ" (page 89). The discipline of meditation is aimed at overcoming hardness of heart and becoming supple to God's grace (page 87). Faith can be described as the opening of the eye of the heart in order to receive the divine light (*New Seeds of Contemplation*, page 130). It is the experience of the disciples on the road to Emmaus, which progresses from the awareness of the heart burning within to a recognition of the risen Christ (*Thomas Merton in Alaska*, page 162). Genuine spiritual renewal, Merton believes, depends on a rediscovery of "the inner discipline of 'the heart,' that is to say, of the 'whole man' — a discipline that reaches down into his inmost ground and opens out to the invisible, intangible, but nevertheless mysteriously sensible reality of God's presence, of His love, and of His activity in our hearts" (*Contemplation in a World of Action*, page 113).

Genuine monastic formation is "education of the heart," a rediscovery of the affirmation and acceptance of God that is the innermost truth of one's being, a recognition Christianity shares, Merton says, with Sufism and the Hasidic tradition of Judaism. "Deep in our hearts is the most profound meaning of our personality, which is that we say 'yes' to God, and the spark is always there. All we need to do is to turn towards it and let it become a flame" (*Thomas Merton in Alaska*, pages 153-54). This reawakening of contact with one's own heart is at the same time an experience of being plunged into the heart of the world, becoming aware of "the deepest and most neglected voices that proceed from its inner depth" (*Contemplative Prayer*, page 25), as Merton himself experienced most notably in his "Fourth and Walnut" experience, when he was able to identify with the people around him, "as if I suddenly saw the secret beauty of their hearts, the depths of their hearts where neither sin nor desire nor self-knowledge can reach, the core of their reality, the person that each one is in God's eyes" (*Conjectures of a Guilty Bystander*, page 142).

See also HESYCHASM; PURITY OF THE HEART.[2]

NOTES

1. William H. Shannon, Patrick F. O'Connell and Christine M. Bochen, *The Thomas Merton Encyclopedia*. (New York: Crossroads Publishing Company, 2002).

2. *Ibid.*

Motif sculpted in outer wall, Monastery of Saint Catherine, Mount Sinai.

7

BREAD IN THE WILDERNESS
The Monastic Ideal in Thomas Merton and Paul Evdokimov[1]

Rowan Williams

Many readers of Merton have probably acquired their only knowledge of the thought of Paul Evdokimov through a long passage in *Conjectures of a Guilty Bystander*[2] in which Merton (mistakenly assuming, by the way, that Evdokimov was a priest) discusses Evdokimov's vision of a "radical tradition of monasticism, both Eastern and Western." It is an impressively sympathetic discussion; Evdokimov's ideal clearly answers to a very great amount in Merton's own thought, already developing with increasing reference to the Eastern tradition in general, and the Desert Fathers in particular. What I hope to do in this essay is to investigate some of the more interesting points of convergence between these two theologians, and thereby to explore a little of what this "radical tradition" implies. Certainly, one of the most significant aspects of such a convergence is that it appears in two thinkers who are at once profoundly rooted in their own traditions and genuinely open to others: Merton's spirituality owes its fundamental orientation to the Cistercian and Carmelite traditions, and, as Evelyn Waugh rightly indicated,[3] to French Catholicism, but it would not be what it is without his devoted and careful study of Greek patristic thought and the Desert Fathers. Evdokimov, a Russian emigré who spent his entire working life in France, is essentially a product of the Russian religio-philosophical and literary ethos of Gogol and Dostoyevsky, Florensky, Bulgakov, and Berdyaev, an ethos itself very much aware of the spirituality of the "desert" which was to become so central to Evdokimov's theology. Yet his understanding of French religious and anti-religious culture, from Bloy and Claudel to Sartre, is remarkable. What we are witnessing is a rapprochement not merely between the "monastic culture" (to borrow Merton's own term[4]) of Catholicism and that of Orthodoxy, but between distinct "religious cultures," in a wider sense; and the interest in Kierkegaard shared by Merton and Evdokimov suggests the possibility of a further convergence, with a particular strand in another "religious culture," that of Continental Lutheranism. That, however, is a subject which would require another paper to itself.

It is Evdokimov's treatment of the question of *authenticity* which seems to interest Merton most in the discussion to which I have referred: "one goes into the desert to vomit up the interior phantom, the doubter, the double"[5] is Evdokimov's phrase, and Merton, as we might expect, responds enthusiastically to the idea of asceticism as "therapy," humanizing therapy, implicit in this formulation. The preoccupation with authenticity is, I think, one of the most consistent unifying themes traceable in Merton's work, from the time of *Elected Silence* onwards; indeed, even further back, in the *Secular Journal*, which contains material written between 1939 and 1941, we find a succession of wryly humorous dialogues with a sceptical interlocutor, in which questions of personal and artistic integrity are obviously much to the fore in Merton's mind.[6] Here, too, we find one of the only two explicit allusions in the *Journal* to Merton's painful decision to risk being refused entry to the Franciscan novitiate in 1940.[7] However, the superb passage on Kierkegaard and the "teleological suspension of ethics"[8] is a moving and revealing commentary on the insights gained through this decision, which was, as *Elected Silence* makes clear, very definitely prompted by considerations of "authenticity." Of his anticipations of life as a friar, Merton dryly comments that "it made a pleasant picture."[9] It represented an attempt to create a new existence essentially divorced from the reality of his previous life, with no attempt at a healing or integration of that previous life; a new existence, therefore, which could not be other than artificial, *inauthentic*. At the same time, his attraction to the Franciscan life is recognized as being no more than a translation into vocational terms of a set of inclinations and attractions purely natural in character, "investing the future with all kinds of natural pleasures and satisfactions which would fortify and defend my ego against the troubles and worries of life in the world."[10] There is no *metanoia* here; any illusion that there is is based upon the superficial divorce from, and sup-pression of, a "sinful" past. It is not difficult to misrepresent this section of *Elected Silence*; Merton's expressions are often obscure, and can be read as suggesting merely a kind of tor-mented scrupulosity, a moralistic awareness of "unworthiness" for the religious life. To some extent, indeed, it is a moralistic vocabulary which he uses here, and a rather conventional lan-guage of "renunciation of natural goods"; but I hope I have shown some reason for seeing his decision as, fundamentally, concerned with a crisis of "integrity." There is here, surely, an implicit recognition that the monastic vocation demands a real encounter with one's own "nothingness," with the false and il-lusory *persona* created by one's betrayal of the true self, the im-age of God, in a concordat with a false and illusory society.

At this point, we may turn to examine Evdokimov's expla-nation of the rise of monasticism; and it is precisely the "concordat" with society and history which Evdokimov sees as driving the monk into the desert: *"Après le concordat qui installait l'Église dans l'histoire et lui offrait son statut légal et une existence paisible, le témoignage que les martyrs rendaient aux choses denières passe au monachisme et s'y transforme en ministère du maximalisme eschatologique."*[11] ["After the Con-cordat had established the Church in history and lent it its legal status along with a peaceful existence, the testimony born by the martyrs concerning final ends went over to monasticism and was transformed there into a mystery of ultimate eschatological commitment."] For "those who love his coming," the Christian city that the Empire of Constantine undertook to build is profoundly ambiguous."[12] What the monk is doing is witnessing to a radical eschatological *folly* in the midst of a church which has learned to sit lightly to the apocalyptic violence of the gospel, to pitch its tent in his-tory, to allow itself to be *defined* by history and by the present *saeculum*. Monasticism is a provisional phenomenon,[13] exist-ing for as long as the Church exists as a function of the city, the state, until the city is truly baptised. Not only Kierkegaard on "Christendom," but Dostoyevsky on Church and state is ech-oed here: "It is not the Church that ought to be turned into a

State, as from a lower to a higher form, but, on the contrary, the State ought to end by being worthy to become only the Church and nothing else."[14] The Church has failed to recognize the devils in the city, and so the monk seeks them out in the desert; the only real reason for the flight to the desert is this impulse to confront the diabolical, the infernal, which threatens all men, be they ever so oblivious of it. In other words, in the more familiar terminology of twentieth-century existentialism, the monk recoils in horror, anguish, and nausea from the possibilities of "bad faith" which life in the city presents to him and other men.[15] The monk is called to face the threat of nothingness, whether in "bad faith" or in the constant awareness of finitude and death, without any of the anodynes provided by life in society: *"Les athlètes de l'ascèse pouvaient se mesurer avec les démons, car seuls ils étaient capables de les voir face à face et de supporter cette vision redoutable (les ascètes parlent de la puanteur insupportable des démons, de la 'nausée de l'esprit' qu'ils provoquent)."*[16] ["The athletes of ascesis could take on demons, for they alone were capable of beholding them face-to-face and bear this fearful sight (the athletes of ascesis mention the stench of the demons, the 'nausea of the spirit' they provoked).»] The monk's service to the city he leaves is the objectification of its demons, so that they become visible and identifiable for men; his immense risk, his total exposure of himself, has a universal "therapeutic" effect,[17] redeeming the Church, and thus, finally, the world, from bondage to blindness and untruth, from submission to the false, "demoniacal" self-image (individual or collective) which is not recognised until it is personalized" in the solitary combat of the ascetic with the devils in the wilderness.

"This is precisely the monk's chief service to the world: this silence, this listening, this questioning, this humble and courageous exposure to what the world ignores about itself — *both good and evil.*"[18] The going-out of the monk into the desert is a sign of hope to the city as well as a sign of judgment, because it testifies to man's ability to face and to reject illusion; it is an act performed in imitation of Christ, partaking in the salvific quality of his temptation in the wilderness. Evdokimov rightly reminds us of the great significance attached by many of the Greek Fathers (especially Justin, Irenaeus and Origen) to the temptations of Christ in the economy of salvation, the ἀνακεφαλάίωσις of human existence and the realisation of the image of God in man;[19] it is the reversal of the consequences of Adam's defeat by the tempter, and thus the opening to man of the new possibility of victory over falsehood and inauthenticity. Christ in the desert prepares the way for the Christian in the desert. Evdokimov's particular use of the temptation narratives, is predictably, very much influenced by the brilliant analysis of the three temptations in Dostoyevsky's parable of the Grand Inquisitor, as temptations to the exercise of "miracle, mystery, and authority."[20] "Satan advances three infallible solutions of human destiny: the alchemist *miracle* of the philosopher's stone, the *mystery* of occult sciences and their boundless powers; and finally one unifying *authority.*"[21] In these temptations is summed up the whole of the diabolical invitation to falsehood and "nothingness," that "self-destruction and non-existence"[22] of which Satan is the personification. And these are the temptations which the Empire offered to the Church, and which the Church, or, at least, the greater part of it, has succumbed, according to Dostoyevsky and Evdokimov. Thus we can see how the monk's rejection of the city is grounded in Christ's victory over the temptor: "If the empire made its secret temptation out of Satan's three invitations, monasticism was openly built on Christ's three immortal answers."[23] We should, Evdokimov suggests, see the three traditional vows of the religious state as corresponding precisely to Christ's three replies to Satan. The refusal to turn stones into bread corresponds to the vow of *poverty*: it is "the primacy . . . of grace over necessity,"[24] the rejection of a scale of values in which the material satisfaction associated with property is considered self-evidently good. The poor man, the monk who possesses nothing, can share nothing but "his *being*, his eucharistic flesh and blood,"[25] is free to be the brother of all men. The refusal of Jesus to cast himself from the pinnacle of the temple corresponds to the vow of *chastity*: it is the "purification of the heart" in love and reverence towards the whole of creation, the refusal of a certain kind of "power" over the cosmos, a power which is a mockery, an abuse and an exploitation of the place which God gives to man in the world. The monk's chastity is an "integration" of his human powers over matter in a new attitude of what Simone Weil would call "attention" to created things. Evdokimov points to the mysterious relationship between woman and the cosmos apprehended in so many of the mystery cults of pre-Christian Europe and Asia, and discernible even in the cult of the Mother of God.[26] Continence towards woman and reverence for creation are intimately connected. Finally, Jesus' refusal to bow down and worship Satan corresponds to the vow of *obedience*: the refusal of slavery to Satan, to illusion and falsehood, is liberation into obedience to him "whose service is perfect freedom." Evdokimov quotes from the *Apophthegmata Patrum* to illustrate his contention that monastic obedience is fundamentally different from the secular model of submission to authority: "Never command, but be for all an example, never a lawgiver,"[27] "I shall say nothing. Do, if you want, what you see me do."[28] "Every counsel of a *staretz* (elder, spiritual father) leads a man to a state of freedom before the face of God."[29]

Merton nowhere (to my knowledge) develops such a close analogy between Our Lord's temptations and the vows of the religious state; but I hope it will become clear that the monastic ideal outlined by Evdokimov is very close indeed to Merton's own. Certainly the type of religious obedience which Evdokimov speaks of is precisely what Merton finds so impressive in the *Apophthegmata*: obedience preserves the monk from the dangers of being a law to himself, of persevering in the falsehood of self-will and self-love which he has fled the city to escape. "His search in the desert is not merely for solitude in which he can simply do as he pleases and admire himself as a great contemplative. There would be no real quiet in such an exploit, or, if there were peace, it would be the false peace of self-assurance and self-complacency."[30] Obedience is a necessary concomitant of *metanoia*, delivery from the worship of the illusory ego; and this, of course, is as much as to say that the mere fact of geographical separation from the city, from society, does not of itself deliver the monk from illusion. What the monastic tradition calls "compunction" (πένθος) and Merton, following the existentialists, calls "dread," is a constantly recurring experience in the monastic life.[31] There is a danger of a wrong sort of objectification of the diabolical, of refusing to recognise its radical presence in *oneself*, and its persistence within oneself, even when the appropriate gestures of renunciation have been made. It is perhaps the new awareness of this that lies underneath the tormented questionings of Part Five of *The Sign of Jonas*, the discovery that a new and more subtle temptation to falsehood and unreality awaits the monk in his community, that it is as easy to yield to the imposition of an illusory definition of the self by the purely external observance of the religious community as to submit to the definition of the self offered by society. It is revealing to look at (what seems to me to be) a climacteric passage in this section of *The Sign of Jonas*: "In order to be not remembered or wanted I have to be a person that nobody knows. They can have Thomas Merton. He's dead. Father Louis — he's half-dead too."[32] The true solitude in which the monk must face his nothingness is to be found, finally, only in the monk himself: "Even though he may live in a community, the monk is bound to explore the inner waste of his own being as a solitary."[33] And in the opening essay of *Raids on the Unspeakable*, one of the places in which he explicitly makes use of the temptation narratives of the Gospels, Merton quotes, from the sixth-century Syrian ascetic, Philoxenos, a passage on the monk following Christ into the desert "to fight the power of error," and comments: "And where is the power of error? We find it was after all not in the city, but in *ourselves*."[34]

The "geographical" desert, then, is adjectival to the true personal solitude of the monk, and to think otherwise is to refuse to see that the flight of the first monks to the desert, although a protest against compromise with history, was itself an *historical* phenomenon, a particular manifestation in a particular period of history: "Certainly *now* there can be no possible return to the desert. We are in different times and above all in different *spiritual ages*."[35] Indeed, Evdokimov suggests that the Fathers of the Desert have paved the way for a return to history, to the city, to society; once the reality of the interior desert has been seen, in the city and in the wilderness, the resultant deep transformation of the human consciousness becomes, to a greater or lesser degree, independent of external circumstances. "Human consciousness was different before the ascesis of the desert from what it was after. Just like the event of Pentecost, this ascesis has modified the dominant energies of the psyche and has renewed the human spirit."[36] The extremism, the "eschatological maximalism" of the desert is a necessary dialectical step in the development of the Christian consciousness toward a position of equilibrium; and because, in the present world order, we cannot hope ever to attain and preserve such a position, the monk's physical or geographical separation from society remains an indispensable witness. However, it is now possible for the monastic state to exist as "interiorised" in the layman: and Evdokimov supports his plea for "interiorised monasticism" with an impressive array of quotations from Chrysostom, Theodore of Studium, and others on the essential unity of all Christian spirituality, whether practiced by priest, monk, or layman. The monastic experience of exposure to the diabolical possibilities inherent in human existence, especially Christian existence in "the world," and the monastic reiteration of Christ's refusal of Satan's temptations are part of the vocation of every believer. What they imply, finally, is a condition of receptivity to the Holy Spirit, the Spirit of Truth, who is alike the giver and the gift of authentic human being. Monasticism is a universal *epiclesis,* an invocation of the Spirit upon all humanity and all creation[37]; there must be no weakening of its demands by any such evasion as the traditional distinction between "counsel" and "precept" in the Gospel. The encounter of the monk with God is the same encounter to which all Christians are called; and here, of course, we are reminded of Merton's constant insistence that contemplative prayer is the vocation of every believer,[38] or, rather, that the "contemplative dimension" (for lack of a better expression) exists in every man, and that the Christian is called upon to realise it as his true identity, his *"identity-in-God."* "Discovering the contemplative life is a new self discovery. One might say it is the flowering of a deeper identity on an entirely different plane from a mere psychological discovery, a paradoxical new identity that is found only in loss of self."[39] This is not the place for a detailed discussion of the central importance for Merton of the doctrine of man as the image of God (for such a discussion, I would commend in particular the first two chapters of Higgins' study), but it should be noted that this explanation of contemplative prayer implies that confrontation with, or awakening to, the true self is awakening to God; so that the condition of inauthenticity, falsehood, clinging to the illusory self-image precludes any real encounter with God.

Noverim Me Noverim Te; to know God in the "coming to ourselves" is to know ourselves as God knows us, to know our true identity. The "opposition" between man and God is done away with, and we may speak of man's "divinisation," "the ultimate in man's self-realisation."[40] To arrive at "true identity" is to arrive at true *personhood,* since one is "not a person in the fullest spiritual sense of the word"[41] if one does not yet truly know oneself. "We must long to learn the secret of our own nothingness (not God's secret first of all, but our own secret). But God alone can show us our own secret."[42] If every man's identity is hidden in God, every man is bound to seek it through that perilous exposure of himself to God in solitude which is the basis of contemplation. Contemplation is not a religious exercise but an ontological necessity in the intense *personalism* of Christian faith, the encounter of the human person with the Divine Council of Persons.

Evdokimov likewise reiterates the profound identity of the mystery of God and the mystery of man: *"Le mystère du Createur vient se refléter dans le miroir de la créature et fait dire à Théophile d'Antioche: "Montre-moi ton homme, et je te montrerai mon Dieu." Saint Pierre parle de l'homocordis absconditus, l'homme caché du coeur. (I P 3:4). Le Deus absconditus, Dieu mystérieux a créé son vis-à-vis: l'homo absconditus, l'homme mystérieux, son icone vivant.*[42] ["The mystery of the Creator is reflected in the mirror of the creature and makes Theophilus of Antioch say: "Show me thy soul and I shall show thee thy Lord." Saint Peter speaks of the homo cordis absconditus, the hidden man of the heart. *The Deus absconditus,* the mysterious God, has created his counterpart: the *homo absconditus*, the mysterious man, his living image."] All human beings have the potential for true personhood, because all have the capacity for self-awareness, which Evdokimov designates as the property of the πρόσωπον; it is when this self-awareness is perfected in communion with God, in the realization of the image of God, that man becomes ὑπόστασις a person whose personhood is analogous to that of the Persons of the Trinity. The πρόσωπον alone can become trapped in individuality, whereas the ὑπόστασις exists in a state of communion with other persons.[44] Thus, if the monk, the solitary, is engaged in the process of becoming a *person*, he cannot be simply an individual pursuing an impossible ideal of individual sanctification in a sort of spiritual solipsism; this is, rather, the condition characteristic of hell.[45] The spirit of man at its deepest level is "intentional," turned toward the other;[46] and again we may say that a denial of this intentionality with regard to other men and to the world in general prevents us from ever realizing our position as partners in dialogue with God. "We can never keep ourselves alone before God; we are saved only together, "collegially," as Soloviev said: "*he will be saved who saves others.*"[47] The purpose of the ascetic life is the attainment of "a heart inflamed with charity for the entire creation,"[48] in the words of Isaac of Nineveh which Evdokimov was so fond of quoting. The Christian is baptized into the death of Christ, into his descent to hell, into a condition of *vulnerability* to the suffering of the whole of humanity; so that the solitary who goes out to face the demons is exploring the consequences of his baptism, his being-in-Christ.[49] Paradoxically, his calling to be alone with Christ in the desert is made possible by his existence in the Church, in "communion," because it is thus that he becomes sensitive and vulnerable to the presence of the demons afflicting mankind; in the desert he has to bear the weight not only of his own interior devils, but of the world's suffering and bondage. The solitary is such because he is a member of Christ's body, and so, ultimately, because he is a human being: and his way must, in some measure, be the way of all members of Christ's body, and so of all human beings.

Solitude, then, is a form of *kenosis*: the solitary is not merely imitating a past event when he follows Christ into the desert, he is *participating* in the whole work of Christ, the *kenosis* of the whole of his existence as "the lamb slain from the foundation of the world." We have already seen, in the first part of this essay, how the life of the monk is grounded in Christ's "recapitulation" of human nature, his perfect realization of the divine image in man; now we may understand also that, just as this restoration of humanity is only achieved by the eternal self-emptying of the Word made flesh, so the monk's refusal of falsehood and his commitment to the search for "authenticity" are made possible only by his baptism into the death of Christ, his sharing in the self-exposure and, if you will, the sheer *risk* of Christ's *kenosis*, He enters into "the radical and essential *solitude of man* – a solitude which was assumed by Christ and which, in Christ becomes mysteriously identified with the solitude of God."[50] He becomes "a poor man with the poor Christ." In a sense, he has nothing to give: and we have seen that, according to Evdokimov, this means that all the monk has to share is his *being*, himself. Here I should like to mention a passage in *The Sign of Jonas*[51] (a passage which, surprisingly, seems to have received no attention in any study of Merton to date), the passage written a few days before his ordination to the priesthood in which Merton reflects on the implications of his vocation to be a priest *and* a contemplative. The priestly state is itself a part of the contemplative life, "an encounter of the substance of my soul with the living God";[52] and thus priesthood is intimately connected with that poverty which is a necessary condition of the contemplative state. "To be a priest means, at least in my particular case, to have nothing, desire nothing, and be nothing but to belong to Christ."[53] Priests who are contemplative monks must recognise "that perhaps we have practically nothing to give to souls in the way of preaching and guidance and talent and inspiration. We are ashamed of any active apostolate that might conceivably come from us. And so we vanish into the Mass."[54] The priestly contemplative is "defined" by the Mass, by the representation of Christ's *kenosis* and sacrifice, and by nothing else, by no "works," no external apostolate; the priest lives Christ's sacrifice, or, rather, the kenotic Christ lives in the priest. We may compare another passage a little later on in *The Sign of Jonas*, written after Merton's ordination to the priesthood: "Day after day I am more and more aware that I am anything but my everyday self at the altar . . . I am superseded by One in whom I am fully real . . . It is at Mass, by the way, that I am deepest in solitude and at the same time mean most to the rest of the universe. This is really the *only* moment at which I can give anything to the rest of men."[55] And what is given is Christ, and therefore the self-in-Christ and the world-in-Christ.

Now I do not think that Merton is suggesting that the canonical state of priesthood is *necessary* for the full living of the contemplative life, but rather that "being a contemplative" is a state of life which has "priestly" implications. The priesthood of the contemplative or the solitary is a very different matter from the priesthood of the pastor, the teacher, the confessor, even if the contemplative is actually in priest's orders (Merton stresses, in the first of the passages to which I have referred,[56] that his interpretation of priesthood is a personal one, bound up with his *particular* vocation: "Not all priests are necessarily committed, by their priesthood, to absolute poverty"[57]). For the monk, who is canonically a priest, his priestly *kenosis*, his gift of himself-in-Christ, is expressed pre-eminently in his offering of the Eucharist, but the significant element here is a *kenosis*, a poverty, which does not depend upon the rite of ordination. Evdokimov notes that "The New Testament uses the term πρεσβύτερος to designate the particular ministry (the clergy) and keeps the term ἱερεύς for the priesthood of the laity . . . Christ abolished the ἱερεύς as a distinct caste."[58] There are, in fact, Evdokimov suggests, *two* priesthoods in the Church, the universal priesthood of the baptised, whose vocation is the consecration of all human existence, the offering of the whole of human being to God, and the "functional" or "ministerial" priesthood, whose vocation is to teaching, leading and explicating the consecration of the world by the performance of the sacraments. The Christian layman is *homo liturgicus*, the man whose whole life is directed to God, and who thus is able to direct all that is in his world to God, "to be in love with all of God's creation in order to decipher the meaning of God in everything,"[59] "Nature's Priest," the "interpretor" of creation to God. The priestly self-oblation of the believer becomes the vehicle of theophany in the world, man becomes transparent to God, and the light of the divine energy shining through him transfigures all things. Thus the *kenosis* of the contemplative is directly linked to the dignity of the priest, the believer is baptized into the priesthood of Christ[60] as he is baptized into the *kenosis* of Christ; and so, finally, the universal priesthood of the laity is identical with the "interiorized monasticism" of the laity.[61] The priest, the monk, the layman (*et hi tres unum sunt*) holds the glass through which God sees the world and the world sees God.

"*Ses saints ne participent pas au dynamisme extérieur des événements ou, s'ils y participent, c'est autrement. Dostoievsky trace un visage de saint et le suspend au mur du fond comme une icone. Mais c'est à sa lumière révélatrice et thérapeutique qu'on déchiffre le sens des événements qui passent sur la scène du monde.*"[62] ["His saints do not participate in the outward dynamism of events; or if they do participate in them, it is in another fashion. Dostoyevsky draws the face of a saint and hangs it on the back wall like an icon. But it is by means of its revelatory and thera-peutic light that one deciphers the meaning of the events tak-ing place on the world's stage."] Thus Evdokimov, writing of the "saints" in Dostoyevsky's novels: the saint is an "icon" not merely in the sense that he "stands for" or "witnesses to" the divine order, but because he is truly the channel through which God's energies enter into the world of men. The saint's vision of the world is *God's* vision of the world, because the saint is "transparent" to God: in the person of the saint contemplat-ing God, God contemplates the world. This divine contem-plation of the world is obviously not *reducible* to any fact in the world, it is a point of reference, in some sense "outside" the world: hence the "uselessness" of the saint, his position on the margin of human existence, his failure to provide practical solutions. Zossima in *The Brothers Karamozov* does not pre-vent the catastrophe that overtakes the Karamazov family; but it is his "vision" of the situation that is ultimately the only real, credible and stable factor in the working out of the brothers' destinies. Tikhon in *The Devils* fails to "save" Stavrogin, who rejects his counsel in mingled fear and contempt; but again, Tikhon is the only character in the novel who is permitted to see Stavrogin whole, to see him as a man and a child of God. The Dostoyevskian saint is a sign of contradiction, a participant in the irony of the Incarnation: at once a fact in the world and a point outside it, useless, yet omnipercipient, the judge of the world and its savior, because he alone knows the "truth" of the world, and his vision can restore it to a reality which is in accord with the purpose of God. His vision is, to take up a favorite expression of Evdokimov, a vision of the "sophianic" world, the world as first formed by the creative Wisdom of God, the world before the Fall. (Of course, this conception is not an insight peculiar to modern Russian thought: in one form or another it is discernible throughout the Eastern patristic tradition, receiving what is probably its fullest and best formulation in the seventh century, in the writings of Maximus the Confessor. The task of Christian man is *reintegration*, the overcoming of the "divisions" (diaipeoeis) caused by the Fall; these divisions are transcended in the first place by the Incarnation, and it is for each man in Christ to realize this victory in his own existence and so partake in the total restoration of the cosmos.[63]

If the restoration of the "sophianic" world is such a fundamental constituent of the calling of every Christian, we might well expect to find Merton underlining its significance as part of his conception of monasticism as "therapy" and "humanization"; and, indeed, there is in his work an increasing interest in the priesthood of man in creation, and its corollary, the "priesthood" of the monk and his reintegration of the world in God. In *Bread in the Wilderness* (1953), for example, there occurs this passage, so very reminiscent of Evdokimov: "David is . . . filled with the primitive sense that man is the *Leitourgos* or the high Priest of all creation, born with the function of uttering in 'Liturgy' the whole testimony of praise which mute creation cannot of itself offer to its God."[64] The "sophianic" theme is even more prominent in his discussion of *Doctor*

Zhivago:[65] "it is as artist, symbolist, and prophet that 'Zhivago' stands most radically in opposition to Soviet society. He himself is a man of Eden, of Paradise. He is Adam, and therefore also, in some sense, Christ. Lara is Eve, and Sophia (the Cosmic Bride of God) and Russia."[66] And "One can see in Pasternak a strong influence from Soloviev's 'Meaning of Love' and his theory of man's vocation to regenerate the world by the spiritualisation of human love raised to the sophianic level of perfect conscious participation in the mystery of the divine wisdom of which the earthly sacrament is love."[67] And it is clear that this conception is one which Merton made very much his own in interpreting the monastic vocation: he can describe monasticism as "recovery of paradisal simplicity,"[68] as "incarnation and eschatology."[69] "Is it," he asks, "too romantic still to suppose the monk can bake the bread he will eat at table and consecrate on the altar — and *bake it well?*"[70] The monk's work, his shaping of the materials of the world, is not merely a prophylactic against acedia, it is an integral part of his being-in-Christ, his sharing in the Word of Christ. To bake bread and bake it well, to till the soil, to carve wood or cast pots — all these are expressions of the monk's efforts to restore man's use of created matter to its proper wholeness: Merton is even prepared to grant that "The instinct that pushes modern monastic experiments toward salaried employment in industry is sure and authentic, though it raises special problems of its own."[71] And here I must refer, in passing to Merton's well-known interest in and admiration for the craftsmanship of the Shakers in their houses and domestic furniture — "a model of what the native American spirit can achieve in the monastic sphere."[72] "The Shaker builders — like all their craftsmen — had the gift of achieving perfect forms."[73]

The monk, the *homo liturgicus*, is icon and iconographer: his material is himself and his personal world; and his "holiness" and that of his world, the measure of their participation in the energies of God, are inseparable. The decay of Christian liturgical art always goes hand in hand with the degeneration of the spiritual life, just as the general decay of beauty and skill in human manufactures is bound up with a process of depersonal-

ization in society at large, and if the Church cannot witness to
the possibility of an integrated personal vision of reality in its
art, who is there left who can?[74]

Evdokimov repeatedly associates the sterile individualistic
emotionalism of late mediaeval and Counter-Reformation
piety with the religiously barren and assertively secularist character of Renaissance and Baroque art,[75] and Merton says categorically that "To *like* bad sacred art, and to feel that one is
helped by it in prayer, can be a symptom of real spiritual disor-
ders."[76] This is not merely an incidental point: the refusal to
bring one's full creative capacities to the service of God is a betrayal of the whole Christian calling to "reintegration" of the
world; it is "a rank infidelity to God the Creator and to the
Sanctifying Spirit of Truth,"[77] a reversion to slavery and
inauthenticity. The Christian — and so, *a fortiori*, the monk —
is bound to be an "artist," in some way, a participant in the
divine πόιησις; and it is of great interest to compare what Merton
has to say about the artist's (especially the poet's) vocation with
his statement of the monastic vocation. The "Message to Poets,"[78] read at a meeting of young Latin American (and some
North American) poets in Mexico City in 1964, speaks of the
poet's task in terms of the rejection of "the political art of pit-
ting one man against another and the commercial art of esti-
mating all men at a price,"[79] the rejection of "infidelity," alienation, the experience of one's existence as "betrayal." The poet
must not even let himself be defined by opposition to the false
society, as this gives a definitive reality to the falsehood: "Let
us remain outside 'their' categories. It is in this sense that *we
are all monks*: for we remain innocent and invisible to publi-
cists and bureaucrats."[80] If art is merely reaction against
philistinism, it is wasted. In "Answers on Art and Freedom"[81]
(first published in a Latin American periodical), Merton contrasts the illusory freedom of the artist "in revolt" against society, *defined* by his revolt and limited by it, who "cultivates anti-
art as a protest against the art cult of the society in which he
lives,"[82] with the true freedom which the artist should enjoy,
"freedom from the *internalized* emotional pressures by which
society holds him down."[83] As for the "use" of art: "The art-

ist must serenely defend his right to be completely useless."[84]
"Today the artist has, whether he likes it or not, inherited the
combined functions of hermit, pilgrim, prophet, priest, show-
man, sorcerer, soothsayer, alchemist and bonze. How could
such a man be free? How can he really 'find himself' if he
plays a role that society has predetermined for him? The freedom of the artist is to be sought precisely in the choice of his
work and not in the choice of the role of 'artist' which society
asks him to play."[85] In other words, the dilemma of the artist
is identical with the dilemma of the monk: each, at one level,
rejects society, but has to guard against being defined by this
rejection, against continuing to play a fore-ordained part (even
though it be a "negative" part) in the social myth. Or again,
reverting to a theme discussed earlier in this essay, the monk
or artist must beware of locating all the demons of the age outside himself: the artist, like the monk, has an interior wilderness to discover.

The importance of refusing the *role* of "monk" or "artist"
lies in the corollary of this refusal, the affirmation of oneself
simply as a person, as a human being: ultimately, I believe, it
is this which is at the heart of the monastic theology of both
Merton and Evdokimov. The monk is, quite simply, man-in-
Christ engaging in his work as "artist," showing the world in
its sophianic truth, by first confronting and rejecting the falsehood in society and in himself. We have seen Merton in particular speaking of the artist and the monk in closely similar
terms: but finally the distinction must be drawn between the
artist (simply *qua* artist) who, in some measure, is bound to be
working "in the dark," and the monk who lives by the light of
Christ. Which is not to say that the monk's task is thereby
made easier or its ends more obvious; only to recall that the
monk knows himself to be sharing in a work of restoration
whose extent neither his nor any other finite mind can grasp,
the ἀνακεφχλάιωσις of all things in Christ. "The necessary
dialectic between eschatology and incarnation"[86] is a fundamental presupposition of all art; for the monk, it is given final and
definitive shape in his baptism into the divine-human existence
of the Incarnate Word, the Alpha and the Omega.

I have written throughout this paper of the monk as "solitary." I should perhaps say that I do not mean thereby to deny true 'monastic" significance to the cenobitic life. Far from it; I have, rather, followed Merton in presupposing that the μόναχος, if he takes his calling seriously, will inevitably be, in some degree, a "solitary," even if he is a member of a community, simply because the refusal of falsehood and the search for identity-in-God involve, by their very nature, a measure of solitude, a solitude often experienced as abandonment, dereliction. And it is equally important to bear in mind Merton's emphasis on the distinction between "person" and "individual" (a distinction very characteristic, as we have seen,[87] of Eastern thought) and the impossibility of attaining true personhood without existing in communion with others.[88] Again, bearing in mind Evdokimov's remarks about the "provisional" character of monasticism, its dependence for its existence upon the imperfection of the present age,[89] I must make it clear that I have not intended to suggest that either Merton or Evdokimov believed the monastic *institution* to have been superseded, simply because the monastic state is seen by them as essentially identical with the calling of all Christians. In this age, the need for radical, concrete witness to the "monastic" ideal by what I have called "physical or geographical separation from society" is as great as ever. However, such a view of monasticism does raise very searching questions for the monastic institution and its attempts at renewal, questions which space (and incompetence) prevents me from entering into here. Perhaps, in conclusion, I may mention a third great theologian of the monastic life, whose name has constantly been in my mind as I write, because his writings seem in so many ways, to adumbrate the positions I have outlined here; I refer, of course, to Charles de Foucauld. To investigate the correspondence of his thought with that of Merton or Evdokimov, and to assess the extent of any influence he may have had upon them would be an undertaking far beyond my capabilities. I mention this in the hope of illumination from those better qualified, and in the conviction that it is to these "Desert Fathers" of our days that we must look for the most authentic statement of the essentials of monasticism, and so also, the most fruitful source for a theology of monastic renewal.

Wadham College, Oxford

NOTES

1. This essay originally appeared in Cistercian Studies, Number 29, *One Yet Two: Monastic Tradition East and West*, 1976.

2. Pages 308-10.

3. In his Foreword to *Elected Silence* (the British edition of *The Seven Storey Mountain)*.

4. See, for example, *The Climate of Monastic Prayer*, note to page 116.

5. *Op. cit.*, page 309. Cf. Evdokimov, *The Struggle with God* (Paramus, New Jersey: Paulist-Newman Press, 1966), pages 99-105.

6. Pages 77-9, 79-80, 84-88.

7. Page 80.

8. Pages 68-71.

9. *Elected Silence*, page 215.

10. *Ibid.*, page 216.

11. *L'Orthodoxie.* page 20.

12. *The Struggle with God*, page 93.

13. *Ibid.*, page 113.

14. *The Brothers Karamazov*, Book II, chapter 5 (I quote from David Magarshack's translation in the Penguin Classics, volume 1, page 69).

15. See *The Struggle with God*, chapter 1, *passim*.

16. *L'Orthodoxie*, page 98.

17. *The Struggle with God*, page 104.

18. *The Climate of Monastic Prayer*, page 37; my italics.

19. *The Struggle with God.* pages 117-18.

20. *The Brothers Karamazov.* Book V, chapter 5; Penguin edition, vol. 1, pages 288-311.

21. *The Struggle with God*, page 118.

22. *The Brothers Karamazov*, Penguin edition, volume 1, page 295.

23. *The Struggle with God*, page 120.

24. *Ibid.*, page 122.

25. *Ibid.*, page 123.

26. Again a theme found in Dostoyevsky; see, for example. *The Devils*, Part I, chapter 4 (Penguin edition, page 154), "The Mother of God is a great mother earth."

27. PG 65:363; 564; quoted in *The Struggle with God*, page 128.

28. PG 65:224; quoted. *ibid*, page 128.

29. *Ibid.*, page 129.

30. *Contemplation in a World of Action*, pages 284-5 (in the essay on "The Spiritual Father in the Desert Tradition").

31. See particularly *The Climate of Monastic Prayer*, page 37.

32. *Op. cit.*, page 246.

33. *The Climate of Monastic Prayer*, page 39; cf. "The Identity Crisis," in *Contemplation in a World of Action*, pages 56-82.

34. *Op. cit.* (New York: New Directions, 1966) page 19.

35. *The Struggle with God*, page 105.

36. *Ibid.*, page 104 (note that the expression "transformation of consciousness is the title of a chapter in Fr. J. Higgins' *Merton's Theology of Prayer* CS 18 [Spencer, Massachusetts: Cistercian Publications, 1971].

37. *Ibid.*, page 130: the concept of *epiclesis* is very important in Evdokimov's thought on a variety of subjects, especially liturgy and iconography.

38. See the essays "Contemplation in a World of Action" and "Is the Contemplative Life Finished?" in *Contemplation in a World of Action*; and cf. Higgins, chapter 3.

39. *Contemplation in a World of Action*, page 340 (cf. pages 205-17).

40. *The New Man* (New York: Farrar, Straus and Cudahy, 1961) page 34.

41. *Ibid.*, page 149

42. *A Secular Journal*, page 98.

43. *La connaissance de Dieu selon la tradition orientale*, page 11 (cf. *The Struggle with God*, page 2); this is well said, but it is only fair to add that, as an exegesis of *I Peter* 3:4, it is somewhat fanciful.

44. See especially *L 'Orthodoxie*, pages 68-72, cf. V. Lossky, *The Mystical Theology of the Eastern Church*, chapter 6.

45. See, for example, *The Struggle with God*, pages 63-4; *La connaissance de Dieu*, page 32.

46. See *L 'Orthodoxie*, pages 312ff.

47. *The Struggle with God*, page 137.

48. *Ibid.*, page 167.

49. See *The Struggle with God*, part II, especially chapters 3 and 4.

50. *Disputed Questions*, page 188.

51. Pages 186-88.

52. *Ibid.*, page 186.

53. *Ibid.*, page 187.

54. *Ibid.*, page 187

55. *Ibid.*, pages 196-97.

56. *A Secular Journal*, pages 186-87.

57. *Ibid.*, page 187.

58. *The Struggle with God*, page 198 (cf. *L'Ortodoxie*, page 165).

59. *Ibid.*, page 208.

60. See Augustine, *De Civ. Dei*, 1. 20, c. 70: *Omnes sacerdotes, quoniam membra sunt unius sacerdotis.*

61. *The Struggle with God.* page 200.

62. *L'art de l'icone*, page 43.

63. For the best exposition in English of Maximus' thought, see *Microcosm and Mediator: the Theological Anthropology of Maximus the Confessor*, by Lars Thunberg.

64. *Bread in the Wilderness* (Collegeville, Minnesota: Liturgical Press, 1953) page 5L.

65. *Disputed Questions.* pages 3-67

66. *Ibid.*, page 18.

67. *Ibid.*, page 49.

68. *Contemplation in a World of Action*, page 188

69. *Ibid.*, page 189.

70. *Ibid.*, page 189; my italics.

71. *Ibid.*, page 189.

72. *Ibid.*, page 189.

73. *Conjectures of a Guilty Bystander*, page 200.

74. See the essays on "Sacred Art and the Spiritual Life" and "Absurdity in Sacred Decoration" in *Disputed Questions*.

75. See, for example. *La connaissance de Dieu*, chapter 8; *L'art de l'icone*, Part I, chapter 7 and *L'Orthodoxie*, pages 220, 229.

76. *Disputed Questions.* page 155.

77. *Ibid.*, page 154.

78. *Raids on the Unspeakable*, pages 155-161.

79. *Ibid.*, page 157.

80. *Ibid.*, page 158, my italics.

81. *Ibid.*, pages 165-175.

82. *Ibid.*, page 166.

83. *Ibid.*, page 167, my italics.

84. *Ibid.*, page 168

85. *Ibid.*, page 173

86. *Contemplation in a World of Action*, page 188

87. See above, n. 44.

88.   See, for example, "The Power and Meaning of Love" *(Disputed Questions*, pages 97-126); *The New Man*, pages 64f., 106, 115; *Life and Holiness* (New York: Herder and Herder, 1963) page 112; and cf. the passage on the different kinds of "solitude," permissible and impermissible, in the cenobitic life, in *The Waters of Siloe* (New York: Harcourt, Brace, 1949) pages 276-282.

89. *The Struggle with God*, page 113.

St. John Damascus. Byzantine fresco fragment, twelfth - fourteenth century.

THEOPHAN THE RECLUSE'S TEACHING ON PRAYER
IN THOMAS MERTON'S MARGINALIA
THROUGHOUT *THE ART OF PRAYER:
AN ORTHODOX ANTHOLOGY*[1]

Edited by Jonathan Montaldo

INTRODUCTION

Thomas Merton's "marginalia" here refers to his highlighting passages, as well as to his writing notes to himself in
the margins, as he read *The Art of Prayer*, a compilation
of instructions on the preconditions of "praying with
one's heart" by Eastern Orthodox authorities. His marginalia
is ample and thus intense in his copy of the 1966 British edition of this work, now archived at Bellarmine University's Thomas Merton Center.

In 1966 Merton was living as a hermit on his Abbey's property. While he offered Sunday conferences down at the monastery to those in his community who wished to attend, he was
no longer preparing the formal classes as a hermit that he had
prepared as Master of Novices from 1955 until his official en-
trance into the hermitage on August 20, 1965. Merton's intense reading of these instructions on the "prayer of the heart"
was thus primarily for his own guidance and for the personal
enrichment of his practice of prayer in solitude.

Although he highlighted passages liberally in *The Art of
Prayer*, Merton's major interest — as evidenced by the number
of passages highlighted — was in the "sayings" of Theophan the
Recluse, to whom contributors to Parts I and II of this volume
have often referred. Because Theophan's "sayings" are most
prominent, almost as if Merton were preparing to transfer them
and form a separate collection of his "sayings," only the passages of Theophan selected by Merton in *The Art of Prayer* are
included below.

Merton's selections from Theophan form a handbook of instructions to prepare for and then accomplish the "descent from

the head into the heart" in *hesychastic* prayer. Theophan's themes are perennial instructions for doing "inner work," which Theophan considers "the one thing necessary" in leading a life that unites one's praying with the Holy Spirit's prayer. These instructions also evidence Theophan's de-emphasis of all "techniques" and "rules" of praying, in order to underline the work of praying unceasingly by remembering God in one's mind and heart. This stability in prayer, this practice of "walking under God's eye," attentive at all times that in all one's experience God is "searching your soul and your heart," is, according to Theophan, the "most powerful lever in the mechanism of the inner spiritual life."

In 1966 and beyond — even perhaps unto his death in 1968 — Merton struggled to live out his vocation to pray in solitude as circumstances, friendships, writing — and even a great, last passionate attachment to a young woman — tested his hermit heart's yearning to abide in focus on "the one thing necessary." Wanting to practice the "prayer of the heart" with all his heart, Merton's experiences recorded in his journals for 1966 witness that, for most of us, there is no such state as a "perfect *heyschasm*." According to the teachings Merton collected, Theophan might agree that one can only pray for the grace to abide in converting one's heart continually through all those vicissitudes that affect one's search for God. The always "getting up again" is more important than the always "falling down." The *hesychast* cannot seek "perfect prayer" but can, at all times and in all states of soul, imperfectly seek God. Our hearts and minds are always "on the way" toward loving God and neighbor.

Additional emphasis within a selected passage below is always Merton's. This gathering represents all selections from Theophan that Merton highlighted as he read *The Art of Prayer*. May Theophan's instruction, as it spoke so strongly to Merton as essential lessons for prayer, be of benefit to all of us.

— *Jonathan Montaldo*

Prayer is the test of everything; prayer is also the source of everything; prayer is the driving force of everything; prayer is also the director of everything. If prayer is right, everything is right. For prayer will not allow anything to go wrong. [51]

The third degree is prayer of feeling: the heart is warmed by concentration so that what hitherto has only been thought now becomes feeling. Where first it was a contrite phrase now it is contrition itself; and what was once a petition in words is transformed into a sensation of entire necessity. [52]

Those who commit themselves irrevocably to grace will pass under its guidance, and it shapes them and forms them in a way known only to it. [60]

For every rank of person, and every degree of drawing near to God, has its own prayer and its own rules. How important it is to have experienced instruction here, and how very harmful it can be to guide and direct oneself. [62]

The principal thing is to stand with the mind in the heart before God, and to go on standing before Him unceasingly day and night, until the end of life. [63]

The state of contemplation is a captivity of the mind and of the entire vision by a spiritual object so overpowering that all outward things are forgotten, and wholly absent from the consciousness. The mind and consciousness become so completely immersed in the object contemplated that it is as though we no longer possess them. [64]

There is prayer which man himself makes; and there is prayer which God Himself gives to him who prays (*I Samuel* II.9). Who is there who does not know the first? And you must also know the second, at least in its inception. Anyone wishing to approach the Lord will first approach Him by prayer. He begins to go to church and to pray at home, with the help of a prayer book or without. But thoughts keep running away. He cannot manage to control them. All the same, the more he strives to pray, the more thoughts will quiet down, and the purer prayer will become. But the atmosphere of the soul is not purified until a small spiritual flame is enkindled in the soul. This flame is the work of the grace of God; not a special grace, but one common to all. This flame appears when a man has attained a certain measure of purity in the general moral order of his life. When this small flame is kindled, or a permanent warmth is formed in the heart, the ferment of thoughts is stilled. The same thing happens in the soul as happened to the woman with an issue of blood: "Her blood stanched" (*Luke* VIII.44). In this state, prayer more or less approaches permanency; and for this the Jesus Prayer serves as an intermediary. This is the limit to which prayer performed by man himself can rise. I think that this is very clear to you.

Further on in this state, another kind of prayer may be given, which comes to man instead of being performed by him. The spirit of prayer comes upon man and drives him into the depths of the heart, as if he were taken by the hand and forcibly led from one room to another. The soul is here taken captive by an invading force, and is kept willingly within, as long as this overwhelming power of prayer still holds sway over it. I know two degrees of such invasion. In the first, the soul sees everything and is conscious of itself and of its outer surroundings; it can reason and govern itself, it can even destroy this state if it so desires. This, too, should be clear to you. [65]

Inner prayer means standing with the mind in the heart before God, either simply living in His presence, or expressing supplication, thanksgiving and glorification. We must acquire the habit of always being in communion with God, without any image, any process of reasoning, any perceptible movement of thought. Such is the true expression of prayer. The essence of inner prayer, or standing before God with the mind in the heart, consists precisely in this.

Inner prayer consists of two states; one *strenuous*, when man himself strives for it, and the other *self-impelled*, when prayer exists and acts on its own. This last happens when we are drawn along involuntarily, but the first must be a constant object of endeavor. Although in itself such endeavour will not be successful because our thoughts are always being dispersed, yet as proof of our desire and effort to attain unceasing prayer, it will attract the mercy of the Lord; and because of this work God fills our heart from time to time with that compelling impulse through which spiritual prayer reveals itself in its true form. [70-71]

The most important thing that the Holy Fathers desired and recommended is the understanding of the spiritual states, and the art of maintaining it. There remains only one ruse for whoever will attain this state: dwell within and worship secretly in the heart. Meditate on the thought of God, on the remembrance of death, and recollect your sins with self-reproach. Be conscious of these things and speak about them often to yourself — for example: Where am I going? Or: I am a worm and no man. Secret meditation consists of pondering on such thoughts as these in our hearts, with due attention and feeling. [79]

Prayer must not be simply an occupation for a certain time, but a permanent state of the spirit. [80]

The Holy Fathers make a distinction, however, between prayer of the mind in the heart and prayer moved by the Spirit. The first is the conscious action of the praying man, but the second comes *to* a man; and although he is aware of it, it works by itself independently of his efforts. This second kind of prayer, moved by the Spirit, is not something that we can recommend people to practice, because it does not lie in our power to achieve it. We can desire it, seek it, and receive it gratefully, but we cannot arrive at it whenever we want to. . . . Pray with the mind in the heart with the desire of attaining to prayer moved by the Spirit. [81]

What is required is a constant aliveness to God — an aliveness present when you talk, read, watch, or examine something. [83]

Standing always before God with reverence in unceasing prayer: such is its exact description; and in this regard the rule of prayer is only fuel for the fire, or the throwing of wood into a stove. [83]

It often happens that no inner activity occupies a person during the fulfillment of outward duties, so that his life remains soul-less. How can we avoid this? Into every duty a God-fearing heart must be put, a heart constantly permeated by the thought of God; and this will be the door through which the soul will enter into active life. All endeavour must be directed towards the ceaseless thought of God, towards the constant awareness of His presence.

"Seek the Lord . . . Seek his face constantly (*Psalms* Civ. 4 Sept)." It is on this basis that sobriety and inner prayer rest.

God is everywhere: see that your thoughts too are always with God. How can this be done? Thoughts jostle one another like swarming gnats, and emotions follow on the thoughts. In order to make their thought hold to one thing, the Fathers used to accustom themselves to the continual repetition of a short prayer, and from this habit of constant repetition this small prayer clung to the tongue in such a way that it repeated itself of its own accord. In this manner their thought clung to the prayer and, through the prayer, to the constant remembrance of God. Once this habit has been acquired, the prayer holds us in the remembrance of God, and the remembrance of God holds us in prayer; they mutually support each other. Here, then, is a way of walking before God.

Inner prayer begins when we establish our attention in the heart, and from the heart offer prayer to God. Spiritual activity starts when we stand with attention in the heart in recollection of the Lord, rejecting every other thought that tries to enter in. [85-86]

The principal monastic rule is to remain constant with God in mind and heart, that is, to pray unceasingly. [86]

The principal thing is to walk before God, or under God's eye, aware that God is looking at you, searching your soul and your heart, seeing all that is there. This awareness is the most powerful lever in the mechanism of the inner spiritual life. [90]

He who has zeal to pray needs no teaching how to perfect himself in prayer. Patiently continued, the effort of prayer itself will lead us to prayer's very summit. [90]

The monk who does not know, or who has forgotten, the practice of the Jesus Prayer, has not the seal of Christ. Books cannot teach us inner prayer. [92]

This prayer alone makes it possible to fulfill the injunction of the Fathers: the hands at work, the mind and heart with God. When this prayer becomes grafted in our heart, then there are no inner interruptions and it continues always in the same, evenly flowing way.

The path to achievement of a systematic interior order is very hard, but it is possible to preserve this (or a similar) state of mind during the various and inevitable duties that you have to perform: and what makes it possible in the Jesus Prayer when it is grafted in the heart. How can it be so grafted? Who knows? But it does happen. He who strives is increasingly conscious of this engrafting, without knowing how it has been achieved. To strive for this inner order, we must walk always in the presence of God, repeating the Jesus Prayer as frequently as possible. As soon as there is a free moment, begin again at once, and the engrafting will be achieved. [92]

The Jesus Prayer and the warmth which accompanies it, helps better than anything else in the formation of the habit of prayer.

Note that these are the means, and not the deed itself.

It is possible for both the Jesus Prayer and the feeling of warmth to be present without real prayer. This does indeed happen, however strange it may seem. [93]

Now what is the meaning of this warmth which accompanies the practice of the Prayer?

In order to keep the mind on one thing by the use of a short prayer, it is necessary to preserve attention and so lead it into the heart: for so long as the mind remains in the head, where thoughts jostle one another, it has no time to concentrate on one thing. But when attention descends into the heart, it attracts all the powers of the soul and body into one point there. This concentration of all human life in one place is immediately reflected in the heart by a special sensation that is the beginning of future warmth. This sensation, faint at the beginning, becomes gradually stronger, firmer, deeper. At first only tepid, it grows into warm feeling and concentrates the attention upon itself. And so it comes about that, whereas in the initial stages the attention is kept in the heart by an effort of will, in due course this attention, by its own vigour, gives birth to warmth in the heart. From this, the two go on supporting one another, and must remain inseparable; because dispersion of attention cools the warmth, and diminishing warmth weakens attention.

From this there follows a rule of the spiritual life: <u>if you keep the heart alive towards God</u>, you will always be in remembrance of God. This rule is laid down by St. John of the Ladder.

The question now arises whether this warmth is spiritual. No, it is *not* spiritual. It is ordinary physical warmth. But since it keeps the attention of the mind in the heart, and thus helps the development there of the spiritual movements described earlier, it is called spiritual — provided, however, that is not accompanied by sensual pleasure, however slight, but keeps the soul and body in sober mood. [94-95]

In all our efforts and ascetic struggles, what we seek is purification of the heart and restoration of the spirit. There are two ways to do this: the active way, the practice of ascetic labours; and the contemplative way, the turning of the mind to God. By the first way the soul becomes purified and so receives God: by the second way the God of whom the soul becomes aware Himself burns away every impurity and thus comes to dwell in the purified soul. The whole of this second way is summed up in the one Jesus Prayer, as St. Gregory of Sinai says: "God is gained either by activity and work, or by the art of invoking the same of Jesus." [96]

The practice of prayer is called an "art," and it is a very simple one. Standing with consciousness and attention in the heart, cry out unceasingly: "Lord Jesus Christ, Son of God, have mercy upon me," without having in your mind any visual concept or image, believing that the Lord sees you and listens to you.

It is important to keep your consciousness in the heart, and as you do so to control our breathing a little so as to keep time with the words of the prayer. But the most important thing is to believe that God is near and hears. Say the prayer for God's ear alone.

At the beginning this prayer remains for a long time only an activity like any other, but in time it passes into the mind and finally takes root in the heart.

There are deviations from this right way of praying; therefore we must learn it from someone who knows all about it. Mistakes occur chiefly from the attention being in the head and not in the heart. He who keeps his attention in the heart is safe. Safer still is he who at times clings to God in contrition, and prays to be delivered from illusion. [96-97]

The various methods described by the Fathers (sitting down, making prostrations, and the other techniques used when performing this prayer) are not suitable for everyone: indeed without a personal director they are actually dangerous. It is better not to try them. There is just one method which is obligatory for all: *to stand with the attention in the heart*. All other things are beside the point, and do not lead to the crux of the matter.

It is said of this prayer, that there is nothing higher in the world. This is wrong. As if it were some talisman! Nothing in the words of the prayer and their uttering can alone bring forth its fruit. All fruit can be received without this prayer, and even without any oral prayer, but merely by directing the mind and heart towards God. . . .

It is most important to realize that prayer is always God-given: otherwise we may confuse the gift of grace with some achievement of our own.

People say: attain the Jesus Prayer, for that is inner prayer. This is not correct. The Jesus Prayer is a good means to arrive at inner prayer, but in itself it is not inner but outer prayer. Those who attain the habit of the Jesus Prayer do very well. But if they stop only at this and go no further, they stop halfway. . . . .

Everything depends on conscious and free turning to God, and on a balanced effort to hold oneself in this. [98-99]

The Jesus Prayer is like any other prayer. It is stronger than all other prayers only in virtue of the all-powerful Name of Jesus, Our Lord and Saviour. But it is necessary to invoke His Name with a full and unwavering faith — with a deep certainty that He is near, sees and hears, pays whole-hearted attention to our petition, and is ready to fulfill it and to grant what we seek. [99]

The essential part is to dwell in God, and this walking before God means that you live with the conviction ever before our consciousness that God is in you, as He is in everything: you live in the firm assurance that He sees all that is within you, knowing you better than you know yourself. [100]

Pray about everything to the Lord, to our most pure Lady, to your Guardian Angel; and they will teach you everything, either directly or through others. [101]

St. Simeon and other writers in the *Philokalia* suggest physical methods to be used in conjunction with the Jesus Prayer. Some people are so much absorbed in these external methods that they forget about the proper work of prayer; in others, prayer itself is distorted because of using these methods. Since, then, for lack of instructors these physical techniques may be accompanied by harmful effects, we do not describe them. In any case they are nothing by an external aid to inner work and are in no way essential. What is essential is this: to acquire the habit of stand-

ing with the mind in the heart — of being within this physical
heart of ours, although not physically. [105]

Do not be led astray by external methods when practicing the
inner Jesus Prayer. For some people they are necessary, but not
for you. In your case, the time for such methods has already
passed. You must already know by experience the place of the
heart about which they speak: do not bother about the rest. The
work of God is simple: it is prayer — children talking to their
Father, without any subtleties. May the Lord give you wisdom
for your salvation.
For someone who has not yet found the way to enter
within himself, pilgrimages to holy places are a help. But
for him who has found it they are a dissipation of energy,
for they force him to come out from the innermost part of
himself. IT IS TIME FOR YOU NOW TO LEARN
MORE PERFECTLY HOW TO REMAIN WITHIN.
YOU SHOULD ABANDON YOUR EXTERNAL PLANS.
[Merton copies these words in the book's margin in capital
letters.] [106]

What [mechanical techniques] would produce you already possessed from the moment you felt the call to practice the Prayer.
But do not come to the wrong conclusion that our journey on
the path of prayer is already completed. Growth in prayer has
no end. If this growth ceases it means that life ceases. [106]

If your heart grows warm through reading ordinary prayers, then
kindle its inner warmth toward God in this way.
The Jesus Prayer, if said mechanically, is valueless: it is no
more help than any other prayer spoken by the tongue and lips.
As you recite the Jesus Prayer, try at the same time to quicken
your realization that our Lord Himself is near, that He stands in
your soul and listens to what is happening within it. Awaken in
your soul the thirst for salvation, and the assurance that our Lord
alone can bring it. And then cry out to Him whom in your
thoughts you see before you: "Lord Jesus Christ, Son of God,
have mercy upon me," or: "O merciful Lord, save me by the

way that Thou knowest." It is not the words that matter, but your feelings toward the Lord.

The spiritual burning of the heart for God springs from our love towards Him. It kindles from the Lord's touch on the heart. Because He is entirely love, His touch on the heart immediately kindles love for Him; and from love comes burning of the heart towards Him. It is this which must be the object of your search.

Let the Jesus Prayer be on your tongue; let God's presence be before your mind; and in your heart let there be the thirst for God, for communion with the Lord. When all this becomes permanent, then the Lord, seeing how you exert yourself, will give you what you ask. [108]

What do you seek through the Jesus Prayer? We seek for the fire of grace to appear in our heart, and we seek for the beginning of unceasing prayer which manifests a state of grace. When God's spark falls into the heart, the Jesus Prayer fans it into flame. The prayer does not of itself produce the spark, but helps us to receive it.

. . . . If anyone should ask me how to carry out the task of prayer, I would say to him: Accustom yourself to walk in the presence of God, keep remembrance of Him, and be reverent. To preserve this remembrance, choose a few short prayers, or simply take the twenty-four short prayers of St. John Chrysostom, and repeat them often with appropriate thoughts and feelings. As you accustom yourself to this, remembrance of God will bring light to your mind and warmth to your heart. And when you attain this state, God's spark, the ray of grace, will fall at last into your heart. There is no way in which you yourself can produce it: it comes forth direct from God. When it comes, dwell in the Jesus Prayer alone, and with this prayer blow the spark of grace into flame. This is the most direct way. [108-109]

This spark is not to be attracted by any artifice, but it is given freely by the grace of God. For this the unwearied effort of prayer is necessary, as St. Makarios says: "If you wish to acquire true prayer, preserve steadfastly in praying, and God, seeing how strenuously you seek, will give it to you." [110]

What is true of this prayer is true of all forms of spiritual growth. A hot-tempered man may be filled with the desire to stamp out irritability and acquire meekness. In the books on asceticism there are instructions how to discipline oneself into achieving this. A man can read these instructions and follow them; but how far will he get by his own efforts? No farther than outward silence during bouts of anger, with only such quelling of the rage itself as self-control can afford him. He will never himself establish the complete extinction of his anger and the establishment of meekness in his heart. This only happen when grace invades the heart and itself places meekness there. [112]

At first this saving prayer is usually a matter of strenuous effort and hard work. But if one concentrates on it with zeal, it will begin to flow of its own accord, like a brook that murmurs in the heart. This is a great blessing, and it is worthy working hard to obtain it. [113]

The warmth of heart or glow of spirit, about which we spoke before, is achieved in just this way. The more the Jesus Prayer penetrates into the heart, the warmer the heart becomes, and the more self-impelled becomes the prayer, so that the fire of spiritual life is kindled in the heart, and its burning becomes unceasing. At the same time the Jesus Prayer will fill the whole heart, and will never cease to move within it. That is why those in whom the perfect inner life is being brought to birth will pray almost exclusively with this prayer alone, making it comprise their entire rule of prayer. [114]

Know that true success is achieved within, unconsciously, and happens as imperceptibly as the growth of the human body. Therefore when you hear an inner voice saying, "Ah, Here it is!" you should realize that this is the voice of the enemy, showing you a mirage rather than the reality. This is the beginning of self-deception. Stifle this voice immediately; otherwise it will resound in you like a trumpet, inflating your self-esteem. [116]

Every struggle in the soul's training, whether physical or mental, that is not accompanied by suffering, that does not require the utmost effort, will bear no fruit. "The kingdom of heaven suffereth violence, and the violent take it by force" (*Matthew* XI.12). Many people have worked and continue to work without pain, but because of its absence they are strangers to purity and out of communion with the Holy Spirit, because they have turned aside from the severity of suffering. Those who work feebly and carelessly may go through the movements of making great efforts, but they harvest no fruit, because they undergo no suffering. According to the prophet, unless our loins are broken, weakened by the labour of fasting, unless we undergo an agony of contrition, unless we suffer like a woman in travail, we shall not succeed in bringing to birth the spirit of salvation in the ground of our heart. [117]

I have often reminded you, my dear sister, about the remembrance of God, and now I tell you again: unless you work and sweat to impress on your heart and mind this awe-inspiring Name, you keep silence in vain, you sing in vain, you fast in vain, you watch in vain. In short, all a nun's work will be useless without this activity, without recollection of God. This is the beginning of silence for the Lord's sake, and it is also the end. This most desirable Name is the soul of stillness and silence. By calling it to mind we gain joy and gladness, forgiveness of sins and a wealth of virtues. Few have been able to find this most glorious Name, save only in stillness and silence. Man can attain it in no other way, even with great effort. Therefore, knowing the power of this advice, I entreat you for the love of Christ always to be still and silent, since these virtues enrich remembrance of God within us. [118]

Do you wish to enter this Paradise as quickly as possible? Here, then, is what you must do. When you pray, do not end your prayer without having aroused in your heart some feeling towards God, whether it be reverence, or devotion, or thanksgiving, or glorification, or humility and contrition, or hope and trust. Also when after prayer you begin to read, do not finish reading without having felt in your heart the truth of what you read. These two feelings — the one inspired by prayer, the other by reading — mutually warm one another; and if you pay attention to yourself, they will keep you under their influence during the whole day. Take pains to practice these two methods exactly and you will see for yourself what will happen. [120]

To pray does not only mean to stand in prayer. To keep the mind and heart turned towards God and directed to Him — this is already prayer, whatever the position in which one may be. Prayer according to the rule is one thing, and this state of prayer is another. The way to it is to attain the habit of constant remembrance of God, of the last hour and the judgment that follows it. Accustom yourself to this, and all will go well. Every step you take will be inwardly consecrated to God. You must direct your steps according to the commandments; and you know what the commandments are. That is all. It is possible to apply these commandments to every event, and to consecrate all your activities inwardly to God; and then all your life will be dedicated to Him. What more is necessary? Nothing. You see how simple it is.

You have zeal for salvation. When you have this zeal, it shows itself in a fervent care for salvation. It is absolutely necessary to avoid lukewarmness. This is how lukewarmness arises: it begins with forgetfulness. God's gifts are forgotten, and so are God Himself, and our salvation in Him, and the danger of being without God; and the remembrance of death disappears — in a word, the whole spiritual realm is closed to us. This is due to the enemy, or to the dispersion of thoughts by business cares and excessive social contacts. When all is forgotten the heart grows cool, and its sensitivity to spiritual things is interrupted: and so we fall into a state of indifference, and then into negligence and carelessness. As a result, spiritual occupations are postponed for a time, and afterwards abandoned completely. And then we begin again our old way of life, careless and negligent, forgetful of God, seeking only our own pleasure. Even if there is nothing disorderly in it, do not look for anything divine. It will be an empty life.

If you do not want to fall into this abyss, beware of the first step — that is, forgetfulness. Therefore walk always in godly recollections — in remembrance of God and divine things. This will keep you sensitive to such things, and these two together — recollection and sensitivity — will set you on fire with zeal. And here will be life indeed. [122-123]

You say that you are afraid of falling in love with spiritual sweetness. But you surely cannot think of doing any such thing. It is not for its sweetness that prayer is practiced, but because it is our duty to serve God in this way, although sweetness goes of necessity with true service. The most important thing in prayer is to stand before God in reverence and fear, with the mind in the heart; for this sobers and disperses every folly and plants contrition before God in the heart. These feelings of fear and sorrow in the sight of God, the broken and contrite heart, are the principal features of true inner prayer, and the test of every prayer, by which we can tell whether or not our prayer is performed as it should be. If they are present, prayer is in order. When they are absent, prayer is not in its true course and must be brought back to its proper condition. If we lack this sense of sorrow and contrition, then sweetness and warmth may breed self-conceit; and that is spiritual pride, and will lead to pernicious illusion. Then the sweetness and warmth will vanish, leaving only their memory, but the soul will still imagine that it has them. Of this you should not be afraid, and so you must increasingly kindle in your heart the fear of God, lowliness, and contrite prostration before Him, walking always in His presence. This is the heart of the matter. [128]

The essential mood of the penitent is this: "In the way Thou knowest, O Lord, save me. For my part I will labour without hypocrisy, without deviation and misinterpretation, but according to a pure conscience, doing everything that I understand and that lies in my power." Whoever can truly feel this in his heart, is accepted by the Lord, who then comes to rule as king within him. [133]

There is no need to be afraid of illusion [in Russian *prelest*]. It overtakes those who become vain, who begin to think that as soon as warmth has come into the heart they are already at the summit of perfection. In fact this warmth is only the beginning and may not prove stable. For this warmth and peace in the heart may be something natural – the fruit of concentrated attention. We have to labour and labour, to wait and wait, until the natural is replaced by the grace-given. It is best never to think of yourself as having attained anything, but always to see yourself as poor, naked, blind, and worthless. [136]

He who in total humility puts himself in the hand of the merciful God, attracts the Lord to himself, and becomes strong in His strength.

Although expecting everything from God and nothing for ourselves, we must nevertheless force ourselves to action, exerting all our strength, so as to create something to which the divine help may come, and which the divine power may encompass. Grace is already present within us, but it will only act after man has himself acted, filling his powerlessness with its own power. Establish yourself, therefore, firmly in the humble sacrifice of your will to God, and then take action without any irresolution or half-heartedness. [136-137]

When you undertake some special endeavour, do not concentrate your attention and heart on it, but look upon it as something secondary; and by entire surrender to God open yourself to God's grace. [137]

Here is some account of the practices which help to strengthen the powers of man's soul and body in goodness, and which enable the life of grace within the spirit to burn more and more brightly. According to the zeal and efforts of the man who gives himself to God, grace will enter and penetrate him increasingly with its power, sanctifying him and making him its own. But one cannot and should not stop at this stage. This is still only a seed, a starting point. It is necessary that this light of life should go further, and permeating the entire substance of the soul and body should in this way sanctify them, claiming them for itself; uprooting the alien and unnatural passionateness which now dominates us, it should raise the soul and body to their pure and natural state. The light should not remain enclosed within itself but should spread over the whole being with all its powers.

But since these powers are all infected with what is unnatural, the pure spirit of grace, coming into the heart, is unable to enter directly and immediately into them, being barred out by their impurity.

Therefore we must establish some channel between the spirit of grace living within us and our own powers, so that the spirit may flow into them and heal them, just as dressings heal the sore places to which they are applied.

It is evident that, to act effectively as a channel, all these means must on the one hand bear the character and qualities of a divine and heavenly origin, and on the other be perfectly adapted to our own powers in their natural arrangement and purpose. Otherwise, they will not act as an effective channel of grace, nor will our powers be enabled to draw healing from them. Such, then, must necessarily be the origin and inner qualities of these means of healing. As to their outward form, they cannot be anything other than activities, exercises, labour; for they are applied to human powers and faculties whose distinctive quality is action.

These, then, are the activities and exercises which are the means of healing our powers and bringing them back to their lost purity and wholeness: fasting, labour, vigil, solitude, withdrawal from the world, control of the senses, reading of the scriptures and the Holy Fathers, attendance at church, frequent confession and communion. [138-139]

When we are quickened by grace, it is impossible not to be conscious of the fact, but it *is* possible not to pay attention to it; and so, living in this quickened state for a while, we descend again into the usual round of activities of the soul and body. The quickening does not complete the act of the sinner's conversion, but only begins it, and there still remains work on oneself; and this work is very complicated. But all that relates to this work will be accomplished in two movements of free will — the turning from the outside world to one's inner self, and the subsequent turning from self towards God. In the first movement, man regains the power over himself which he had lost, and in the second he brings himself as an offering to God — the free will offering of burnt sacrifice. In the first he decides to abandon sin, and in the second, drawing near to God, he vows to belong to Him alone all the days of his life. [140]

God's grace, coming first at a man's initial awakening, and afterwards visiting him during the whole period of is conversion, cleaves him in two. It makes him aware of a duality within himself, and enables him to distinguish between what is unnatural and what should be natural; and thus it makes him resolve to sift or winnow all that is unnatural, so that his God-like nature should be brought fully to light. But obviously such a decision is only the beginning of the undertaking. At this stage it is only with his will and intention that he has left the domain of alien unnaturalness, rejecting it, and aiming at the naturalness which he expects and desires. But in fact his whole structure remains as before — that is, saturated with sin; and passions dominate his soul in all its faculties and his body in all its functions, just as they did before — with only this difference, that formerly he chose and embraced all this with desire and pleasure, but now it is not desired or chosen, but is hated, trampled on, rejected. In this state a man has emerged from himself as from a putrefying corpse; he sees how the reek of passion flows from different parts of himself against his will, and sometimes he experiences the stench given off by himself so strongly that it stifles his mind.

Thus the true life of grace in man is in its beginning only a seed, a spark; but a seed sown among tares, a spark constantly smothered by ashes. It is still only a feeble candle glimmering in the densest fog. Man by his consciousness and will has attached himself to God, and God has accepted him, has united with him in this self-awareness and point of free choice, within his mind — what is termed the spirit, in St. Antony of Egypt and St. Makarios the Great. And this is the only part of him which is healthy, agreeable to God, and saved. All the other parts are still held prisoner and do not want and cannot be obedient to the demands of the new life: the mind as a whole does not yet know how to think in the new way but thinks as before; the will does not yet know how to desire in the new way, but desires as before; the heart does not know how to feel in the new way, but feels as before. It is the same in the body in all its functions. Consequently man is as yet wholly impure except at the one point which is the conscious power of free choice within his mind — what we termed the spirit. God, being wholly pure, enters into union only with this one part; but all the other parts, being impure, remain outside Him and estranged from Him. He is ready to fill the entire man, but does not do so because man is impure. Afterwards, as soon as he is cleansed, God makes known His full dwelling in him. [140-141]

Before the birth of the inner life — before the palpable manifestation of the action of grace and union with God — it frequently happens that a man still acts on his own initiative, up to the limit of his powers. But when he is exhausted by the failure of his efforts he at last casts aside his own activity, and whole-heartedly gives himself up to the all-embracing action of grace. Then the Lord visits him with His mercy, and kindles the fire of inner spiritual life in him, and he knows from experience that it is not his own former efforts which have effected this great transformation. Afterwards, the more or less frequent withdrawals of divine grace teach him by experience that sustaining this fire of life is likewise not dependent on his own efforts.

The frequent appearance of good thoughts and intentions, his frequent infusion by the spirit of prayer — coming he knows not whence or how — similarly convince him by experience that all this good is possible for him only through the action of divine grace, which is always present in him, by the mercy of the Lord, who saves all who are striving for salvation. He gives himself to the Lord, and the Lord alone acts in him. Experience shows that he only succeeds in everything when he entrusts himself wholly to God. So he never turns back, but guards this grace in every way possible. [142]

He who bears grace in his heart surrenders himself wholly to the action of grace, and it is grace that acts in him. For him this truth is more evident, not only than any mathematical truth, but even than any experience of his exterior life, because he has already ceased to live outside himself and is wholly concentrated within. <u>He has now only one care, always to be faithful to the grace present within him</u>. Unfaithfulness offends grace, causing it either to retreat, or to reduce its action. Man testifies to his faithfulness to grace or to the Lord by not permitting — either in thoughts, feelings, actions, or words — anything which he knows to be contrary to the will of the Lord. [142]

When a fire is kindled, movement of air is necessary to keep the flame alight and to strengthen it: in exactly the same way, when the fire of grace is kindled in the heart, prayer is necessary, for it acts as a kind of current of spiritual air in the heart. [142]

The first state in the life of prayer can be likened to the bare trees during winter; the second, to the same trees covered with leaves and blossoms brought out by the spring warmth. <u>In both states repentance must be the soul and aim of the prayer</u>. As a reward for the repentance which a man offers while still proceeding by his own endeavours, God grants, in His own good time, a repentance that comes full of grace; and the Holy Spirit, having entered the man, "maketh intercession" for him "with groanings which cannot be uttered . . . He maketh intercession for the saints according to the will of God," which He alone knows (*Romans* VIII:26-27).

It is thus quite clear that the beginner's search for the place of the heart, that is, his untimely and premature attempts to kindle the manifest action of grace, is a most mistaken undertaking, perverting the due order and system of the science of prayer. Such an undertaking is one of pride and foolishness. In the same way it is not right for a beginner to use the practices recommended by the Holy Fathers for advanced monks and hesychasts. [144]

Work, exert yourself, seek and you shall find; knock, and it shall be opened unto you. Do not relax and do not despair. But at the same time remember that these efforts are no more than attempts on our part to attract grace; they are not grace itself, which we still have to go on seeking. The principal thing we lack is the quickening power of grace. It is very noticeable that when we reason, or pray, or do something else of this nature, it is as though we are forcing into our heart something foreign from outside. This is what sometimes happens: our thoughts or prayers make an impression on us, and their efforts descend into the heart to a certain depth, depending on the strength of the efforts we make; but then, after a while, this impression is cast out again — as a stick which is thrust vertically into water is forced up once more — because of a kind of resistance in the heart which is disobedient and unaccustomed to such things. Immediately following this, coolness and coarseness begin again to take hold of the soul: a sure sign that it was not the action of grace that we experienced there, but only the effects of our own work and effort. Therefore do not be content with these efforts alone; do not rest on them as if they were what you have to find. This is a dangerous illusion. It is equally dangerous to think that in these labours there is merit, which grace is bound to reward. Not at all: these efforts are only the preparation for receiving grace; but the gift itself depends entirely on the will of the Giver. Therefore, with careful use of all the means already mentioned, he who seeks must still walk in the expectation of the divine visitation, which gives no warning of its coming, and arrives from whence no one knows.

Only when this quickening power of grace comes will the inner work of the transformation of our life and character really begin. Without it, we cannot expect success; there will only be unsuccessful attempts. [145]

Let no one, hearing great tidings about the action of the Spirit from the lips of a sinner, hesitate in unbelief and be troubled in thought, considering that the action he hears about is the work of devils and an illusion. He must cast aside any such blasphemous thought. No! No! Not such is the action of illusion, nor its attributes. Tell me: is it possible for the devil, the enemy and murderer of man, to become his physician? Is it possible for the devil to unite in one the parts and powers of man which were severed by sin, to liberate them from the domination of sin, to lead them out from the state of contradiction and civil war into the state of holy peace in the Lord? Is it possible for the devil to deliver a man from the deep abyss of his ignorance of God, and to give him living knowledge of God, based on experience, which no longer needs any proofs from outside? Is it possible for the devil to preach and explain in detail about the Saviour — to preach and explain how we can draw near to Him through repentance? Is it possible for the devil to restore the lost image in man, to set the distorted likeness in order? Is it possible for him to impart the savour of spiritual poverty, and along with it, the savour of resurrection, of renewal and union with God? Is it possible for the devil to raise man to the height of communion with God, a communion in which man becomes as nothing, without thoughts, without desires, totally immersed in wondrous silence? This silence is the absorption of all the powers of a human being: they are all drawn towards God, and as it were disappear before His endless majesty. [146-147]

Illusion, when it approaches man in thought or in dream, in some subtle idea, by some apparition which can be seen with the physical eyes, or by a voice from on high heard by the physical ears, never approaches as an absolute master, but comes as a charmer who seeks acceptance by man, and from his acceptance gains power over him. The action of illusion inside our outside man is always action from without; it is open to man to repel it. Illusion is always met at first by a certain doubt in the heart: only those whom it has conquered decisively accept it without question. Illusion never untied a man who is divided by sin, it does not stop the upsurge of blood, does not lead the ascetic to repentance, does not make him small in his own eyes; on the contrary it fires his imagination, encourages the rush of blood, brings him a certain tasteless, poisonous enjoyment and flatters him insidiously, inspiring him with self-conceit and establishing in his soul an idol — "I." [147]

He who has sought the help of grace and now feels its presence must be firmly resolved, not only to correct himself, but also to begin to do this at once. This desire to correct himself has already directed him in all his previous efforts, but there is still something to be added to its composition or to its perfecting. For there are various kinds of desire. There is mental desire: the mind demands something and the man makes the effort; such a desire directs the preparatory labour. There is compassionate desire: this is born under the influence of the affections and feelings induced by grace. Finally, there is active desire: consent of the will to begin at once in the task of rising from one's fallen state. Supported by God's grace, you should start now. [148-149]

When the query arises "Is this it?," make it your rule once and for all mercilessly to drive away all such questions as soon as they appear. They originate from the enemy. If you linger over this question the enemy will pronounce the decision without delay, "Oh yes, it certainly is — you have done very well!" From then on you stand on stilts and begin to harbour illusions about yourself and to think that others are good for nothing. Grace will vanish: but the enemy will make you think that grace is still with you. This will mean that you think you possess something, when really you have nothing at all. The Holy Fathers wrote, "Do not measure yourself." If you think you can decide any question about your progress, it means that you are beginning to measure yourself to see how much you have grown. Please avoid this as you would avoid fire. [158-159]

At this point the zealous man looks inward, and what do you think he finds there? Ceaseless wandering of thoughts, constant onslaughts from the passions, hardness and coldness of heart, obstinacy and disobedience, desire to do everything according to his own will. In a word, he finds everything within himself in a very bad state. And seeing this, his zeal is inflamed, and he now directs strenuous efforts to the development of his inner life, to controlling his thoughts and the dispositions of his heart.

From directions on inner spiritual life he discovers the necessity of paying attention to oneself, of watching over the movements of the heart. In order not to admit anything bad, it is necessary to preserve the remembrance of God.

And so he sets to work to achieve this remembrance. But his thoughts can no more be arrested than the wind; his bad feelings and worthless impulses can no more be evaded than the stench of a corpse; his mind, like a wet and frozen bird, cannot rise to the remembrance of God.

What is to be done? Be patient, they say, and go on working. Patience and labour are exercised, but all within remains
the same. At last someone of experience is found who explains
that all is inwardly in disorder because the forces within
are divided: mind and heart each go their own way. Mind and
heart must be united; then wandering of thoughts will cease,
and you will gain a rudder to steer the ship of your soul, a
lever by which to set in movement all your inner world. But
how can one unite mind and heart? Acquire the habit of praying these words with the mind in the heart, "Lord Jesus Christ,
Son of God, have mercy upon me." And this prayer, when you
learn to perform it properly, or rather when it becomes grafted
to the heart, will lead you to the end which you desire. It will
unite your mind with your heart, it will cut off your wandering
thoughts, and give you the power to govern the movements of
your soul. [167]

From the psychological point of view, this must be said of the
kingdom of God: it is born in us when the mind is united with
the heart, both alike adhering steadfastly to the remembrance
of God.

Then man surrenders to the Lord his consciousness and freedom as a sacrifice pleasing to Him, and receives from God power
over himself; and by strength received from Him he rules over
all his inner and outer life as God's vice-regent. [169]

There are, in fact, three kinds of communion with God: a first
in thought and intention, which happens at the time of conversion; and two others which are actual, of which one is hidden,
invisible to others and unknown to oneself, and the other is evident both to oneself and to others.

The whole of our spiritual life consists in the transition
from the first kind of communion with God — in thought and
intention — to the third kind — a real, living, and conscious communion. [171]

You dream of a hermitage. But you already have your hermitage, here and now! Sit still, and call out, "Lord, have mercy!"

When you are isolated from the rest of the world, how will you fulfill the will of God? Simply by preserving within yourself the right inner state. And what is this? It is a state of unceasing remembrance of God in fear and piety, together with the remembrance of death. The habit of walking before God and keeping Him in remembrance — such is the air we breathe in the spiritual life. Created as we are in the image of God, this habit should exist in our spirit naturally: if it is absent, that is because we have fallen away from God. As a result of this fall, we have to fight to acquire the habit of walking before God. Our ascetic struggle consists essentially in the effort to stand consciously before the face of the ever-present God; but there are also various secondary activities, which likewise form part of the spiritual life. Here too there is work to be done, in order to direct these activities to their true aim. Reading, meditation, prayer, all our occupations and contacts, must be conducted in such a way as not to blot out or disturb the remembrance of God. The seat of our consciousness and attention must also be concentrated on this remembrance of God. [185]

Maybe in your case God asks for a final surrender of your heart, and your heart longs for God. For without God it can never be content but remains forever unsatisfied. Examine yourself from this point of view. Perhaps you will find here the door to God's dwelling place. [187]

You seek the Lord? Seek, but only within yourself. He is not far from anyone. The Lord is near all those who truly call on Him. Find a place in your heart, and speak there with the Lord. It is the Lord's reception room. Everyone who meets the Lord, meets him there; He has fixed no other place for meeting souls. [187]

You preserve inner attention and solitude in the heart. May the Lord help you always to remain thus. This is the most important thing in our spiritual life. When consciousness is within the heart, there too is the Lord; and so the two become united and the work of salvation progresses successfully. The entry is barred to evil thoughts, and still more to emotions and mood. The Name of the Lord by itself disperses everything alien to it and attracts everything akin.

What have you to fear above all else? Self-satisfaction, self-appreciation, self-conceit, and all other things beginning with *self*.

Work out your salvation with fear and trembling. Kindle and maintain a contrite spirit, a humble and a contrite heart. [187]

For you, the path of salvation is still dark. Read the first paragraphs of Philotheus of Sinai in the *Philokalia*, and see what is said there. One act is required — and that is all: for this one act pulls everything together, and keeps everything in order. Try to organize yourself as Philotheus directs, and you will receive the right order within, as you will clearly realize. This one act is to stand with attention in your heart, and to remain there before God in worship. This is the beginning of spiritual wisdom.

You wish to grow wise in discernment of thoughts. Descend from the head into the heart. Then you will see all thoughts clearly, as they move before the eye of your sharp-sighted mind. But until you descend into the heart, do not expect to have due discrimination of thoughts. [189]

The heart is the innermost man or spirit. Here are located self-awareness, the conscience, the idea of God and one's complete dependence on Him, and all the eternal treasures of the spiritual life. [190]

The spirit of wisdom and revelation, and heart that is cleansed, are two different matters; the former is from on high, from God, the latter is from ourselves. But in the process of acquiring Christian understanding they are inseparably united, and this understanding cannot be gained unless both of them are present together. The heart alone, despite all purification — if purification is possible without grace — will not give us wisdom; but the spirit of wisdom will not come to us unless we have prepared a pure heart to be its dwelling-place.

The heart is to be understood here, not in its ordinary meaning, but in the sense of the "inner man." We have within us an inner man, according to the Apostle Paul, or a hidden man of the heart, according to the Apostle Peter. It is the God-like spirit that was breathed into the first man, and it remains with us continuously, even after the Fall. It shows itself in the fear of God, which is founded on the certainty of God's existence, and in the awareness of our complete dependence on Him, in the stirrings of conscience and in our lack of contentment with all that is material. [191]

No one has power to command the heart. It lives its own special life. It rejoices of itself, it is sad of itself; and no one can do anything about this. Only the Master of all, holding all in His right hand, has power to enter the heart, to put feelings into it independently of its naturally changing currents. [192]

One must not be without work for a single moment. But there is work performed by the body, visibly, and there is work which is done mentally, invisibly. And it is this second kind that constitutes real work. It consists primarily in the unceasing remembrance of God, with the prayer of the mind in the heart. Nobody sees it, yet those who are in this state work with ceaseless vigour. This is the one thing necessary. Once it is there, do not worry about any other work. [192]

NOTE

1. Compiled by Igumen Chariton of Valamo. Translated by E. Kadloubovsky and E.M. Palmer. Edited with an Introduction by Timothy Ware. Translated for this edition by Elizabeth M. Palmer. London: Faber and Faber Limited, 1966.

9

THOMAS MERTON AND THE SILENCE OF ICONS

Jim Forest

If our ancestors were to visit us, perhaps the biggest single shock that the world of the third millennium would pose for them would be the noise. I wonder if it wouldn't drive some of them mad? The noise of traffic. The noise of jet planes overhead. The noise of television and radio. The canned music in so many stores. The strange sounds emitted by the earphones of people plugged into Walkmans. The noise of one-way conversations of people talking on their mobile phones. The various noises made by mobile phones as they announce incoming calls. The noise of passing cars in which the driver is playing his radio full blast. We live in a world of millions of sound addicts. Real silence for most of us, at least those of us living in cities and large towns, is a stunning experience. For some, it is unbearable.

Years ago a friend of mine, an announcer working for one of New York City's most popular radio stations, lost his job. This was a big surprise to everyone who knew him. José was a jovial man with a cello-like voice who had a gift for warming the ears and heart — caring, funny, original, who played with words with the flair of a circus juggler. But several times he had allowed as much as ten seconds of silence to go out over the air. The station manager was truly sorry about firing someone so gifted, and a personal friend as well. He explained that the main thing the station's listeners required from him was constant sound. Silence could last no more than milliseconds. Otherwise too many listeners become anxious or frightened or turned the dial to find noise somewhere else. Broadcasting silence was something the station could not allow. José had been warned twice before. "Three times and you're out," the station manager said.

Monasteries are places where meaningless noise is avoided, with the Trappists being on the cutting edge of silence. It was in part the massive silence he met at the Abbey of Gethsemani that knocked Merton's socks off when he first visited the abbey in the spring of 1941. After becoming a Trappist monk, he occasionally was drawn to other monasteries where the silence was even more absolute. Imagining the ultimate monastic silence, he would sometimes take illustrated books about Carmoldolese and Carthusian monasteries off the library shelves, looking at the photos much the way a teen-age boy might look at certain photos in very non-monastic magazines.

One might say there were times when Merton lusted for silence. It was an attraction to what in the Orthodox Church is called the way of *hesychasm* — the path of silence. As is often the case with writers, Merton was painfully aware of the limitations of words. "He who follows words is destroyed," is a Chinese proverb Merton quoted approvingly to the novices. Icons were part of the word-free, God-charged silence toward which Merton was so powerfully drawn.

The first mention of icons in Merton's autobiographical writings occurs at his father Owen's deathbed in London. Owen was suffering from a brain tumor that made him unable to speak, yet he did manage "a last word" to his 16-year-old son. Young Merton came to see his father in his London hospital room and, to his amazement, found the bed littered with drawings of "little, irate Byzantine-looking saints with beards and great halos," as he wrote in *The Seven Storey Mountain*. Tom had no eye for icons at the time. He then regarded Byzantine art, he confessed in an unpublished autobiographical novel, *The Labyrinth*, as "clumsy and ugly and brutally stupid."

Two years later Merton was in Rome, which he seems generally not to have liked. The architecture, statuary and painting of the Empire, the Renaissance and the Counter-Reformation struck him as vapid and melodramatic. "It was so evident, merely from the masses of stone and brick that still represented the palaces and temples and baths, that imperial Rome must have been one of the most revolting and ugly and depressing cities the world has ever seen," Merton wrote in *The Seven Storey Mountain*.[1]

Perhaps we would never have heard of Thomas Merton had it not been for what happened when he found his way to the city's most ancient churches — San Clemente, Santa Sabina, Santa Maria Maggiore, Saints Cosmas and Damian, the Lateran, Santa Costanza, Santa Maria in Trastevere, the Basilica of San Prassede. In Santa Maria Maggiore, there are icons that date from the fourth century. These are all churches of sober design whose main decoration is mosaic iconography, images of simplicity and quiet intensity that astonished him.

"I was fascinated by these Byzantine mosaics," he wrote in his autobiography. "I began to haunt the churches where they were to be found." Through icons, he began to understand who Christ is: "For the first time in my whole life I began to find out something of whom this Person was that men call Christ. . . . It is the Christ of the Apocalypse, the Christ of the Martyrs, the Christ of the Fathers. It is the Christ of Saint John, and of Saint Paul, and of St. Augustine and St. Jerome and all the Fathers — and of the Desert Fathers. It is Christ God, Christ King."[2]

The teen-age Merton was so moved that he wanted to pray, to light a candle, to kneel down, but it was not easy to move from longing to fulfillment.

He describes a particular morning when he climbed the Aventine Hill, crowned by the fifth century church of Santa Sabina. "Although the church was almost empty, I walked across the stone floor mortally afraid that a poor devout old Italian woman was following me with suspicious eyes." He knelt down at the altar rail and, with tears, again and again recited the *Our Father.*

Leaving the church, Merton felt a depth of joy he hadn't known in years, if ever before. He was no longer "a heretic tourist," he commented in *The Labyrinth.* He put it more positively in *The Seven Storey Mountain:* "Without knowing anything about it, I became a pilgrim."

In *Art and Worship,* an unpublished text by Merton mainly written in the late fifties, he tried to put in words some of the characteristics of icons, one of which of course is silence. It was to have gone to press in 1959. The galley sheets survive at the Thomas Merton Center at Bellarmine University in Louisville, Kentucky. Also on file there is the correspondence about the project. It makes for diverting reading to see various friends struggling to bring Merton up-to-date on religious art. The art historian Eloise Spaeth was enlisted as a kind of professor-by-post to escort Merton into the modern world. In the end she could see no way to rescue either Merton or his book. She was appalled with Merton's "sacred artist" who keeps "creeping out with his frightful icons."[3]

Merton's aesthetic heresy was his view that Christian religious art had been more dead than alive for centuries. What he had hoped to do with his small book was to sensitize his readers to an understanding of religious art that, in the west at least, had been abandoned in the Renaissance and afterward simply forgotten. It was, in brief, a work in praise of icons.

"It is the task of the iconographer," he wrote in *Art and Worship*, "to open our eyes to the actual presence of the Kingdom in the world, and to remind us that, though we see nothing of its splendid liturgy, we are, if we believe in Christ the Redeemer, in fact living and worshiping as 'fellow citizens of the angels and saints, built upon the chief cornerstone with Christ'."

Half a century ago, Merton was one of the few non-Orthodox Christians to appreciate that silence and stillness of icons. What he wrote on this topic, unfashionable at the time, has proved to be prophetic. These days it is hard to find a Catholic church or monastery in which icons are not present or even placed in principal locations. Icons are often found in Protestant environments as well. Increasingly we find in many Christian homes the creation of icon corners — an area where icons are used to create a place of prayer where one lives. Many non-Orthodox Christians have sought to learn the art of icon painting — a much harder tradition than is usually imagined.

Let us consider some of the key characteristics of icons. In doing so, I am following the broad outlines Merton drew in *Art and Worship*.

It is hieratic. That is, it is concerned solely with the sacred, seeking to convey the awesomeness of the invisible and divine reality and to lead the beholder to awareness of the divine presence.

It is traditional. Far from being merely conventional, tradition constantly renews the everlasting newness of revelation. The icon is not the personal meditation of an individual artist but the fruit of many generations of belief uniting us to the witnesses of the resurrection. The icon is as much an instrument of the transmission of Christian tradition as the written or spoken word. Such art has much in common with bread-baking. No loaf of bread is signed and none is the work of a single generation.

It is living. Icons communicate a life of prayer, a life rooted in worship. They are connected to the Eucharist. There is a deep sense in icons of communion. It is communication without words not about the past or future
but the present.

It is sincere. Icons are simple, direct, unaffected, unmanipulative, and unpretentious.

It is reverent, not seeking to draw attention to itself or sell anything.

Icons guard against a too easy or too human familiarity with the divine. For example, a Savior icon is not a painting merely of "our dear friend Jesus" but at once portrays both his divinity as well as his manhood, his absolute demands on us as well as his infinite mercy.

It is spiritual. The icon is not an art object and has nothing to do with the commercial world, but exists only as an evangelical expression and an aid to worship. "The Spirit of God speaks to the faithful in between the lines of divine revelation, telling us things that are not evident to the inspection of scholarship or reason," Merton comments. "So too the Spirit of God speaks behind the lines and colors of a sacred painting, telling the worshiper things the art critic cannot see."

It is pure. It is not the work of a person who seeks to draw attention to himself. The iconographer, having been blessed by the church to carry on this form of silent evangelical activity, willingly and with gratitude works under the guidance of tradition.

It is silent. Post-iconographic western religion has often tended toward action and drama. In the icon there is a conscious avoidance of movement or theatrical gesture. It is rendered in the simplest manner. The stillness and silence of the icon, in the home setting no less than the church, creates an area of silence. The deep silence characteristic of a good icon is nothing less than the silence of Christ. One of the ways that silence is expressed in icons is the closed mouths. In fact no physical detail suggests sound.

But the silence is not empty. It is the very opposite of the empty stillness of the tomb. It is the silence of Mary's contemplative heart, the silence of the transfiguration, the silence of the resurrection, the silence of the Incarnate Word. St. Ignatius, Bishop of Antioch, the disciple of St. John the Evangelist who was martyred in Rome in the year 107, made the comment: "He who possesses in truth the word of Jesus can hear even its silence."

It bears witness to the incarnation. The iconoclastic heresy of the seventh and eighth centuries, which resulted in the destruction of countless icons and persecution of those making or using them, was rooted in the idea that the humanity of Christ had been absorbed into his divinity; therefore to draw an image of Christ, representing as it did aspects of his physical appearance, stressed his humanity while obscuring his divinity. The great theologian affirming the place of icons in Christian life was St. John of Damascus, writing from Mar Saba Monastery in the desert southeast of Jerusalem. In his essay *On the Divine Images*, he argues:

> If we made an image of the invisible God, we would certainly be in error . . . but we do not do anything of the kind; we do not err, in fact, if we make the image of God incarnate who appeared on earth in the flesh, who, in his ineffable goodness, lived with men and assumed the nature, the volume, the form, and the color of the flesh. . . . Since the invisible One became visible by taking on flesh, you can fashion the image of him whom you saw. Since He who has neither body nor form nor quantity nor quality, who goes beyond all grandeur by the ex-

cellence of his nature, He, being of divine nature, took on the condition of a slave and reduced himself to quantity and quality by clothing himself in human features. Therefore, paint on wood and present for contemplation Him who desired to become visible.

The icon is a revelation of transfiguration. We were made in the image and likeness of God but the image has been damaged and the likeness lost. The icon shows the recovery of wholeness. Over centuries of development, iconographers gradually developed a way of communicating physical reality illuminated by Christ. The icon suggests the transfiguration that occurs to whomever has acquired the Holy Spirit. The icon is thus a witness to theosis, meaning deification. It is an ancient Christian teaching that "God became man so that man could become God." Not that we become our own Creator but that we actually participate in God's life.

From time to time Merton returned to the subject of sacred art in his letters. In the last year of his life, for example, there are two letters of importance to us that were addressed to a Quaker correspondent, June Yungblut. She had sent him the manuscript of a book by her husband on great prophets of history, in which one chapter was devoted to Jesus of Nazareth. June hoped Merton might read and comment on the Jesus chapter.

Merton replied with the confession that he was still "hung up in a very traditional Christology." He wasn't drawn, he went on, to a Christ who was merely an historical figure possessing "a little flash of the light" but to "the Christ of the Byzantine icons."[4]

In her response June Yungblut expressed dismay with the phrase, "the Christ of the Byzantine icons." Didn't Merton feel a shiver to use the word Byzantine? Didn't "Byzantine" signify the very worst in both Christianity and culture? And weren't icons of about as much artistic significance as pictures on cereal boxes?

In March 1968 Merton replied, explaining what he meant in linking himself with the "Christ of the Byzantine icons." "The whole tradition of iconography," he said, "represents a traditional experience formulated in a theology of light, the icon being a kind of sacramental medium for the illumination and awareness of the glory of Christ within us. . . . What one 'sees' in prayer before an icon is not an external representation of a historical person, but an interior presence in light, which is the glory of the transfigured Christ, the experience of which is transmitted in faith from generation to generation by those who have 'seen,' from the Apostles on down. . . . So when I say that my Christ is the Christ of the icons, I mean that he is reached not through any scientific study but through direct faith and the mediation of the liturgy, art, worship, prayer, theology of light, etc., that is all bound up with the Russian and Greek tradition."

It is with such words as these, still bearing the stamp of his experience of many years before in Rome, that we can better understand the significance for Merton of the handwritten icon, originally from Mount Athos, that he was given in 1965, the year he was beginning his hard apprenticeship as a hermit living in a small cinderblock house in the woods near the monastery.

The icon of the Mother of God and the Christ Child – the unexpected gift of his Greek Orthodox friend, Marco Pallis, a scholar of Tibetan Buddhism – was for Merton like a kiss from God. He wrote Pallis in response:

How shall I begin? I have never received such a precious and magnificent gift from anyone in my life. I have no words to express how deeply moved I was to come face to face with this sacred and beautiful presence granted to me. . . . At first I could hardly believe it. . . . It is a perfect act of timeless worship. I never tire of gazing at it. There is a spiritual presence and reality about it, a true spiritual "Thaboric" light, which seems unaccountably to proceed from the Heart of the Virgin and Child as if they had One heart, and which goes out to the whole universe. It is unutterably splendid. And silent. It imposes a silence on the whole hermitage . . . [This] icon of the Holy Mother came as a messenger at a precise moment when a message was needed, and her presence before me has been an incalculable aid in resolving a difficult problem.[5]

Merton traveled light on his journey to Asia in 1968. It is striking that among the few things that he brought with him during the last weeks of his life was a hand-painted icon of Christ and his mother. On the back he had written, in Greek, a short passage from the *Philokalia*, a collection of patristic texts that was very dear to him:

"If we wish to please the true God and to be friends with the most blessed of friendships, let us present our spirit naked to God. Let us not draw into it anything of this present world (no art, no thought, no reasoning, no self-justification) even though we should possess all the wisdom of this world."[6]

NOTES

1. Thomas Merton, *The Seven Storey Mountain* (New York: Harcourt Brace, 1948), page 107.

2. *The Seven Storey Mountain*, page 109.

3. For details, see Donna Kristoff's essay, "Light That Is Not Light: A Consideration of Thomas Merton and the Icon," *The Merton Annual*, volume 2. (New York: AMS Press, 1989), pages 84-117.

4. *The Hidden Ground of Love: The Letters of Thomas Merton on Religious Experience and Social Concerns*, edited by William H. Shannon (New York: Farrar Straus & Giroux, 1985), pages 637, 642-3.

5. *The Hidden Ground of Love*, pages 473-74.

6. The quotation is from the *Philokalia*, a collection of writings on the spiritual life, especially prayer of the heart, widely read in the Orthodox Church. A three-volume translation of the complete text is published by Faber & Faber.

ΑΓΙΑΣΟΦΙΑ

HAGIA SOPHIA

One day, Father Louis (Thomas Merton) our friend, came from his
monastery at Trappist, Kentucky, to bring an ill novice to the hospital in
Lexington. (I had known Father Louis since 1955 when I visited him
for the first time. Later we printed several of his books.) We had
prepared a simple luncheon and I welcomed him to sit with us at table.
From where he sat he had a good view of the triptych on the chest and he
often looked at it. After a while he asked quite abruptly, "And who is
the woman behind Christ?" I said, "I do not know yet." Without further
question he gave his own answer. "She is Hagia Sophia, Holy Wisdom,
who crowns Christ." And this she was — and is.

— Victor Hammer

10

MERTON AND "HAGIA SOPHIA" (HOLY WISDOM)

Susan McCaslin

Wisdom will honour you if you embrace her
She will place on your head a fair garland
She will bestow on you a crown of glory.
— *Proverbs 4:8-9*

When visiting his friend Victor Hammer, Vienna-born artist, printmaker and typographer in Lexington, Kentucky in 1959, Merton noticed a triptych depicting a dark-haired young woman crowning a youth. Hammer had begun painting a Madonna and child but said he no longer knew exactly who the woman was, as she had turned out quite differently than originally intended.

Immediately Merton interjected, "I know who she is. I have always known her. She is Hagia Sophia." A similar mysterious figure of Wisdom makes her first appearances in Merton's journals of 1958 as a recurrent dream persona he called "Proverb," based on the figure of Wisdom in *Proverbs* 8.

In his scattered journal entries and especially in the long poem "Hagia Sophia," completed in the Spring of 1961 during Pentecost, Merton explores this ancient feminine figure of God. The poem grew out of a letter Merton wrote in response to Hammer's request for more detail on the identity of Sophia. In "Hagia Sophia," Merton invokes the sophianic character of Eastern Orthodoxy, anticipating later feminist reconfigurations of the divine by embracing a sense of the reciprocity and unity of male and female polarities in God, the world, and the self.

THE IDENTITY OF HAGIA SOPHIA

Merton's letter to Hammer, dated May 2, 1959, develops in more detail the identity of the young Madonna in the triptych:

The first thing to be said, of course, is that Hagia Sophia is God Himself. God is not only a Father but a Mother.

He is both at the same time. . . . [T]o ignore this distinction is to lose touch with the fullness of God. This is a very ancient intuition of reality which goes back to the oldest Oriental thought. . . . For the "masculine-feminine" relationship is basic in all reality — simply because all reality mirrors the reality of God.

The poem "Hagia Sophia" names Wisdom as "the dark, nameless *Ousia* [essence or ground of being] of the Father, the Son, and the Holy Ghost, the 'primordial' darkness which is infinite light," "the wisdom of God," "the Tao, the nameless pivot of all being and nature," "the feminine child playing before God," "the mercy of God," "the feminine, dark, yielding, tender counterpart of the power, justice, creative dynamism of the Father."

The poem was printed privately by Hammer in January of 1962 as a limited edition imprint (Stamperia del Santuccio, Library Press) and reprinted in a second edition with Hammer's icon, based on a woodcut engraving, illustrating the text. The poem appeared in the magazine *Ramparts* in March of 1963, and became finally the centerpiece of Merton's book of poems, *Emblems of a Season of Fury* (New Directions, 1963). "Hagia Sophia" was written during a period in the early sixties when Merton was moving from a more parochial sensibility based on a sense of *fuga mundi* (flight from the world) to a universal, politically engaged, ecumenical Catholicism in which contemplation enters a dialectic with social action. In this poem he remains within the lyrical-meditative mode, experimenting with the long prose-poem, but not yet turning to the "anti-poetry" or more experimental forms of his later years evidenced in *Cables to the Ace* and *The Geography of Lograire*.

"Hagia Sophia" is an extended poetic meditation on Holy Wisdom. It alternates between a heightened, first-person lyric voice and the tone of a more formal hymn to Wisdom, blending private and public utterance. Set in the framework of the canonical hours of monastic prayer, it enacts the daily passage from morning to evening, waking to sleep. Each section corresponds to one of the liturgical hours: Dawn or *Lauds*, early morning or *Prime*, high morning or *Tierce*, and sunset or

Compline when the *Salve Regina* was sung at Gethsemani. The poem links Sophia to the Eternal Feminine, the cycles of the day, and the cycles of liturgical prayer.

Hagia Sophia, or Holy Wisdom, is invoked through a complex nexus of symbols. She is Wisdom, Sister, Bride, Mother, Nurse, Child, Muse, Lady Poverty (of St. Francis), Eve, Mary (Our Lady, the Blessed Virgin, Incarnation, Virgin), Mercy, Gift (*Donum Dei*), *Ousia*, *Natura Naturans* (creating nature as opposed to created nature or *Natura Naturata*), and the "unseen pivot of all nature." The names are archetypes embedded in the particularity of the poet-speaker's existential situation. Merton foregrounds the gentler qualities associated with woman in many cultures, such as tenderness, receptivity, pardon, grace, peacemaking and mercy. Yet Sophia is not simply the passive pole of a binary in which Spirit is privileged over matter, male over female, light over darkness, and strength over meekness — but a comprehensive and evolving presence best expressed in the mystical language of paradox. She is, for instance, both "God-given and God Himself as Gift" (III, 368). Experiencing her requires an "unknowing" or apophatic approach to language. As Merton puts it in the letter to Hammer, "[T]o arrive at her beauty we must pass through an apparent negation of created beauty." This is so because she is part of the uncreated ground of all Being. She is not merely one Person of a Hypostatic union in God (one of the Persons of the Trinity), but the ontological base of all things known and unknown. She is the mystery of the Godhead in both essence and existence, being and becoming. She cannot be known through her names or signs, but only approached through contemplation that moves toward oneness with her. She is, indeed, a figure of contemplation, since Merton makes it clear she is the ontological ground of both being and knowing in the self and in creation. As the *Ousia* of God in the world she is the silent center (pivot) in which the interior self and the Divine self converge. Merton writes in Section III:

> Perhaps in a certain very primitive aspect Sophia is the unknown, the dark, the nameless *Ousia*. Perhaps she is even the Divine Nature, One in Father, Son and Holy

Ghost. And perhaps she is in infinite light unmanifest, not even waiting to be known as Light.

MERTON'S SOURCES FOR "HAGIA SOPHIA":
BIBLICAL AND MYSTICAL

What is the provenance of this profoundly mysterious figure of whom Merton speaks so tentatively, using the word "perhaps"? His sources include his own interior and psychological awakening to the feminine as charted in his dreams and reflections, the figure of Wisdom in Judeo-Christian Wisdom literature, and the figure of Sophia in nineteenth-century Eastern Orthodox Russian mystical theology. His primary source, however, is the Wisdom tradition in the Hebrew Bible, allegorized both in Talmudic commentary and in Christianity. The original Hebrew words *Ruah* (Spirit), *Hokhmah* (Wisdom) and *Shekinah* (the female aspect of God) are either feminine or grammatically inclusive of both genders, suggesting what later feminists have seen as a repressed feminine aspect to the Godhead within patriarchal Judaism. Merton's principal source is *Proverbs* 8 and the Wisdom literature of the Bible such as the *Books of Wisdom* and *Ecclesiasticus*, where Wisdom is personified as a woman standing at the crossroads calling to humankind to follow her way of justice. She is also portrayed as a presence at creation, God's partner dancing the world into being. As a cosmological presence at creation, she was subsequently associated in the Gospel of John and the Pauline writings with Jesus as the *Logos* or Wisdom of God, similarly co-eternal with God in the beginning. Though Christ as the *Logos* or Word of God is masculine in his incarnation, he has been seen as a son of Wisdom, embodying her values of peace-making and mercy in the world. In the Jewish Wisdom literature Sophia is linked to both creative power and justice (judgment), not simply the traditional feminine role of gentle nurturer. Like the Christ as divine *Logos*, she represents God as cosmic Mediator.

Sophia in Merton's poem is also associated with the Bride, and Merton was, of course, well acquainted with the tradition of Christian ecclesiological symbolism drawn from both the *Song of Songs* and the book of *Revelation* in which the Church is the Bride of Christ. He had studied the long tradition of patristic commentary on the *Song of Songs* going back to Origen. Allegorically, the female beloved has been interpreted variously as Israel, the Church and as the soul in union with God. He knew Boethius' famous *Consolation of Philosophy*, featuring the figure of Sophia, and would have been familiar with the medieval use of feminine metaphors for God by both male and female monastics of the eleventh and twelfth centuries. Merton was immersed also in Christian mysticism which took up nuptial symbolism as an expression of the most intimate union of God and the soul in writers such as Bernard of Clairvaux, Catherine of Siena, John of the Cross and Teresa of Avila.

The fourteenth century English mystics, like the anonymous author of *The Cloud of Unknowing*, however, figure the most prominently in the poem, particularly Julian of Norwich. In March of 1961, around the time "Hagia Sophia" was written, Merton reflects in his journal, "I am still a 14th century man: the century of Eckhart, Ruysbroek, Tauler, the English recluses, the author of the *Cloud* . . . a lover of the dark cloud in which God is found by love." In section III of the poem he alludes parenthetically to the 14th century mystics, highlighting the mystical theology of Julian, who develops the image of Jesus as Mother in her *Revelations of Divine Love*:

> (When the recluses of fourteenth-century England heard their Church Bells and looked out upon the wolds and fens under a kind sky, they spoke in their hearts to "Jesus our Mother." It was Sophia that had awakened in their childlike hearts.) (III, 367)

THE RUSSIAN MYSTICAL THEOLOGIANS

Another wellspring for Merton's "Hagia Sophia" is Eastern Orthodoxy and, especially, the Russian Orthodox mystical theologians of the nineteenth and twentieth centuries. Merton's journals indicate he was reading Macarius Bulgakov and Nicholas Berdayev between 1957 - 1959, a few years prior to writing "Hagia Sophia," and around the time of his famous "Fourth and Walnut" epiphany recorded in *Conjectures of a Guilty By-*

stander. Merton reflects on Bulgakov's Sophianism in his journal, August 7, 1957, suggesting that if God as Sophia is immanent in creation, then all of nature is a theophany of God.

Matter and spirit, nature and God, immanence and transcendence are not severed into inseparable categories. Here Merton distances himself from the dualism of his youth toward a much more sacramental worldview in which Sophia is that in God which longs for incarnation:

> I think this morning I found the key to Bulgakov's Sophianism. His idea is that the Divine Sophia, play, wisdom, is by no means a fourth person or hypostasis, yet in creation . . . hypostasized, so that creation itself becomes the "Glory of God" . . .

Moving on from his reading of Bulgakov's *The Wisdom of God*, Merton implies that, if God is "hypostasized" (of one substance) with Sophia or the feminine principle in creation, then humankind's posture should not be one of control over nature, but of humility in light of our interconnectedness with her. Humankind's utter dependence on Sophia as Nurse, Mother, Sister, Beloved is, indeed, the central theme of "Hagia Sophia." Merton reflects in a journal entry of April 25, 1957:

> They [Bulgakov and Berdyaev] have dared to accept the challenge of the sapiential books, the challenge of the image of *Proverbs* where Wisdom is "playing in the world" before the face of the Creator.

For the Russians Sophia is God's *Ousia*, the matrix of the three hypostases – the Father, Son and Spirit. She is the Ground of Being of the created cosmos and the basis of the image of God in creation and humanity. She is humanly manifest in the maternity of Mary whose receptivity to God's purpose can only be understood as an expression of Holy Wisdom. In section IV of the poem, Merton celebrates Mary, the mother of Christ, as the earthly medium of the heavenly Sophia. Bulgakov's theory on the close relation between the Blessed Virgin and Sophia brought him under investigation by the Church in 1922 when he was accused of "promulgating the doctrine of an androgynous Christ" and characterizing God equally as "Father" and "Mother." In exploring the notion that Sophia is a disclosure of God in creation, these theologians were challenging the boundaries of the patriarchal orthodoxy of their times and re-introducing the feminine into an understanding of the Godhead.

Vladimir Soloviev (1853 - 1900), another Russian mystical theologian Merton was reading around this time, posits that God's other or feminine self is the universe, the world in which Wisdom desires to be incarnate.

Such a realization and incarnation is also the aspiration of the eternal Femininity itself, which is not merely an inert image in the Divine mind, but a living spiritual being possessed of all the fullness of powers and activities.

Soloviev sees Sophia as a cosmic feminine presence — both transcendent and immanent in the world. He suggests that all beings, like Adam and Eve made in God's image, are inwardly both male and female. This implies that God contains a balance of both male and female attributes. Like Soloviev, Merton in "Hagia Sophia" places much emphasis on littleness, meekness, hiddenness and childlikeness as powerful, transformative qualities in Sophia and in those who incarnate her presence.

The Russian mystical theologian who had the most impact on Merton's thought at this time was Paul Evdokimov (1901 - 1970), who taught at Saint-Serge in Paris, and wrote *La femme et le salut du monde* or *The Feminine and the Salvation of the World* (1945). Merton made a notation in his journal on this book on September 18, 1959 and spent much of his retreat in January of 1960 reading Evdokimov in the original French. Jonathan Montaldo calls this book "required reading . . . for appreciating the appearance of the dream figure 'Proverb' [Wisdom] in Merton's journals" of 1958 and points to Merton's "copious marginalia" in the original French edition of his copy. Evdokimov was also an expert on Greek Orthodox iconography and took the Orthodox perspective that a sacred *ikon* can mediate Divine Presence. It is significant that Merton's "Hagia Sophia" grew out of an act of gazing at a sacred image of Holy Wisdom. Through an act of participation in which the image mediates ultimate reality, the viewer may experience the actual presence of the saint, Christ, or — in this case — God revealed as Holy Wisdom.

For Evdokimov, as for Merton in "Hagia Sophia," Mary's virginity is not a sign of her difference from other women or her need for detachment from the "evils" of the flesh, but rather is symbolic of a state of "integrated being" (whole-ness) or child-like purity attainable by all. The Greek term *sophronsyne*, meaning, "integrity that is in conformity with Wis-dom," denotes a state of "ontological chastity." Hagia Sophia is a figure of immense power in Merton's poem precisely be-cause of such ontological purity. She is that in the human spirit which is incorruptible. God's purpose in Eastern Orthodox thought, as Evdokimov characterizes it, is not merely humankind's salvation from the effects of the Fall, but the res-toration of the original Divine Image in each person through the Incarnation. Like the *Logos* crowned and sent forth into the world by Mary-Sophia in Merton's poem, each person is born into the world to incarnate the lost or corrupted *Imago Dei*. In Eastern Orthodoxy the deification or *theosis* of human-kind is possible through mystical or interior transformation. Evdokimov calls Sophiology "the glory of Eastern Orthodoxy" because of its sacramental view of nature, writing that "the in-wardness of nature unfolds into the infinite." Sophia is this inward aspect of nature that opens out into the eternal pres-ence of God.

Psychological Nexus:
Hagia Sophia as Merton's Feminine Self

Merton's developing sense of an inward feminine principle also suggests a psychological level to the poem, where he em-braces the feminine not only theologically, but personally. As the son of a mother perceived as strong, distant and sometimes critical, and who died when he was six, Merton needed to reconnect to the feminine self or *anima* in his own psyche.

Yet the poem "Hagia Sophia" is only one stage in a slowly developing trajectory that began as early as his experience of the Virgin in Cuba, reflected in his early poem, "Song for Our Lady of Cobre," the product of his visit to the Basilica of Our Lady of Cobre as recorded in *The Seven Storey Mountain*.

Wisdom (as Proverb) figures prominently as well in Merton's well-known "Fourth and Walnut" epiphany described in *Conjectures of a Guilty Bystander* (1965), where he acknowledges himself not as someone set apart because of his religious vocation, but only a man among others with faces "shining like the sun." In a journal entry of February 28, 1958 that precedes the epiphany by eighteen days, he writes:

> I am embraced with determined and virginal passion by a young Jewish girl. She clings to me and will not let go, and I get to like the idea. I see that she is a nice kid in a plain, sincere sort of way. I reflect, "She belongs to the same race as St. Anne." I ask her name and she says her name is Proverb. I tell her that is a beautiful and significant name, but she does not appear to like it — perhaps the others have mocked her for it.

In his journal, where Merton expresses poignantly his sudden sense of profound interconnection with ordinary people on the street (including women), he reflects on the nature of this dream figure tied to St. Anne, the mother of Mary. It is clear from the context of the "letters" to Proverb in his journals preceding and following the well-known epiphany, that Proverb is for him a personalized figure of Wisdom. It is significant that his epiphany takes place at the public "crossroads" of Fourth and Walnut in downtown Louisville, for in *Proverbs* Wisdom cries out to men at the crossways or marketplace of life. It is as if Wisdom herself in the form of "Proverb" calls Merton the solitary monk to a sense of his deep involvement with the world and with women:

> For the woman-ness that is in each of them [each woman he saw on the street] is at once original and inexhaustibly fruitful bringing the image of God into the world. In this each one is Wisdom and Sophia and Our Lady — (my delights are to be with children of men!).

MERTON AND KARL STERN

A final contribution to Merton's developing sense of involvement with womankind (and with individual women) was his encounter with psychologist Karl Stern, a Jewish convert to Catholicism who visited the monastery in March 1958 and later published a book called *The Flight from Woman* (1965).

Stern critiques six western male writers — Descartes, Schopenhauer, Sartre, Ibsen, Tolstoy, Kierkegaard and Goethe — for harbouring an almost pathological fear of the feminine expressed both in their writings and in their personal lives. Though Stern assumes the archetypal feminine as essentially soft and receptive, he traces what he sees as an irrational misogyny ingrained in western culture, suggesting that fear-based attitudes toward woman and the earth with which she has been associated have led to the victimization and "colonization" of actual women. He argues that God is the ultimate ground of reciprocity of male and female powers in each person, and that mankind is essentially androgynous in origin and destination.

Jonathan Montaldo suggests that Merton's series of dreams of Proverb needs to be read in the context of Merton's exposure to these ideas, since the dreams and "the epiphany" on Fourth and Walnut Streets occur around the same time that Karl Stern visited Gethsemani and spoke to Merton's novices.

AN EXEGESIS OF "HAGIA SOPHIA"

I. Dawn. The Hour of *Lauds*.

This brief survey of Merton's personal and theological sources for "Hagia Sophia" allows for a richer tracing of the layered metaphors for Wisdom played out in the poem. The "*Lauds*" section, celebrating the Feast of Our Lady's Visitation (July 2), opens at 5:30 a.m. in a hospital where the speaker awakens to the gentle voice of "Hagia Sophia, speaking as my sister, Wisdom":

> There is in all visible things an invisible fecundity, a
> dimmed light, a meek namelessness, a hidden wholeness.

This mysterious Unity and Integrity is Wisdom, the Mother of all, *natura naturans*. (I, 363)

In July of 1960 Merton was hospitalized for several days. This section is strangely premonitory of Merton's encounter six years later with the student nurse called M. whom he met in a hospital in Louisville in 1966, and with whom he fell deeply in love. In a sense, "Hagia Sophia," with its passages about the soft voice of the Nurse awakening a hospitalized man, anticipates Merton's actual relationship with the student nurse called M. in the journals. The similarities in his language describing Sophia and M. certainly seem to suggest a Jungian "synchronicity" in which archetype and reality merge. In Merton's "Midsummer Diaries" (June 23, 1966), where he struggles with his love for M., he speaks of her in the same tone used to describe Proverb-Sophia:

I will never be without the mysterious, transcendent presence of her essential self that began to speak to me so stirringly and so beautifully those early mornings in May between sleeping and waking. She [M.] will always be to me her soft voice speaking out of the depths of my own heart saying that the central reality of all is found in our love that no one can touch and no one can alter.

"Hagia Sophia" opens in the early morning in a similar hypnogogic state where the soft voice of the Nurse arouses the patient from sleep. This section attempts to answer the question, "What is it like to awaken to the voice of Wisdom?" Oxymorons like "invisible fecundity" and "dimmed light" enable Merton to suggest that Wisdom is an active power deliberately tempered to meet human capacity. She is God's mercy encountering our poverty with her own "indescribable humility." The speaker compares this moment at dawn to humankind's stirring from a dream, Christ awakening in "all the separate selves," Adam first hearing the voice of Eve in paradise, and humanity (Christ) being awakened by the Blessed Virgin. Sophia's power to quicken through her voice echoes the divine "*Fiat*" of God at creation, the calling forth of new life through the Word. Here Merton may have in mind as well the Kabbalistic myth of "Adam

Kadmon," the primordial man whose fragments are drawn together at the voice of the Shekinah:

> It is like the first morning of the world (when Adam,
> at the sweet voice of Wisdom awoke from nonentity
> and knew her), and like the Last Morning of the world
> when all the fragments of Adam will return from death
> at the voice of Hagia Sophia, and will know where they
> stand. (I, 364)

Sophia is an eschatological presence active at both beginning
and ending – an *Alpha* and *Omega*. In Christian typology,
of course, it is common to read Eve as a type of Mary. In
the poem, however, Eve, Mary and Sophia form a kind of
Triune Feminine with Hagia Sophia taking the part of the
Holy Spirit as a feminine unifying presence. It is interesting
that the unification of the fragmented man and reintegration
of male and female powers in each person through love
and "mutual forgiveness" is the central myth of the later
William Blake, the Romantic poet who most continuously influenced Merton throughout his lifetime. In Blake's
mythos the reunion of male and female counterparts (the
Zoas with their feminine Emanations) resolves itself in the
final union of Albion with his bride Jerusalem. In this poem,
Merton emphasizes the utter dependency of humanity on the
feminine, its maternal "Nurse" Sophia, through a series of rhe-
torical questions:

> Who is more little, who is more poor than the help-
> less man who lies asleep in his bed without awareness and
> without defense? Who is more trusting than he who must
> entrust himself each night to sleep? (I, 364)

If Merton's central myth, like that of Blake, is the loss of an
original paradisal unity, this is a poem that enacts the possibility of healing (wholeness) through the presence of the feminine.

II. Early Morning. The Hour of *Prime*.

In Section II, or "*Prime*," the tone shifts from that of a
dreamer in the hypnogogic state describing Wisdom in tentative symbols and metaphors to that of prayer-like apostrophe:

"Oh blessed, silent one, who speaks everywhere!" The motif of awakening continues, but the tone turns to lament as the poet decries the community's collective rejection of Wisdom. In Evdokimov this renunciation is described in terms of the "darkening" of the image of Sophia in the world through man's overthrow of the sacred order. As in *Proverbs* 8, she cries out at the crossroads, but we seal our ears.

Merton uses *anaphora*, or repetition of initial phrases, to grieve this human resistance to Mercy who is, in a lovely turn of phrase, "the candor of God's light":

> We do not hear the soft voice. . . . We do not hear Mercy, or yielding love, or non-reprisal. . . . . We do not hear the uncomplaining pardon that bows down the innocent visages of flowers to the dewy earth. . . . . We do not see the Child. . . . (II, 365)

Section II is the most lyrical part of the poem. Drawing on the nature personification of the *Psalms* where setting stars and rising sun rejoice in the cycle of creation, the speaker advances from darkness into the light of consciousness by admitting "the clear silence of Sophia in his own heart" (II, 366). The archetypes of Wisdom as Mother and Sister modulate into that of the Child as incorruptible innocence, not the naïve innocence that refuses experience, but the inviolable purity of utmost interiority. Here Wisdom is something like what Merton elsewhere called the *point vierge*, or virgin center, of the heart. The Child is Wisdom playing before the throne of God in her elements of creativity and spontaneity.

> She [the Child] smiles, for though they have bound her, she cannot be a prisoner. Not that she is strong, or clever, but simply that she does not understand imprisonment. (II, 366)

Having awakened to the "pure simplicity" of Wisdom as the Child, the speaker prepares for the light of the rising sun.

III. High Morning. The Hour of *Tierce*.

In Section III (*Tierce* or High Morning), the Sun as the "Face of God" is again "diffused" into the softer light of Hagia Sophia, which shines from within each individual and in the created order ("in ten thousand things").

Though Merton accepts as unproblematic the traditional binaries of male and female as direct light versus mediated light, he emphasizes that God as Sophia is incarnate in creation as Mercy and Tenderness:

> He is at once Father and Mother. As Father He stands in solitary might surrounded by darkness. As Mother His shining is diffused, embracing all His creatures with merciful tenderness and light. The Diffuse Shining of God is Hagia Sophia. . . . In Sophia His power is experienced only as mercy and as love. (III, 367)

A feminist reading of the poem might find the identification of the feminine with mercy and tenderness problematic if doing so restricts the feminine to the "softer" virtues, or subordinates the feminine to the masculine in a hierarchical order. Feminist theorists have pointed out how God-language affects the lives of actual women. Such subordination of Sophia to a masculine God does not, in fact, occur in the poem, since qualities of tenderness and mercy are also demonstrable in God the Father when united with Sophia. We are told "He speaks to us gently in ten thousand things . . . " (III, 366). Also, Sophia exercises power and authority when she crowns the *Logos* and sends him forth into the world in section IV.

Ultimately, Sophia represents the darkness of "unknowing" as well as the dawn light. The metaphors for male and female are interconnected and interchangeable in the poem. God is not simply transcendent and Sophia immanent, or God active and Sophia passive. Gender metaphors are an expression of two aspects of a single dynamic at play, like Wisdom at the foundation of the world.

It is paradoxical that in section III, which celebrates high morning, Merton's poem turns to metaphors of darkness. The efforts to name Sophia, to catch her in the net of language defer to the apophatic tradition of "unnaming." Every naming becomes an unnaming, a backing off from language, and an insistence that words and names are inadequate before mystery. Sophia herself becomes "the unknown, the dark, the nameless." The "I" speaker summons words to back away from words: "I do not know where she is, in this Beginning. I do not speak of her as a Beginning, but as a manifestation." The entire section moves repeatedly from naming to unnaming: The speaker's struggle with language reminds us that all gender-bound metaphors for ultimate reality are inadequate, since God is not an object of knowledge. The God who is male and female, father and mother, is simultaneously neither male nor female, transcending gender categories.

Because Merton's metaphors move into the mystical language of *apophasis* or "unsaying," they remain fluid. Sophia is the "nameless *Ousia*," the unmanifest or unknown being of God.

IV. Sunset. The Hour of *Compline*. *Salve Regina*.

In the "*Compline*" section, Merton invokes the monks' evening singing of the *Salve Regina* and Sophia in her manifestation as "the Blessed Virgin Mary."

The *Salve Regina* is one of the seasonal *antiphons*, at the close of which the monks at the Abbey of Gethsemani extinguish all lights in the abbey church except one, directed at the image of the Virgin in a window over the altar. The poem ends with the return to sleep and darkness; yet the ending is the beginning of a new cycle in which the Virgin crowns Christ (mankind) and sends him forth into the world. In one of the monographs of "Hagia Sophia" printed by Hammer, Merton placed the following text from *Proverbs* 4:8-9, establishing the biblical source for the image: "Wisdom will honour you if you embrace her. She will place on your head a fair garland. She will bestow on you a crown of glory."

In "Hagia Sophia," Mary-Sophia, dressed in a simple Greco-Roman robe, crowns Christ as well as the Merton-speaker. She is not portrayed as the mother of an infant or as a royal Queen of Heaven. The poem establishes, through her sending forth of the *Logos* or Son, that we share a common humanity as ones who have undergone birth. As Christ or the *Logos*, the Incarnation of Wisdom, the Child goes forth to His destiny: crucifixion and resurrection. As humanity the child goes forth, an Everyman or Everywoman, into exile from paradise. The conclusion suggests the speaker's sense of his own homelessness, vagrancy and destitution as well as the position of Christ (born to us and in us) as an Incarnation of Feminine Wisdom. Wisdom's child, like Christ, "has nowhere to lay his head." The final passage presents a strangely modern figure of the exile or God as exile in us:

> A vagrant, a destitute wanderer with dusty feet, finds his way down a new road. A homeless God, lost in the night, without papers, without identification, without even a number, a frail expendable exile lies down in desolation under the sweet stars of the world and entrusts Himself to sleep. (IV, 371.)

The image of Sophia or the Divine Feminine crowning the *Logos* is an act of feminine power. The more traditional depictions of "the Coronation of the Virgin" in Christian art show Mary being crowned by Christ rather than she actively bestowing the crown upon Him. In Hammer's triptych and Merton's poem, the usual relation is inverted so that Sophia's tenderness and gentleness "crowns Him [Christ] not with what is glorious, but with what is greater than glory: the one thing greater than glory is weakness, nothingness, poverty" (IV, 370). In her crowning of Christ with his "human nature," she reminds us that all men and women come from a common womb (the earth, the Feminine) and are alike vulnerable, frail, and utterly dependent on the earth and the feminine matrix. The Christ-like potential in each is crowned (reaches its maturity or fulfillment) through gentleness and tenderness. Christ in this depiction is not external to us and apart, but within, poor and homeless in the world. What Wisdom requires is an utter extinguishing of ego, like the nightly entrusting of the self to sleep. The ego is a nameless "nobody" through whose *kenosis* or self-emptying Wisdom enters the world.

MERTON'S ANTICIPATION OF FEMINIST CONCERNS

Some feminists have expressed concern that the figure of Mary has been used to oppress women by holding up an impossible ideal of woman as both virgin and mother.

More recent feminist theorists of the "liberation theology" schools, however, see Mary as a *locus* of power for the disempowered because of her willing consent to the purpose of God and because of her *Magnificat*, which speaks of an eschatological reversal of the positions of oppressors and oppressed when God "[puts] down the mighty from their seats, and [exalts] them of low degree" (*Luke* 1:52). Merton exalts Mary for her humility, linking her to the cosmological creativity of Sophia as an image of the fullness of God. How gendered metaphors for God are contextualized culturally is significant, and the political and social implications of God-talk are crucial. Certainly, Merton's poetic texts on the feminine divine have to be read within a mystical tradition in which the ground of each person's being is consubstantial with the center of God. In this context, Wisdom offers to all (both men and women) a way of becoming divine or awakening to the divine Wisdom within.

"Hagia Sophia," though employing traditional polarities of male and female, avoids a dualistic framework that subordinates the female to the male or objectifies the feminine. Merton is aware of the radical unconventionality of the poem in terms of its treatment of the feminine in his journals (July 8, 1962): "The Hammers were here yesterday. Brought . . . the little paper of Hagia Sophia. . . . It is pretty, but my theology is strange in it. It needs revision and reformulation." Michael Mott, one of Merton's chief biographers, notes that "Hagia Sophia" was a kind of "secret work," circulated in mimeographed letters primarily to non-monastic artists and friends because it expressed Merton's "deepest and most unorthodox thought."

In what sense is "Hagia Sophia" unorthodox? Firstly, Merton celebrates the feminine in a culture where the feminine has been feared, denigrated and suppressed. Secondly, the poem implies that the salvation of humanity through the feminine is due to the values of peace, mercy and forgiveness that Sophia represents in her expressions of softness, tenderness and non-retaliation. Merton writes on Evdokimov in his journal:

> [T]he icon of wisdom, the dancing ikon — the summit
> reached by so many non-Christian contemplatives (would

that it were reached by a few Christians!) Summit of Vedanta – Faith in Sophia, *Natura naturans*, the great stabilizer today – for peace.

If one looks at the poem"Hagia Sophia" in the context of the book in which it was published, *Emblems of a Season of Fury*, the way in which Sophia calls for the transformation of the world through non-violence and non-retaliation is even more evident. Many poems about injustice, war and corruption lead up to and emerge from "Hagia Sophia," including some of Merton's most powerful poems, [such as], "There Has to be a Jail for Ladies," "And the Children of Birmingham," and "Chant to be Used in Procession Around a Site with Furnaces" Of all his books of poetry, *Emblems* is perhaps Merton's best at establishing the inseparability of the socio-political and the spiritual and striking a balance between his lyrical and ironic voices. Sophia becomes in the book the unifying ground of political action.

As a dissident within a patriarchal structure, Merton revives ancient feminine metaphors for the divine. Though he may be less conscious than later feminist theorists about projecting feminine images of God to correct a perceived imbalance, Merton's "Hagia Sophia," read in the context of his work as a whole, complements the work of later feminists by recovering lost feminine images and voices. Merton is aware that the sapiential (Sophiological) tradition had been marginalized within Western Christianity and attempts to restore it. Later, more radical forms of feminism have gone further in appropriating methods of deconstruction to destabilize and dismantle naïve forms of essentialism – the association of the feminine with stereotypical qualities. Later feminists would examine how social and linguistic constructions of the feminine affect power relations between men and women and contribute to the oppression of women. If God is idolized as a male authority figure, then women can be excluded from positions of power.

In terms of Cartesian dualisms of spirit over matter, transcendence over immanence, and so on, woman has been associated with the flesh, earth, matter (*mater*) and mothering, but not as much with spirit, power, justice. Some feminists have argued that the emphasis on transcendence as a flight from the body, nature, woman and the earth has led to a disembodied spirituality and a related devaluation of woman, while ecofeminists tie the devaluation of woman to the devaluation of nature.

CONCLUSION

Merton's use of feminine metaphors for God is part of a larger *nexus* in his work. "Hagia Sophia" is part of a long process of development in which he embraces not only feminine metaphors for God but opens himself to the feminine at many levels of being — through dreams and recollections, through intellectual engagement with feminist theologians [such as] Rosemary Ruether, through his relationship with M., through retreats and conferences with communities of religious women shortly before his death, and through his sense of Sophia in the earth and in the self. Merton is not interested in simply reversing the positions of oppressors and oppressed by replacing God the Father with "the Goddess." He uses gendered metaphors interchangeably to suggest a presence and a power beyond gender. What prevents "Hagia Sophia" from reinforcing gender stereotypes is the way Merton uses metaphors as tentative approximations of a nameless mystery. Merton's Sophia is not just the feminine face of a masculine God, or a masculine God with feminine attributes (God in a skirt), but an active power permeating all things.

In "Hagia Sophia" Merton is not a systematic philosopher or theologian, but a poet intuitively receiving and shaping images and symbols for the divine. A poem is a play of metaphors and silences rather than a theological construct. Unlike critical theory or philosophy of religion, his poem does not deconstruct gender paradigms, but makes "old things new" through the transforming power of imagination. While Merton recognizes the limitations of language, he assumes a metaphysical and ontological ground of being beyond language; that is, the "real presence" of Wisdom behind and within the signs.

WORKS CITED

- Paul Evdokimov, *Woman and the Salvation of the World*. Crestwood, New York: St. Vladimir's Seminary Press, 1994.
- Sister Therese Lentfoehr, *Words and Silence: On the Poetry of Thomas Merton*. New York: New Directions, 1979.
- Caitlin Matthews, *Sophia, Goddess of Wisdom: the Divine Feminine from Black Goddess to World-Soul*. Hammersmith, London: Mandala Press, 1991.
- Thomas Merton, *The Collected Poems of Thomas Merton*. New York: New Directions, 1977.
- Thomas Merton, *Conjectures of a Guilty Bystander*. New York: Doubleday & Co., 1968.
- Thomas Merton, *Learning to Love (Journals VI): Exploring Solitude and Freedom, 1966-1967*. Edited by Christine Bochan. New York: HarperCollins, 1997.
- Thomas Merton, *A Search for Solitude (Journals III): Pursuing the Monk's True Life, 1952-1960*. Edited by Lawrence S. Cunningham. San Francisco: HarperCollins, 1996.
- Thomas Merton, *The Seven Storey Mountain*. New York: Harcourt Brace & Co., 1948.
- Thomas Merton, *Turning Toward the World (Journals IV): The Pivotal Years, 1960-1963*. Edited by Victor A. Kramer. San Francisco: HarperCollins, 1996.
- Thomas Merton, *Witness to Freedom: Letters in Times of Crisis*. Edited by William H. Shannon. San Diego: Harcourt Brace & Co., 1994.
- Jonathan Montaldo, "A Gallery of Women's Faces," in *The Merton Annual: Studies in Culture, Spirituality and Social Concerns*, Vol. 14. (Sheffield Academic Press, 2001), pages 155-172.
- Michael Mott, *The Seven Mountains of Thomas Merton*. Boston: Houghton Mifflin, 1984.
- Rosemary Radford Ruether, *New Woman, New Earth: Sexist Ideologies and Human Liberation*. San Francisco: Harper & Row, 1975.
- Vladimir Solovyov, *The Meaning of Love*. Introduction by Owen Barfield. Hudson, New York: Lindisfarne Press, 1985.
- Karl Stern, *The Flight from Woman*. New York: Farrar, Straus & Giroux, 1965.
- Robert G. Waldron, *Thomas Merton in Search of His Soul: A Jungian Perspective*. Notre Dame, Indiana: Ave Maria Press, 1994.

11

HAGIA SOPHIA[1]

Thomas Merton

I. Dawn. The Hour of *Lauds.*

There is in all visible things an invisible fecundity, a dimmed light, a meek namelessness, a hidden wholeness. This mysterious Unity and Integrity is Wisdom, the Mother of all, *Natura naturans.* There is in all things an inexhaustible sweetness and purity, a silence that is a fount of action and joy. It rises up in wordless gentleness and flows out to me from the unseen roots of all created being, welcoming me tenderly, saluting me with indescribable humility. This is at once my own being, my own nature, and the Gift of my Creator's Thought and Art within me, speaking as Hagia Sophia, speaking as my sister, Wisdom.

I am awakened, I am born again at the voice of this my Sister, sent to me from the depths of the divine fecundity.

Let us suppose I am a man lying asleep in a hospital. I am indeed this man lying asleep. It is July the second, the Feast of Our Lady's Visitation. A Feast of Wisdom.

At five-thirty in the morning I am dreaming in a very quiet room when a soft voice awakens me from my dream. I am like all mankind awakening from all the dreams that ever were dreamed in all the nights of the world. It is like the One Christ awakening in all the separate selves that ever were separate and isolated and alone in all the lands of the earth. It is like all minds coming back together into awareness from all distractions, cross-purposes and confusions, into unity of love. It is like the first morning of the world (when Adam, at the sweet voice of Wisdom awoke from nonentity and knew her), and like the Last Morning of the world when all the fragments of Adam will return from death at the voice of Hagia Sophia, and will know where they stand.

Such is the awakening of one man, one morning, at the voice of a nurse in the hospital. Awakening out of languor and darkness, out of helplessness, out of sleep, newly confronting reality and finding it to be gentleness.

It is like being awakened by Eve. It is like being awakened by the Blessed Virgin. It is like coming forth from primordial nothingness and standing in clarity, in Paradise.

Thus Wisdom cries out to all who will hear (*Sapientia clamitat in plateis*) and she cries out particularly to the little, to the ignorant and the helpless.

Who is more little, who is more poor than the helpless man who lies asleep in his bed without awareness and without defense? Who is more trusting than he who must entrust himself each night to sleep? What is the reward of his trust? Gentleness comes to him when he is most helpless and awakens him, refreshed, beginning to be made whole. Love takes him by the hand, and opens to him the doors of another life, another day.

(But he who has defended himself, fought for himself in sickness, planned for himself, guarded himself, loved himself alone and watched over his own life all night, is killed at last by exhaustion. For him there is no newness. Everything is stale and old.)

When the helpless one awakens strong at the voice of mercy, it is as if Life his Sister, as if the Blessed Virgin, (his own flesh, his own sister), as if nature made wise by God's Art and Incarnation were to stand over him and invite him with unutterable sweetness to be awake and to live. This is what it means to recognize Hagia Sophia.

II. Early Morning. The Hour of *Prime*.

O blessed, silent one, who speaks everywhere!

We do not hear the soft voice, the gentle voice, the merciful and feminine.

We do not hear mercy, or yielding love, or non-resistance, or non-reprisal. In her there are no reasons and no answers. Yet she is the candor of God's light, the expression of His simplicity.

We do not hear the uncomplaining pardon that bows down the innocent visages of flowers to the dewy earth. We do not see the Child who is prisoner in all the people, and who says nothing. She smiles, for though they have bound her, she cannot be a prisoner. Not that she is strong, or clever, but simply that she does not understand imprisonment.

The helpless one, abandoned to sweet sleep, him the gentle one will awake: Sophia.

All that is sweet in her tenderness will speak to him on all sides in everything, without ceasing, and he will never be the same again. He will have awakened not to conquest and dark pleasure but to the impeccable pure simplicity of One consciousness in all and through all: one Wisdom, one Child, one Meaning, one Sister.

The stars rejoice in their setting, and in the rising of the Sun. The heavenly lights rejoice in the going forth of one man to make a new world in the morning, because he has come out of the confused primordial dark night into consciousness. He has expressed the clear silence of Sophia in his own heart. He has become eternal.

III. High Morning. The Hour of *Tierce*.

The sun burns in the sky like the Face of God, but we do not know his countenance as terrible. His light is diffused in the air and the light of God is diffused by Hagia Sophia.

We do not see the Blinding One in black emptiness. He speaks to us gently in ten thousand things, in which His light is one fullness and one Wisdom.

Thus He shines not on them but from within them. Such is the loving-kindness of Wisdom.

All the perfection of created things are also in God; and therefore He is at once Father and Mother. As Father He stands in solitary might surrounded by darkness. As Mother His shining is diffused, embracing all His creatures with merciful tenderness and light. The Diffuse Shining of God is Hagia Sophia. We call her His "glory." In Sophia His power is experienced only as mercy and as love.

(When the recluses of fourteenth-century England heard their Church Bells and looked out upon the wolds and fens under a kind sky, they spoke in their hearts to "Jesus our Mother." It was Sophia that had awakened in their childlike hearts.)

Perhaps in a certain very primitive aspect Sophia is the unknown, the dark, the nameless *Ousia*. Perhaps she is even the Divine Nature, One in Father, Son and Holy Ghost. And perhaps she is in infinite light unmanifest, not even wanting to be known as Light. This I do not know. Out of the silence Light is spoken. We do not hear it or see it until it is spoken.

In the Nameless Beginning, without Beginning, was the Light. We have not seen this Beginning. I do not know where she is, in this Beginning. I do not speak of her as a Beginning, but as a manifestation.

Now the Wisdom of God, Sophia, come forth, reaching from "end to end mightily." She wills to be also the unseen pivot of all nature, the center and significance of all the light that is *in* all and *for* all. That which is poorest and humblest, that which is most hidden in all things is nevertheless most obvious in them, and quite manifest, for it is their own self that stands before us, naked and without care.

Sophia, the feminine child, is playing in the world, obvious and unseen, playing at all times before the Creator. Her delights are to be with the children of men. She is their sister. The core of life that exists in all things is tenderness, mercy, virginity, the Light, the Life considered as passive, as received, as given, as taken, as inexhaustibly renewed by the Gift of God. Sophia is Gift, is Spirit, *Donum Dei*. She is God-given and God Himself as Gift. God as all, and God reduced to Nothing: inexhaustible nothingness. *Exinanivit semetipsum*. Humility as the source of unfailing light.

Hagia Sophia in all things is the Divine Life reflected in them, considered as a spontaneous participation, as their invitation to the Wedding Feast.

Sophia is God's sharing of Himself with creatures. His outpouring, and the Love by which He is given, and known, held and loved.

She is in all things like the air receiving the sunlight. In her they prosper. In her they glorify God. In her they rejoice to reflect Him. In her they are united with him. She is the union between them. She is the Love that unites them. She is life as communion, life as thanksgiving, life as praise, life as festival, life as glory.

Because she receives perfectly there is in her no stain. She is love without blemish, and gratitude without self-complacency. All things praise her by being themselves and by sharing in the Wedding Feast. She is the Bride and the Feast and the Wedding. The feminine principle in the world is the inexhaustible source of creative realization of the Father's glory. She is His manifestation in radiant splendor! But she remains unseen, glimpsed only by a few. Sometimes there are none who know her at all.

Sophia is the mercy of God in us. She is the tenderness with which the infinitely mysterious power of pardon turns the darkness of our sins into the light of grace. She is the inexhaustible fountain of kindness, and would almost seem to be, in herself, all mercy. So she does in us a greater work than that of Creation: the work of new being in grace, the work of pardon, the work of transformation from brightness to brightness *tamquam a Domini Spiritu*. She is in us the yielding and tender counterpart of the power, justice and creative dynamism of the Father.

IV. Sunset. The Hour of *Compline*. *Salve Regina*.

Now the Blessed Virgin Mary is the one created being who enacts and shows forth in her life all that is hidden in Sophia. Because of this she can be said to be a personal manifestation of Sophia, Who in God is *Ousia* rather than Person.

Natura in Mary becomes pure Mother. In her, *Natura* is as she was from the origin from her divine birth. In Mary *Natura* is all wise and is manifested as an all-prudent, all-loving, all-pure person: not a Creator, and not a Redeemer, but perfect Creature, perfectly Redeemed, the fruit of all God's great power, the perfect expression of wisdom in mercy.

It is she, it is Mary, Sophia, who in sadness and joy, with the full awareness of what she is doing, sets upon the Second Person, the *Logos*, a crown which is His Human Nature. Thus her consent opens the door of created nature, of time, of history, to the Word of God.

God enters into His creation. Through her wise answer, through her obedient understanding, through the sweet yielding consent of Sophia, God enters without publicity into the city of rapacious men.

She crowns Him not with what is glorious, but with what is greater than glory: the one thing greater than glory is weakness, nothingness, poverty.

She sends the infinitely Rich and Powerful One forth as poor and helpless, in His mission of inexpressible mercy, to die for us on the Cross.

The shadows fall. The stars appear. The birds begin to sleep. Night embraces the silent half of the earth.

A vagrant, a destitute wanderer with dusty feet, finds his way down a new road. A homeless God, lost in the night, without papers, without identification, without even a number, a frail expendable exile lies down in desolation under the sweet stars of the world and entrusts Himself to sleep.

NOTE

1. Thomas Merton, *The Collected Poems of Thomas Merton*. (New York: New Directions Publishing Co., 1977), pages 363-371.

PART III

HESYCHASM IN THE WRITING OF THOMAS MERTON

A hermit of Mount Athos.

1

THE CLIMATE OF MONASTIC PRAYER[1]

Thomas Merton

"He who walks in darkness, to whom no light appears,
let him trust in the Name of Yahweh, let him rely upon his God."
— *Isaiah 50:10*

"I will give them a heart to understand that I am Yahweh,
and they shall be my people and I will be their God
when they return to me with all their heart."
— *Jeremiah 24:7*

INTRODUCTION

The monk is a Christian who has responded to a special call from God, and has withdrawn from the more active concerns of a worldly life, in order to devote himself completely to repentance, "conversion," *metanoia*, renunciation and prayer. In positive terms, we must understand the monastic life above all as a life of prayer. The negative elements, solitude, fasting, obedience, penance, renunciation of property and of ambition, are all intended to clear the way so that prayer, meditation and contemplation may fill the space created by the abandonment of other concerns.

What is written about prayer in these pages is written primarily for monks. However, just as a book about psychoanalysis by an analyst and primarily for analysts may also (if it is not too technical) appeal to a layman interested in these matters, so a practical, non-academic study of monastic prayer should be of interest to all Christians, since every Christian is bound to be in some sense a man of prayer. Though few have either the desire for solitude or the vocation to monastic life, all Christians ought to be able to read and make use of what is here said for monks, adapting it to the circumstances of their own vocation. Certainly, in the pressures of modern urban life, many will face the need for a certain interior silence and discipline simply to keep themselves together, to maintain their human and Christian identity and their spiritual freedom. To promote this they may often look for moments of retreat and prayer in which to deepen their meditative life. These pages discuss prayer in its very nature, rather than special restricted techniques. What is said here is therefore applicable to the prayer of any Christian, though perhaps with a little less emphasis on the intensity of certain trials which are proper to life in solitude.

Monastic prayer is, first of all, essentially simple. In primitive monasticism prayer was not necessarily liturgical, though liturgy soon came to be regarded as a specialty of monks and canons. Actually, the first monks in Egypt and Syria had only the most rudimentary liturgy, and their personal prayer was direct and uncomplicated. For example, we read in the sayings of the Desert Fathers[2] that a monk asked St. Macarius how to pray. The latter replied: "It is not necessary to use many words. Only stretch out your arms and say: Lord, have pity on me as you desire and as you well know how! And if the enemy presses you hard, say: Lord, come to my aid!" In John Cassian's *Conferences on Prayer*[3] we see great stress laid by the early monks on simple prayer made up of short phrases drawn from the Psalms or other parts of Scripture. One of the most frequently used was *Deus in adjutorium meum intende*, "O God, come to my aid!"[4]

At first sight one might wonder what such simple prayers would have to do with a life of "contemplation." The Desert Fathers did not imagine themselves, in the first place, to be mystics, though in fact they often were. They were careful not to go looking for extraordinary experiences, and contented themselves with the struggle for "purity of heart" and for control of their thoughts, to keep their minds and hearts empty of care and concern, so that they might altogether forget themselves and apply themselves entirely to the love and service of God.

This love expressed itself first of all in love for God's Word. Prayer was drawn from the Scriptures, especially from the Psalms. The first monks looked upon the Psalter not only as a kind of compendium of all the other books of the Bible, but as a book of special efficacy for the ascetic life, in that it revealed the secret movements of the heart in its struggle against the forces of darkness.[5] The "battle Psalms" were all interpreted as referring to the inner war with passion and with the demons. Meditation was above all *meditatio scripturarum.*[6] But we must not imagine the early monks applying themselves to a very intellectual and analytical "meditation" of the Bible. Meditation for them consisted in making the words of the Bible their own by memorizing them and repeating them, with deep and simple concentration, "from the heart." Therefore the "heart" comes to play a central role in this primitive form of monastic prayer.

St. Macarius was asked to explain a phrase of a Psalm: "The meditation of my heart is in your sight." He proceeded to give one of the earliest descriptions of that "prayer of the heart" which consisted in invoking the name of Christ, with profound attention, in the very ground of one's being, that is to say in "the heart" considered as the root and source of all one's own inner truth. To invoke the name of Christ "in one's heart" was equivalent to calling upon him with the deepest and most earnest intensity of faith, manifested by the concentration of one's entire being upon a prayer stripped of all non-essentials and reduced to nothing but the invocation of his name with a simple petition for help. Macanus said: "There is no other perfect meditation than the saving and blessed Name of Our Lord Jesus Christ dwelling without interruption in you, as it is written: 'I will cry out like the swallow and I will meditate like the turtledove!' This is what is done by the devout man who perseveres in invoking the saving Name of Our Lord Jesus Christ."[7]

The monks of the Oriental Churches in Greece and Russia have for centuries used a handbook of prayer called the *Philokalia.* This is an anthology of quotations from Eastern monastic Fathers from the third century to the Middle Ages, all concerned with this "prayer of the heart" or "prayer of Jesus." In the school of hesychastic contemplation which flourished in the monastic centers of Sinai and Mount Athos, this type of prayer was elaborated into a special, almost esoteric, technique. In the present study we will not go into the details of this technique which has at times (rather irresponsibly) been compared to yoga. We will only emphasize the essential simplicity of monastic prayer in the primitive "prayer of the heart" which consisted in interior recollection, the abandonment of distracting thoughts and the humble invocation of the Lord Jesus with words from the Bible in a spirit of intense faith. This simple practice is considered to be of crucial importance in the monastic prayer of the Eastern Church, since the sacramental power of the Name of Jesus is believed to bring the Holy Spirit into the heart of the praying monk. A typical traditional text says:

> A man is enriched by the faith, and by the hope and humility with which he calls on the most sweet Name of Our Lord Jesus Christ; and he is enriched also by peace and love. For these are truly a three-stemmed life-giving tree planted by God. A man touching it in due time and eating of it, as is fitting, shall gather unending and eternal life, instead of death, like Adam. . . . Our glorious teachers . . . in whom liveth the Holy Spirit, wisely teach us all, especially those who have wished to embrace the field of divine silence (i.e. monks) and consecrate themselves to God, having renounced the world, to practice *hesychasm* with wisdom, and to prefer his mercy with undaunted hope. Such men would have, as their constant practice and occupation, the invoking of his holy and most sweet Name, bearing it always in the mind, in the heart and on the lips . . . . [8]

The practice of keeping the Name of Jesus ever present in the ground of one's being was, for the ancient monks, the secret of the "control of thoughts," and of victory over temptation. It accompanied all the other activities of the monastic life imbuing them with prayer. It was the essence of monastic meditation, a special form of that practice of the presence of God which St. Benedict in turn made the cornerstone of monastic life and monastic meditation. This basic and simple practice could of course be expanded to include the thought of the passion, death and resurrection of Christ, which St. Athanasius was among the first to associate with the different canonical hours of prayer.[9]

However, in the interests of simplicity, we will concentrate upon the most elementary form of monastic meditation, and will discuss prayer of the heart as a way of keeping oneself in the presence of God and of reality, rooted in one's own inner truth. We will appeal to ancient texts on occasion, but our development of the theme will be essentially modern.

After all, some of the basic themes of the existentialism of Heidegger, laying stress as they do on the ineluctable fact of death, on man's need for authenticity, and on a kind of spiritual liberation, can remind us that the climate in which monastic prayer flourished is not altogether absent from our modern world. Quite the contrary: this is an age that, by its very nature as a time of crisis, of revolution, of struggle, calls for the special searching and questioning which are the work of the monk in his meditation and prayer. For the monk searches not only his own heart: he plunges deep into the heart of that world of which he remains a part although he seems to have "left" it. In reality the monk abandons the world only in order to listen more intently to the deepest and most neglected voices that proceed from its inner depth.

This is why the term "contemplation" is both insufficient and ambiguous when it is applied to the highest forms of Christian prayer. Nothing is more foreign to authentic monastic and "contemplative" (e.g. Carmelite) tradition in the Church than a kind of gnosticism which would elevate the contemplative above the ordinary Christian by initiating him into a realm of esoteric knowledge and experience, delivering him from the ordinary struggles and sufferings of human existence, and elevating him to a privileged state among the spiritually pure, as if he were almost an angel, untouched by matter and passion, and no longer familiar with the economy of sacraments, charity and the Cross. The way of monastic prayer is not a subtle escape from the Christian economy of incarnation and redemption. It is a special way of following Christ, of sharing in his passion and resurrection and in his redemption of the world. For that very reason the dimensions of prayer in solitude are those of man's ordinary anguish, his self-searching, his moments of nausea at his own vanity, falsity and capacity for betrayal. Far from establishing one in unassailable narcissistic security, this way of prayer brings us face to face with the sham and indignity of the false self that seeks to live for itself alone and to enjoy the "consolation of prayer" for its own sake. This "self" is pure illusion, and ultimately he who lives for and by such an illusion must end either in disgust or in madness.

On the other hand, we must admit that social life, so-called "worldly life," in its own way promotes this illusory and narcissistic existence to the very limit. The curious state of alienation and confusion of man in modern society is perhaps more "bearable" because it is lived in common, with a multitude of distractions and escapes — and also with opportunities for fruitful action and genuine Christian self-forgetfulness. But underlying all life is the ground of doubt and self-questioning which sooner or later must bring us face to face with the ultimate meaning of our life. This self-questioning can never be without a certain existential "dread" — a sense of insecurity, of "lostness," of exile, of sin. A sense that one has somehow been untrue not so much to abstract moral or social norms but to one's own inmost truth. "Dread" in this sense is not simply a childish fear of retribution, or a naive guilt, a fear of violating taboos. It is the profound awareness that one is capable of ultimate bad faith with himself and with others: that one is living a lie.

The peculiar monastic dimension of this struggle lies in the fact that society itself, institutional life, organization, the "approved way," may in fact be encouraging us in falsity and illusion. The deep root of monastic "dread" is the inner conflict which makes us guess that in order to be true to God and to ourselves we must break with the familiar, established and secure norms and go off into the unknown. "Unless a man hate his father and mother . . . " These words of Christ give some indication of the deep conflict which underlies all Christian conversion — the turning to a freedom based no longer on social approval and relative alienation, but on direct dependence on an invisible and inscrutable God, in pure faith.

It must be said at once that this struggle does not end at the gate of a monastery, and often it may come to light again in a conflict over one's monastic vocation. The purpose of monastic renewal and reform is to find ways in which monks and sisters can remain true to their vocation by deepening and developing it in new ways, not merely sacrificing their lives to bolster up antique structures, but channeling their efforts into the creation of new forms of monastic life, new areas of contemplative experience.

This is precisely the monk's chief service to the world: this silence, this listening, this questioning, this humble and courageous exposure to what the world ignores about itself — both good and evil. If, in the latter part of this study, we speak frequently of the concept of "dread," it will be in this existential sense.

The monk who is truly a man of prayer and who seriously faces the challenge of his vocation in all its depth is by that very fact exposed to existential dread. He experiences in himself the emptiness, the lack of authenticity, the quest for fidelity, the "lostness" of modern man, but he experiences all this in an altogether different and deeper way than does man in the modern world, to whom this disconcerting awareness of himself and of his world comes rather as an experience of boredom and of spiritual disorientation. The monk confronts his own humanity and that of his world at the deepest and most central point where the void seems to open out into black despair. The monk confronts this serious possibility, and rejects it, as Camusian man confronts "the absurd" and transcends it by his freedom. The option of absolute despair is turned into perfect hope by the pure and humble supplication of monastic prayer. The monk faces the worst, and discovers in it the hope of the best. From the darkness comes light. From death, life. From the abyss there comes, unaccountably, the mysterious gift of the Spirit sent by God to make all things new, to transform the created and redeemed world, and to re-establish all things in Christ.

This is the creative and healing work of the monk, accomplished in silence, in nakedness of spirit, in emptiness, in humility. It is a participation in the saving death and resurrection of Christ. Therefore every Christian may, if he so desires, enter into communion with this silence of the praying and meditating Church, which is the Church of the Desert.

NOTES

1. Thomas Merton's Introduction to *The Climate of Monastic Prayer* was first published by Cistercian Publications in *Cistercian Studies* Number 1 in 1973.

2. *Apothegmata*, 19, P.G. 34:249.

3. *Conference 10.*

4. Psalm 69:2.

5. St. Athanasius, *Ep. ad Marcellinum.*

6. Cf. Dom Jean Leclercq, *Love of Learning and the Desire of God* (New York: Fordham University Press, 1961), Chapters I and IV.

7. From Arnelineau, quoted by *Reach in Doctrine Ascetique des Premiers Maitres Egyptiens*, page 151.

8. Kadloubovsky and Palmer, *Writings from the Philokalia on Prayer of the Heart*, pages 172-173.

9. *De Virginitate 12-16.*

Nineteenth century Russian icon.

2

THE WISDOM OF THE DESERT[1]
Sayings from the Desert Fathers of the Fourth Century

Thomas Merton

INTRODUCTION

In the fourth century A.D. the deserts of Egypt, Palestine, Arabia and Persia were peopled by a race of men who have left behind them a strange reputation. They were the first Christian hermits, who abandoned the cities of the pagan world to live in solitude. Why did they do this? The reasons were many and various, but they can all be summed up in one word as the quest for "salvation." And what was salvation? Certainly it was not something they sought in mere exterior conformity to the customs and dictates of any social group. In those days men had become keenly conscious of the strictly individual character of "salvation." Society — which meant pagan society, limited by the horizons and prospects of life "in this world" — was regarded by them as a shipwreck from which each single individual man had to swim for his life. We need not stop here to discuss the fairness of this view: what matters is to remember that it was a fact. These were men who believed that to let oneself drift along, passively accepting the tenets and values of what they knew as society, was purely and simply a disaster. The fact that the Emperor was now Christian and that the "world" was coming to know the Cross as a sign of temporal power only strengthened them in their resolve.

It should seem to us much stranger than it does, this paradoxical flight from the world that attained its greatest dimensions (I almost said frenzy) when the "world" became officially Christian. These men seem to have thought, as a few rare modern thinkers like Berdyaev have thought, that there is really no such thing as a "Christian state." They seem to have doubted that Christianity and politics could ever be mixed to such an extent as to produce a fully Christian society. In other words, for them the only Christian society was spiritual and extramundane: the Mystical Body of Christ. These were surely extreme views, and it is almost scandalous to recall them in a time like ours when Christianity is accused on all sides of preaching negativism and withdrawal — of having no effective way of meeting the problems of the age. The Desert Fathers did, in fact, meet the "problems of their time" in the sense that *they* were among the few who were ahead of their time, and opened the way for the development of a new man and a new society. They represent what modern social philosophers (Jaspers, Mumford) call the emergence of the "axial man," the forerunner of the modern personalist man. The eighteenth and nineteenth centuries with their pragmatic individualism degraded and corrupted the psychological heritage of axial man with its debt to the Desert Fathers and other contemplatives, and prepared the way for the great regression to the herd mentality that is taking place now.

The flight of these men to the desert was neither purely negative nor purely individualistic. They were not rebels against society. True, they were in a certain sense "anarchists," and it will do no harm to think of them in that light. They were men who did not believe in letting themselves be passively guided and ruled by a decadent state, and who believed that there was a way of getting along without slavish dependence on accepted, conventional values. But they did not intend to place themselves above society. They did not reject society with proud contempt, as if they were superior to other men. On the contrary, one of the reasons why they fled from the world of men was that in the world men were divided into those who were successful, and imposed their will on others, and those who had to give in and be imposed upon. The Desert Fathers declined to be ruled by men, but had no desire to rule over others themselves. Nor did they fly from human fellowship — the very fact that they uttered these "words" of advice to one another is proof that they were eminently social. The society they sought was one where all men were truly equal, where the only authority under God was the charismatic authority of wisdom, experience and love. Of course, they acknowledged the benevolent, hierarchical authority of their bishops: but the bishops were far away and said little about what went on in the desert until the great Origenist conflict at the end of the fourth century.

What the Fathers sought most of all was their own true self, in Christ. And in order to do this, they had to reject completely the false, formal self, fabricated under social compulsion in "the world." They sought a way to God that was uncharted and freely chosen, not inherited from others who had mapped it out beforehand. They sought a God whom they alone could find, not one who was "given" in a set, stereotyped form by somebody else. Not that they rejected any of the dogmatic formulas of the Christian faith: they accepted and clung to them in their simplest and most elementary shape. But they were slow (at least in the beginning, in the time of their primitive wisdom) to get involved in theological controversy. Their flight to the arid horizons of the desert meant also a refusal to be content with arguments, concepts and technical verbiage.

We deal here exclusively with hermits. There were also cenobites in the desert — cenobites by the hundred and by the thousand, living the "common life" in enormous monasteries like the one founded by St. Pachomius at Tabenna. Among these there was a social order, almost military discipline. Nevertheless the spirit was still very much a spirit of personalism and freedom, because even the cenobite knew that his Rule was only an exterior framework, a kind of scaffolding with which he was to help himself build the spiritual structure of his own life with God. But the hermits were in every way more free. There was nothing to which they had to "conform" except the secret, hidden, inscrutable will of God which might differ very notably from one cell to another! It is very significant that one of the first of these *Verba* (Number 3) is one in which the authority of St. Anthony is adduced for what is the basic principle of desert life: that God is the authority and that apart from His manifest will there are few or no principles: "Therefore, whatever you see your soul to desire according to God, do that thing, and you shall keep your heart safe."

Obviously such a path could only be traveled by one who was very alert and very sensitive to the landmarks of a trackless wilderness. The hermit had to be a man mature in faith, humble and detached from himself to a degree that is altogether terrible. The spiritual cataclysms that sometimes overtook some of the presumptuous visionaries of the desert are there to show the dangers of the lonely life — like bones whitening in the sand. The Desert Father could not afford to be an illuminist. He could not dare risk attachment to his own ego, or the dangerous ecstasy of self-will. He could not retain the slightest identification with his superficial, transient, self-constructed self. He had to lose himself in the inner, hidden reality of a self that was transcendent, mysterious, half-known, and lost in Christ. He had to die to the values of transient existence as Christ had died to them on the Cross, and rise from the dead with Him in the light of an entirely new wisdom. Hence the life of sacrifice, which started out from a clean break, separating the monk from the world. A life continued in "compunction" which taught him to lament the madness of attachments to unreal values. A life of solitude and labor, poverty and fasting, charity and prayer which enabled the old superficial self to be purged away and permitted the gradual emergence of the true, secret self in which the Believer and Christ were "one Spirit."

Finally, the proximate end of all this striving was "purity of heart" — a clear unobstructed vision of the true state of affairs, an intuitive grasp of one's own inner reality as anchored, or rather lost, in God through Christ. The fruit of this was *quies*: "rest." Not rest of the body, not even fixation of the exalted spirit upon some pious point or summit of light. The Desert Fathers were not, for the most part, ecstatics. Those who were have left some strange and misleading stories behind them to confuse the true issue. The "rest" which these men sought was simply the sanity and poise of a being that no longer has to look at itself because it is carried away by the perfection of freedom that is in it. And carried where? Wherever Love itself, or the Divine Spirit, sees fit to go. Rest, then, was a kind of simple nowhereness and no-mindedness that had lost all preoccupation with a false or limited "self." At peace in the possession of a sublime "Nothing," the spirit laid hold, in secret, upon the "All" — without trying to know what it possessed.

Now the Fathers were not even sufficiently concerned with the nature of this rest to speak of it in these terms, except very rarely, as did St. Anthony, when he remarked that "the prayer of the monk is not perfect until he no longer realizes himself or the fact that he is praying." And this was said casually, in passing. For the rest, the Fathers steered clear of everything lofty, everything esoteric, everything theoretical or difficult to understand. That is to say, they refused to talk about such things. And for that matter they were not willing to talk about anything else, which accounts for the laconic quality of these sayings.

In many respects, therefore, these Desert Fathers had much in common with Indian Yogis and with Zen Buddhist monks of China and Japan. If we were to seek their like in twentieth-century America, we would have to look in strange, out of the way places. Such beings are tragically rare. They obviously do not flourish on the sidewalk at Forty-Second Street and Broadway. We might perhaps find someone like this among the Pueblo Indians or the Navahos: but there the case would be entirely different. You would have simplicity, primitive wisdom: but rooted in a primitive society. With the Desert Fathers, you have the characteristic of a clean break with a conventional, accepted social context in order to swim for one's life into an apparently irrational void.

Though I might be expected to claim that men like this could be found in some of our monasteries of contemplatives, I will not be so bold. With us it is often rather the case of men leaving the society of the "world" in order to fit themselves into another kind of society, that of the religious family they enter. They exchange the values, concepts and rites of the one for those of the other. And since we now have centuries of monasticism behind us, this puts the whole thing in a different light. The social "norms" of a monastic family are also apt to be conventional, and to live by them does not involve a leap into the void — only a radical change of customs and standards. The words and examples of the Desert Fathers have been so much a part of the monastic tradition that time has turned them into stereotypes for us, and we are no longer able to notice their fabulous originality. We have buried them, so to speak, in our own routines, and thus securely insulated ourselves against any form of spiritual shock from their lack of conventionality. Yet it has been my hope that in selecting and editing these "words" I may have presented them in a new light and made their freshness once again obvious.

The Desert Fathers were pioneers, with nothing to go on but the example of some of the prophets, like St. John the Baptist, Elias, Eliseus, and the Apostles, who also served them as models. For the rest, the life they embraced was "angelic" and they walked

the untrodden paths of invisible spirits. Their cells were the furnace of Babylon in which, in the midst of flames, they found themselves with Christ.

They neither courted the approval of their contemporaries nor
sought to provoke their disapproval, because the opinions of others had ceased, for them, to be matters of importance. They had
no set doctrine about freedom, but they had in fact become free
by paying the price of freedom.

In any case these Fathers distilled for themselves a very practical and unassuming wisdom that is at once primitive and timeless, and which enables us to reopen the sources that have been
polluted or blocked up altogether by the accumulated mental and
spiritual refuse of our technological barbarism. Our time is in desperate need of this kind of simplicity. It needs to recapture something of the experience reflected in these lines. The word to emphasize is *experience*. The few short phrases collected in this volume have little or no value merely as information. It would be
futile to skip through these pages and lightly take note of the fact
that the Fathers said this and this. What good will it do us to
know merely that such things were once *said?* The important thing
is that they were lived. That they flow from an experience of the
deeper levels of life. That they represent a discovery of man, at
the term of an inner and spiritual journey that is far more crucial
and infinitely more important than any journey to the moon.

What can we gain by sailing to the moon if we are not able to
cross the abyss that separates us from ourselves? This is the most
important of all voyages of discovery, and without it all the rest are
not only useless but disastrous. Proof: the great travelers and colo-
nizers of the Renaissance were, for the most part, men who perhaps were capable of the things they did precisely because they were
alienated from themselves. In subjugating primitive worlds they
only imposed on them, with the force of cannons, their own confusion and their own alienation. Superb exceptions like Fray
Bartolome de las Casas, St. Francis Xavier, or Father Matthew Ricci,
only prove the rule.

These sayings of the Desert Fathers are drawn from a classical
collection, the *Verba Seniorum*, in Migne's *Latin Patrology* (Volume
73). The *Verba* are distinguished from the other Desert Fathers'

thing that savoured of punishment and revenge, however hidden it might be.

The charity of Desert Fathers is not set before us in unconvincing effusions. The full difficulty and magnitude of the task of loving others is recognized everywhere and never minimized. It is hard to really love others if love is to be taken in the full sense of the word. Love demands a complete inner transformation — for without this we cannot possibly come to identify ourselves with our brother. We have to become, in some sense, the person we love. And this involves a kind of death of our own being, our own self. No matter how hard we try, we resist this death: we fight back with anger, with recriminations, with demands, with ultimatums. We seek any convenient excuse to break off and give up the difficult task. But in these *Verba Seniorum* we read of Abbot Ammonas, who spent fourteen years praying to overcome anger, or rather, more significantly, to be delivered from it. We read of Abbot Serapion, who sold his last book, a copy of the Gospels, and gave the money to the poor, thus selling "the very words which told him to sell all and give to the poor." Another Abbot severely rebuked some monks who had caused a group of robbers to be thrown in jail, and as a result the shamefaced hermits broke into the jail by night to release the prisoners. Time and again we read of Abbots who refuse to join in communal reproof of this or that delinquent, like Abbot Moses, that great gentle Negro, who walked into the severe assembly with a basket of sand, letting the sand run out through many holes. "My own sins are running out like this sand," he said, "and yet I come to judge the sins of another."

If such protests were made, there was obviously something to protest against. By the end of the fifth century Scete and Nitria had become rudimentary monastic cities, [with] laws and penalties. Three whips hung from a palm tree outside the church of Scete: one to punish delinquent monks, one to punish thieves and one for vagrants. But there were many monks like Abbot Moses who did not agree: and these were the saints. They represented the primitive "anarchic" desert ideal. Perhaps the most memorable of all were the two old brothers who had lived together for years without a quarrel, who decided to "get into an argument like the rest of men" but simply could not succeed.

Prayer was the very heart of the desert life, and consisted of psalmody (vocal prayer — recitation of the Psalms and other parts of the Scriptures which everyone had to know by heart) and contemplation. What we would call today contemplative prayer is referred to as *quies* or "rest." This illuminating term has persisted in Greek monastic traditions as *hesychia*, "sweet repose." *Quies* is a silent absorption aided by the soft repetition of a lone phrase of the Scriptures — the most popular being the prayer of the Publican: "Lord Jesus Christ, Son of God, have mercy on me a sinner!" In a shortened form this prayer became "Lord have mercy" (*Kyrie eleison*) — repeated interiorly hundreds of times a day until it became as spontaneous and instinctive as breathing.

When Arsenius is told to fly from the Cenobium, be silent and rest (*fuge, tace, quiesce*) it is a call to "contemplative prayer." *Quies* is a simpler and less pretentious term, and much less misleading. It suits the simplicity of the Desert Fathers much better than "contemplation" and affords less occasion for spiritual narcissism or megalomania. There was small danger of quietism in the desert. The monks were kept busy, and if *quies* was a fulfillment of all they sought, *corporalis quies* ("bodily rest") was one of their greatest enemies. I have translated *corporalis quies* as "an easy life," so as not to give the impression that agitated action was tolerated in the desert. It was not. The monk was supposed to remain tranquil and stay as much as possible in one place. Some Fathers even frowned on those who sought employment outside their cells and worked for the farmers of the Nile valley during the harvest season.

Finally, in these pages we meet several great and simple personalities. Though the *Verba* are sometimes ascribed only to an unidentified *senex* (elder) they are more often attributed by name to the saint who uttered them. We meet Abbot Anthony, who is no other than St. Anthony the Great. This is the Father of all hermits, whose biography, by St. Athanasius, set the whole Roman world afire with monastic vocations. Anthony was indeed the Father of all the Desert Fathers. But contact with his original thought reminds us that he is not the Anthony of Flaubert — nor do we find here anyone like the Paphnutius of Anatole France. Anthony, it is true, attained *apatheia* after long and somewhat spectacular contests with demons. But in the end he concluded that not even the devil was purely evil, since God could not create evil, and all His works are good. It may come as a surprise to learn that St. Anthony, of all people, thought the devil had some good in him. This was not mere sentimentalism. It showed that in Anthony there was not much room left for paranoia. We can profitably reflect that modern mass-man is the one who has returned so whole-heartedly to fanatical projections of all one's own evil upon "the enemy" (whoever that may be). The solitaries of the desert were much wiser.

Then in these *Verba* we meet others like St. Arsenius, the dour and silent stranger who came to the desert from the far-off court of the Emperors of Constantinople and would not let anybody see his face. We meet the gentle Poemen, the impetuous John the Dwarf, who wanted to "become an angel." Not the least attractive is Abbot Pastor, who appears perhaps most frequently of all. His sayings are distinguished by their practical humility, their under-standing of human frailty and their solid common sense. Pastor, we know, was himself very human, and it is said of him that when his own blood brother seemed to grow cold to him and preferred the conversation of another hermit, he became so jealous that he had to go to one of the elders and get his sights adjusted.

These monks insisted on remaining human and "ordinary." This may seem to be a paradox, but it is very important. If we reflect a moment, we will see that to fly into the desert in order to be extraordinary is only to carry the world with you as an implicit standard of comparison. The result would be nothing but self-contemplation, and self-comparison with the negative standard of the world one had abandoned. Some of the monks of the Desert did this, as a matter of fact: and the only fruit of their trouble was that they went out of their heads. The simple men who lived their lives out to a good old age among the rocks and sands only did so because they had come into the desert to be themselves, their *ordi-nary* selves, and to forget a world that divided them from them-selves. There can be no other valid reason for seeking solitude or for leaving the world. And thus to leave the world, is, in fact, to help save it in saving oneself. This is the final point, and it is an important one. The Coptic hermits who left the world, as though escaping from a wreck, did not merely intend to save themselves. They knew that they were helpless to do any good for others as long as they floundered about in the wreckage. But once they got a foothold on solid ground, things were different. Then they had not only the power but even the obligation to pull the whole world to safety after them.

This is their paradoxical lesson for our time. It would perhaps be too much to say that the world needs another movement such as that which drew these men into the deserts of Egypt and Palestine. Ours is certainly a time for solitaries and for hermits. But merely to reproduce the simplicity, austerity and prayer of these primitive souls is not a complete or satisfactory answer. We must transcend all those who, since their time, have gone beyond the limits which they set. We must liberate ourselves, in our own way, from involvement in a world that is plunging to disaster. But our world is different from theirs. Our involvement in it is more complete. Our danger is far more desperate. Our time, perhaps, is shorter than we think.

We cannot do exactly what they did. But we must be as thorough and as ruthless in our determination to break all spiritual chains, and cast off the domination of alien compulsions, to find our true selves, to discover and develop our inalienable spiritual liberty and use it to build, on earth, the Kingdom of God. This is not the place in which to speculate what our great and mysterious vocation might involve. That is still unknown. Let it suffice for me to say that we need to learn from these men of the fourth century how to ignore prejudice, defy compulsion and strike out fearlessly into the unknown.

NOTE

1. Thomas Merton's "Introduction" to his *The Wisdom of the Desert: Sayings of the Desert Fathers*. New York, New York: New Directions, 1960.

St. Paul and St. Anthony in the Eastern Desert of Egypt, twentieth century.

†

صلاة القلب

يا ربي يسوع المسيح أرحمني

يا ربي يسوع المسيح أعني

يا ربي يسوع المسيح ساعدني

أنا الخاطئ

Prayer of the Heart
O My Lord Jesus the Messiah have mercy upon me,
O My Lord Jesus the Messiah help me,
O My Lord Jesus the Messiah assist me,
I am a sinner.

The Jesus Prayer in Arabic,
written by a monk at the monastery in the Eastern Desert of Egypt,
where St. Anthony lived in his cave in view of the Red Sea.

3

THE SPIRITUAL FATHER IN THE DESERT TRADITION[1]

Thomas Merton

The place of the "Director of Conscience" or "Spiritual Director" in modern Catholic practice since the Council of Trent need not be treated here in details, but it must as least be mentioned as the term of a long evolution of which we wish to discuss the beginning.[2] The "Director of Conscience" as his title suggests is usually a confessor and also by implication a "specialist" with an appropriate theological and spiritual training. If he is called a "Director of *Conscience*," this suggests that he is adept in settling *casus conscientiae*, or special cases and problems, for which he provides professional solutions. But this imposes rather unfortunate juridical limitations upon the traditional concept. The term "Spiritual Director" is broader, and suggests one who, by virtue of his learning and experience, is equipped to help others make progress in the spiritual life. Ideally speaking, the "spiritual director" will help others reach the heights of spiritual and mystical perfection. In the lives of Saints since the Middle Ages, for instance St. Teresa of Avila,[3] the importance of the spiritual director is sufficiently underlined. His influence may be positive or negative. He may prove to be a great obstacle to progress, or he may remove obstacles and help one to attain the mysterious action of the Holy Spirit and attain to union with God. But in any case the director, if not essential for the spiritual life, is considered in practice to have had a decisive part to play in the lives of saints and mystics, with a few notable exceptions. St. Francis de Sales may be taken as the typical saintly "director" who, by his prudence, learning, experience, good sense and intuitive understanding of others, helped many to find their spiritual path, leading them safely to high contemplation and mystical union. Such directors have clearly exercised a providential function in the lives not only of individuals but also of religious congregations and of certain social milieux, indeed of the Church herself.

However, it is not of these modern directors that we are writing here. Rather we wish to return to the *archetypal* figure of the "spiritual Father" as depicted in the literature of early monasticism, that is to say, the monasticism of Egypt, Palestine and Syria in the fourth and fifth centuries. Particularly valuable as source material are the *Apophthegmata* or sayings of the Desert Fathers.[4] Even though these are "typical" stories of figures that have become quasi-legendary, we need not question the fact that they represent an authentic spirit and indeed an historical attitude, a view of life that was so profound and so real that it exercised a permanent influence on centuries of Christian spirituality.

The Abba or spiritual Father was first of all one who by long experience in the desert and in solitude had learned the secrets of desert life. He was, by reason of his holiness, endowed with charismatic gifts, which enabled him to detect and dispel the illusions that would inevitably tempt the beginner — or even the experienced monk who had not yet fully attained to the full maturity and perfection of the monastic life. But the function implied by the name "Father" is not fully accounted for in spiritual advice and instruction. The spiritual Father exercised a genuine "paternity" — in the name of God — engendering the life of the Spirit in the disciple. Of course, this concept must not be exaggerated (as it has sometimes been in later monastic circles, for instance in Byzantine cenobitism). The only source of the spiritual life is the Holy Spirit. The spiritual life does not come from men. The Holy Spirit is given in Baptism. However, as we know too well, the seeds of the spiritual life planted in Baptism too often remain dormant or die altogether. The Abba or "spiritual Father" was one who was recognized as a charismatic and "life-giving" influence, under whose care these mysterious seeds would truly grow and flourish. The Fathers attracted disciples who came not only for lectures and counsel, but seeking *life* and *growth* in a special relationship of filial love and devotion — indeed, in later times, of actual veneration.

The sayings of the Fathers show us in simple, often naïve terms, the archetypal life-giving *charismata* of these quiet, humble, often very humorous, always human figures. To such experienced and spiritually gifted *seniors* or "elders," even though they might

literature by their total lack of literary artifice, their complete and honest simplicity. The *Lives* of the Fathers are much more grandiloquent, dramatic, stylized. They abound in wonderful events and in miracles. They are strongly marked by the literary personalities to whom we owe them. But the *Verba* are the plain, unpretentious reports that went from mouth to mouth in the Coptic tradition before being committed to writing in Syriac, Greek and Latin.

Always simple and concrete, always appealing to the experience of the man who had been shaped by solitude, these proverbs and tales were intended as plain answers to plain questions. Those who came to the desert seeking "salvation" asked the elders for a "word" that would help them to find it — a *verbum salutis*, a "word of salvation." The answers were not intended to be general, universal prescriptions. Rather they were originally concrete and precise keys to particular doors that had to be entered, at a given time, by given individuals. Only later, after much repetition and much quotation, did they come to be regarded as common currency. It will help us to understand these sayings better if we remember their practical and, one might say, existential quality. But by the time St. Benedict in his Rule prescribed that the "Words of the Fathers" were to be read aloud frequently before Compline, they were traditional monastic lore.

The Fathers were humble and silent men, and did not have much to say. They replied to questions in few words, to the point. Rather than give an abstract principle, they preferred to tell a concrete story. Their brevity is refreshing, and rich in content. There is more light and satisfaction in these laconic sayings than in many a long ascetic treatise full of details about ascending from one "degree" to another in the spiritual life. These words of the Fathers are never theoretical in our modern sense of the word. They are never abstract. They deal with concrete things and with jobs to be done in the everyday life of a fourth-century monk. But what is said serves just as well for a twentieth-century thinker. The basic realities of the interior life are there: faith, humility, charity, meekness, discretion, self-denial. But not the least of the qualities of the "words of salvation" is their common sense.

This is important. The Desert Fathers later acquired a reputation for fanaticism because of the stories that were told about their ascetic feats by indiscreet admirers. They were indeed ascetics: but when we read their own words and see what they themselves thought about life, we find that they were anything but fanatics. They were humble, quiet, sensible people, with a deep knowledge of human nature and enough understanding of the things of God to realize that they knew very little about Him. Hence they were not much disposed to make long speeches about the divine essence, or even to declaim on the mystical meaning of Scripture. If these men say little about God, it is because they know that when one has been somewhere close to His dwelling, silence makes more sense than a lot of words. The fact that Egypt, in their time, was seething with religious and intellectual controversies was all the more reason for them to keep their mouths shut. There were the Neo-Platonists, the Gnostics, the Stoics and Pythagoreans. There were the various, highly vocal, orthodox and heretical groups of Christians. There were the Arians (whom the monks of the Desert passionately resisted). There were the Origenists (and some of the monks were faithfully devoted followers of Origen). In all this noise, the desert had no contribution to offer but a discreet and detached silence.

The great monastic centers of the fourth century were in Egypt, Arabia and Palestine. Most of these stories concern hermits of Nitria and Scete, in northern Egypt, near the Mediterranean coast and west of the Nile. There were also many colonies of monks in the Nile Delta. The Thebaid, near ancient Thebes, further inland along the Nile, was another center of monastic activity, particularly of the cenobites. Palestine had early attracted monks from all parts of the Christian world, the most famous of them being St. Jerome, who lived and translated the Scriptures in a cave at Bethlehem. Then there was an important monastic colony around Mount Sinai in Arabia: founders of the monastery of St. Catherine which has recently broken unto the news with the "discovery" of the works of Byzantine art preserved there.

What kind of life did the Fathers lead? A word of explanation may help us understand their sayings better. The Desert Fathers are usually referred to as "Abbot" (*abbas*) or "Elder" (*senex*). An Abbot was not then, as now, a canonically elected superior of a community, but any monk or hermit who had been tried by years in the desert and proved himself a servant of God. With them, or near them, lived "Brethren" and "Novices" — those who were still in the process of learning the life. The novices still needed the continuous supervision of an elder, and lived with one in order to be instructed by his word and example. The brethren lived on their own, but occasionally resorted to a nearby elder for advice.

Most of the characters represented in these sayings and stories are men who are "on the way" to purity of heart rather then men who have fully arrived. The Desert Fathers, inspired by Clement and Origen, and the Neo-Platonic tradition, were sometimes confident that they could rise above all passion and become impervious to anger, lust, pride and all the rest. But we find little in these sayings to encourage those who believed that Christian perfection was a matter of *apatheia* (impassivity). The praise of monks "beyond all passion" seems indeed to have come from tourists who passed briefly through the deserts and went home to write books about what they had seen, rather than from those who had spent their whole life in the wilderness. These latter were much more inclined to accept the common realities of life and be content with the ordinary lot of man who has to struggle all his life to overcome himself. The wisdom of the *Verba* is seen in the story of the monk John, who boasted that he was "beyond all temptation" and was advised by a shrewd elder to pray to God for a few good solid battles in order that his life might continue to be worth something.

At certain times, all solitaries and novices would come together for the liturgical *synaxis* (Mass and prayers in common) and after this they might eat together and hold a kind of chapter meeting to discuss communal problems. Then they returned to their solitude, where they spent their time working and praying.

They supported themselves by the labor of their hands, usually weaving baskets and mats out of palm leaves or reeds. These they sold in the nearby towns. There is sometimes question in the *Verba* of matters relating to the work and to the commerce involved. Charity and hospitality were matters of top priority, and took precedence over fasting and personal ascetic routines. The countless sayings which bear witness to this warm-hearted friendliness should be sufficient to take care of accusations that these men hated their own kind. Indeed there was more real love, understanding and kindliness in the desert than in the cities, where, then as now, it was every man for himself.

This fact is all the more important because the very essence of the Christian message is charity, unity in Christ. The Christian mystics of all ages sought and found not only the unification of their own being, not only union with God, but union with one another in the Spirit of God. To seek a union with God that would imply complete separation, in spirit as well as in body from all the rest of mankind, would be to a Christian saint not only absurd but the very opposite of sanctity. Isolation in the self, inability to go out of oneself to others, would mean incapacity for any form of self-transcendence. To be thus the prisoner of one's own selfhood is, in fact, to be in hell: a truth that Sartre, though professing himself an atheist, has expressed in the most arresting fashion in his play *No Exit* (*Huis Clos*).

All through the *Verba Seniorum* we find a repeated insistence on the primacy of love over everything else in the spiritual life: over knowledge, *gnosis*, asceticism, contemplation, solitude, prayer. Love in fact *is* the spiritual life, and without it all the other exercises of the spirit, however lofty, are emptied of content and become mere illusions. The more lofty they are, the more dangerous the illusion.

Love, of course, means something much more than mere sentiment, much more than token favors and perfunctory almsdeeds. Love means an interior and spiritual identification with one's brother, so that he is not regarded as an "object" to "which" one "does good." The fact is that good done to another as to an object is of little or no spiritual value. Love takes one's neighbor as one's other self, and loves him with all the immense humility and discretion and reserve without which no one can presume to enter into the sanctuary of another's subjectivity. From such love all authoritarian brutality, all exploitation, domineering and condescension must necessarily be absent. The saints of the desert were enemies of every subtle or gross expedient by which the "spiritual man" contrives to bully those he thinks inferior to himself, thus gratifying his own ego. They had renounced every-

not be priests, the young would spontaneously direct themselves with their questions, asking for those "words of salvation" that would awaken new life and growth in their hearts.

In the *Apophthegmata* we are concerned chiefly with the desert hermits, rather than with the cenobites. In fact the distinction is important, for the heads of the cenobitic communities tended to give their guidance first of all by a Rule and observances which doubtless implemented a spiritual doctrine, but which were by their nature general rather than personal. The *Apophthegmata* on the other hand represent the direct and personal answers to the question of individuals. The "word" becomes, in each case, endowed with a general validity for "everyone" in the same or in analogous circumstances. Among the hermits these individual directives tended to take the place of general written rules: or rather they were intended to help the monk discover his own rule of life, or God's will *for him* in particular.

In order to understand these directives, we must first understand the objective of the solitary in the desert. It would be an oversimplification to say that the Egyptian and Syrian hermits went into the desert "to find solitude and lead the contemplative life." It is true that many of them were Greeks, or had a Greek outlook on life (acquired in Constantinople, Rome or Alexandria) and for these the search for a primarily intellectual intuition of God was the most important thing about desert life. This particular tradition is represented in the writings of Evagrius Ponticus[5] and was doubtless prevalent at Nitria and Scete. But the term contemplation, *theoria*, is not prominent in the *apophthegmata* or other popular stories of the Fathers, though we read of them "seeing the glory of God" or having prophetic visions. There is, then, another term which is at once simpler, more profound, and more general, and which embraces all the different modes of desert spirituality — whether the intellectual or the volitional, the Platonic or the Biblical: that term is "tranquility," in Greek *hesychia* and in Latin *quies*. This repose is essentially "contemplative" if you like, but it is more: in its deepest meaning it implies perfect sonship of God, union with God by a complete renunciation of self, and total surrender to the word and will of God in faith and love. This is exemplified in a classic anecdote about the vocation of the desert father St. Arsenius.

When Abba Arsenius was in the palace, he prayed to God and said, "O Lord, direct me how to live" and a voice came to him, saying, "Arsenius, flee from men and thou shall live." And when Arsenius was living the ascetic life in the monastery, he prayed to God the same prayer, and again he heard a voice saying to him, "Arsenius, flee, keep silence and lead a life of silent contemplation, for these are the fundamental causes which prevent man from committing sin."[6]

The *fuge, tace, quiesce* of Arsenius became a classical trope of the contemplative life. The "flight" was of course from the monastery into complete desert solitude as a hermit. The silence is self-explanatory, and the *quies*, as we have said above, is the real goal of the solitary life: the rest and "purity of heart" which comes from complete liberation from worldly care, from the concerns of a life devoted to the assertion of a social ego and from the illusions consequent upon such a life. John Cassian, in his first conference, defining the whole purpose of the monastic life, brings together three things which he identifies with monastic perfection. These three are simply aspects of the same spiritual reality. Perfection does *not* consist merely in solitude, asceticism, prayer, or other practices. All these may be sought for basically selfish motives, and they may in the end be simply more subtle and more stubborn ways of affirming one's own ego. True perfection is found only when one renounces the "self" that seems to be the subject of perfection, and that "had" or "possesses" perfection. For Cassian this perfection is "charity . . . which consists in purity of heart alone" and which he identifies with *quies*, since it consists in "always offering to God a perfect and most pure heart, and in keeping that heart untouched by all perturbations."[7] Behind this formula we must recognize the doctrine of Evagrius, for whom the monastic life was a purification first from all passionate desires, then from all disturbing thoughts, then finally from all conceptualization, leading thus to the attainment of *theologia*. The highest "rest" is the direct intuition of the Trinity. If the Greek tradition gave this *quies* some sophisticated and intellectual implications which the simple Coptic hermits never knew, the fact remains that all sought this tranquility and liberty of spirit in one form or other and all identified with love of God. In all the different traditions – Greek, Coptic, Palestinian and Syriac – we find a common agreement in this: that in the desert the monk renounces his own illusory ego-self, he "dies" to his worldly and empirical existence, in order to surrender completely to the transcendent reality which, though described in various terms, is always best expressed in the simple Biblical expression: "the will of God." In his surrender of himself and of his own will, his "death" to his worldly identity, the monk is renewed in the image and likeness of God, and becomes like a mirror filled with divine light.

This doctrine of man finding his true reality in his remembrance of God, in whose image he was created, is basically Biblical and was developed by the Church Fathers in connection with the theology of grace, the sacraments, and the indwelling of the Holy Spirit. In fact, the surrender of our own will, the "death" of our selfish ego, in order to live in pure love and liberty of spirit, is effected not by our own will (this would be a contradiction in terms!) but by the Holy Spirit. To "recover the divine likeness," to "surrender to the will of God," to "live by pure love," and thus to find peace, is summed up as "union with God in the Spirit," or "receiving, possessing the Holy Spirit." This, as the nineteenth century Russian hermit St. Seraphim of Sarov declared, is the whole purpose of the Christian (therefore *a fortiori* the monastic) life. St. John Chrysostom says: "As polished silver illumined by the rays of the sun radiates light not only from its own nature but also from the radiance of the sun, so a soul purified by the Divine Spirit becomes more brilliant than silver; it both receives the ray of Divine Glory and from itself reflects the ray of this same glory."[8] Our true rest, love, purity, vision and *quies* is not something in ourselves, it is God the Divine Spirit. Thus we do not "possess" rest, but go out of ourselves into him who is our true rest.

In the Coptic life of St. Pachomius we read a touching episode in which Pachomius, not yet the founder of his community, but living as a hermit with his brother, is praying to know the "will of God." He and his brother are living in an abandoned village, Tabbenese, and they are occupied in harvesting for neighboring farmers, thus earning their bread. One night, after their common prayers, Pachomius falls apart and "he was desolate and broken hearted about the will of God which he desired to learn." A luminous personage appears before him and asks, "Why are you desolate and broken hearted?" "Because I seek the will of God," Pachomius replies. The personage tells him: "It is the will of God that you serve the human race, in order to reconcile it with him." Pachomius is at first shocked: "I ask about the will of God and you tell me to serve men?" The personage repeats three times: "It is God's will that you serve men in order to bring them to him."[9]

The story is interesting from many points of view. First of all it contrasts in some respects with the *fuge, tace, quiesce* of Arsenius. The spirituality of the Pachomian communities was more active than contemplative, and in any case Pachomius is here being called to the task of being a Father and Founder of cenobitism. It is characteristic of St. Pachomius's thought that in the cenobitic life the monk is brought to perfection not so much by an isolated ascetic struggle directed by an enlightened spiritual master, as by participation in the life of the holy community, the brotherhood of those gathered together "in the spirit." Pachomius is said by his disciple Theodore to have declared: "This Congregation . . . is the model for all those who wish to gather together souls according to God, in order to help them until they become perfect."[10]

But in the Pachomian system too the goal is peace, *quies*, the spiritual security that comes from complete detachment and self-renunciation. The Abba regulates the life and work of the monks in the way that seems to him best for their spiritual advancement and they in turn, trusting completely in him as God's instrument, find peace in following his regulations.[11]

Meanwhile, however, we find Pachomius himself seeking peace, tranquility and *quies* in the clear perception of and surrender to God's will. What is important for us in the story we have quoted is the fact that in "desolation and with a broken heart" Pachomius is seeking the *ultimate meaning of his life*. This is characteristic of all the Desert monks. They have come out into the desert tormented by a need to know the inner meaning of their own existence, which to them has lost all significance and purpose in the cities of man. And though the individual answers may take different and even contradictory forms, yet they all have this one thing in common: all authentic answers come from God and are the expression of his will, manifested in his word, and when one received and obeys this word one has peace, *quies*. These answers are not easily come by. One must seek them in repentance, suffering and patience, for no one can demand an answer as by right, and each one must be prepared to accept an answer that may be in many ways disconcerting. The suffering and solitude of the desert life are, in the eyes of the Egyptian monks, the price that has to be paid for such an ultimate solution to the question of existence. The price is not too high.

Meanwhile, though the stories may tell us that some of the pioneers like Arsenius, Pachomius, Anthony, received their answers by interior inspiration or from "luminous personages," the other Desert Fathers had to be content with a more prosaic and ultimately more secure source of information: they had to ask other monks who had found their answer. They had to approach a "spiritual Father."

Anecdotes about the Desert Fathers are more often than not direct and succinct reports of spiritual consultations; and the "sayings" (*Apophthegmata*) of the Fathers are generally solutions of problems or difficulties. These may have been presented by a disciple living in the same cell as the Master or in a neighboring cell, in order to be taught and formed by him; or they may be posed by a stranger who has traveled a long distance with the precise purpose of getting this answer from a famous Abba. Sometimes the questions are general and fundamental, involving what we would call today a vocational decision, changing the entire course of the questioner's life. In the terminology of the "sayings" such questions are formulated: "What ought I to do?" "Speak to me a word" (i.e. "a word of salvation," manifesting the will of God and thereby showing the way to the goal of my existence). The answer to such a question is a program of life in the desert, or, if you like, a "Rule" expressed in three or four words appropriate to the needs of the one asking. In each case, the reply of the Master is intended to meet the personal need of the inquirer, but it is also a fundamental statement about the monastic life.

One of the best examples of this kind of statement is found in the Coptic life of St. Pachomius. It is the story of Pachomius's first encounter with the hermit Abba Palemon, his request to become the old man's disciple, and Abba Palemon's reply.[12]

Pachomius knocks at the cell door. The old man cries out rudely, "Why are you knocking?" The youth says, "Father, I desire you to let me be a monk with you."

The old man then launches on a sobering, if not discouraging, account of the solitary vocation: "Many have come here for that very purpose and were not able to stand it; they turned back shamefully . . . " Nevertheless, he briefly exposes the purpose of the monastic life ("Scripture orders us to pray and fast in order that we may be saved"), and the actual Rule that is followed by the monks. "The Rule of monasticism, as we have been taught by our predecessors, is as follows: at all times we spend half the night — and often from evening to morning — in vigils, reciting the words of God, and doing much manual work, with thread, hair or palm-fibre, so as not to be importuned by sleep and to provide for our bodily needs; whatever remains over and above what we need, we give to the poor." He continues with details about the fasting and prayers and concludes: "Now that I have taught you the law of monasticism, go and examine yourself on all these points. See if you are capable of doing what I have said . . . " He also says, "go to your own house, stay there and hold fast to what you have received. See . . . if you are capable of enduring."

This passage is a paradigm for monastic formation and the deciding of vocations.[13]

Other simpler examples:

A cenobite comes to the hermit Abba Bessarion and asks advice about how to live in his community: "The old man said unto him, 'Keep silence and consider thyself to be nothing.'"[14]

"A brother asked Abba Muthues saying: 'Speak a word to me'; and the old man replied, 'Cut off from thee contention concerning every matter whatsoever, and weep and mourn, for the time hath come.'"[15]

This "compunction," and the eschatological perspective which saw all things in the light of their end, was sufficient to revolutionize a man's whole outlook on himself and on life.

Notice that in these two examples, chosen at random, emphasis is laid on being at peace with others, "not contending" with them, even in thought. This is a very common theme in the saying of the Fathers. Retirement into solitude is of no use if the hermit is to live alone with aggressive and hostile fantasies. A prerequisite for this tranquility (*quies*) of the true solitary is the renunciation of all judgments, all criticisms of others and all interior argumentation. Living in the presence of the divine judge of all was the beginner's way to reduce all these things to their true dimensions.

Sometimes the question concerns a particular problem in the ascetic life. The solution given constitutes a principle which has a certain importance in analogous cases. not able to perform ascetic labours: speak to me a word whereby I may live." And the old man said unto him: "Art thou able to rule thy thought and not to permit it to go to thy neighbour in guile?"[16]

A brother asked the same Abbot Poemen: "What shall I do, for I am troubled when I am sitting in my cell?" The old man said unto him, "Think lightly of no man: think no evil in thy heart, condemn no man and curse no man; then shall God give thee rest, and thy habitation shall be without trouble."[17]

There are some sayings in which the Master is, so to speak, certifying that the disciple has reached a certain state of perfection and that he is now able, with spiritual freedom, to go forth and help others. Thus Theodore, himself an "old man" and therefore experienced, asked Abba Pambo saying, "Tell me a word." And with much labor he said to him, "Theodore, get thee gone and let thy mercy be poured out on every man, for thy loving-kindness hath found freedom of speech before God."[18]

An answer of an anonymous Abba covers the whole field of monastic asceticism, according to his view of it:

In my opinion the work of the soul is as follows: to live in silence, persistent endurance, self denial, labor, humility of body, and constant prayer. And a man should not consider the shortcomings of men, but his own lapses; if now a man will persist in these things the soul will after no great time make manifest the fruits of spiritual excellence.[19]

If the Fathers answered different questioners to their needs, it followed that sometimes they solved the same problem in different ways or gave seemingly contradictory answers to identical questions. Once Abba Joseph was reproached with this. When asked how to deal with tempting thoughts, he told one monk to resist them forcefully and thrust them out, and another to pay no attention to them. It was this second who complained of the contradiction. The answer of the Abba was: "I spoke to you as I would have spoken to myself"[20] – in other words he knew that his questioner was experienced, and that forceful resistance was not necessary as the tempting thoughts made no real appeal to his will, while direct resistance would only cause him to be unnecessarily concerned with them, devoting his attention to them when it would be better occupied elsewhere.

This purpose is well stated in a Syrian work of the fifth or sixth century, outside the context of Egyptian monasticism, and more speculative than the practical "sayings" of the Fathers. Yet the gist of it is much the same.

A disciple asks the question: "What is the beginning of the conduct of the interior man?"

Master: "Renunciation of the love of money. After renunciation of the love of money, it is necessarily required of him that he strip himself of the love of praise. Then after that it is possible for him to be in the virtue of understanding: in humility and in patience, in quietude and lucidity of spirit, in the joy of his hope, in the vigilance of noble concerns, in the perfect love of God and of men: by these things he will come to purity of soul which is the crowning of all the conduct God has enjoined upon man to attain in this life."[21]

This fact will help us to understand the various statements of principle which are made by the Fathers: all must be understood in the light of concrete situations. At one moment stern asceticism is declared essential, at another non-essential. Everything depends on the concrete case. In a word, the sayings of the Fathers are not to be taken as hard and fast rules which apply in the same way in every situation: they are applications of broad general principles, which we have already considered. The most fundamental of them is stated clearly in the first Conference of Cassian: every practice, every decision, every change in one's mode of life is to be judged in terms of the purpose of the solitary life. That purpose is purity of heart, perfect charity, and *quies*, or the tranquility of the selfless and detached spirit.

The worth and meaning of every ascetic practice is to be estimated in terms of quietude, lucidity of spirit, love, and purity of heart. Anything that does not lead to these is worthless, for instead of liberating us from self-preoccupation, it only reinforces our illusory and obsessive concern with our own ego and its victory over the "not-I." True quietude and purity of heart are impossible where this division of the "I" (considered as right and good) and the "not-I" (considered as threatening) governs our conduct and our decisions.

When one has been liberated from this obsession with self, says the same text, one attains to *integrity*, to the "conduct of the new man." This is the "beginning" of the true life, the life of the interior or spiritual man who lives entirely as a son of God and not as a slave.

Is there one principle above all which can be said to cover almost every case, a basic norm of the solitary life? Yes, there is one. Its observance is practically synonymous with *quies* because it is the essential condition for tranquility. It is the key principle of the solitary life and is sometimes stated with such finality that it even seems to dispense with further advice. Here is a classic statement of it:

> "A certain brother went to Abba Moses in Scete, and asked him to speak a word; and the old man said, '*Get thee gone, and sit in thy cell, and thy cell shall teach you all things.*'"[22]

This saying has obvious implications for the practice of spiritual direction. As stated here, it clearly implies that there is no use in the monk leaving his cell and running about asking advice, if he is not first prepared *to face his own solitude in all its naked reality.*

Though we cannot go into all the depth of this idea at present, let us at least say this much: it is in solitude that the monk most completely comes to discover the true inner dimensions of his own being, at once "real" and "unreal." The conviction of one's "self" as a static, absolute and invariable reality undergoes a profound transformation and dissolves in the burning light of an altogether new and unsuspected awareness. In this awareness we see that our "reality" is not a firmly established ego-self already attained that merely has to be perfected, but rather that we are a "nothing," a "possibility" in which the gift of creative freedom can realize itself by its response to the free gift of love and grace. This response means accepting our loneliness and our "potentiality" as a gift and a commission, as a *trust* to be used — as a "talent," in the language of the parables. Our existence is then at once terrible and precious because radically it belongs not to us but to God. Yet it will not be fully "His" unless we freely make it "ours" and then offer it to Him in praise. This is what Christian tradition means by "obedience to the Word of God." The monk must learn this for himself.

Of course he needs the assistance of others but he cannot be helped by others if he is not first determined to help himself. Others will be of little use as mediators between himself and God if he does not have enough faith to give first place to prayer and solitude in his own eremetical life. In other words, it is the solitude of the cell itself that teaches one how to face illusion, how to resist temptation, how to pray. All other advice and direction is first of all contingent upon the young hermit's willingness to accept this basic principle. One might say that all other advice assumes that one is ready and willing to sustain the purifying silence and loneliness of the cell, in which one is stripped of his illusory image of himself and forced to come to terms with the nothingness, the limitation, the infidelity, the defectibility, or as we might say today the "void" of his own life.

St. Anthony, who knew better than anyone the meaning of this solitary combat with thoughts ("demons"),[23] said that life in the cell was at times like being in a fiery furnace. Yet in that furnace one came face to face with God. The saying recalls that of a modern monk of Mount Athos, Staretz Silouan, who lived "as though in hell" but did not despair.[24] Anthony left us a most important saying, with deep implications about the mystical life (of which little is said explicitly in the *Apophthegmata*): "The cell of the monk is the furnace of Babylon wherein the three children found the Son of God, and it is also the pillar of cloud wherefrom God spoke with Moses."[25]

The monk who faces this fire and darkness will not be able to continue in the cell at all unless he lives as a man of faith and prayer. A monastic saying has it that when you do not live worthily in your cell, the cell of its own accord vomits you out. This accounts, perhaps, for the fact that the Desert Fathers were not carried away with enthusiasm over the specious zeal to convert others which often presented itself as an honorable evasion from the solitude of the cell and from the *acedia* caused by the "noonday demon."[26]

A young monk, tormented by this kind of problem, confesses to Abba Arsenius:

My thoughts vex me and say: "thou canst not fast; and thou art not able to labour; therefore visit the sick which is a great commandment." The Abba Arsenius, after the manner of one who was well acquainted with the war of devils said to him: "Eat, drink and sleep and toil not but on no account go out of thy cell," for the old man knew that dwelling constantly in the cell induceth all the habits of the solitary life.[27]

The rest of this charming story tells how the young monk, remaining in the cell, gradually found himself working and praying more and more steadily and finally won the ascetic battle — the great battle of the solitary — against all his "thoughts." (That is to say he found *quies* by resolving the division caused in himself by useless interior activity and self-projection into words and ideas which were obstacles between himself and his life.)

Another old man discussed the problem of wandering thoughts in the following terms:

"The matter is like unto that of a she-ass which hath a sucking foal. If she be tied up, however much the foal may gambol about or wander hither and thither, he will come back to her eventually, either because he is hungry or because of other reasons which drive him to her; but if it happen that his mother be also roaming about loose, both animals will go to destruction. And thus is it in the matter of the monk. If the body remain continually in its cell the mind thereof will certainly come back to it after all its wanderings, for many reasons which will come upon it, but if the body as well as the soul wander outside the cell both will become a prey and a thing of joy to the enemy."[28]

If the Fathers place so much emphasis on staying in the cell, this does not mean that there are no other rules to follow and that the beginner, provided he stays out of sight, can do anything he pleases. "Become not a lawgiver to thyself," said one of the elders.[29] Another saying of monastic tradition is, "those who are not under the law of the governors shall fall like leaves."[30] The reason for this is not only that the beginner is inexperienced and needs to be instructed and helped. Everywhere in the sayings of the Fathers we find men who are themselves experienced and yet follow the guidance of others, not trusting their own judgment. Though the solitary must certainly develop a certain ability to take care of himself, this does not mean that he trusts in his own strength or in his own ideas. His search in the desert is not merely for solitude in which he can simply do as he pleases and admire himself as a great contemplative. There would be no real *quies* in such an exploit, or if there were peace, it would be the false peace of self-assurance and self-complacency.

Hence we have another story which qualifies the saying: "Stay in thy cell and it shall teach thee all things." One must be in the cell for the right reason.

A certain brother had recently received the garb of a monk and he went and shut himself up in a cell and said, "I am a desert monk." And when the Fathers heard this, they came and took him out of his place and made him go about the cells of the brethren and to make apologies to them saying, "I am not a desert monk, and have only just begun as a disciple."[31]

The monk does not come into the desert to reinforce his own ego-image, but to be delivered from it. After all, this worship of the self is the last and most difficult of idolatries to detect and get rid of. The monk knows this, and therefore he determines to take the proper means to destroy instead of reinforcing the image. For this purpose he renounces his own will in order to be taught and guided by another, even though he may live alone. Still he consults a spiritual Father and as we have seen above in the story of Abbot Theodore, he may be an old man himself before he is told by the spiritual Father that he can now go out on his own because he has obtained the freedom and confidence, not of the self-opinionated proud man who believes in his own ascetic prowess, but of the humble man who has perfect trust in God.

A brother confessed to an elder:

"In my cell I do all that one is counselled to do there, and I find no consolation from God." The elder said: "This happens to you because you want your own will to be fulfilled." The brother said: "What then do you order me to do, Father?" The elder said: "Go, attach yourself to a man who fears God, humble yourself before him, give up your will to him, and then you will receive consolation from God."[32]

The term "consolation from God" is not explained. In the normal context of monastic spirituality it means "compunction." Now, compunction is a sign of valid and authentic repentance, that is to say of *metanoia* or *conversatio*. This means much more than simply a "feeling" of sorrow for sin expressed in the "gift of tears." It is, more basically, a sense of *truth*, a sense of having reached the ground of one's being (or if you prefer, of one's "nothingness") in the crucial realization that one is completely defectible, that one is "*he who is not*" in the presence of "*him who is*." The heart of "consolation" lies precisely in this sense that in the center of one's nothingness one meets the infinitely real. In a word, humility and consolation go together, for humility is truth experienced in its concrete and existential factuality in our own life. One who simply "runs his own life" by putting into effect ideal projects designed to establish his own ego-image more and more firmly, cannot possibly taste "consolation from God." He is not debarred from other consolations — those which come from the image he has constructed for himself! But these consolations are laborious fabrications, ambivalent and nauseating to anyone with a sense of truth.

Merely reading books and following the written instructions of past masters is no substitute for direct contact with a living teacher.[33] The Master does not merely lecture or instruct. He has to know and to analyze the inmost thoughts of the disciple. The most important part of direction is the openness with which the disciple manifests to the spiritual Father not only all his acts but all his thoughts.

An apothegm attributed to St. Anthony declares: "The monk must make known to the elders every step he takes and every drop of water he drinks in his cell, to see if he is not doing wrong."[34]

Since the real "work of the cell" is not a matter of bodily acts and observances, but of interior struggle with "thoughts" (that is, in the last analysis, with the ego-thinking-centered passions and pride), it is most important for the disciple to be able to make known to the Spiritual Father all that is going on in his heart. The purpose of this is to learn *diacrisis*, the discernment of the spirits, which identifies these motions in their very beginning and does not mistake proud, vain, illusory or obsessive drives for "the will of God" and "inspirations of the Spirit." The stories of the Desert Fathers abound in examples of monks who were stern ascetics but who, for lack of discernment (*diacrisis*) went to fantastic extremes or completely wrecked their lives.

Cassian, using an expression which had become current in monastic circles because it had even been attributed to Christ in a *logion*, said that monks should, "according to the commandment of the Lord become as wise money-changers,"[35] able to distinguish gold from brass, and to accept only genuine coin. Cassian applies this to the testing of thoughts.

Seemingly spiritual thoughts may indeed be only illusions or superstitions. Or they may be merely superficial. Sometimes monks are dazzled by words, or by subtle-sounding methods that promise to bring them to a new kind of illumination. Or else they are too ready to follow a train of thought that, in the end, is entirely contrary to the true purpose of the monastic life (i.e. detachment from self and *quies*).

Since the appetite for novel doctrines and for curious new methods provides an outlet for self-will, which can defeat the monk's own purpose, or at best induce him to waste his time in trivialities, the spiritual Father will not tolerate any such fantasies. He severely demands the renunciation of all these subterfuges by which the disciple is merely trying to flatter his own ego. Conversely, a monk who takes pains to avoid having a master shows by that fact that he prefers his own will and his own illusions.

Is it therefore possible to think a man leads a Divine life, in accordance with the Word of God, if he lives without a guide, pandering to himself and obeying his own self-will? Naturally not . . . [To such monks St. John of the Ladder says] "know that you are attempting a short but hard way which has only one road, leading into error."[36]

The monk should of course be free to choose his own Spiritual Father, but he will only deceive himself if, in making the choice, he seeks out a Master who will never tell him anything except what he wants to hear, and never commands him anything against his own will. In fact the Spiritual Father must if necessary be uncompromisingly severe, and make extremely difficult demands upon the disciple in order to test his vocation to solitude and to help him make rapid progress. It was naturally of the greatest importance for the disciple to accept these trials and face them squarely. The young monk was expected to give uncompromising and complete obedience to the demands and advice of the Spiritual Father no matter how disconcerting some might appear. In this hard school of training — and here alone — the monk would learn to "get rid of three things: self-will, self-justification and the desire to please."[37] If he can put up with rough treatment, realizing that the Spiritual Father knows what he is doing, he will rapidly come to a state of detachment from his own will and his own ego. He will then enter a state of spiritual liberty in which, instead of being guided by his own subjective fantasies and desires, he completely accepts objective reality and conforms to it with no other purpose than to "walk in truth." This implies a state of complete indifference to his own subjective purposes, to his desire to be praised and accepted by others, and to have a respected place in the society of men. In the language of the Fathers, this transformation was the result of a complete substitution of God's will for the will of the individual ego.[38]

Such is the spiritual freedom without which there is no tranquility, no *quies*, no purity of heart. In other words, the purpose of the spiritual training given by the Fathers was to bring their disciples as quickly as possible to this state of inner liberty which made them able to live as sons of God.

Nevertheless, a loose and irresponsible reading of the Fathers has sometimes led less discerning ascetics of a later age to place undue emphasis on arbitrary and unreasonable commands, systematically insulting the intelligence and the essential human dignity of the subject, as if the sole purpose of ascetic training were to break down his personal integrity by so-called blind obedience. Fr. Hausherr points out that the term "blind obedience" is not found in the *Vitae Patrum*, and that the Fathers in any case would certainly not have thought that one who was following a guide endowed with a charismatic gift of understanding, was obeying blindly.[39] A more accurate expression would be "uncritical" or "unquestioning" obedience. This is not blind, unreasoning and passive obedience of one who obeys merely in order to let himself be "broken," but the clear-sighted trusting obedience of one who firmly believes that his guide knows the true way to peace and purity of heart and is an interpreter of God's will for him. Such obedience is "blind" only in the sense that it puts aside its own limited and biased judgment: but it does so precisely because it sees that to follow one's own judgment in things one does not properly understand is indeed to walk in darkness.

At this point, passing from the viewpoint of the disciple to that of the Master, we see that the Master must be extraordinarily humble, discerning, kind, and in no sense a despotic character. The "hard sayings" which he administers must spring from genuine kindness and concern for the interests of the disciples and not from a secret desire to dominate and exploit them for his own egotistic ends. The Master must, in other words, be himself one who is no longer in the least attracted by "superiorship" or by the desire to rule and teach others. In fact, we may find many of the Apothegms devoted to stories of monks who refused to take on the role of Abba, or who fled from those who attempted to gather around them as disciples. However, as in the case of St. Pachomius and the other great Masters, they eventually gave in and accepted, realizing that this service of others was a further step in their own self-renunciation. But they always taught first by example, and only after that by their words.

A brother said to Abba Poeman: "Some brothers are living with me: do you wish me to command them?" The old man replied: "Not at all. Act first, and if they wish to 'live', they will put the lesson into effect themselves." The brother said: "Abba, they themselves want me to command them." The old man said: "No, become a model for them, and not a lawgiver."[40]

One remarkable characteristic of the Desert hermits as reflected in the "sayings" is their great respect for the variety of personal vocations and "ways." They did not seek to impose hard and fast rules, reducing all to an arbitrary uniformity. Far from seeking security in a kind of servile conformism, they were able to appreciate the diversity of gifts which manifested the One Spirit dwelling in them all (I Corinthians 12:4).

Abba John used to say: "The whole company of the holy men is like unto a garden which is full of fruit-bearing trees of various kinds, and wherein the trees are planted in one earth and all of them drink from one fountain; and thus it is with all the holy men, for they have not one rule only, but several varieties, and one man laboureth in one way and another man in another, but it is one Spirit which operateth and worketh in them."[41]

Finally, to sum up, we can say that the Spiritual Father must indeed be "spiritual" in the technical sense of pneumatikos, a man entirely guided and illuminated by the Divine Spirit, one who has totally surrendered himself to God, and who is therefore guided by love and not by merely external or logical norms. John the Solitary distinguishes the "spiritual man" (pneumatikos) from the merely rational and virtuous man who he calls psychicos. Actually he is simply following the terminology of St. Paul (I Corinthians 2:14) where the psychicos is sometimes translated the "natural man," and where the Apostle says: "The psychicos does not receive what comes from the Spirit of

God, for it is folly to him." The spiritual man is he who has received the Spirit of God and knows the "things of the Spirit" (see *I Corinthians* 2:6-13).

For John the Solitary, transferring the Pauline teaching into the monastic context, the *psychicos* is the well-meaning but literal-minded monk who seeks to gain much merit by his good works, and estimates everything by the yardstick of human respect. "If his good works are eclipsed (by the superior action of the Spirit) he falls into a kind of despair."[42] He is unable to give genuine spiritual guidance, for all he knows about are the externals of asceticism and cult, which are good in themselves, but which he does not know how to relate to their true end.

We can sum up the teaching of the Fathers on spiritual direction by saying that the monk who is merely a *psychicos* lacks the wisdom required to make a true spiritual Father. He cannot liberate minds and hearts, he cannot open them to the secret action of the Spirit. He trusts entirely in an external and legalistic knowledge of mere rudiments, and does not "give life" by an insistence on non-essentials and by consistent neglect of the living needs of the disciple, he tends to stifle life and to "extinguish the Spirit" (*I Thessalonians* 5:19).

John the Solitary observes very acutely that while the *psychicos* has overcome his grosser passions and lives virtuously, he does not really love God and men. He is in a kind of intermediate state in which he has ceased to be moved by passion and crude self-interest (which would make him "love" those who accorded with his own interests) and he has not attained to the spiritual freedom which loves all men perfectly in and for God. "The love of God is not acquired by bodily asceticism but by insight into the mysteries; and since he has not attained to this he fails to love all men."[43] He does indeed have love for some men, but what is the basis of this love? It is, says John, his love for *his own doctrine*, his own ascetic system, "his rule, his way." He is capable of loving *only those who acquiesce in his teaching.* Hence this charity is not authentic. He loves his disciples *for the sake of his own doctrine,* that is to say he makes use of the disciple to affirm the truth and rightness of his own system, or in the end, to show that he himself is a good director!

On the contrary, a truly spiritual Father is sought out not only by beginners but by those who are themselves advanced, because he has the "words of life," and loves men as God does. They see that he loves not a doctrine, not a method, but men. Since he loves not his ideal but them, they say to him:

We have hastened to come to you . . . because we have found in your words so many things that had never even entered our minds. For although for many years we had never gone out of our cell, the fact of coming to see you has been of much greater profit to us than our stability. We had fixed certain customs for ourselves and now we have set them aside as trivial on account of the knowledge you have shown us. We feel as St. Paul must have felt . . . who at first gained credit for himself and took satisfaction in living according to the law, thinking that there was no other way of perfection until he received the knowledge of Christ. So we also thought that what we had was perfection . . . . [44]

Since in fact one of the pitfalls of the strictly regulated ascetic life of the monks was this spirit of legalism and trust in external works, the true spiritual Father was necessary to insure that the solitaries did not forget the "freedom of the sons of God" which was so ardently preached by Paul and is at the very heart of the New Testament. It was in this freedom alone that they could find authentic purity of heart and true *quies*. This freedom and tranquility are the "good ground" in which the seed of grace and wisdom can bring forth fruit a hundredfold. The state of purity and rest is not what one can call the "summit of perfection," what-ever that may mean. It is simply the last stage of development that can be observed and discussed in logical terms. It is what John the Solitary calls "integrity," but his integrity is not the end, it is really only the *beginning* of the true spiritual (*pneumatikos*) life. "Beyond integrity is mystery which cannot be defined."[45]

They used to say that one of the old men asked God that he might see the Fathers, and he saw them all with the exception of Abba Anthony; and he said to him that showed them to him: "Where is Abba Anthony?" And he said to him, "Wheresoever God is, there is Anthony."[46]

NOTES

1. Chapter IV from *Contemplation in a World of Action.* Garden City, New York: Doubleday & Company, Inc., 1971.

2. For an excellent survey of the whole history of spiritual direction in the Christian context see the article "Direction Spirituelle" in the *Dictionnaire de Spiritualité,* Volume III, cols. 1002-1214.

3. See the *Life,* St. Teresa's autobiography, where for instance in Chapter 28 she speaks of the great help she received from Dr. Balthasar Alvarez. In her *Interior Castle,* VI Mansion, she speaks of the injury done to mystics, during their time of purifying trial, by bad directors, and how the fears and scruples of confessors can add to the suffering of one who is already disconcerted by inexplicable experiences.

4. The *Apophthegmata* are to be found in Migne's Greek patrology, Volume 65, and many of the same stories are reproduced in the *Verba Seniorum* in the Latin Patrology, Volume 73, col. 739 ff. For the sake of convenience the excellent English version of E. Wallis Budge, in the *Paradise of the Fathers* (from Syriac) 2 volumes (London, 1907), will be used here.

5. The most characteristic work of Evagrius — as well as the most influential — is his treatise on prayer, *De Oratione,* long ascribed to St. Nilus, and available in a French translation by Père I. Hausherr, S.J.

6. *Paradise of the Fathers,* II, 3. This saying is the first in the entire series and thus acquires a certain importance as a paradigm for the whole monastic ascesis.

7. Cassian, *Collatio* I. 6. Migne P.L. 49: 488. Cf. St. Peter Damian: "As the proper office of the priest is to apply himself completely to offer sacrifice, and the doctor's function is to preach, so no less is the hermit's office to rest in fasting and silence — *in jejunio silentioque quiescere.*" Opus XV. 5. P.L. 145: 339.

Dom J. Leclercq, O.S.B., has developed the theme of *quies* in *Otia Monastica,* Studia Anselmiana, Rome, 1963.

8. Serm. VII on II Epistle to Corinthians. Quoted by Callistus and Ignatius in *Writings from the Philokalia on Prayer of the Heart,* edited by Kadlubovsky and Palmer, London, 1953, page 166.

9. L. Th. Lefort, *Les Vies Coptes de Saint Pachôme,* Louvain, 1943, pages 60, 61.

10. Lefort, *op. cit., Avant Propos,* page 1.

11. Lefort, *op.cit.,* page 74.

12. Lefort, *Les Vies Coptes,* pages 84-85.

13. See *Rule of St. Benedict,* chapter 58.

14. *Paradise*, II, 13.

15. *Ibid.*, page 32.

16. *Ibid.*, page 83.

17. *Ibid.*

18. *Ibid.*, page 97.

19. *Ibid.*, page 199.

20. *Ibid.*, page 198.

21. John the Solitary, *Dialogue sur l'Ame et les Passions*, translated by I. Hausherr, S.J., Orientalia Christiana Analecta, 120, Rome, pages 31-32.

22. *Paradise*, II, 16.

23. In all spiritual traditions there is recognized a stage in which thoughts and desires, whether good or bad, are projected and objectified as external beings or person. This stage has to be transcended, but the experiences that belong to it have to be taken into account even it "illusory." The question of the metaphysical reality of angels or demons is another matter.

24. See *The Undistorted Image* by Archmandrite Sophrony, London, 1962.

25. *Paradise*, II, 14, for the pillar of cloud as a mystical symbol. See St. Gregory of Nyssa, *De Vita Moysis*, French translation by J. Daniélou, S.J., *Sources Chrétiennes*, 2nd edition, Paris, 1955.

26. See Cassian, *De Cenobiorum Institutis*, Lib. X, P.L.49, volumes 359 ff.

27. *Paradise*, II, 4.

28. *Ibid.*, page 12. Here we see that the importance of "staying in the cell" is analagous to the emphasis on *Zazen* (sitting in meditation) in Zen Buddhism. Dom J. Leclercq has an important essay, "Sedere" (sitting) in the volume *Le Millenaire du Mont Athos*, Chevetogne, 1963.

29. *Ibid.*, page 161.

30. Palladius, *Historia Lausiaca* 24. *Paradise*, I, 136.

31. *Paradise*, II, 240.

32. Paul Evergetinos. See I. Hausherr, S.J. *Direction Spirituelle en Orient autrefois*, Orientalia Christiana Analecta 144, Rome, 1955, page 162.

33 *Ibid.*, pages 167-168 (quoting St. Gregory of Nyssa).

34. *Apophthegmata*, Alpha Antonii, note 8, Migne P.G. 65: col. 88.

35. Cassian, Conference I, c. 20. Migne P.L. 49: 514-516.

36. Callistus and Ignatius in *Writings from the Philokalia*, P. 175.

37. Barsanuphius, quoted in Hausherr, *op.cit.*, page 165.

38. Hausherr, *ibid.*

39. *Op. cit.*, page 197.

40. *Apophthegmata*, Alph. Poemen, 174, P.G. 65: 364; see Hausherr, *op cit.*, page 190.

42. *Paradise*, II, 148.

42. John the Solitary, *op. cit.*, page 34. Compare St. John of the Cross, *Living Flame of Love*, III, 29 ff.

43. *Op. cit.*, page 43.

44. John the Solitary, *op. cit.*, page 39.

45. *Op. cit.*, page 46.

46. *Paradise*, II, 165.

"The Virgin of the Sign represents the Holy Virgin in an attitude of prayer. . . The Virgin is a model of the soul in its state of primordial purity, and the Child is like the germ of the Divine Light in the heart."
— Titus Burckhardt, *Sacred Art in East and West*

4

MOUNT ATHOS[1]

Thomas Merton

For over a thousand years Mount Athos has been one the greatest monastic centers in all Christendom. Perhaps those who have heard of this ancient republic have cherished a vague idea that Athos was simply a "monastery." Actually, the 35-mile-long peninsula near Thessalonica, in north Greece, is a whole nation of monks and monasteries. The capital of this small country, which for a long time enjoyed a completely independent political existence, is a town called Karyes in the center of the peninsula; it is the seat of Synaxis or Synod, the representative body of monks elected by the various monasteries at the beginning of each year. Karyes is a town of monks with a monastic school, a small hotel, and various shops and stores run by monks and men, plus a small force of Greek policemen who are obliged to remain celibate as long as they serve on Athos. The peninsula is absolutely forbidden to all women, for, as legend says, the Blessed Virgin excluded all other women from Athos when she claimed it as "her garden," after she was driven ashore by a storm, near the site of the present monastery of Iviron.

Whether or not the Blessed Virgin ever came there, Athos has been for a thousand years a "desert" cut off from the world and a jealously guarded stronghold of asceticism and contemplation. The mountain itself stands at the south end of the peninsula, and rises to a height of 5,000 feet. The rest of the territory is rugged, stony, wooded and truly wild. Wolves and wild boars still roam there. The mountain is crisscrossed by mule tracks. Automobiles, trucks, and tractors do not exist on Athos; there are no motor roads. Some of the monasteries have telephone connections with each other. Only one has electric lights, and in consequence is despised by the others. Some of the communities make their living by selling timber. Others survive by the production of wine or olive oil. All are poor and even the best of them does not measure up to minimum standards of comfort for Western Europeans, let alone for Americans. Recent books written about Athos tend to be at once exciting and deceptive. Often they are illustrated by magnificent photographs which one can contemplate with insatiable wonder. But the text is generally trivial by comparison. We find the sardonic remarks of hardened tourists who are ready for anything, and who will not hesitate to ride miles on mule back, drink ouzo and eat octopus fried in olive oil (provided that they can regard all this with the amused detachment of westerners dropping, as it were, from another planet). In such books one rarely receives any insight into the profound religious mystery of Athos. Even one of the most sympathetic and understanding accounts, that written by a Scot, the late Sidney Loch, who lived for years just outside the borders of Athos and knew its monks and hermits very well, nevertheless lacks a deep religious perspective. Nowhere has any modern western writer given us a witness to the spirit of Athos comparable to the profoundly moving pages of Henry Miller about Epidaurus, Mycenae and especially Phaestos (in Crete). It is perhaps true that Athos is out of touch with our times, more so than any monastery in the Western world. But precisely because of this it has much to teach us, since our salvation consists not in keeping up with the times but in transcending them or, as St. Paul would say, in redeeming them.

Athos is the last important Christian survival of the typical ancient monastic colonies which flourished in the fourth and fifth centuries when monasticism began in the Church. In those days men did not enter this or that religious order (there were no "orders") — they fled to a "desert" or to mountain area in the wilderness where monks gathered in twos or threes, or in small colonies of ten, twenty, or fifty, or even in large groups of several hundred. Others lived alone as hermits and recluses. There the monastic way was followed not according to a fixed legislative code, but according to traditional customs which could be adjusted very flexibly to the needs of each one in his spiritual journey to God. So too at Athos, even today. The different monasteries, *skites* and cells are not representatives of "orders" in the Orthodox Church. There are still no formal orders, in our sense, in the Greek Church, only varieties of monks.

At Athos the two main groups are cenobitic and idiorrhythmic monks. The cenobites live a systematic community life resembling that of Cistercians or Benedictines in the Western Church. Yet they do not, as one might suppose "follow the Rule of St. Basil" or any other rule. The Rule of St. Basil is in any case rather a "spiritual directory" than a formal rule like that of St. Benedict. The Athonites are bound to keep the *typicon* (monastic customs) of their individual monasteries, and the cenobite's life is still in many ways much stricter than the strictest observance in the Western Church. The monks sometimes chant in choir sixteen or eighteen hours at a stretch for the offices of the greater feasts, and their fasts are more numerous and more arduous than ours. The general condition of poverty in the cenobitic monasteries is all the more notable now that these once prosperous houses have been gradually ruined. The monks work hard to earn a meager living. Wars, revolutions and iron curtains have cut off their supply of vocations as well as their revenues. And if life in the monasteries themselves is austere, it is all the more so out in the cells and hermitages where men live on the rugged mountainside in conditions on a level with those of the poorest of the poor in the Balkan countries.

The idiorrhythmic monks are peculiar to the Oriental Church, if we except those modern religious congregations in the West whose members are allowed to retain title to their property and to keep their individual earnings. The idiorrhythmic monks, whether in monasteries or out of them, retain proprietorship of what property they have, and live on the income from their labor. The monastery furnishes them with shelter and work in a rudimentary organization which is controlled not by an abbot but by an elected committee. The monks chant the office together in choir, but work and live on their own, in or out of the monastery, cooking their own meals which can include meat on certain days. The monastic shops in Karyes are run by idiorrhythmic monks. It is a loose kind of life, not necessarily decadent, though it dates from a period of relaxation in the history of Athos, in the days when it was ruled by the Turks. Monasteries can choose to be either idiorrhythmic or cenobitic and some have passed back and forth from one to other several times in the course of centuries.

There are twenty large autonomous monasteries on Athos.

The oldest of these is Lavra, founded by St. Athanasius of Athos in 963. Though there were hermits and small groups of monks on the Mountain before this time, and though St. Athanasius himself first came to Athos in 958, the thousandth anniversary of Athonite monasticism will probably be celebrated in 1963. The monastery of Simopetra, standing on a high cliff overhanging the sea, is probably familiar to many who have seen photographs of Mount Athos; the flimsy balconies on which the monks may sit suspended hundreds of feet above the sea leave one with an indelible impression of the Holy Mountain. Another ancient monastery is Iviron, founded in 980 by three knights from Georgia. The community was originally Georgian, and chanted the liturgy in its own tongue, though for centuries now Iviron has been under the control of Greeks. Later I will mention the once flourishing Russian monastery on Athos, St. Panteleimon.

The score of smaller groups, *skites, kalybes, kellia* and hermitages, all depend on one or other of the main monasteries, which alone can be represented by delegates (one each) in the synod at Karyes.

The general level of life for the idiorrhythmic monks is a little more comfortable and a great deal more independent than it is for the cenobites. The largest and most prosperous Greek monasteries are idiorrhythmic. Cenobitism flourished most of all among the Russians, who are now rapidly declining in numbers and significance. The idiorrhythmic monastery of Vatopedi, one of the largest and least primitive, is the only one that has electric light and a few water closets which may or may not work. It is also the only Athonite community that has adopted the Gregorian calendar, so that Vatopedi celebrates the feasts of the liturgical year with the Western Church, thirteen days ahead of the other monasteries on Athos.

Only at Vatopedi does twelve o'clock mean noon. Other monasteries, following the Turkish practice, put twelve at sunset. Iviron, different from all the rest, puts twelve at sunrise, as it used to be done in Persia. The atmosphere of independence on Athos is therefore something quite unusual in this world of ours where no one dreams of disregarding the clocks of his time-belt, no matter how nonconformist he may be in other respects.

The so-called *skites* are dependent monasteries, not necessarily smaller than the twenty autonomous communities that have a voice in the synod. On the contrary, Stavronikita, which today numbers only twenty-two monks, is an autonomous house, while the Russian *skite* of St. Andrew once outnumbered it by several hundred but never managed to become autonomous.

Besides the *skites,* the Holy Mountain is dotted with *kalybes* (cottages) where two or three monks live and work together, and then there are caves and cells for hermits, some of whom still live in the same seclusion and austerity as the primitive monks of the desert. The great variety of vocations on Athos, the respect for individual differences of vocation, the liberty allowed to the grace of the Holy Spirit: all this remains a significant characteristic of this monastic nation, and a sign of its vitality.

Not everyone can become a hermit: this depends on the permission of monastic superiors who jealously guard the privilege and grant it only to those who have proved the spiritual strength and purity of heart and are ready to be "kissed by God."

At the same time we must not take too romantic a view of the solitaries on Athos. They lead a life that is, from our Western viewpoint, utterly squalid, filthy and miserable. Yet they seem to get along well enough at it, and they really are, for the most part, deeply spiritual men. (In fact it is quite possible that they are more spiritual than the monks of our more hygienic and up-to-date monasteries with their spotless dairy cows and well-washed pigs.) The hermits on Athos are, generally, men of peasant extraction who are physically prepared to live a life exposed to heat, cold, vermin and near-starvation.

The population of Athos has had its ups and downs since the tenth century. Perhaps the highest number was reached in the sixteenth century when it is estimated that from 15,000 to 20,000 monks and hermits lived on the Holy Mountain. This was when the monastic republic enjoyed its greatest material prosperity, in spite of the fact that Turkish government imposed a levy on the monks, in return leaving them in peace. There was a sharp decline after the Greek revolution in 1821. Many monks joined the army and fought for Greece, leaving the monasteries half empty.

The nineteenth century saw the great tide of Russian vocations

to Athos, astutely promoted by the Tsars who took over a ruined, abandoned Greek monastery (St. Panteleimon) and built it
up into a powerful community of 1,500 Russian cenobites. The
Russikon, as this cenobium is called, became a kind of political
nightmare for all the rest of Athos. The Greeks fought with all
their power to prevent the populous and wealthy Russian *skites*,
like that of St. Andrew, from becoming independent monasteries and thus gaining a seat in the synod. They already suspected
that half the monks of the Russikon were Tsarist soldiers in dis-
guise, and were afraid that the Russians might gain control of
the governing body of the peninsula.

In 1912, the population of Athos was about 7,000, of whom
over half were Russians. By 1930 this number had been cut
almost in half, and of course the biggest decline of all was among
the Russians, who had received no vocations since the Bolshevist revolution. One by one the dependent cells and *kalybes* closed
down and the aging Russian monks fell back upon the larger
monasteries which, even with these reinforcements, remained half
empty and began to go to ruin.

Vocations from other Iron Curtain countries have also rapidly declined. The Serbian idiorrhythmic monastery of Chilandari
has dwindled from eighty monks in 1930 to forty-three in 1950.
The same rate of decline is found in Zographou (Bulgarian) and
the Rumanian *skite* of Prodromos. But the Greek monasteries
themselves are in no better condition. The population of the
Holy Mountain was 4,600 in 1930 and must be little more than
half that number today.

Lavra, one of the most flourishing Greek idiorrhythmic houses,
and said to be the best on Athos, had six hundred monks in
1930 and only two hundred in 1953 – a drastic loss in twenty-
three years. The outlook for the future of Athos is not reassur-
ing and, in parentheses, the Russian ambassador in Athens has
taken a discreet, disquieting interest in the Russikon. (The remaining monks are all loyal to the memory of the Tsars whose
portraits are everywhere at St. Panteleimon.) It is known that
monasticism is tolerated today within the U.S.S.R. for reasons
of political expediency. Perhaps the Kremlin might suddenly one
day find it dialectically correct to take over the Russikon for its
own monastic purposes – and revive the nightmare that kept the

Greeks of Athos uneasy all through the nineteenth century.

The typical Athos monastery is a fortified village of rambling, balconied buildings centered around the main building or *katholikon*. There are always other churches and chapels — seventeen, for example, at Vatopedi. In these churches and chapels are innumerable ikons, some of which represent the best of Byzantine painting and many of which figure in miraculous legends.

The sacred art of Mount Athos is hieratic but resplendent in the darkness and silence of churches where there is no room for curiosity and aestheticism, only for worship. We of the west have become so unaccustomed to seeing sacred painting in its proper situation — the sanctuary of the Living God, and are so familiar with the bare lighted wall of the museum, that we might at first fail to appreciate the mystical technique of the great painters of Athos. Here the saints, the angels, the Mother of God and Christ the *Pantokrator* shine at us dimly from the shadowy walls lit by candles and votive lamps. Their beauty is part of the mystery of the liturgy and speaks to us in harmony with the Greek hymns. In such frescoes we look in vain for realism or anecdote. We find instead the powerful language of prayer and of spiritual vision. It is true that on Athos as everywhere else, sacred art has declined into vulgarity and pastiche. As far as I know there has not yet been any significant attempt at a revival of the ancient spirit and the pure tradition of Greek sacred painting.

Sculpture is an altogether negligible element in Eastern Church art. We find nothing at Athos to correspond to the *tympan* of Vezelay or of Autun, nor to the saints around the doors of Rheims and Chartres. Fortunately we find nothing that corresponds to the sculpture of Saint Sulpice.

Most of the monasteries, particularly those near the sea-shore, have arsenals as well as crenelated walls, a reminder of the days when they had to be ready to defend themselves at any time against pirates or Latin raiders from the West. Though in the earliest days of Athos, before the schism of 1054, there was a monastery of Italian Benedictines on Athos, the Western Church has not been popular there since the Crusades. Too often parties of Crusaders or other groups of Western knights raided and sacked the monasteries of Athos, and the memory of these events has not died.

Theological suspicion of the west has also been kept alive on the Holy Mountain by memory of the Palamite controversy in the fourteenth century. Athos in the Middle Ages was the center of a powerful mystical revival — the so-called hesychast movement. The *hesychasts* were contemplatives, solitaries for the most part, who followed a tradition supposed to have originated on Mount Sinai and which later flourished in Russia. The term *hesychasm* has had a very bad press in the west where it has been grossly misunderstood. St. Gregory Palamas, a monk of Athos who later became Archbishop of Salonika, was the chief defender of *hesychasm*, in the fourteenth century, against a Greek from Italy called Barlaam of Calabria. Barlaam has sometimes been represented as a westernizing pseudo-Thomist. In actual fact, he was a humanist who, in the name of classical ideals, turned the weapon of his skeptical nominalism against the mystical theology of Palamas. Barlaarn, in practice, considered all mystical experience more or less illusory. At best, it was only a product of refined aesthetic fervor enkindled by symbols. St. Gregory Palamas, on the other hand, defended the thesis that the "divine light" — the same light that was seen by the three Apostles who saw the vision of the Transfigured Savior on Mount Thabor — could be experienced directly in this present life. He held that this light was not a mere symbol of the divinity, but an experience of the "divine energies" — though not of the divine essence. Barlaam was formally defeated in the lists of theological controversy and the Oriental Church upheld the teachings of Palamas. At this, Barlaam withdrew to the west and went over to Rome (or rather to Avignon) — not so much because of devotion to Church unity, as because he found the climate of nominalism in the west at that time more congenial to his own mentality.

Hesychasm, which has always been regarded with extreme caution, if not outright suspicion, by Western writers, has perhaps been treated too shabbily by them. It is clearly something more than a technique of autohypnosis by which one pretends to "procure" or "induce" a state of mystic illumination. *Hesychasm* has some technical points in common with hatha-yoga, but it is an authentically Christian and deeply simple way of prayer.

Gregory Palamas taught that the "uncreated energies" of God

could communicate themselves directly to men in the present life (he rejected the idea of created grace). All these points are questionable and might seem, to Western theologians, to be unacceptable. But perhaps we should not reject them without first having made sure we know what they really mean. In practice, the *hesychast* "way of contemplation" is simply a method of recollection which relies on slow, rhythmical breathing and silent repetition of an aspiratory prayer like "Lord Jesus Christ have mercy on me a sinner."

It would be a great mistake to idealize the monasticism of Mount Athos. But it would be a far greater one to underestimate it. Here, as everywhere, human frailty and the miseries of man as a political animal have made themselves evident from age to age. And yet Athos remains, for all its deficiencies, one of the most authentic and integral examples of Christian monasticism. After a thousand years it is still quite close to the original pattern of monastic life that was first developed in the deserts of Egypt and Syria. It is above all the fullness and variety of Athos that impress us. Like everything else in the West, our monasticism has been subject to fragmentation — it has been atomized. We have broken up into different orders, none of which retain the many-sided completeness of the monastic ideal.

The free growth that has been permitted on Athos for a thousand years has extended in all directions and sometimes the branches that should have been pruned have been allowed to wander too far. The fruit has not always been sweet. The branches have not always been strong enough to resist storms. The fact that Athonite monachism has sedulously ignored all modern developments in technology or hygiene is not necessarily in its favor. There should be a reasonable adaptation to the times — though the obvious danger is not lack of adaptation to, but submersion in, the spirit of these times. In the main, the spiritual growth of Athos has been normal, healthy and supremely varied. Such rich variety is a noble, desirable thing. There is room for the weak and the strong. There are all kinds of levels of observance. There are all kinds of opportunities for contemplative perfection. The horizons are not those of one four-walled enclosure. The monk is never shut up within the limits of a rigidly confined outlook. There are always possibilities for unexpected growth; one can always aspire to new — or old directions. However, these new directions are always purely contemplative. The monks of Athos have never engaged in any kind of active apostolate, and never even seem to have considered it necessary. Their apostolate of prayer and example has been unexcelled. For centuries the ambition of every devout Orthodox Christian man was to make a pilgrimage to the Holy Mountain — an objective second, in this respect, to Jerusalem alone. Adaptation to the times should not mean abandonment of a contemplative ideal.

What if someday there were to be an Athos for the Western Church, the Western world? Some island, some mountain jutting out into the sea, a "nation" of contemplatives with room for Benedictines and Carthusians and Cistercians and Camaldolese, for cenobites and hermits, for small and large groups with diversified observances, with free access to one another, with reasonable opportunities for mutual stimulation, transit and exchange. Is this a heresy? Is this a dream? Have we reached the point where all dreams are regarded as dangerous and forbidden? When life has no more risk in it and no more dreams, it is no longer life.

Still, though one may dream, one must also be realistic if he hopes to see those dreams come somewhere near actuality. It is evident that with the various contemplative orders structured as they are, and with each one jealous of its own usages, its own interpretations of the Rule, and its own exclusiveness, it would be over-optimistic to expect them to get along together in a monastic "republic" like Athos. They could co-exist, no doubt, and be good friends. But there could never be a real compenetration and mutuality of ideals. One wonders if they could really form a large, homogeneous group, a real intermonastic family. Whatever may be the answer, speculation on the point is perhaps useless. A group of communities and individuals living the monastic life at different levels and with varying tempos could be formed of lay contemplatives, gathered in groups around about a nucleus of one formally established monastic family — say, a community of Primitive Benedictines. Here there would be plenty of flexibility, plenty of opportunity for growth in new directions. Organization ought not be the first and most important consideration. What we really ought to do is what the first monks did: go off somewhere into the wilderness (approved by a qualified director) and see how long and how well we can stand it — with or without companions — and then go on to build upon a foundation of experience.

Each year on the Feast of the Transfiguration of Christ, monks and pilgrims climb to the summit of Athos and there in a small chapel, built upon the peak, the office of the feast is solemnly chanted and the sacred liturgy of the day is celebrated at dawn. Far out at sea, the ships can see the light of a huge fire triumphantly kindled on the Mountain. The flames dancing in the dawn wind and reaching into the purple sky to mingle with the stars speak a far different message from those which we receive from the artificial earth satellites which man has hurled into orbit by the power of his science. It is certainly right and fitting that the mind of man should reach out to explore the cosmos. But in that case, he must be prepared for what he finds there. He must be prepared that the void into which he has projected his mind could in turn take possession of his heart. He must be prepared to find his pseudo-humanism undermined and have it collapse under him while he plunges into the darkness and emptiness of a nominalist abyss. As long as it is only the light of our own mind that peers into infinite spaces, the cosmic depths will reflect nothing but our own vacuity. But when from the heavens come fire and light into our heart — not the light of the sun or of the stars, but the Light that transfigured Christ on Tabor, then man, strong in the love created within him by God, can safely stand as a god upon the earth. Then the light that comes to him from God transfigures and ennobles the whole of creation and all that is in it.

Then the emptiness of man no longer surrounds him and invades him from the outside. On the contrary, his own emptiness, assumed by the God who "emptied Himself" out of love for man, becomes an infinite fullness in which there can be no longer any darkness or any void. Admittedly, faith is still dark. But this is the night of nights, the paschal night, the passage of the Red Sea, in which man follows the Risen Savior through the tomb and the hell in the center of his own being to emerge in the heaven which is the very heart of his own nothingness. The light of Tabor is the light of the Resurrection. The meaning of Athos is the mystery of Easter. The flames that spring up in the summer night, on top of the Holy Mountain, are flames that mutely proclaim the message of God's love for man in Christ: the light that has shone upon us all "in the face of Christ Jesus," the light that dawns in our hearts to the day of eternity. The light of Athos is the light of a daystar that knows no setting. But if, at some future time, the flame of the symbolic bonfire fails to appear on the mountain, like the signal that heralded the fall of Troy, then we shall know for certain that the time of battle has come, a dreadful time in which the pillar of fire and cloud must rise in our own hearts to lead us out of the chaos of radioactivity around that other mushroom-like pillar of death which the world has decided to parody a glorious sign of God, the sign of the passage out of Egypt into the Kingdom of Life.

NOTE

1. "Mount Athos" was first published in Thomas Merton's *Disputed Questions*. Farrar, Straus & Giroux, 1960.

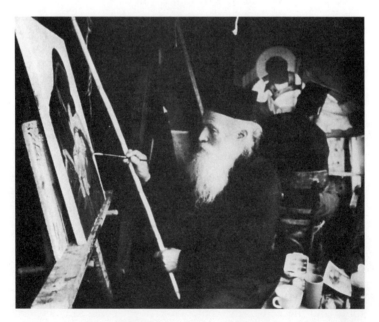

Icon painter at work on Athos.

5

THE SPIRITUALITY OF SINAI[1]
Saint John of the Ladder

Thomas Merton

The Oriental Church has no book strictly comparable to the *Imitation of Christ*, a characteristic flowering of medieval Western Christianity, human, tender, devotional, often criticized today as "individualistic." In the Eastern Church, the admirable *Life in Christ* by Nicholas Cabasilas may be a kind of opposite number to the *Imitation*. But it is theological, sacramental, embracing the whole mystery of Christ and of the Church, though lacking nothing in warmth, love, personal devotion. In any case, it never enjoyed the vast popularity of the *Imitation*.

From the point of view of popularity, the most widely read spiritual book in Eastern Christendom, apart perhaps from the *Philokalia*, is the *Holy Ladder* of St. John Climacus, recently published in a new and first-rate English translation.[2] The influence and the importance of this remarkable book makes it the Eastern counterpart of our *Imitation*. And this suggests an interesting comparison between the two.

First of all, the *Ladder* is seldom, if ever, tender. It is a tough, hard-hitting, merciless book. Climacus was a kind of sixth-century desert Hemingway. Except, of course, that he is not entirely disillusioned with everything — he is no victim of *acedia*. But he sees through the weaknesses of men and monks, and cannot resist the temptation to caricature them without mercy. He never stops. Even when he gets to the last, supposedly serene rungs of the *Ladder*, on which all is sweet repose and *hesychia*, he restlessly yields to the same wild reflex and keeps lashing out on all sides. You cannot keep the man quiet. He is an irrepressible fighter.

You will look in vain, in the *Ladder*, for the gentle and affective devotion to Christ Crucified that is the very heart of the *Imitation*. In fact little is said about the Person of the Redeemer — except in one, rare, exceptional little line which is doubtless the most significant in the book, perhaps beyond all awareness and intention on the part of the author. I will postpone discussion of this point to the end of the article.

Meanwhile, if we consider the matter of "individualism," the *Ladder* is certainly as individualistic as the *Imitation*, if not more so. There is scarcely a word about liturgy, sacraments, corporate unity in Christ. Indeed, there is not much explicitly said about charity, though for all his violence, Climacus has a deep undercurrent of friendly and fraternal understanding. The *Ladder* is almost exclusively concerned with the problems, struggles and conquests of the individual monk, seeking his own salvation. And in this it is completely faithful to and characteristic of the desert tradition. Hence we must not be too eager to say that all "individualism" in Christian piety began with the *devotio moderna* and has nothing to do with the Patristic spirit.

Both the *Imitation* and the *Ladder* call for a complete dedication of oneself to the pursuit of spiritual perfection. But in the *Imitation*, the emphasis is all on God's grace and on His merciful help. In the *Ladder* the basic concern is with the will and energy of the monk himself. The spiritual life is a holy war, a death struggle with the devil, in which one must kill or be killed. One fights desperately under the eye of a severe and, it is implied, somewhat detached Judge. Even the most heroic of penances cannot guarantee to move Him to pity. This is a spirituality as severe, as inflexible, as rugged as the landscape in which it was written.

The desert of Sinai is, of course, the scene of the most dramatic and terrible episode in the history of Israel. The burnt, forbidding cliffs of Djeb-el-Moussa frown pitilessly on a waste of sand, rock and waterless scrub. In this desert, the children of Israel danced madly around the Golden Calf while Moses came down and smashed the Tables of the Law which he had just received from Yahweh in the thundercloud. It is the setting for contradiction, blasphemy, struggle and despair: the despair of man faced with an inhuman command, and finding nothing in himself with which to fulfill it. And yet the thunder roars "Thou *shalt* . . . "

At the same time, the Mountain of God is the great symbol of mystical contemplation. Here Moses saw God in the Burning Bush. Here he spoke to God face to face in darkness, in the cloud, as to a friend. Philo Judaeus, followed by Origen and St. Gregory of Nyssa, had worked out these symbols in a theology of *apophatic* (dark) contemplation. But to reach that dark vision, the spirit had to be utterly sinless, perfectly pure, free from all taint of inordinate passion. Brute beasts and defiled sinners were not to touch the smoking mountain, on pain of death by stoning!

Fugitives from the persecutions of the third and fourth centuries made the desert of Sinai a center of eremitical monasticism when Nitria and Scete became the lights of the Christian world. The fact that Justinian founded a monastery there in A.D. 527 only proves that Sinai was a famous nation of monks in his time. The monastery has existed and flourished ever since. It has never been destroyed by the Moslems. Legend ascribes this to the fact that the monks once gave hospitality to Mohammed. Whether or not they did so literally, they have never ceased to do so in spirit: the monastery of Sinai has for centuries aided and supported with alms and medical aid the Moslem nomads of the desert.

St. John Climacus was abbot of this monastery in the sixth century and here he wrote his famous *Holy Ladder*. It was addressed to the monks of a nearby monastery of Raithu. But actually it was to spread from monastery to monastery all over the Christian world. In the East it exercised a decisive influence in the lives of such important figures as St. Anthony, founder of the monastery of the Caves at Kiev, St. Symeon the "New Theologian," and closer to our time Paissy Velichkovsky, the leader of the great monastic revival in Russia at the end of the eighteenth century, which produced the movement of the *stareizki*, or charismatic, prophetic monks of nineteenth-century Russia.

The *Ladder* has also been well known in the West at least since the fifteenth century when it was first printed in Venice. The reformer of La Trappe, Abbot de Rancé, knew it well and imbibed its spirit, probably from a Greek edition published in France in 1633. A Trappist monk of Mount Saint Bernard, England, was the author of the only English translation in existence before the present text. It is interesting to notice that the Trappist edition highlights the ascetic severity of the original, while suppressing some of the chapter on "solitude," which contains the heart of St. John's doctrine on mystical contemplation. This earlier English edition, published just over a hundred years ago in 1858, was read within the last decade at the Abbey of Gethsemani, in the refectory. In the main, the monks seem to have found it either funny or unpleasant, and some unfledged ascetics openly complained to the present writer that Climacus was nuts. I think this effect was mainly due to the old translation. The new one is much more impressive. It clearly proves that St. John Climacus was no fanatical windbag but a very astute observer of human nature, a man of violent and passionate sanctity, and in his better moments a very fine writer.

II.

The *Holy Ladder* is a compilation and popularization of all the spirituality of the Desert. St. John Climacus was not one of the great originators of the monastic tradition. He came three to four centuries after Anthony, Macanus, Evagrius and Cassian. He merely collected what had been taught and lived in the golden age, enlivening the collection with stories from his own experience, with his own caustic observations, and with his sensational style!

It is interesting to compare Climacus with the *Apothegmata* — that is with the collection of sayings *(Verba)* of the early Desert Fathers. The contrast is striking. The originators, the first Fathers, were silent, humble men who seemed unable to say anything except in the fewest possible words. Their statements are as laconic, as sober as they can be. And yet they are full of inner life and warmth. They overflow with an inexhaustible spirituality. They are as simple, as direct, and as mysterious as the *mondo* of the Zen Masters. And even more charming.

For this laconic charm St. John Climacus has substituted what I am sometimes tempted to regard as repetitious bluster. The reason for this is, I think, that Climacus has a strong and vener-able institution behind him. He is speaking with the full sup-port of a powerful monastic organization. The early Fathers had behind them nothing but the Desert.

The *Ladder*, as its name suggests, starts at the bottom with renunciation of the world and works up to mystical union with God. By far the greater part of the book is concerned with vices, passions, temptations and wiles of the devil, and, of course, with the proper means of unmasking the enemy and busting him in the teeth. It is here that St. John Climacus is his characteristic self, and without doubt this is the aspect of the book that will most impress the modern, casual reader. Even this violent and colorful aspect of the *Ladder* is significant. The book is a literary monument to a very important aspect of religious culture, much too important to be ignored. It throws light on such writers as Dostoievsky, for example. *Crime and Punishment* has a lot to do with the spirituality of St. John Climacus, in a perverse and in-verted sort of way. In fact all Russian literature and spirituality is tinged with the ferocity and paradox of Sinai — though it com-pensates with a tenderness and a depth of human feeling un-known to St. John of the Ladder. You will search the *Ladder* in vain for the compassion of a Staretz Zossima.

The intensity and seriousness of this book's demand for un-compromising battle with sin and with self-indulgence will nec-essarily frighten modern Christians, always anxious for compro-mise. That is why Father Georges Florovsky, quoted on the jacket, wisely declares: "The *Ladder* is an invitation to pilgrimage. Only those who have resolved to climb and ascend will appreciate this book." That is true. The others will be fighting it, and if you resist a man like Climacus, you get in the way of his flying fists.

At his best, Climacus sometimes suggests Theocritus and La-Bruyère. Here is his pungent description of the "insensible" man — that is, of the man for whom spirituality has become a matter of mere words and routine, rather than of serious practice:

"He talks about healing a wound, and does not stop ir-ritating it. He complains of sickness, and does not stop eating what is harmful. He prays against it, and immedi-ately goes and does it. And when he has done it, he is angry with himself; and the wretched man is not ashamed of his own words. 'I am doing wrong,' he cries, and eagerly continues to do so. His mouth prays against his passion, and his body struggles for it. He philosophizes about death, but he behaves as if he were immortal. He groans over the separation of soul and body, but drowses along as if he were eternal. He talks of temperance and self-control, but he lives for gluttony. He reads about the judgment and begins to smile. He reads about vainglory, and is vainglorious while actually reading. He repeats what he has learnt about vigil, and drops asleep on the spot. He praises prayer, but runs from it as from the plague. He blesses obedience, but he is the first to disobey. He praises detachment, but he is not ashamed to be spiteful and to fight for a rag. When angered he gets bitter, and he is angered again at his bitterness; and he does not feel that after one defeat he is suffering another. Having overeaten he repents, and a little later again gives way to it. He blesses silence, and praises it with a spate of words. He teaches meekness, and during the actual teaching frequently gets angry. Having woken from passion he sighs, and shaking his head, he again yields to passion."

As might be expected, one of the best chapters in book deals with *anger*, a subject on which Climacus might be trusted to say the last word. Actually he has some interesting observations. "Sometimes singing, in moderation, successfully relieves the temper," remarks the hermit in him. And the cenobite and abbot, remembering the monastery choir, hastens to point out that much can be lost in solitude that might have been saved in the cenobium, and his description of the angry hermits, fighting alone like caged partridges, is by all standards a classic:

"When for some reason I was sitting outside a monastery near the cells of those living in solitude, I heard them fighting by themselves in their cells like caged partridges from bitterness and anger, and leaping at the face of their offender as if he were actually present. And I devoutly advised them not to stay in solitude in case they should be changed from human beings into demons."

However, he is quite impartial. If the angry man should come back to the community and *face* it, the sensual man ought to go into the desert.

III.

Like all Oriental Christians, St. John Climacus is a great faster, and he does not hesitate to pour scorn on every form of gluttony. He may shock us, but perhaps this is one of the matters in which we ought to take him a little more seriously, although he is often at his funniest in treating it.

"The preparing of the table exposes gluttons, but the work of prayer exposes lovers of God. The former dance on seeing the table, but the latter scowl."

He has a subtle and interesting chapter on lust, another on the spirit of blasphemy which is important as a psychological document. The hair-raising description of the monastery prison, and the penitents incarcerated there, reads today like a report on a badly-run mental institution. One hermit can neatly check off symptoms of all the various kinds of schizophrenia and manic depression.

"Others were continually beating their breasts and recalling their past life and state of soul. Some of them watered the ground with their tears; others, incapable of tears, struck themselves. Some loudly lamented over their souls as over the dead, not having the strength to bear the anguish of their heart. Others groaned in their heart, but stifled all sound of their lamentation. But sometimes they could control themselves no longer, and would suddenly cry out.

"I saw there some who seemed from their demeanour and their thoughts to be out of their mind. In their great disconsolateness they had become like dumb men in complete darkness, and were insensible to the whole of life. Their minds had already sunk to the very depths of humility, and had burnt up the tears in their eyes with the fire of their despondency.

"Others sat thinking and looking on the ground, sway-ing their heads unceasingly, and roaring and moaning like lions from their inmost heart to their teeth . . . .

"One could see how the tongues of some of them were parched and hung out of their mouths like a dog's. Some chastised themselves in the scorching sun, others tor-mented themselves in the cold. Some, having tasted a little water so as not to die of thirst, stopped drinking; others, having nibbled a little bread, flung the rest of it away, and said that they were unworthy of being fed like human beings, since they had behaved like beasts."

However, do not be misled by the gusto with which he lets his pen run away with him. This "Prison" section, always con-sidered one of the most sensational and popular, has in it a deep spiritual truth. Climacus is trying to say that the most spiritual people he knew in the desert were not the ones who thought themselves to be great ascetics and contemplatives but those who were sincerely convinced that they were worthless monks, failures in their vocation. Naturally, this does not mean that spiritual perfection is to be sought in psychotic melodrama. We must pardon the vehement pleasure derived by this saint from pure exaggeration.

Little space is left in which to praise the last chapters, on solitude and *Hesychasm* (contemplation). Here the fiery writer becomes more quiet and even discreet, and deftly, in few words, exposes the mystery of pure prayer, that prayer without thoughts and without words in which the solitary clings to an experience of what cannot be experienced. "The cat keeps hold of her mouse, and the thought of the solitary holds his spiritual mouse. Do not call this example rubbish; if you do, then you do not know what solitude means."

We have said "prayer without words." That is not quite ac-curate. St. John Climacus is not one of those who, like Evagrius and St. Gregory of Nyssa, take us to the heights of obscure *theologia*, the contact with God in darkness, beyond even the purest of concepts. Rather he seems to speak of that contem-plative union achieved by the rhythmic repetition of the Holy Name of Jesus, synchronized with deep and controlled breathing, which became the favorite way to contemplation for monks of Mount Athos. This *hesychasm* came to Athos from Sinai, and one of the chief authorities for it was St. John Climacus himself. Actually, whatever is contained in his *Ladder* on this subject is fairly well hidden and had to be worked out by minds familiar with the more esoteric elements in the Sinaite tradition. The fact remains that the Greeks seem to have been quite justified in their interpretation of that one line which, I said above, turned out to be more influential than all the rest of the book put together: "Let the remembrance of Jesus be present with each breath, and then you will know the value of solitude."

Our just evaluation of St. John Climacus depends on our understanding of a few lines like this. They contain his mystical doctrine, which, by all means, balances the pages of garrulous asceticism. But we have to realize this fact. When we do, we see the real importance of the *Ladder*. Neglect of this truth makes the book little more than a religious and literary curiosity.

NOTES

1. "The Spirituality of Sinai" was first published in Thomas Merton's *Disputed Questions*. Farrar, Straus & Giroux, 1960.

2. *The Ladder of Divine Ascent*, by St. John Climacus, translated by Archimandrite Lazarus Moore, with an introduction by M. Heppell.

Palm motifs and cross, carved into the outer wall of
Saint Catherine's Monastery, Mount Sinai.

The gold and blue domes of the cathedral at Zagorsk, the center of the Eastern Orthodox Church in Russia.

6

RUSSIAN MYSTICS[1]

Thomas Merton

Russian mysticism is predominantly monastic (though one meets an occasional exception like the modern non-monastic mystics, Father John of Kronstadt — recently canonized by the Orthodox Church — and Father Yelchaninov). It therefore thrives in solitude and renunciation of the world. Yet anyone who has even the most superficial acquaintance with Russian Christendom is aware that the monasteries of Russia, even more than those of the West, exercised a crucially important influence on society, whether as center of spiritual life and transformation to which pilgrims flocked from everywhere, or as bases for missionary expansion, or, finally, as powerful social forces sometimes manipulated — or suppressed — for political advantage. Such struggles as those between St. Nilus of Sora and St. Joseph of Volokolamsk speak eloquently of the age-old conflict, within monasticism itself, between the charismatic drive to solitary contemplation plus charismatic pastoral action, and the institutional need to fit the monastic community into a structure of organized socio-religious power, as a center of liturgy and education and as a nursery of bishops.

Other conflicts, such as that between Eastern Orthodox spirituality and Westernizing influences, play an important part in the lives of the monks and mystics of Russia. Many students of Russian spirituality will be surprised to learn what a great part Western theological attitudes and devotions played in the formation of St. Tikhon in the eighteenth century. The seminary which Tikhon attended was organized on the Jesuit pattern and yet he was not influenced by post-Tridentine Catholic thought. Dr. Bolshakoff identifies him rather with German pietism. In any case, we must not be too quick to assume that St. Tikhon's spirituality is purely and ideally "Russian." Yet, paradoxically, this combination of

Western and Eastern holiness is a peculiarly Russian phenomenon. St. Tikhon was perhaps the greatest mystic of the age of rationalist enlightenment.

Russian mysticism is to be traced largely to the greatest monastic center of Orthodox mysticism, Mount Athos. Ever since the eleventh century the Russian monastic movement had been nourished by direct contact with the "Holy Mountain" — interrupted only by the Tatar invasions of the Middle Ages. Liturgy, asceticism, and mysticism in Russia owed their development in great part not to literary documents but to the living experience of pilgrim monks who spent a certain time at Athos, either in the "Rossikon" (the Russian monastery of St. Panteleimon) or in various sketes and cells, before returning to found new monasteries or renew the life of old ones in their country. Periods when, for one reason or another, communication with Athos has diminished have also been periods of monastic decline in Russia.

One of the characteristic fruits of Russian monachism on Athos is the "Prayer of Jesus," the constant repetition of a short formula in conjunction with rhythmic breathing and with deep faith in the supernatural power of the Holy Name. This was a Russian development of the Greek *Hesychast* way of prayer taught by St. Gregory Palamas. The "Prayer of Jesus" became the normal way of contemplative prayer in Russian monasticism, but, more important still, it was adopted on all sides by devout lay people, especially among the masses of the poor peasantry.

Until recently, Western theologians were highly suspicious of Athonite *Hesychasm* and regarded it as perilous, even heretical. Deeper study and a wider acquaintance with non-Western forms of spirituality have made *Hesychasm* seem a little less outlandish. It is now no longer necessary to repeat the outraged platitudes of those who thought that the *Hesychasts* were practicing self-hypnosis, or who believed that, at best, the monks of Athos were engaged in a kind of Western Yoga.

The "Prayer of Jesus," made known to Western readers by the "Tale of the Pilgrim," surely one of the great classics of the literature of prayer, is now practiced not only by characters in Salinger's novels but even at times by some Western monks.

Needless to say, a way of prayer for which, in its land of origin, the direction of a staretz was mandatory, is not safely to be followed by us in the West without professional direction.

The mystical Russian "pilgrim" received from his staretz an anthology of patristic quotations on prayer: the famous *Philokalia*. The monastic reformer, Paisius Velichkovsky (1722 - 1794), after living for some time in a skete on Mount Athos during a period of monastic decline, translated the *Philokalia* into Slavonic and introduced it to Russia. It was then done into Russian by another mystic, Bishop Theophane the Recluse.

Paisius and his disciples also translated other works of the Fathers and in addition to this exercised a direct and living influence on Russian monachism through the numerous pilgrims who constantly visited in monasteries reformed by him in Moldavia and Walachia. Here visitors from all parts of Russia encountered not only a pure and austere monastic discipline but also the spiritual direction of specialists in asceticism and *Hesychast* prayer, who came to be known as startzy. The translations of the *Philokalia*, the monastic reform of Paisius, and especially *Starchestvo*, the direction of the startzy, set in motion the great development that was to make the nineteenth century the golden age of Russian mysticism. This was also the time when the Rossikon on Mount Athos reached its peak in numbers, fervor, and prosperity.

One of the best-known (or least-unknown) of the Russian mystics is St. Seraphim of Sarov, who lived the life of a Desert Father in the forests at the beginning of the nineteenth century. He affords a striking contrast to other post-medieval saints and ascetics who have tried to imitate the Desert Fathers. In many of these, together with a sincere ascetic and monastic purpose and devotion to authentic ideals, we seem to encounter a spirit of willfulness that is often violent and artificial even to the point of obsession. As a result, we find a negative, gloomy, and tense spirituality in which one is not sure whether the dominant note is hatred of wickedness or love of good — and hatred of wickedness can so easily include hatred of human beings, who are perhaps less wicked than they seem. The study of ascetic tradition and the passion for austerity do not suffice by themselves to make monastic saints, although it must be admitted that a specious "humanism" which turns its back on all austerity and solitude is hardly more effective in this regard!

Whether or not Seraphim had studied ancient monastic tradition, it is certain that he was a living and spontaneous exemplar of the most authentic monastic ideal. His solitary life in the forest was extremely austere and yet his spirituality was marked by pure joy. Though he gave himself unsparingly to each ascetic exploit *(podvig)*, he remained simple, childlike, meek, astonishingly open to life and to other men, gentle, and profoundly compassionate.

He is without doubt the greatest mystic of the Russian Church, and the *Hesychast* tradition is evident in his mysticism of light. Yet *Hesychasm* is, so to speak, absorbed in the evangelical and patristic purity of his experience of the great Christian mystery, the presence of the Spirit given by God through the Risen Christ to His body, the Church.

Seraphim's simplicity reminds us in many ways of Francis of Assisi, though his life was more like that of Anthony of the Desert. But like every other great contemplative saint, Seraphim had his eyes wide open to the truth of the Gospel, and could not understand how the rest of men could be content with an "enlightenment" that was, in reality, nothing but ignorance and spiritual blindness. The only contemporary figure in the West who speaks so eloquently and with such ingenuous amazement of the divine light shining in darkness is the English poet William Blake. But there is in Seraphim none of Blake's gnosticism: only the pure and traditional theology of the Church.

Seraphim of Sarov is then the most perfect example of that mysticism of light which is characteristic of the Orthodox Church: completely positive and yet compatible with, indeed based on, the apophatic (negative) theology of Pseudo-Dionysius and St. Maximus the Confessor. It is perhaps this which distinguishes Russian mysticism in its pure state. Not an intellectualist and negative ascent to the Invisible above all that is visible, but more paradoxically an apprehension of the invisible as visible insofar as all creation is suddenly experienced as transfigured in light for which there is no accounting in terms of any philosophy, a light which is given directly by God, proceeds from God, and in a sense *is* the Divine Light. Yet this experience is not a substantial vision of God, because in Oriental theology the light experienced by the mystic is a divine "energy," distinct from God's nature but which can be apprehended in contact with the *Person* of the Holy Spirit in mystical love and grace.

Thus, it is easy to see that though there are in Russia some instances of negative mysticism comparable to the Dark Night in St. John of the Cross, yet they are not characteristic of Russian mystical theology, which is a theology not of suffering but of transfiguration.

Nevertheless, this theology of resurrection and joy is firmly based on repentance and on tears, and one does not easily find in it the impertinences of a devout sentimentality which simply assumes that "everything is bound to turn out all right." The reality of redemption and transfiguration depends on the most basic experience of the evil of sin.

Not all the Russian mystics were able to experience this evil as totally consumed in the flames of Redemptive Love. Bishop Ignatius Brianchaninov, an aristocrat and an army engineer converted to the monastic life, looked out upon the world with profound pessimism. The world of matter was not, for him, transfigured by the divine light: it was purely and simply the subject of corruption. For him (as for so many others in the nineteenth century), science and religion were in conflict, and to know Christ one had to reject all earthly knowledge as false and totally misleading. And yet science does nevertheless contribute something of positive value to the meditations of Bishop Brianchaninov. However, we observe with regret in Brianchaninov a tendency to impose a kind of unnatural constraint upon the body and the mind, and we are not surprised when he informs us that he considers visions of devils rather a usual thing in the monastic life. His pessimism and suspicion toward women as such blend with the rest of his dark view of things. Yet, even where his negative attitude repels us, we must admit he often displays remarkable psychological insight. All in all, Brianchaninov is too rigid, too suspicious of the light, too closed to ordinary human experience to impress us as St. Seraphim does. And yet it would seem that the negativism of Brianchaninov had a deeper influence on nineteenth-century Russian monasticism than the marvelous Gospel optimism of St. Seraphim. The works of Brianchaninov will help us to understand the conservative reaction of Leontiev and of the monks of Optino against Dostoevsky's idealized and forward-looking portrait of Staretz Zosima.

This portrait was supposed to have been based on the living figure of Staretz Ambrose of Optino, but the monks in general rejected its optimism, its "humanism," as untrue to the genuine monastic tradition of Russia. Perhaps the generality of monks were more disposed to look at life through the embittered and blazing eyes of the fanatical ascetic Ferrapont, in whom Dostoevsky himself evidently intended to portray the kind of negativism typified by the old school, the critics and opponents of the Startzy.

It is curious that the Russian revolution was preceded not by a century of monastic decadence and torpor, but by a monastic Golden Age. But if the term "Golden Age" is to mean anything, it must mean a time of vitality. Vitality means variety, and this, in turn, may imply conflict. In nineteenth-century Russian monasticism we find darkness and light, world-denial and loving affirmation of human values, a general hardening of resistance to forces of atheist humanism and revolution, and yet an anguished concern at the sinful oppression of the poor. We cannot with justice dismiss the whole Russian monastic movement as negative, pessimistic, world-hating. Nor can we identify its deep and traditional contemplative aspirations with mere political or cultural conservatism. There was an unquestionably prophetic spirit at work in the movement, and St. Seraphim is only one among many examples that prove this. There was also a profound concern for "the world" and for humanity, a wonderful, unequaled compassion that reached out to all mankind and indeed to all living creatures, to embrace them in God's love and in merciful concern. It cannot be doubted that the great startzy, in their humane and tender simplicity, were sometimes completely identified with the humble and the poor. It would be ludicrous to class them as obscurantists and reactionaries.

On the other hand, there was a less prophetic, but nonetheless amazing spirit of ascetic fervor, of discipline, of order, which, while it was undeniably one of the things that made the age "Golden," still had rather more human and even political implications. And here monasticism was, indeed, more deeply involved in social structures and national aspirations, even where it most forcefully asserted its hatred of "the world." Here, too, contempt for the world and pessimistic rigorism were in fact inseparable from social and political conservatism. The ascetic who renounced the city of man in order to lament his sins in the *Poustyna* (desert) may well have been giving his support to a condition of social inertia by implicitly affirming that all concern with improvement was futile and even sinful. We may cite as an example Constantin Leontiev, Dostoevsky's adversary and critic, who entered a monastery, gloried in extreme austerity, and doubtless expressed monastic views that were those of most monks of the time.

Leontiev actually stated that the Orthodoxy on Mount Athos depended on the peace of the harmonious interaction of Turkish political power, Russian wealth, and Greek ecclesiastical authority. Most of his compatriots, monks included, were probably too nationalistic to follow this "realist" view all the way. They were Pan-Slavist and therefore anti-Greek as well as anti-Western. But the point is that their monastic fervor formed part of a complex Russian nationalist mystique and contributed much energy to it. The average good monk, who was not raised by sanctity above this level, tended to identify himself and his religious ideal with this mystique of Holy Russia. It would be very interesting to compare this with the ideas of such lay theologians as Soloviev, who was very open to Rome and the West, but space does not permit here.

The doctrine of the Russian startzy of the last hundred and fifty years is rich in monastic wisdom, as well as in ordinary religious psychology and plain good sense. It is interesting to see that they were concerned with many traditional monastic problems which are being rather warmly discussed in Western monasteries today. The answers to the startzy can be of special value to Western monks who are interested in discovering the deepest meaning of their monastic vocation, and ways to live that vocation more perfectly in the spirit and teaching of the Russian mystics can be of great help to us in carrying on the work of reunion which demands charity.*

One cannot refrain from observing, in this same connection, how much Pope John XXIII displayed this same charismatic and evangelical openness. His life as Pope is filled with incidents in which this great warmhearted man unquestioningly obeyed the spirit of goodness that was in him, and met with consternation when he expected others to obey the same spirit with equal readiness! So many Christians exalt the demands and rigors of law because, in reality, law is less demanding than pure charity. The law, after all, has reasonable safe limitations! One always knows what to expect, and one can always hope to evade, by careful planning, the more unpleasant demands!

The mention of Pope John naturally suggests a conclusion to this brief article. Pope John's love for the Church of the Orient, of Greece and Russia, is well known. His idea of calling the Second Vatican Council was prompted in large part by this love of our separated Orthodox brothers. Knowledge of the spirit and teaching of the Russian mystics can be of great help to us in carrying on the work of reunion which Pope John has bequeathed to us.**

*[The following two paragraphs were omitted for publication in *Mystics and Zen Masters* but were included in the original essay in Sergius Bolshakoff's *Russian Mystics.*]

This is a book that becomes more absorbing as it progresses, and the most interesting pages are those which deal with the Startzy of the last hundred years. Their doctrine is rich in monastic wisdom, as well as in ordinary religious psychology and plain good sense. It is interesting to see that they were concerned with many traditional monastic problems which are being rather warmly discussed in Western monasteries today. The answers of the Startzy can be of special value to Western monks who are interested in discovering the deepest meaning of their monastic vocation, and ways to live that vocation more perfectly.

The reason for this is perhaps simpler than one might expect. It is not so much that the Startzy were exceptionally austere men, or that they had acquired great learning, but that they had surrendered themselves completely to the demands of the Gospel and to evangelical charity, totally forgetting themselves in obedience to the Spirit of God so that they lived as perfect Christians, notable above all for their humility, their meekness, their openness to all men, their apparently inexhaustible capacity for patient and compassionate love. The purpose of *Starchesteve* is then not so much to make use of daily spiritual direction in order to inculcate a special method of prayer, but rather to keep the heart of the disciple open to love, to prevent it from hardening in self-centered concern (whether moral, spiritual or ascetical). All the worst sins are denials and rejections of love, refusals to love. The chief aim of the Staretz is first to teach his disciple not to sin against love, then to encourage and assist his growth in love until he becomes a saint. This total surrender to the power of love was the sole basis of their spiritual authority; and on this basis the Startzy demanded complete and unquestioning obedience. They could do so because they themselves never resisted the claims and demands of charity.

**This is therefore a very timely book for an age of ecumenism and of renewal. Full of interesting historical material and of spiritual wisdom, written for the ordinary reader, it provides a much-needed popular introduction to a subject of great interest and importance to all Christians.

NOTE

1. This essay was originally published as an introduction to *The Russian Mystics* by Sergei Bolgakov, and later appeared as Chapter 9 in Thomas Merton's *Mystics and Zen Masters*. (Toronto: Collins Publishers, 1961.)

Holy Patriarchs, Russia.

7

THE PASTERNAK AFFAIR[1]

Thomas Merton

I. IN MEMORIAM

On the night of Monday, May 30, 1960, the Pasternak Affair was finally closed. The lonely Russian poet's mysterious life of seventy years came to a peaceful end in the *dacha* at the writer's colony which he had made famous — Peredelkino, twenty miles outside of Moscow.

A year and a half had passed since the brief orgy of political animosity and righteous indignation which had celebrated the award of the Nobel Prize for Literature in the fall of 1958. The prize had been offered to Pasternak, not for his novel *Dr. Zhivago* alone but for his whole life work in poetry, for his other prose works and presumably also for his translations. Under Soviet pressure Pasternak refused the prize. He also refused a proffered opportunity to "escape" from Soviet Russia, pointing out that he did not want to "get away" from his native country because he did not feel that he could be happy anywhere else.

There was a great deal of excitement everywhere. The press made much of the Pasternak case, with the usual gesticulations on both sides of the iron curtain. While the smoke was still thick, and the excitement over the explosion still general, all one could do was to hope and pray that Pasternak would survive. There seems to have been every expectation, both in the west and in Russia, that Pasternak was about to become a "non-person." The Russian writers fell all over one another in their eagerness to become as disassociated from him as they possibly could. Western writers, in appeals that were probably more effective than anyone expected them to be, asked that Pasternak's case be examined with the cool objectivity of non-partisan fairness. Although the poet was menaced in every way, especially when his case was front-page news, after the excitement died down he was left alone. The visits of foreign newsmen, the "pilgrimages" of western men of letters to Peredelkino, were suffered to continue. Pasternak's immense correspondence was apparently not much interfered with, and things went on "as usual" except that the poet could not write poetry or work on the historical play or on the new novel which he had planned. He was kept too busy with visitors and the writing of letters. The last phase of his extraordinary life was the most active of all. The whole world (including many of the younger writers in the Soviet Union) had turned to him as to a prophetic figure, a man whose ascendancy was primarily spiritual. The impact of this great and sympathetic figure has been almost religious, if we take that term in a broad and more or less unqualified sense.

It is true that there are striking and genuinely Christian elements in the outlook of Pasternak, in the philosophy that underlies his writing. But of course to claim him as an apologist for Christianity would be an exaggeration. His "religious" character is something more general, more mysterious, more existential. He has made his mark in the world not so much by what he said as by what he was: the sign of a genuinely spiritual man. Although his work is certainly very great, we must first of all take account of what is usually called his personal "witness." He embodied in himself so many of the things modern man pathetically claims he still believes in, or wants to believe in. He became a kind of "sign" of that honesty, integrity, sincerity which we tend to associate with the free and creative personality. He was also an embodiment of that personal warmth and generosity which we seek more and more vainly among the alienated massmen of our too organized world. In one word, Pasternak emerged as a genuine human being stranded in a mad world. He immediately became a symbol, and all those who felt it was important not to be mad attached themselves in some way to him. Those who had given up, or sold out, or in one way or another ceased to believe in this kind of human quality turned away from him, and found appropriate slogans or catchwords to dismiss him from their thoughts.

This does not mean, of course, that everyone who was "for" Pasternak was a real human being and all the rest were squares. On the contrary, one of the most salient characteristics of the Pasternak Affair in its most heated moments was the way

Pasternak got himself surrounded by squares coming at him from all directions with contradictory opinions. Naturally, those who "believed" in Pasternak were not thereby justified, sanctified, or reborn. But the fact remains that he stirred up the unsatisfied spiritual appetites of men for ideals a little more personal, a little less abstract, than modern society seems to offer them.

But what, after all, has been the precise importance of Pasternak? Is this the last, vivid flareup of the light of liberal and Christian humanism? Does he belong purely to the past? Or is he in some way the link between Russia's Christian past and a possibly Christian future? Perhaps one dare not ask such questions, and the following two studies are not by any means attempts to do so.

The first essay is the more literary of the two. The second examines, in detail, the development of the "Pasternak Affair" and tries to assess its significance for the spiritual and intellectual life of our time. In neither do I try to appropriate Pasternak for any special cultural or religious movement, to line him up with any religious position that may be familiar in the west, or to claim that he stands four-square for culture and democracy as against barbarism and dictatorship.

I might as well admit that, looking at the divisions of the modern world, I find it hard to avoid seeing somewhat the same hypocrisies, the same betrayals of man, the same denials of God, the same evils in different degrees and under different forms on either side. Indeed, I find all these things in myself. Therefore I cannot find it in myself to put on a mentality that spells war. These studies of Pasternak are by no means to be interpreted as my contribution to the cold war, because I don't want any part of the war, whether it is cold or hot. I seek only to do what Pasternak himself did: to speak my mind out of love for man, the image of God — not to speak a set piece dictated by my social situation.

I am happy to record the fact that Pasternak himself read the first of these two studies, and accepted it with kind approval.[2] The second was not sent to him, being to a great extent "political." Because of my own warm personal admiration for this great poet, and because of the debt of gratitude I owe him for many things, this book is dedicated to his memory. I am persuaded that Russia will one day be as proud of Pasternak as she is of all her other great writers, and that *Dr. Zhivago* will be studied in Russian schools among the great classics of the language. I can think of no better and more succinct comment upon the life and death of Pasternak than these words of his own which express his belief in immortality and which I have quoted again in the second study. Because of the coming of Christ, says Zhivago, speaking the mind of Pasternak himself: "Man does not die in a ditch like a dog — but at home in history, while the work toward the conquest of death is in full swing; *he dies sharing in this work.*"

II. The People with Watch Chains

My sister-called-life, like a tidal wave breaking
Swamps the bright world in a wall of spring rain:
But people with watch-chains grumble and frown
With poisoned politeness, like snakes in the corn.
— From *My Sister Life*

It is perhaps not quite fair to start a discussion of Pasternak with lines from an early poem. He repudiated his earlier style, together with much that was written by the futurists and symbolists who were his friends forty years ago. (He did not, of course, repudiate his friends. For someone like Pasternak, friends cannot become "non-persons.") He may or may not have pardoned us for enjoying the freshness of this early verse, but in any case it is clear that Life who was his "sister" in 1917 became his bride and his very self in *Doctor Zhivago* ("Doctor Life"). Life is at once the hero and the heroine (Lara) of this strange, seemingly pessimistic but victorious tragedy: not, however, Life in the abstract, certainly not the illusory, frozen-faced *imago* of Life upon which Communism constructs its spiritless fantasies of the future. Life for Pasternak is the painful, ambivalent, yet inexhaustibly fecund reality that is the very soul of Russia. A reality which, with all its paradoxes, has certainly manifested itself in the Russian revolution and all that followed, but which overflows all the possible limits of recorded history. Hundreds of pages of turbulent and exquisite prose give us some insight into the vastness of that reality as it was experienced, quite providentially, by one of the few sensitive and original spirits that survived the storm. And since Life cannot be confined within the boundaries of one nation, what Pasternak has to say about it overflows symbolism, into every corner of the world. It is the mystery of history as passion and resurrection that we glimpse obscurely in the story of the obscure Doctor who gives his name to the novel. This frustrated, confused and yet somehow triumphant protagonist is not only Pasternak himself and even Russia, but mankind — not "twentieth-century man" but man who is perhaps too existential and mysterious for any label to convey his meaning and his identity. We, of course, are that man.

That is the mark of a really great book: it is in some way about everybody and everybody is involved in it. Nothing could be done to stop the drab epic of *Zhivago*, like the downpour in the 1917 poem, from bursting on the heads of all and swamping them whether they liked it or not. For that is exactly what Life cannot refrain from doing.

The appearance of *Doctor Zhivago*, and all the confused and largely absurd reactions which followed upon it, forms a very meaningful incident at the close of an apparently meaningless decade. Certainly the surprise publication and instant success of the novel everywhere (including Russia, where it has been avidly read in manuscript by all the young intellectuals who could get hold of it) has more to say in retrospect than all the noise and empty oratory of the Soviet fortieth anniversary. This significance will of course be missed by all those who insist on taking a purely partisan and *simpliste* view of events, and who therefore interpret the book as all black or all white, all good or all bad, all left or all right. The dimensions of Pasternak's world view are more existential and spiritual and are decidedly beyond left and right.

In bursting upon the heads of all, *Zhivago* inevitably deluged first of all those simple and pontifical souls whose Gospel is passive conformity with the politicians and bigshots, with the high priests of journalism and the doctors of propaganda: upon those who, though they no longer decorate their paunches with cheap watch chains, still thrive on conformity with the status quo, on either side of the iron curtain.

Zhivago is one of those immensely "popular" books that has not really been popular. It has been bought by more people than were able to read it with full understanding. No doubt many of those who have had Pasternak's heavy volume in their hands have approved of it only vaguely and for the wrong reasons. And others who have read it have put it down with the unquiet feeling that it was somehow not sufficiently business-like. For such as these, "life" has ceased to mean what it means to Pasternak. For the people with watch chains, a life that gets along independently of the plans of politicians and economists is nothing but a reactionary illusion. This has been brought home to Pasternak in no uncertain terms by his devoted confrères in the Soviet Writers' Union. But the same judgment has finally worked its way out in the West also, where Isaac Deutscher, the biographer of Stalin, has accused *Zhivago* of being another Oblomov and scolded him for considering the revolution "an atrocity." Let us face it, the people with watch chains can easily reconcile themselves with any atrocity that serves their own opportunism, whether it be in the form of a revolution or of an atomic bomb. Life (claimed as a sister by escapists and cosmopolitan mad-dogs) had better learn to get along in these new circumstances. The atrocities are here to stay.

All great writing is in some sense revolutionary. Life itself is revolutionary, because it constantly strives to surpass itself. And if history is to be something more than the record of society's bogging down in meaningless formalities to justify the crimes of men, then a book that is at the same time great in its own right, and moreover lands with a tremendous impact on the world of its time, deserves an important place in history. The reason why *Doctor Zhivago* is significant is precisely that it stands so far above politics. This, among other things, places it in an entirely different category from Dudintsev's *Not by Bread Alone*. Attempts to involve Pasternak in the cold war have been remarkable above all by their futility. The cloud of misunderstandings and accusations that surrounded the affair did not engulf Pasternak:

the confusion served principally to emphasize the distance which separated him from his accusers and his admirers alike.

Both as a writer and as a man, Pasternak stands out as a sign of contradiction in our age of materialism, collectivism and power politics. His spiritual genius is essentially and powerfully solitary. Yet his significance does not lie precisely in this. Rather it lies in the fact that his very solitude made him capable of extraordinarily intimate and understanding contacts with men all over the face of the earth. The thing that attracted people to Pasternak was not a social or political theory, it was not a formula for the unification of mankind, not a collectivist panacea for all the evils in the world: it was the man himself, the truth that was in him, his simplicity, his direct contact with life, and the fact that he was full of the only revolutionary force that is capable of producing anything new: he is full of love.

Pasternak is then not just a man who refuses to conform (that is to say, a rebel). The fact is, he is not a rebel, for a rebel is one who wants to substitute his own authority for the authority of someone else. Pasternak is one who *cannot* conform to an artificial and stereotyped pattern because, by the grace of God, he is too much alive to be capable of such treason to himself and to life. He is not a rebel but a revolutionary, in the same way that Gandhi was a revolutionary. And in fact those who have said: "Passive resistance is all right against the English but it would never work against Russia" must stop and consider that in Pasternak it did, to some extent, work in Russia. Pasternak is certainly a man to be compared even with Gandhi. Though different in so many accidental ways, his protest is ultimately the same: the protest of life itself, of humanity itself, of love, speaking not with theories and programs but simply affirming itself and asking to be judged on its own merits.

Like Gandhi, Pasternak stands out as a gigantic paradox in a world of servile and mercenary conformities. His presence in such a world has had an inescapable effect: it has struck fear into the hearts of everyone else, whether in Russia or in America. The reaction to Pasternak, the alternate waves of love, fear, hate, and adulation that have rushed toward him from every part of the world, were all set in motion by the *guilt* of a society that has consciously and knowingly betrayed life, and sold itself out to falsity, formalism and spiritual degradation. In some (for instance, the pundits of Soviet literature) this guilt has produced hatred and rage against Pasternak. The fear he aroused was intolerable. His colleagues in the Soviet Writers' Union began to yell for his blood, and yelled all the more loudly in proportion as they were themselves servile and second rate. There were a few notable exceptions, rare writers of integrity and even talent, like Ilya Ehrenburg.

The politicians of the Kremlin, on the other hand, not being writers, not thoroughly understanding what it was all about anyway, were less moved to guilt, felt less fear, and were slow to do much about the case at first.

In the West the reaction was different. We felt the same guilt, the same fear, but in a different mode and degree. On the whole our reaction was to run to Pasternak with fervent accolades: to admire in him the courage and integrity we lack in ourselves. Perhaps we can taste a little vicarious revolutionary joy without doing anything to change our own lives. To justify our own condition of servility and spiritual prostitution we think it sufficient to admire another man's integrity.

I think that later pages of this study will show that Pasternak's witness is essentially Christian. That is the trouble: the problematical quality of Pasternak's "Christianity" lies in the fact that it is reduced to the barest and most elementary essentials: intense awareness of all cosmic and human reality as "life in Christ," and the consequent plunge into love as the only dynamic and creative force which really honors this "Life" by creating itself anew in Life's — Christ's — image.

As soon as *Doctor Zhivago* appeared everybody began comparing Pasternak with Tolstoy and Dostoievsky. The comparisons were obvious, sometimes trite, but basically legitimate. However, they run the risk of creating misconceptions. Pasternak does not merely work on an enormous canvas, like the classical novelists of the nineteenth century. Sholokov also has done that, and Pasternak is immensely more important than Sholokov, competent as the latter may be. But to be a twentieth-century Tolstoy is in fact to disqualify oneself for comparison with one who was an original and unique genius of his own age. The thing that makes Pasternak a new Tolstoy is precisely the fact that he is *not* Tolstoy, he is Pasternak. He is, that is to say, a writer of great power, a man of new and original vision, whose work takes in an enormous area, creates a whole new world. But it is not the world of *War and Peace* and it is not constructed in the same way. In fact, Pasternak has as much in common with Joyce and Proust as he has with Tolstoy. He is a poet and a musician which Tolstoy was not, and the structure of *Zhivago* is symphonic, thematic, almost liturgical. Both writers are "spiritual" in a very deep way, but the spirituality of Tolstoy is always more ethical and pedestrian.

Like Dostoievsky, Pasternak sees life as a mystic, but without the hieratic kenoticism of the *Brothers Karamazov*. The mysticism of Pasternak is more latent, more cosmic, more pagan, if you like. It is more primitive, less sophisticated, free and untouched by any hieratic forms. There is therefore a "newness" and freshness in his spirituality that contrasts strikingly with the worn and mature sanctity of Staretz Zossima purified of self-consciousness by the weariness of much suffering. Pasternak's simple and moving poem on "Holy Week" illustrates this point. It is the death and resurrection of Christ seen in and through nature. Only discreetly and for a brief moment do ritual forms present themselves, as when we see a procession emerge from a country church. The birch tree "stands aside" to let the worshippers come forth but the procession soon returns into the church.

> And March scoops up the snow on the porch
> And scatters it like alms among the halt and lame—
> As though a man had carried out the Ark
> And opened it and distributed all it held.

All the reality of Holy Week is there, but in a very simple, elementary shape — a shape given to it by Pasternak's humility and contact with the "sacred" earth.

The very scarce and slight expressions of explicit spirituality in *Doctor Zhivago* are uttered by people who might have qualified for a place in the *Brothers Karamazov* (Uncle Nikolai and the seamstress of Yuriatin), but they have about them the ingenuousness of a spirituality that has never yet become quite conscious of it-self and has therefore never needed to be purified.

If Pasternak's view of the universe is liturgical, it is the cosmic liturgy of *Genesis*, not the churchly and hierarchal liturgy of the Apocalypse, of pseudo-Dionysius and of the Orthodox Church. And yet Pasternak loves that liturgy, and belongs to that Church. It even occurs to him to quote from the liturgy frequently and in strange places: for instance, these words which he declared indicate a basic liturgical inspiration in the poets Blok and Mayakovsky:

"Let all human flesh be silent and let it remain in ter-ror, and in trembling, and let no living being think within itself. For behold, there cometh the King of Kings and the Lord of Lords to offer Himself in immolation and to be-come the food of the faithful."

Notice, though, in what a subdued and apologetic manner Pasternak himself makes use of this powerful text. In the last stanza of the poem on "Holy Week," we read his lines on the Easter Vigil:

And when midnight comes
All creatures and all flesh will fall silent
On hearing Spring put forth its rumor
That just as soon as there is better weather
Death itself can be overcome
Through the power of the Resurrection.

To say then that *Zhivago* has a liturgical character is not to accuse it of hieratic ceremoniousness. On the contrary, it is to praise the spontaneity with which cries of joy and reverence spring up on every page to hymn the sanctity of Life and of that Love which is the image of the Creator.

And so, though Pasternak is deeply and purely Christian, his simplicity, untainted by ritualistic routine, unstrained by formal or hieratic rigidities of any sort, has a kind of *pre-Christian* char-acter. In him we find the ingenuous Christianity of an *anima naturaliter Christiana* that has discovered Christianity all by itself. It is a Christianity that is not perfectly at home with dogmatic formulas, but gropes after revealed truth in its own clumsy way. And so in his Christianity and in all his spirituality Pasternak is exceedingly primitive. This is one of his most wonderful qualities and we owe it no doubt to the persecution of Christianity by the State in Russia. Where the Church was free we got the complex, tormented Christianity of Dostoievsky. Where the Church is confined and limited we get the rudimentary, "primitive" Christianity of Pasternak.

What Zhivago opposes to Communism is therefore not a defense of Western democracy, not a political platform for some kind of liberalism, and still less a tract in favor of formal religion. Zhivago confronts Communism with life itself and leaves us in the presence of inevitable conclusions. Communism has proposed to control life with a rigid system and with the tyranny of artificial forms. Those who have believed in this delusion and yielded themselves up to it as to a "superior force" have paid the penalty by ceasing to be complete human beings, by ceasing to live in the full sense of the word, by ceasing to be men. Even the idealistic and devoted Strelnikov becomes the victim of his own ideals, and Lara can say of him:

> It was as if something abstract had crept into his face and made it colorless. As if a living human face had become the embodiment of a principle, the image of an idea . . . . I realized that this had happened to him because he had handed himself over to a superior force that is deadening and pitiless and will not spare him in the end. It seemed to me that he was a marked man and that this was the seal of his doom.

The fact that this judgment is so closely akin to Freudianism and is yet explicitly Christian gives one much food for reflection. The Christian note is sounded in a strong and definite way at the very beginning of the book, as one of the themes which will recur most strongly in all its various parts. The "beast in man" is not to be tamed by threats, but must be brought into harmony with life and made to serve creativeness and love by the influence of inner and spiritual music.

What has for centuries raised man above the beast is not the cudgel but an inward music; the irresistible power of unarmed truth, the powerful attraction of its example. It has always been assumed that the most important things in the Gospel are the ethical maxims and commandments. But for me the most important thing is that Christ speaks in parables taken from life, that He explains the truth in terms of everyday reality. The idea that underlies this is that communion between mortals is immortal, and that the whole of life is symbolic because it is meaningful.

The words about the "irresistible power of unarmed truth" are pure Gandhi. The rest, about the inextricable union of symbolism and communion, in life itself, is what gives Pasternak's vision of the world its liturgical and sacramental character (always remembering that his "liturgy" is entirely nonhieratic and that in him sacrament implies not so much established ritual form as living mystery).

Everyone has been struck, not to mention embarrassed, by the overpowering symbolic richness of *Doctor Zhivago*. In fact, Pasternak, whether he knows it or not, is plunged fully into midstream of the lost tradition of "natural contemplation" which flowed among the Greek Fathers after it had been set in motion by Origen. Of course the tradition has not been altogether lost, and Pasternak has come upon it in the Orthodox Church. The fact is clear in any case: he reads the Scriptures with the avidity and the spiritual imagination of Origen and he looks on the world with the illuminated eyes of the Cappadocian Fathers — but without their dogmatic and ascetic preoccupations.

However, it is not with scriptural images that Pasternak is primarily concerned. The Fathers of the Church declared that the Scriptures are a recreated world, a Paradise restored to man after Adam had disturbed the cosmic liturgy by his fall. Pasternak is not the prophet of this regained Paradise, as were Origen and Gregory and Nyssa. Rather he is a prophet of the original, cosmic revelation: one who sees symbols and figures of the inward, spiritual world, working themselves out in the mystery of the universe around him and above all in the history of men. Not so much in the formal, and illusory, history of states and empires that is written down in books, but in the living, transcendental and mysterious history of individual human beings and in the indescribable interweaving of their destinies.

It is as artist, symbolist and prophet that *Zhivago* stands most radically in opposition to Soviet society. He himself is a man of Eden, of Paradise. He is Adam, and therefore also, in some sense, Christ. Lara is Eve, and Sophia (the Cosmic Bride of God) and Russia. One should examine, for instance, the description of the Eden-like garden at Duplyanka in the very beginning of the book. The fragrant fields, the heat, the flowerbeds, the lonely coppice where Yurii speaks with his angel or his mother whose presence (again a sophianic presence) seems to surround him here. Here too Lara, as a girl, is shown to us in the beginning of the book (in one of those innumerable coincidences which Pasternak himself regards as of supreme significance in his novel):

Lara walked along the tracks following a path worn by pilgrims and then turned into the fields. Here she stopped and, closing her eyes, took a deep breath of the flower-scented air of the broad expanse around her. It was dearer to her than her kin, better than a lover, wiser than a book. For a moment she rediscovered the purpose of her life. She was here on earth to grasp the meaning of its wild enchantment, to call each thing by its right name, or, if this were not in her power, to give birth out of love for life to successors who would do it in her place.

The allusion to that primeval, Edenic existence in which Adam gave the animals their names, is transparently obvious. And Eve is the "Mother of all the living."

Yurii and Lara will be united in another Eden, at Varykino, but a strange Eden of snow and silence, lost in a vast landscape wasted by armies. There Yurii will give himself, in the night, to his most fruitful work of poetic creation.

In contrast to the Eden image which symbolizes the sophianic world of Yurii and Lara, of Adam, of Christ, stands the House of the Sculptures in Yuriatin. One of the most significant chapters of the book is called "Opposite the House of the Sculptures." It is the one where the seamstress develops the typological figures of the Old Testament, speaking by lamplight in the same enchanted atmosphere of warmth that pervaded the fields of Duplyanka. The opposition is obvious.

(Lara) Antopova lived at the corner of Merchant Street opposite the dark, blue-grey house with sculptures. . . . It did indeed live up to its name and there was something strange and disturbing about it. Its entire top floor was surrounded by female mythological figures half as big again as human beings. Between two gusts of the dust storm it seemed to him as if all the women in the house had come out on the balcony and were looking down at him over the balustrade. . . .

At the corner there was a dark grey house with sculptures. The huge square stones of the lower part of its facade were covered with freshly posted sheets of government newspapers and proclamations. Small groups of people stood on the sidewalk, reading in silence. . . .

With uncanny insight, the poet has portrayed the bourgeois world of the nineteenth century, a grey facade covered with "sculptures" — enormous and meaningless figures of nothingness, figures for the sake of figures. Yet a dust storm gives them an illusory life. Decorations with no inner reference: advertisements of a culture that has lost its head and has run soberly raving through its own backyards and factories with a handful of rubles. All that remained was for the house itself behind the facade to be gutted and emptied of its semi-human content: then everything was set for the Posters and Proclamations of the Red state. If the editors of *Novy Mir* read *Doctor Zhivago* with understanding they would have found in this passage a much more profound condemnation of Communism than in the description of the Partisan battle which they picked out for special reproof.

On the one hand we have the revolution: "what they mean by ideas is nothing but words, claptrap in praise of the revolution and the regime. . . . " Against this pseudo-scientific array of propaganda clichés, stands the doctor and poet, the diagnostician. One of his greatest sins (the term is chosen advisedly) is his belief in intuition. By his intuition, he is able to get "an immediate grasp of a situation as a whole" which the Marxists vainly hope to achieve by pseudo-science. But what does he seek most of all? What is his real work? As poet, his function is not merely to express his own state of mind and not merely to exercise his own artistic power. Pasternak's concept of the poet's vocation is at once dynamic and contemplative: two terms which can only be synthesized in the heat of a prophetic ardor.

Language is not merely the material or the instrument which the poet uses. This is the sin of the Soviet ideologist for whom language is simply a mine of terms and formulas which can be pragmatically exploited. When in the moment of inspiration the poet's creative intelligence is married with the inborn wisdom of human language (the Word of God and Human Nature — Divinity and Sophia) then in the very flow of new and individual intuitions, the poet utters the voice of that wonderful and mysterious world of God-manhood — it is the transfigured, spiritualized and divinized cosmos that speaks through him, and through him utters its praise of the Creator.

Language, the home and receptacle of beauty and meaning, itself begins to think and speak for man and turns wholly into music, not in terms of sonority but in terms of the impetuousness and power of its inward flow. Then, like the current of a mighty river polishing stones and turning wheels by its very movement, the flow of speech creates in passing, by virtue of its own laws, meter and rhythm and countless other relationships, which are even more important, but which are as yet unexplored, insufficiently recognized, and unnamed. At such moments, Yurii Adreievitch felt that the main part of the work was being done not by him but by a superior power that was above him and directed him, namely the movement of universal thought and poetry in its present historical stage and in the one to come. And he felt himself to be only the occasion, the fulcrum, needed to make this movement possible.

This is the very key to Pasternak's "religious philosophy." He is a complete existentialist (in the most favorable and religious sense of the word). One might ask, in the light of this passage, if his Christian images were nothing more than secondary symbols, subordinated to this great, dynamic worldview. The answer is no. What we have here is a Christian existentialism like that of Berdyaev, and of course far less articulate and less developed than that of Berdyaev. The Christian cosmology of Dante, for example, was static and centripetal. But Christianity is not bound up with Ptolemaic astronomy. Pasternak is absorbed in his vision of a fluid, ever moving, ever developing cosmos. It is a vision appropriate to a contemporary of Einstein and Bergson: but let us not forget that it is also akin to the vision of St. Gregory of Nyssa.

It is not necessary at this point to investigate further the depth and genuineness of the Christian elements in Pasternak. They are clearly present, but their presence should not delude us into any oversimplifications in his regard. There are many differences between his Christianity and the Protestant, or even the Catholic Christianity of the West. To what extent are these differences fundamental? We may perhaps return to this question elsewhere. Sufficient to remember that if in the first pages of the book Christ becomes a kind of ideological or symbolic center for the whole structure, this does not alter the fact that Uncle Nikolai propounds his belief in the following terms, which cannot help but perplex the average believer:

> One must be true to Christ. . . . What you don't under-
> stand is that it is possible to be an atheist, it is possible
> not to know whether God exists or why, and yet believe
> that man does not live in a state of nature but in history,
> and that history as we know it now began with Christ, and
> that Christ's Gospel is its foundation.

Without commenting on this passage, let us simply remark that it is typical of the "religious statements" made here and there in the book which very frequently are much tamer and more simple than they appear to be at first sight. Here the difficulty arises largely from a misuse of the word "atheist." What Pasternak really means, in our terminology, is "agnostic," as is clear from his own explanation. Note that Pasternak does not necessarily make himself personally answerable for the theology of Uncle Nikolai, and that he records with full approval the remarkable discourse of Sima on the miracles of the Old Testament as "types" of the greatest miracle, the Incarnation. It is clear that Christ, for Pasternak, is a transcendent and Personal Being in the sense generally understood by such orthodox theologians as Soloviev or the Russian existentialist Berdyaev. The Christ of Pasternak is the Christ of Soloviev's "God-manhood."

His view of the cosmos is, like Berdyaev's, "sophianic" and his "sister Life" has, in fact, all the characteristics of the Sancta Sophia who appeared to Soloviev in Egypt. His protestations that for him "believing in God" or in "the Resurrection" is not quite the same thing as it might be to the popular anthropomorphic mind is, after all, a quite legitimate self-defense for one who has no pretension of talking like a professional theologian. So much for his terms. But as for his intentions and his spirit, of these there can be no doubt: they are genuinely religious, authentically Christian and all the more so for their spontaneous unconventionality.

But the important thing to realize is that here, as with all deeply spiritual thinkers, to concentrate on a strict analysis of concepts and formulas is to lose contact with the man's basic intuitions. The great error, the error into which the Communists themselves plunge headlong at the first opportunity, is to try to peg genius down and make it fit into some ready-made classification. Pasternak is not a man for whom there is a plain and definite category. And we must not try to tag him with easy names: Christian, Communist; anti-Christian, anti-Communist; liberal, reactionary; personalist, romanticist, etc.

As Lara says, in one of her most "sophianic" moods: "It's only in mediocre books that people are divided into two camps and have nothing to do with each other. In real life, everything gets mixed up! Don't you think you'd have to be a hopeless nonentity to play only one role all your life, to have only one place in society, always to stand for the same thing?" Both the admirers and the enemies of Pasternak have tried to do him this great dishonor: to write him into one of their own "mediocre books," and to make of him a stereotype to fit and to excuse their own lamentable prejudices. Thus do the "people with watch chains" complain — and not too politely — "like snakes in the corn."

It is true that some names fit Pasternak better than others, and that he is certainly very much of a Christian and not very much of a Communist. Nevertheless his Christianity is first of all quite personal, then quite Russian. His politics are personal first of all and then again Russian, though it might be a lot safer to say that he is anti-political rather than political. But it would be utterly false to say (as his accusers said) that he had rejected the Russian revolution as a whole.

Where precisely does he stand? The answer is that like life itself he stands nowhere, but *moves*. He moves in a definite direction, however, and this is what must be taken into account if he is to be properly understood. From the very first we must realize that this direction does not lie, simply, west of Russia. Pasternak's tendencies are neither geographical nor political. His movement is into the new dimension of the future which we cannot yet estimate because it is not yet with us. He looks beyond the rigid, frozen monolith of Soviet society; he looks beyond the more confused, shifting and colliding forms that make up the world of the West. What does he see? Freedom. Not the freedom of Soviet man after the mythical "withering away of the state." Not the chaotic irresponsibility that leaves Western man the captive of economic, social and psychological forces. Not even that vision which has been irreverently described as "pie in the sky," but really the freedom of the sons of God, on earth, in which "individual life becomes the life story of God and its contents fill the vast expanses of the universe."

III. SPIRITUAL IMPLICATIONS

Boris Pasternak established himself in 1958 as one of the very few unquestionably great writers of our century. For forty years this deeply sensitive and original poet had remained hidden and practically unknown in a Russia that seemed entirely alien to his genius. It would be an understatement to say that Soviet official criticism relegated him to oblivion, scorning him as a bourgeois individualist and an internal émigré. But the events of October and November 1958 were to bring out the fact that Pasternak had remained one of the most admired and loved Russian poets, even in Russia itself. It is true, both in Russia and outside it, he was a poet's poet. But that was precisely his importance. He was a rare, almost miraculous being, who had survived the Stalin purges not only with his life but with his full spiritual independence: a kind of symbol of freedom and creativity in the midst of an alienated society — an alienated world.

The fact that the prize award followed closely on the publication and the world-wide success of *Dr. Zhivago* made it easy for politicians to say that the whole thing was a plot, a new gambit in the Cold War. This popular oversimplification obscured the literary importance of the novel which represented the final maturing of a great talent that had been waiting in silence for many years, unable to express itself. A long discipline of sorrowful gestation had given the book a kind of unruly, explosive sincerity that demanded to be heard. And it was heard, in spite of the fact that critics took occasion to complain of many things in it. Was the story too involved? Were the characters really characters? Did the book really have a structure? Was it absurd to compare such a writer to Tolstoy? And above all, why so many curious and arbitrary coincidences? When all these things were said, it was still evident that the people who said them were wasting their time in doing so. It was somehow clear to anyone who had really penetrated the meaning of *Dr. Zhivago* that all these questions were really irrelevant. The book was much too big and too vital a creation for such criticisms to have much meaning. It swept them all away by its own overwhelming strength and conviction. The story was involved because life is involved: and what mattered was that the book was alive. You could not only forgive the complexity of the plot, but you were drawn to lose yourself in it, and to retrace with untiring interest the crossing paths of the different characters. *Dr. Zhivago* is one of those books which are greater than the rules by which critics seek to condemn them: and we must remember that it is precisely with such books as this that literature advances. In the end, when everyone had had his say, and the first pronouncements on the book could be evaluated and summed up, it was clear that the deeper and more original critical minds were sold on it. They were obviously preparing to undertake a deeper and more detailed study of the work. This was the case with Edmund Wilson, for example, who came out with one of the most serious and favorable studies of the novel (*The New Yorker*, November 15, 1958) and who later plunged more deeply into what he believed to be the book's symbolism (*The Nation*, April 25, 1959.) It is interesting that Wilson's enthusiasm led him into a kind of Joycean labyrinth of allegory which he imagined he had discovered in the book, and this evoked an immediate protest on the part of the author. Pasternak emphatically denied any intention of creating the allegorical structure Wilson had "discovered." But the effect of this protest was to increase one's respect for *Dr. Zhivago*. It is not by any means another *Ulysses* or *Finnegans Wake*. The genius of Pasternak is quite other than the genius of Joyce, and to imagine him plotting out and landscaping his symbolism is to miss what he is really doing.

In any case, it is quite clear that the publication of *Zhivago* was one of the most significant literary events of the century. This is confirmed by the fact that every scrap of poetry or prose Pasternak ever published is being dug up, translated and printed in every language and that his great novel is already beginning to be the object of exhaustive study. We shall now undoubtedly have a lush crop of doctoral dissertations on every aspect of Pasternak's life and work, and this is certainly no cause for rejoicing. The perfectionistic critics, the group who have been turning over and over the least relics of Melville and Henry James will probably leave Pasternak alone, which is fortunate for everyone concerned. But a great many sensitive and alert writers are going to dive into Pasternak and come up with wonderful things for the rest of us, because Pasternak is a great sea full of sunken treasures and in him we have, for once, riches that are not fully expended in a column and a half of the Sunday Book Section.

It is not out of place to start by this affirmation: that the award of the 1958 Nobel Prize for Literature was a *literary* event. Last year it was treated almost exclusively, both in Russia and out of it, as a political event. It was to be expected that Soviet officialdom would react a little hysterically to the prize award. Since Marxists think entirely in political categories, their hysteria was necessarily political. The publication of the book was a vile and sweeping attack on the Revolution. The prize award was a direct blow at the Soviet Union. The whole thing was a reactionary plot cooked up on Wall Street. Pasternak was an unregenerate relic of the bourgeois past who had somehow been suffered to survive and to pollute the pure air of a new Soviet world. The capi-

talist wolves had taken advantage of this occasion to howl for Soviet blood. One mixed metaphor after another denounced the
shameless author.

No one was, or should have been, surprised at this mechanical routine. It was inevitable, and so familiar as to have been
supremely boring to everyone except the author and to those who
appreciated his talent and personality enough to fear for his life.
Nor was it entirely surprising that our side picked up the ball
and got into the same game without moment's delay. To the
Western journalists, Pasternak at once became a martyr, a symbol of democracy fighting for recognition under Red tyranny, another proof of the arbitrary perversity of Soviet dictatorship. And
of course all this was partly true. But it was slanted and given a
political emphasis that was not really there, because *Dr. Zhivago*
is in no sense a defense of Western democracy or of the political
and economic systems that prevail here. The liberty that Pasternak
defends is a liberty of the spirit which is almost as dead in the
West as it is behind the Iron Curtain. Perhaps, in a certain way,
it is *more* dead in those situations where men fondly believe that
the spirit can continue to live in an atmosphere of crass materialism. Let us remember that the vilest character in *Dr. Zhivago*
is not one of the Communist automatons but the shrewd, lech-
erous businessman, Komarovsky.

The fact that Christ is mentioned with sympathetic approval
in all parts of the book and that there are quotations from the
Bible and from the liturgy was perhaps overstressed by those who
were too eager to find in *Dr. Zhivago* an *apologia* for a vague and
superficial Christianity. Here too, Pasternak does not lend himself so easily to exploitation in favor of a cause. This is not a
book that can be used to prove something or to sell something,
even if that something happens to be the Christian faith. The
dogmatic ambiguity of Pasternak's religious statements takes good
care of that. Pasternak himself denies that there is an explicitly
religious "message" in his book. But this does not mean that
the book is not deeply religious and even definitely Christian.
The sincerity of the author's own religious feeling is over-
poweringly evident, even though it is not always easy to see how
that feeling is to be translated into clear theological propositions.

But can we not believe that this too is not only understandable, but much to be desired? Who would think of asking a citizen of the Soviet Union today to burst out periodically with a little homily, couched in the exact technical language of a manual of Catholic moral or dogma? Is it not perhaps all too evident that to demand such a thing would be to put ourselves unconsciously on the same footing as the Soviet Writers' Union who insisted that Pasternak must have secret connections in the West, and must be engaged in an ideological plot?

To me, on the contrary, one of the most persuasive and moving aspects of Pasternak's religious mood is its slightly off-beat spontaneity. It is precisely because he says practically nothing that he has not discovered on his own, that he convinces me of the authenticity of his religious experience. When one is immersed in a wide and free-flowing stream of articulate tradition, he can easily say more than he knows and more than he means, and get away with it. One can be content to tell his brethren in Christ what they devoutly desire and expect, no more and no less. But *Dr. Zhivago*, and the deeply religious poems printed in its final section, is the work of a man who, in a society belligerently hostile to religion, has discovered for himself the marvels of the Byzantine liturgy, the great mystery of the Church, and the revelation of God in His word, the Sacred Scriptures. The newspapermen who interviewed Pasternak in his *dacha* were all struck by the big Russian Bible that lay on his desk and gave evidence of constant use.

Pasternak's Christianity is, then, something very simple, very rudimentary, deeply sincere, utterly personal and yet for all its questionable expressions, obviously impregnated with the true spirit of the Gospels and the liturgy. Pasternak has no Christian message. He is not enough of a Christian "officially" to pretend to such a thing. And this is the secret to the peculiar religious strength that is in his book. This strength may not be at all evident to most of us who are formally and "officially" members of the visible Church. But it is certainly calculated to make a very profound impression on those who think themselves unable to believe because they are frightened at the forbiddingly "official" aspects our faith sometimes assumes. *Dr. Zhivago* is, then, a deeply spiritual event, a kind of miracle, a humble but inescapable portent.

It is my purpose to bring out and to emphasize the essentially spiritual character of the Pasternak affair. That is precisely its greatest importance for it is one of the few headline-making incidents of our day that has a clearly spiritual bearing. The literary significance of *Dr. Zhivago* and of Pasternak's verse would never have accounted for the effect they have had on our world. On the other hand, the real political content of Pasternak's work is negligible, and the brief political upheaval that accompanied his prominence in the news was quite accidental, except in so far as it was a tacit recognition of Pasternak as a *spiritual* influence in the world. Those who have been struck by the religious content of his work have been responding, consciously or otherwise, not so much to a formal Christian witness as to a deep and uncompromising *spirituality*.

Pasternak stands first of all for the great spiritual values that are under attack in our materialistic world. He stands for the freedom and nobility of the individual person, for man the image of God, for man in whom God dwells. For Pasternak, the person is and must always remain prior to the collectivity. He stands for courageous, independent loyalty to his own conscience, and for the refusal to compromise with slogans and rationalizations imposed by compulsion. Pasternak is fighting for man's true freedom, his true creativity, against the false and empty humanism of the Marxists — for whom man does not yet truly exist. Over against the technological jargon and the empty scientism of modern man, Pasternak sets creative symbolism, the power of imagination and of intuition, the glory of liturgy and the fire of contemplation. But he does so in new words, in a new way. He speaks for all that is sanest and most permanently vital in religious and cultural tradition, but with the voice of a man of our own time.

This is precisely what makes him dangerous to the Marxists, and this is why the more intelligent and damning pro-Soviet critics (for instance Isaac Deutscher) have done all they could to prove that *Dr. Zhivago* is nothing but a final, despairing outburst of romantic individualism — a voice from the dead past.

On the contrary, however, the fervor with which writers and thinkers everywhere, both in the West and in Russia, have praised the work and the person of Pasternak, quickly made him the center of a kind of spontaneous spiritual movement. This has not received much publicity in the press, but it still goes on. Pasternak became the friend of scores of men still capable of sharing his hopes and fighting for the same ideal. The beauty of this "movement" is that it has been perfectly spontaneous and has had nothing to do with any form of organized endeavor: it has simply been a matter of admiration and friendship for Pasternak.

In a word, it is not a "movement" at all. There were none of the "secret connections" the Soviet Police are always hopefully looking for. There was no planned attempt to make systematic fuss about anything. The protests of Western writers like Camus, T.S. Eliot, Bertrand Russell, and so on, were perfectly spontaneous. And, at the same time, it is not generally known that in Moscow several of the leading members of the Writers' Union conspicuously refused to take part in the moral lynching of Pasternak. The most important of these was Ilya Ehrenburg.

The peculiar strength of Pasternak lies then not only in his own literary genius and in his superb moral courage, but in the depth and genuineness of his spirituality. He is a witness to the spirituality of man, the image of God. He is a defender of everything that can be called a spiritual value, but especially in the aesthetic and religious spheres. He is a thinker, an artist, a contemplative. If at times he seems to underestimate the organized ethical aspect of man's spiritual life it is for two reasons: first because he is portraying a world that has become an ethical chaos, and secondly because in that chaos ethics have been perverted into a non-sensically puritanical system of arbitrary prohibitions and commands. There are moments when Dr. Zhivago seems so much a creature of impulse as to have lost his ethical orientation. But this is deliberate: and we shall see that it is part of a protest against the synthetically false "moralism" that is inseparable from the totalitarian mentality today.

In order to understand the events of 1958, it is necessary to review briefly Pasternak's own career and the part played by him in the literary history of twentieth-century Russia. In particular we must examine his real attitude toward the Russian revolution which has been by no means simple. For Pasternak was one of those poets who, in 1917, received the Revolution with hopeful, though perhaps not unmixed, enthusiasm and who, though he never succeeded in confining his genius within the paralyzing limitations of the Communist literary formulary, at times attempted to write in praise of the Revolution. There are in fact many passages in *Dr. Zhivago* itself which favor the Revolution in its early stages. In a word, Pasternak was one of that legion of writers, artists and intellectuals who, though they began by a more or less fervent acceptance of the Revolution, were forced sooner or later to reject it as a criminal perversion of man's ideals — when they did not pay with life itself for their fidelity to it. The special importance of Pasternak lies in the symbolic greatness of the protest of one who, having survived the worst of the purges conducted under Stalin, emerged after Stalin's death to say exactly what he thought of Stalinism and to say it not in France, or in England, or in America, but in the heart of Soviet Russia.

Everyone is familiar by now with the salient facts of Pasternak's life. He was born in 1890, in Moscow, the son of a painter, Leonid Pasternak, who was the friend and illustrator of Tolstoy. His mother was a concert pianist. In his early years, young Pasternak conceived a great admiration for two friends of his father — the poet Rilke and the musician Scriabin, and at first the boy planned to become a musician. He wrote: "I love music more than anything else, and I loved Scriabin more than anyone else in the world of music. I began to lisp in music not long before my first acquaintance with him. . . . " In other words, he had already begun to compose, and he soon played some of his compositions for Scriabin who "immediately began to assure me that it was clumsy to speak of talent for music when something incomparably bigger was on hand and it was open to me to say my word in music" (*Safe Conduct*, page 23).

In 1912 Pasternak studied Kantian philosophy under Cohen at the University of Marburg in Germany, and returning to Russia became involved in the futurist movement, publishing poems in the review *Tsentrifuga*. He had already long since been under the spell of the symbolist, Alexander Blok, and Blok plays an

important, though hardly noticeable part, in the symbolic structure of *Dr. Zhivago*. The crucial symbol of the candle in the window, which flashes out to illuminate a kind of knot in the crossing paths of the book's main characters, sets Zhivago to thinking
about Blok. The connection of ideas is important, because the
candle in the window is a kind of eye of God, or of the Logos
(call it if you like *Tao*), but since it is the light in the window of
the sophianic figure, Lara, and since Blok in those days (1905)
was absorbed in the cult of Sophia he had inherited from
Soloviev, the candle in the window suggests, among other things,
the Personal and Feminine Wisdom Principle whose vision
has inspired the most original Oriental Christian theologians of
our day.

Among the futurists, the one who seems to have made
the greatest impression on Pasternak is Mayakovsky. In the
early autobiographical sketch, *Safe Conduct*, Pasternak speaks
of admiring Mayakovsky with all the burning fervor which he
had devoted to Scriabin. Later, however, in his more recent
memoir, *I Remember*, he has corrected the impressions created
by his earlier sketch. "There was never any intimacy between
us. His opinion of me has been exaggerated." The two had
"quarreled" and Pasternak says that he found Mayakovsky's
propagandist activities for the Communists "incomprehensible."
Mayakovsky devoted a turbulent and powerful talent to the
Bolshevist cause and turned out innumerable *agitkas* (political
playlets) and a long propaganda poem in honor of Lenin. But
Pasternak himself wrote a fine poem about the bleak days of the
Revolution, in which he traces a vigorous and sympathetic portrait
of Lenin.

> I remember his voice which pierced
> The nape of my neck with flames
> Like the rustle of globe-lightning.
> Everyone stood. Everyone was vainly
> Ransacking that distant table with his eyes:
> And then he emerged on the tribune,
> Emerged even before he entered the room,
> And came sliding, leaving no wake
> Through the barriers of helping hands and obstacles,

Like the leaping ball of a storm
Flying into a room without smoke.
(From *The High Malady*, translated by Robert Payne.)

This, however, is no propaganda poem. Nowhere in it does Pasternak betray the truth in order to conform to some preconceived idea about the Revolution. His vision is direct and sincere: he says what he sees. He describes not what he thinks he feels or "ought to feel," but what he actually feels.

These facts are important since Pasternak, who has been accused by the Communists of having always been an inveterate reactionary, obviously felt sympathy and admiration for Lenin and for the October Revolution. As for the 1905 Revolution, his position is unequivocal. Lara, for instance, walks down the street listening to the guns in the distance and saying to herself, "How splendid. Blessed are the down trodden. Blessed are the deceived. God speed you, bullets, You and I are of one mind" (page 53). Her exultation is symbolic. The revolution means that she is temporarily delivered from her captivity to Komarovsky, the smart lawyer, the opportunist and man of business who, all in all, is the most sinister figure in the whole book and who typifies the wealthy ruling class. It is significant of course that after the Revolution Komarovsky remains a powerful, influential figure: he is the type that revolutions do not get rid of but only strengthen.

All that Pasternak has to say both for and against the Bolshevik Revolution — and there is very much of it — is summed up in a paragraph spoken by Sima, in Yuriatin (a very minor character who nevertheless expresses the clear ideological substance of the whole book). She says:

> With respect to the care of the workers, the protection of the mother, the struggle against the power of money, our revolutionary era is a wonderful, unforgettable era of new, permanent achievements. But as regards the interpretation of life and the philosophy of happiness that is being propagated, it is simply impossible to believe that it is meant to be taken seriously, it's such a comic survival of the past. If all this rhetoric about leaders and peoples had the power to reverse history it would set us back thousands of years

to the Biblical times of shepherd tribes and patriarchs. But fortunately this is impossible (*Dr. Zhivago*, page 413).

Pasternak's writing in the twenties is by no means purely an evasion of contemporary reality. It is true that in the collection of stories by him printed in 1925 there is only one, "Aerial Ways," which has anything to do with the revolution and this is by no means a glorification of the new order. That is in fact the thing that Pasternak has never really been able to do. He has not been able to believe in Communism as any kind of an "order." He has not been able to accept the myth of its dialectical advance toward an ever saner and better world. Even in his most sanguine moments he always viewed the revolution as a chaotic surging of blind forces out of which, he hoped, something new and real might perhaps evolve. *Dr. Zhivago* by and large represents his judgment that the whole thing was a mountain that gave birth to a mouse. No new truth has been born, only a greater and more sinister falsity. It is for this that the Communists cannot forgive him. They do not seem to realize that this very fact confirms his judgment. If Communism had really achieved what it claims to have achieved, surely by now it could tolerate the expression of such opinions as are to be found in *Dr. Zhivago*.

In 1926 Pasternak published a poem on the 1905 Revolution and in 1927 he followed with another revolutionary poem, "Lieutenant Schmidt." The former of these received a lengthy and favorable exegesis from Prince Dimitry Mirsky who had at that time returned to Russia and was temporarily in favor as a Marxist critic — prior to his exile and death in one of the far north camps of Siberia.

Pasternak's writings about the revolution never quite succeeded with the Party because he was always interested too much in man and not enough in policies and the party line. It cannot really be said that he ever seriously attempted to write about the Revolution from a Communist viewpoint and it is certainly false to think that he ever sacrificed any of his integrity in order to "be a success." The fact remains that he has been consistently criticized for "individualism," "departure from reality" and "formalist refinement." In other words he remained an artist and refused to prostitute his writing to politics.

No original work from Pasternak's pen was to appear from 1930 until 1943 when "Aboard the Early Trains" appeared and was condemned by Zhdanov as "alien to socialism." During the rest of these years he worked at translations.

That Pasternak fell silent was not a matter of isolated significance. Blok had died in 1921, disillusioned by the Revolution. The Party's literary authorities were discussing whether or not "The Twelve" was really a Communist poem. Gumilyov had been executed in 1922. Esenin had written his last poem in his own blood and killed himself in 1925. Mayakovsky, at the height of fame and success as a "proletarian poet," committed suicide at the precise moment when, in the words of a historian, he was considered "the embodiment of socialist optimism." The last remaining representatives of the poetic ferment of the war years and the early twenties disappeared into the background and remained silent, if they were not liquidated in the thirties. Pasternak was one of the few to survive. He was able to find support and expression for his genius by publishing remarkable translations of Shakespeare, Rilke, Verlaine, Goethe and other poets of the West.

One of the most mysterious aspects of the Pasternak story is his survival during the great purges of the 1930s. The current guesses as to how he escaped death are barely satisfactory. Some allege that since Pasternak was supposed to have been Mayakovsky's "best friend," and Mayakovsky was now canonized, Stalin allowed Pasternak to live. But anyone who knows anything of Stalin and the purges knows perfectly well that the fact of being the "best friend" of someone who had died might just as well have meant a one-way ticket to the far-north camps. Others believe that because Pasternak had translated the Georgian poets so brilliantly, Stalin could not kill him. But Stalin found it no hardship to kill the Georgian poets themselves — like Pasternak's friend Tabidze. Why then should he spare a translator?

By all the laws of political logic, or lack of logic, Pasternak should have died in the thirties and in fact he nearly did so, for the strain of living through those times undermined his health. Not only was he obviously suspect as a nonpolitical, antipolitical and therefore automatically reactionary poet, but he also distinguished himself by openly defying official literary dogmas in meetings and conferences. Not only that, but he refused to sign several official "petitions" for the death of "traitors," and his friends barely saved him by covering up his defection. The general opinion is that Pasternak could not possibly have survived the purges unless Stalin himself had given explicit orders that he was to be spared. Why?

There has been much speculation, and an article by Mr. Mikhail Koryakov, published in Russian in the *Novy Zhurnal* (in America) and quoted by Edmund Wilson (*The Nation, loc. cit.*), seriously lines up some of the quasi-legendary possibilities. What they add up to is that because of some cryptic statement made by Pasternak in reference to the mysterious death of Stalin's wife, Allelueva, Stalin conceived a superstitious fear of the poet. The Georgian dictator is said to have imagined that Pasternak was endowed with prophetic gifts, was a kind of dervish, and had some kind of unearthly insight into the cause of Allelueva's death. Since Stalin himself has been credited with the murder of his wife, this does not make the mystery of Pasternak's survival any less mysterious.

The intolerably dreary history of art and literature under Stalin might have seemed hopeful to those who firmly believed that the Leader could really make Russia over and create a new, mass-produced Soviet man in his own image and likeness. But the death of Stalin and the "thaw" that followed showed on all sides that the need for originality, creative freedom, and spontaneity had not died. Even men like Ehrenburg and Simonov, successful Communist writers who could be relied upon to do exactly what the Party leaders wanted, discreetly began to suggest the possibility of a rebirth of initiative and even a certain frankness on the part of the writer. As if socialist realism might soon be replaced with something remotely related to real life!

The history of the "thaw" is well known. A few months proved that the slightest relaxation in favor of individual liberty and self-determination, in any field whatever, would bring about the collapse of everything that had been built up by Stalin. The events in Poland and Hungary in the fall of 1956 make this abundantly clear. In both these countries, outspoken writers had led the resistance against Moscow. There was no choice but a hasty and devout return to principles used so effectively by Stalin. While notable ex-members of the Praesidium began to wend their way to places like Outer Mongolia, the millionaire novelist and editor, Simonov, became overnight a leading literary figure of Uzbekistan.

Yet no show of official severity has yet been able to discourage the determined resistance of a younger generation of writers. This resistance is in no sense overtly political; it takes the form of a dogged, largely passive protest against the dreariness and falsity of Communist life. It is a silent, indirect refusal to seek any further meaning in copybook formulas and in norms handed down from above by politicians. A young poet of today, Evgeny Evtushenko, has been publicly scolded by Khrushchev in person. Evtushenko, as a kind of prophet of the New Generation, defies the limitations imposed on his spiritual and artistic freedom. He describes a friend returning from a forced labor camp bursting with interest in everything new, listening to the radio and seeking out all kinds of information: "everything in him breathes character." Evtushenko himself cries out in protest at not being able to fraternize and speak with the people of Buenos Aires, New York, London, or Paris. He wants art, but not socialist realism. He wants to defy the directives of a dying generation and "speak new words." He actively resents the attempts of the Party to regiment his talent, and replies to official criticism with startling lines:

> Many do not like me
> Blaming me for many things
> And cast thunder and lightning at me.
> Sullen and tense they pour scorn on me
> And I feel their glares on my back.
> But I like all this
> I am proud that they cannot handle me,
> Can do nothing about me.[3]

One cannot help but admire the courage of this young poet — it is a fact of deep significance. It shows that the boots of the MVD have never succeeded in stamping out the fires of independent thought in Russia: and that these fires can, at any time, blaze out more brightly than ever.

We are reminded of the revolutionists of a century ago. But there is one significant difference: the resistance of Russian youth so far has been largely nonpolitical. It is not revolutionary in the nineteenth-century sense. It is moral and personal. Even when there is protest against the pharisaism and obscurantism of Soviet propaganda and censorship, it is not the protest of men who want to overthrow the regime. It is singularly free from attempts to exercise political pressure. It is this special innocence from political bias that strikes us most forcibly, for this is a resistance of people who have become *utterly fed up with everything that savors of politics.* This is the most significant thing about the protest, and it is the key to the Pasternak affair.

To try to place in a well-defined political category the moral rebellion of Russian youth against Communism is not only to misunderstand that rebellion: it is the very way by which the Communists themselves would try to frustrate it. Communism is not at home with nonpolitical categories, and it cannot deal with a phenomenon which is not in some way political. It is characteristic of the singular logic of Stalinist-Marxism, that when it incorrectly diagnoses some phenomenon as "political," it corrects the error by forcing the thing to *become* political. Hence the incessant cries of treachery and attack on all sides. Everything that happens that is unforeseen by Russia, or somehow does not fit in with Soviet plans, is an act of capitalist aggression on the Soviet Union. If a late frost ruins the fruit trees of the Ukraine, this is a political event, fomented by Wall Street. When Pasternak writes a great novel, which for political reasons cannot be printed in the U.S.S.R.; and when this novel is hailed as a masterpiece outside the U.S.S.R. — even though the novel is obviously not a political tract against the Soviet system, its success becomes an act of political betrayal on the part of the author. Reasons: for propaganda purposes, the U.S.S.R. has to appear to be the home of all true literature and the only sound judge of what is and what is not a masterpiece. To produce a book that is hailed as a masterpiece after it has been rejected by the Soviet publishers is therefore an act of treachery, for which Pasternak was publicly and officially called "a pig who dirties the place where he sleeps and eats." No one thinks of admitting that it was a sign of weakness and impotency on the part of the Soviet publishers not to be able to print this great work themselves!

Dr. Zhivago was written in the early fifties and finished shortly after Stalin's death in 1953. In 1954, the Second Congress of Soviet writers, with its rehabilitation of condemned writers living and dead, seemed to offer hope for the future. *Dr. Zhivago* was offered for publication to *Novy Mir*. In 1954 some of the poems from *Dr. Zhivago* appeared in a literary magazine and the prospects for the publication of the entire book really seemed to be good. Ilya Ehrenburg had read it, apparently with enthusiasm, as had many other writers. Meanwhile the manuscript had been given personally by Pasternak to the publisher Feltrinelli, of Milan.

In 1956, *Dr. Zhivago* was rejected by *Novy Mir* with a long explanation which we shall discuss in a moment. But Feltrinelli refused to give up the manuscript and manifested his intention to go ahead and publish it. From that time on, guarded attacks on Pasternak were frequent in the Soviet literary magazines. He was reminded that though he might have talent he "had strayed from the true path" and one critic, Pertsov, accused him of a happy acceptance of "chaos" and of being in his element in confusion. Nevertheless in June, 1958, a sympathetic discussion of *Dr. Zhivago* was held over Radio Warsaw. Meanwhile of course the book had appeared in Italy, France and Germany and had taken Europe by storm. The English edition came out in late summer of 1958 and the Nobel Prize was awarded to Pasternak on October 23.

This was hailed by an immediate uproar in the Russian press. The decision was regarded as an act of open hostility, a new maneuver in the Cold War. The award was "steeped in lies and hypocrisy" and *Dr. Zhivago* was a "squalid" work in which Pasternak manifested his "open hatred of the Russian people. He does not have one kind word to say about our workers." *Pravda* discussed the whole thing under the delightfully confusing headline: "A Reactionary hue and cry about a Literary Weed."

On October 27 Pasternak was solemnly expelled from the Soviet Writers' Union. This automatically made it impossible for him to be published or to make any kind of a living by his pen. On October 30 Pasternak, seeing the political storm that had been raised about the award, communicated to Stockholm his regretful decision not to accept the prize. Nothing had been said officially one way or another by the Kremlin. Of all the attacks on Pasternak, the most concentrated and bitter were those which came from his colleagues in the Union of Soviet Writers. The day after his refusal of the Prize, 800 members of the Union which had already expelled him now passed a resolution demanding that he be deprived of Soviet citizenship.

At the same time, the issue continued to be discussed with a certain amount of frankness in Moscow. Pasternak was visited by newspapermen and friends. Poems and parts of *Zhivago* continued to circulate from hand to hand in typewritten or mimeographed editions.

The reports in the Western press tended, by and large, to miss the nuances and gradations of the Pasternak affair in Russia. Everything was presented as either black or white. The Russians were *all* against Pasternak. The Kremlin was completely opposed to him, and would have done away with him if the protest of the West had not been so strong. In the West, on the contrary, everything was white, everyone was *for* Pasternak.

It is true that the protest of Western thinkers and intellectuals was decisive in arresting the all-out campaign against Pasternak in Russia, and in helping to keep him free. Nevertheless, his friends inside Russia were by no means idle. Efforts to organize a positive movement in his behalf were not very successful. But several of the most influential members of the Writers' Union refused to participate in the meetings where Pasternak was condemned. Ilya Ehrenburg sent word that he was "absent from Moscow" when everyone knew he was in his Gorky Street apartment. Leonid Leonov remained conspicuously aloof. Another writer tried actively to bring about Pasternak's rehabilitation and used his influence with Khrushchev for this end. A well-informed Western observer in Moscow reported that the Kremlin in general was disturbed by the fact that the Moscow intelligentsia remained at least passively pro-Pasternak, and that the campaign was met with deep anxiety and even mute protest on the part of the young writers who admired him. Mute protest is not much, of course. But in Russia, any protest at all is significant.

It is said that Pasternak received a fair number of letters from people in the U.S.S.R. who deplored the attacks on him. Later, many of the Soviet writers who had participated in the voting at the Writers' Union privately expressed their regrets to him. All this is true. But at the same time it must not be forgotten that a real wave of indignation and hostility toward Pasternak swept the Soviet Union, incited by the speeches and articles against him, and one night a resentful crowd put on a demonstration outside his *dacha* and even threatened to burn it down.

The political noise that has surrounded *Dr. Zhivago* both in the East and in the West does nothing whatever to make the book or its author better or worse. As far as politics are concerned, Pasternak takes the position of a "non-participant," or *obyvatel*, and as *Life* comments, "Pasternak's detachment sounds a little like the faraway voice of a monk in a beleaguered Dark Age monastery, a mood with which Americans cannot easily sympathize." For my own part, being not only an American, but also a monk, I do not find sympathy so terribly hard. On the contrary, it would seem that Pasternak's ability to rise above political dichotomies may very well be his greatest strength. This transcendence is the power and the essence of *Dr. Zhivago*. One of the more important judgments made by this book is a condemnation of the chaotic meaninglessness of all twentieth-century political life, and the assertion that politics has practically ceased to be a really vital and significant force in man's society. This judgment is pronounced upon the political confusion of the nineteen-twenties in Soviet Russia, but it also falls by implication, and with proper modifications, on the West as well as on the East. What Pasternak says about Russia goes, in a different way, for the Western Europe of Hitler and Mussolini, and for the whole world of the last war — not to mention the America of the '50s.

The protest of *Dr. Zhivago* is spiritual, not political, not sociological, not pragmatic. It is religious, aesthetic and mystical. We cannot fully understand the author's view of the modern world if we insist on interpreting him by standards which have nothing to do with his work and his thought. We cannot fit into simple political categories one for whom the whole political chaos of our world is a kind of enormous spiritual cancer, running wild with a strange, admirable and disastrous life of its own and feeding on the spiritual substance of man. The deep interest of *Dr. Zhivago* is precisely its diagnosis of man's spiritual situation as a struggle for freedom *in spite of* and *against* the virulence of this enormous political disease. For, to be more accurate, since man's spiritual substance is his freedom itself, it is precisely this freedom which is devoured by politics and transmuted into a huge growth of uncontrollable precocity. Hope of attaining true freedom by purely political means has become an insane delusion.

The great success of *Dr. Zhivago* is by no means attributable to the mere fact that it happens to contain sentences which level devastating blows against the Communist mentality. Anyone with any perception can see that these blows fall, with equal power, on every form of materialistic society. They fall upon most of the gross, pervasive and accepted structures of thought and life which go to make up our changing world. The book is successful not because these blows are dealt, but because, as they land, we gradually begin to realize that Pasternak seems to know what is wrong. He seems to know what has happened to our spiritual freedom. He seems to realize why it is that most of the world's talk about freedom, peace, happiness, hope for the future is just talk and nothing more. He knows all too well that such talk is only a palliative for despair. But at the same time he has a true and solid hope to offer.

The author who most reminds me of Pasternak in this respect is Ignazio Silone. His heroes too, perhaps on a smaller scale and in a more restricted area, travel the same road as Dr. Zhivago, but with a more explicitly political orientation. Silone's men, with all the pathetic yet admirable smallness of genuinely human heroes, are true to man, true to his real history, true to man's vocation to "be Christ."

Zhivago of course is not a saint or a perfect hero. He is weak-willed, and his life is a confused and unsatisfactory mess. He himself knows that he has not been able to make a success of it. But the point is, he sees that in the circumstances in which he lives it is not possible to make a success out of life — that the only honest thing is to face meaninglessness and failure with humility, and make out of it the best one can. Under such conditions his tragic life is lived "successfully" under the sign of wisdom.

It seems that the main difference between Pasternak and Western authors who have sensed the same futility, is that he is not defeated by it as they are. Nowhere in Pasternak does one get the impression that his heroes are up a blind alley, beating their heads against a wall. In the West one sees very little else. For a great majority of Western writers, though in varying degrees, man finds himself as he does in Sartre, with "No Exit" — Huis Clos — that is to say, in hell. The Communists would explain this as a feature of capitalist decay. Yet their own society is up the same blind alley, pretending that the wall at the end is not there, and that the business of beating your head against it is proof of optimism and progress. Pasternak sees the blind alley and sees the wall, but knows that the way out is not through the wall, and not back out by the way we came in. The exit is into an entirely new dimension — finding ourselves in others, discovering the inward sources of freedom and love which God has put in our nature, discovering Christ in the midst of us, as "one we know not."

This exit is not a mere theoretical possibility. Nor is it even a mere escape. It is a real and creative solution to man's problems: a solution that can bring meaning out of confusion and good out of evil. It is something that has been sought after with hope and conviction by the greatest Russian minds of the past century: Dostoievsky, Tolstoy, Soloviev, and by Russians of our own time like Nicholas Berdyaev.

The solution is *love* as the highest expression of man's spirituality and freedom. Love and Life (reduced to one and the same thing) form the great theme of *Dr. Zhivago*. In proportion as one is alive he has a greater capacity and a greater obligation to love. Every degree of true and false love makes its appearance in the book — from the self-assured and bestial selfishness of Komarovsky, the businessman, to the different shades of compulsive and authoritarian falsity in the various revolutionaries. There are all aspects of parental and conjugal love (Zhivago really loves his wife Tonia, for example). Lara though seduced by Komarovsky in her girlhood remains the embodiment of a love that is simple, unadulterated spontaneity, a love that does not know how to be untrue to itself or to life. Her love is perfectly aware of the difference between sin and goodness, but her repentance (the Magdalen theme) has a creative power to transcend limitations and to emerge into a new world. Lara is thus the embodiment of the goodness and love of God immanent in His creation, immanent in man and in Russia, and there left at the mercy of every evil. Far from being a trite and prissy concept, this is both deep and original. One can see in Pasternak a strong influence from Soloviev's *Meaning of Love* and his theory of man's vocation to regenerate the world by the spiritualization of human love raised to the sophianic level of perfect conscious participation in the mystery of the divine wisdom of which the earthly sacrament is love.

At the same time we must remember that Zhivago's victory is tragic. Lara vanishes "without a trace" to die, probably, in a concentration camp. Nothing has been "transformed." It is the victory that shines forth in apparent defeat — the victory of death and resurrection. We notice too, that resurrection remains curiously implicit in the strange, impoverished death of the unsuccessful doctor who falls to the pavement with a heart attack while getting out of a Moscow streetcar. There is a strange parallel between the double death rite of Marina and Lara for Zhivago and the terribly impressive scene of lamentation at the end of *Safe Conduct* in which Mayakovsky's sister raves with Oriental passion over the body of the suicide. There is a gleam of hope in the Epilogue where Tania, the child of Zhivago and Lara, the "child of the terrible years" is seen, for a moment, in her own simplicity. The things she has had to go through have not ruined her. And we realize that the strange mystical figure of Evgraf, the "guardian angel," "will take care of her." She is the Russia of the future.

One of the singularly striking things about *Dr. Zhivago* is its quality of tragedy without frustration. Here everything is clean and free from ambivalence. Love is love and hate is hate. Zhivago says and does what he means, and when he is uncertain he is not dishonest about it. It is this spiritual cleanliness, this direct vision and fidelity to life here and now which Pasternak opposes to the grandiose and systematic ravings of politicians who turn all life into casuistry and bind man hand and foot in the meticulous service of unrealities.

It is time to quote. These are the thoughts of Zhivago, half starved and faint from hardships and exposure, as he reads a political proclamation pasted on a wall:

> Had (these words) been composed last year, the year before? Only once in his life had this uncompromising language and single-mindedness filled him with enthusiasm. Was it possible that he must pay for that rash enthusiasm all his life by never hearing year after year, anything but these unchanging, shrill, crazy exclamations and demands which became progressively more impractical, meaningless and unfulfillable as time went by? . . . What an enviable blindness, to be able to talk of bread when it has long since vanished from the face of the earth! Of propertied classes and speculators when they have long since been abolished by earlier decrees! Of peasants and villages that no longer exist! Don't they remember their own plans and measures, which long since turned life upside down? What kind of people are they, to go on raving with this never cooling feverish ardor, year in, year out, on non-existent, long-vanished subjects, and to know nothing, to see nothing around them. (*Dr. Zhivago*, page 381.)

Pasternak was morally compelled to refuse the Nobel Prize in order to remain in Russia. Writers in England, France and the United States protested against Russia's flat rejection of her only great writer since the Revolution. *Pravda* devoted eighteen columns to an unprecedented publication of the "original letter" which had been sent to Pasternak by the magazine *Novy Mir* refusing to serialize the novel in Russian. The letter was signed, curiously enough, by a poet, A.T. Tvardovsky, who, since writing it, had himself fallen under an official ban. The document is notable for its surprising lack of abusiveness and its relatively sympathetic effort to reason with the author. Pasternak was evidently respected in this case by a devoted colleague. The chief objection is not made against the passages in which Marxism is explicitly condemned, for these are relatively few and could have been expunged. The whole fault of the book, from the Soviet point of view, is something "which neither the editors nor the author can alter by cuts or revision the spirit of the novel, its general tenor, *the author's view of life.*"

This view of life, as we have indicated above, is that the individual is more important than the collectivity. His spirit, his freedom, his ability to love, raise him above the state. The state exists for man, not man for the state. No man has the right to hand himself over to any superior force other than God Himself. Man has no right to alienate his own liberty to become a cog in a machine. Man is of no use to man if he ceases to be a person and lets himself be reduced to the status of a "thing." A collectivity that reduces the members to the level of alienated objects is dooming both itself and its members to a sterile and futile existence to which no amount of speeches and parades can ever give a meaning. The great tragedy of the revolution, for Pasternak, was the fact that the best men in Russia submitted to mass insanity and yielded up their own judgment to the authority of Juggernaut.

It was then that untruth came down on our land of Russia. The main misfortune, the root of all evil to come, was the loss of confidence in the value of one's own opinion. People imagined that it was out of date to follow their own moral sense, that they must all sing in chorus, and live by other people's notions, notions that were being crammed down everybody's throat. . . . The social evil became an epidemic. It was catching, and it affected everything, nothing was left untouched by it. Our home too became infected. . . . Instead of being natural and spontaneous as we had always been, we began to be idiotically pompous with each other. Something showy, artificial, forced, crept into our conversation — you felt you had to be clever in a certain way about certain world-important themes. . . . . (*Dr. Zhivago*, page 404.)

Like Dostoievsky, Pasternak holds that man's future depends on his ability to work his way out from under a continuous succession of authoritarian rulers who promise him happiness at the cost of his freedom. Like Dostoievsky, also, Pasternak insists that the fruit of Christ's Incarnation, Death and Resurrection, is that true freedom has at least become possible: but that man, ignoring the real meaning of the New Testament, prefers to evade the responsibility of his vocation and continues to live "under the law." This is not a new complaint: it goes back to St. Paul.

Ironically enough, one of the most brilliant analyses of man's alienation came from the pen of Marx. Modern Russia, while paying lip-service to Marx's theory on this point, has forgotten his full meaning. Yet in so doing, the Soviets have brought out the inner contradiction of Marx's thought: for the complete spiritual alienation of man which Marx ascribed in part to religion has been brought about by militant atheism, as well as by the economic system which claims to be built on an orthodox Marxian foundation. It is of course not fair to blame Stalin's police state directly on Marx, though Marx cannot be absolved from indirect responsibility.

At any event, Pasternak's "view of life" is what has brought upon him the outraged and unanimous condemnation of Soviet officialdom. While the letter from *Novy Mir* reproves Pasternak as immoral, the Soviet critics after the Nobel Prize award did not hesitate to find in *Dr. Zhivago* and in its author every possible kind of moral depravity. Pasternak, the lowest of the low, could not even be compared to a pig. He could no longer claim a right to breath the pure air of Soviet Russia.

It would be a great mistake to think that for the Communists such accusations are taken as mere words without specific reference, to be used with cynical opportunism. The curious fact is that Communism today has forged its own rigid and authoritarian code of morals, which can be called "an ethic" only by doing violence to the meaning of words, but which nevertheless claims with puritanical self-assurance to show men how to "live."

The ideal Communist is a combination of a beaver and wolf. He unites machine-like industry with utter insensitiveness to deep human values whenever they come into conflict with political duty. He either knows at all times the course of history and "the one correct thing" to do at the moment, or, if he does not know it, he obeys someone else who claims to know it. In either case, he "acts" with all the complacent self-assurance of a well-adjusted machine, and grinds to pieces anything that comes in his way, whether it be his own idea of truth, his most cherished hopes for this world or the next, or the person of a wife, friend, or parent.

All through *Dr. Zhivago* we find an extraordinary and subtle range of such characters portrayed: some of them pure Communist types, others much more complicated and hard to label. The hero himself, Yurii Zhivago, *is in all respects the exact opposite to the New Soviet Man.* This, of course is what constitutes, in Soviet eyes, the depth of moral degradation. To have human feelings, to follow the lead of spontaneous inner inspiration, to be moved by love and pity, to let oneself be swayed by appreciation of what is *human* in man — all this is nothing but bourgeois depravity and shameless individualism.

It almost seems that Pasternak has gone out of his way to make Zhivago act on impulse in a way that would seem utterly foolish to Communists. It always remains clear that this yielding to impulse is not presented (as it sometimes is in Western novels) as the ideal of freedom. No, freedom is something higher and more spiritual than that. But Pasternak makes the point that if one does at times follow a crazy urge and do something completely pointless, it is not an act to be ashamed of. Must one always be reasonable? Must one always have a ponderous ethical justification for every action he performs? Must one fear spontaneity and never do anything that is not decreed by some program, some form or other of duty? On the contrary, it is compulsiveness that warps life and makes it pointless. The apparent pointlessness of man's impulses may perhaps show the way to what he is really seeking.

This, for a Marxist, is deadly heresy: everyone knows that for a Marxist everything has to fit in with his fantasies of omniscience.

Everything has to have a point, everything has to be guided toward some specific purpose. To this, Zhivago replies:

You find in practice that what they mean by ideas is nothing but words — claptrap in praise of the revolution and the regime. . . . One of my sins is a belief in intuition. And yet see how ridiculous. They all shout that I am a marvelous diagnostician, and as a matter of fact it's true that I don't often make mistakes in diagnosing a disease. Well, what is this immediate grasp of the situation as a whole supposed to be if not this intuition they find so detestable? (*Dr. Zhivago*, page 407.)

It is therefore understandable that *Novy Mir* should have singled out with horror the passage where Yurii Zhivago finds himself accidentally in the middle of a battle between Red Partisans and White Russian volunteers (pages 332-6). There can be no question that such a passage would make any good Communist squirm in his chair with acute moral discomfort. It would repel and horrify him in much the same way as a chapter of Sartre or Moravia might horrify a nun. It is the kind of thing he would take not only as alien and unpleasant, but as a threat to the whole foundation of moral security and peace of mind. I do not doubt that Pasternak wrote this section deliberately with his tongue in his cheek. The Reds have responded admirably. The *Novy Mir* letter as reprinted in *Pravda* contains the whole passage quoted *in extenso*, in order to let each loyal Communist taste the full deliciousness of scandalized horror.

What happens? Zhivago, as a doctor, is not supposed to fight. But he is caught in this battle which like all battles is a silly and tragic mess. Zhivago impulsively takes the gun of a fallen comrade, but deliberately aims at a dead tree trunk and only hits one of the enemy by accident. After the skirmish, he finds that his fallen Red comrade and the White soldier he has wounded each wear a locket containing the text of Psalm 90, which was devoutly believed to be a protection against death. The Red soldier, with a corrupt text of the Psalm, is dead. The White, with a correct text, is alive. Taking pity on him, Zhivago clothes him in the uniform of the fallen Red Partisan and looks after him among the Communist fighters, until he escapes, threatening that he will continue to fight the Reds.

This scene, which is essentially comical, contains just about every mortal sin in the Communist code. I leave the reader to discover them for himself.

The situation being what it was, the Soviet Leaders were faced with the problem of blackening Pasternak in the eyes of East and West at the same time. He had to be regarded not only as a dangerous criminal by Russia, but as a hypocrite and coward by the West. Realistic politicians knew well enough that denunciations would not be enough to ruin Pasternak in the eyes of the young writers who undoubtedly looked up to him as a model and a hero. Soviet attacks on Pasternak could only add to his prestige in the West. For this reason, far from categorically forbidding him to accept the prize, they left the door wide open and urged him to leave Russia as long as he did not try to return. It would have been admirable, from their viewpoint, to have "proof" that Pasternak was a traitor to his country. At the same time their benevolence would remain to "prove" that "Pasternak has been left perfectly free to accept the Nobel Prize." Pasternak refused to abandon Russia, not out of political astuteness but merely because he loved his own country and did not feel that he would be able to write anywhere else.

Once again, he was acting with perfect consistency as one who is the exact opposite of a Communist. His staying in Russia was another victory for his personal integrity as an artist and as a human being. But perhaps there was some advantage to be gained here by the Reds. Perhaps Pasternak could be pressed a little further, and so diminished in the eyes of the West. Pasternak came out in *Pravda* with a letter of "apology," declared that he had made a "mistake" in accepting the Nobel Prize, and that his subsequent refusal of it had been "entirely voluntary." He stated that he had not been threatened and that his life had not been imperiled. This letter, which saddened and shocked readers in the West, but which could have been regarded as inevitable, was probably extracted from him in order to save face for the Soviet Government and pay the price of his moral victory.

If one reads the letter carefully, he can detect the difference between passages written by Pasternak and those inserted by others to "make his meaning clear." The passages obviously written by Pasternak are clear and consistent with his position. He asks to be dissociated from the "political campaign around my novel" which he regrets and did not intend. "I never had the intention of causing harm to my state and my people." That is only a reaffirmation of the obvious fact that the book is not a political tract. In regard to the "political errors" of which he "might be accused," he declares that they are not to be found in the novel. This passage is interesting and entirely true. Here is what Pasternak writes: "*It would appear* that I am *allegedly maintaining* the following erroneous principles. *I am supposed to have alleged* that any revolution is an historically illegal phenomenon, that the October Revolution was such, and that it brought unhappiness to Russia and the downfall of the Russian intelligentsia." It is quite obvious that Pasternak nowhere holds that all revolution is "historically illegal" — nor does anybody else. Nor does he maintain that the October Revolution was "illegal." The texts we have quoted certainly show that Russia after the revolution is not portrayed in *Dr. Zhivago* as a bed of roses and that Pasternak plainly ascribes many bad effects to Communism. At the same time we have seen clearly that he accepted the necessity of the Revolution, first of all in 1905, then in 1917. No one in his right senses could imagine that Pasternak was trying in *Dr. Zhivago* to lead Russia back to capitalism or to the old regime. But it is equally clear that he has maintained a perfect independence and objectivity with regard to the revolution, and after living through Stalin's five-year plans and the purges, he has concluded (with the vast majority of intellectuals everywhere in the world) that the Bolshevik Revolution was a failure and that Marxism had nothing to offer man but a Gospel of delusions. His apology as it stands does nothing to alter the substance of this belief. All that he regrets, about *Zhivago*, is the manner in which it was published and the way it was exploited by anti-Communist journalism. These two things were obviously not the fault of the author.

Pasternak's letter ends with a pious sigh which is utterly alien to his thought and his style and was almost certainly inserted by somebody else: "I firmly believe that I shall find the strength to redeem my good name and restore the confidence of my comrades."

The mystery of this letter has not fully been cleared up, but after its publication and the publication of other similar statements, Pasternak cautioned a friend against believing any statement that was supposed to have emanated from him.

Meanwhile, November and December 1958 were months of bitterness and conflict. We have already considered the open explosions of hostility which occurred at the time of the Prize award, when the Soviet authorities were trying to get Pasternak out of Russia. These explosions soon ceased, and the case vanished from the pages of *Pravda*. It ceased to be front-page news in the West and soon disappeared altogether but for a few sporadic flare-ups.

Meanwhile, Pasternak was exhausted and ill. In order to forget his troubles, he kept himself busy on a translation of a Polish play, a job that had been deliberately steered his way by sympathetic friends in the Polish Writers' Union. Letters continued to arrive from the West. Friends and even reporters continued to visit the *dacha* — where the presence of newspapermen did nothing to improve the peace of the household. Mrs. Pasternak strenuously objected to them, and uttered vigorous protests, all of which were dutifully reported in the Western newspapers.

December came, and with it the distribution of the Noble Prizes. Western journalists gloated over the possibility it might turn into a good show — with an empty chair evidence for Pasternak. No such thing was done, fortunately. It would have been very entertaining for minds that rejoice in devious forms of moral aggression, but it would not have made life any more comfortable for Pasternak.

At the end of the year a story broke in the Western press stating that a Spanish exile in London, José Vilallonga, had arranged to tour free Europe and America with Pasternak giving lectures. It was alleged that Pasternak's life had been insured for three million dollars. The Russians seem to have taken this story seriously and *Pravda* reported a telegram in which Pasternak was supposed to have rejected the offer. In reality, as Pasternak himself made clear, he had never been in contact with Vilallonga and everything about the story was "pure invention" including the supposed telegram.

Early in the new year, Pasternak was again featured in a disturbing story. A reporter of the London *Daily Mail* printed a poem in which Pasternak complained bitterly at being rejected by his own countrymen. Pasternak did not deny having written the poem but protested against its publication as a breach of confidence. Once again it was felt that his life might be in danger. When in February Pasternak suddenly disappeared from his *dacha*, many came to the conclusion that he had been imprisoned and that the game was now up. The explanation given by the Soviet Press was that he had gone away for a "vacation" and in order "to avoid the newspapermen who were coming from London to Moscow with Prime Minister Macmillan." As it turned out, this explanation may have been substantially true.

Actually, Pasternak had left Peredelkino of his own free will and had gone to spend a few weeks at Tiflis, Georgia, as the guest of Mrs. Tabidze, the widow of the Georgian poet shot by Stalin's police. He returned home in good health, and gradually, as the affair ceased to appear in the press and began to be forgotten in the West, prospects began to look good for the harassed writer. In May, for example, a shake-up in the Soviet Writers' Union led to the replacement of Pasternak's enemy Surkov, as head of the Union, by Fedin who is friendly to Pasternak.

This was not a mere coincidence. The removal of Surkov was certainly a consequence of the Pasternak Affair, and those who interpreted this change in the Writer's Union as evidence that Pasternak's friends had won over the favor of Khrushchev are perhaps not too far wrong. Whatever may be the real facts, which remain to be discovered and made public, we can agree with the writer of the *New York Times* who said: "It was apparent that there were profound second thoughts about the persecution of Mr. Pasternak. All of the leading literary and party figures who participated in the verbal lynching were downgraded or demoted."

And this is highly significant. It shows at least that the qualities of freedom and integrity for which Pasternak stood in the eyes of west and east alike were able in some measure to get themselves recognized in Soviet Russia.

This is no small achievement. It is quite clear that Pasternak emerged from the whole affair as the moral and spiritual conqueror of Stalinism, and that he conquered, not for himself alone but even for those of his compatriots who were able to share to some degree in his outlook. And if he did this, it was not only because of his natural and human qualities but, I might venture to say, because of the depth and clarity of his Christian faith. Not that Pasternak is an explicit witness for the Christian message, in the face of Communism: his faith was never directly involved in the debate at all. And yet his resistance was spiritual and his spirit was essentially Christian not only because of his belief in "Christ as the center of history" but because of his existential dedication to the supreme inner value of personalism, which is one of the characteristic Christian contributions to western humanistic thought.

Let us now draw a few conclusions.

Pasternak's book was offered for publication in Russia after the death of Stalin, during the "thaw" when, at the Twentieth Party Congress, Khrushchev openly admitted the "crimes and errors" of Stalin, implicitly showing that Russia needed to move back from extreme dictatorial authoritarianism to a freer and more flexible way of life. Pasternak obviously thought that his book could claim to represent the thought and aspirations of the intelligentsia, including many Communists, at that time. No doubt there would have to be changes, but the *substance* of his book was, it seemed, just what Russia was waiting for. As far as the young intellectuals are concerned, this may have been true.

Unfortunately, as regards the Party, he was premature! The fact that *Dr. Zhivago* could never be made acceptable by editing showed that Soviet Russia could never accept so fundamental an idea of freedom. The end of the thaw soon made this very plain.

A providential accident led to the publication of the novel outside the U.S.S.R. by an Italian publisher who refused obedience to Moscow when the edition was condemned. When Pasternak was awarded the Nobel Prize, it showed that the whole world was glad that at last a great book had come out of Russia. The acclaim of critics and readers was certainly not primarily a political matter. Unquestionably Western readers have not studied Pasternak's estimate of Communism without satisfaction. And of course the newspapers have turned the book into a political weapon, which was not the intention of the author. But the Nobel Prize was awarded on nonpolitical grounds to a book great in its own right.

The fact remains that, if Soviet Russia had been strong enough to absorb the powerful contents of this book in the first place, and had been able to publish it, even in a somewhat edited version, the prestige achieved by this act would have been tremendous. One Nobel Prize winner in literature is of more value to Russia than a thousand winners in physics, no matter how set the Soviet government is on science. It is one thing to produce atomic counters or to win the pentathlon, and another to be recognized as a leader in the field of literature. If Russia wins the Nobel award in science, it is because she has good scientists. If her athletes excel, it is because they are good. But her scientists and athletes are good because dialectical materialism cannot directly interfere in their speciality. (The attempt to do so in biology has been given up.) What remains but the conclusion that, if Russian writers were not forced to sabotage their talent and their integrity and grind out political clichés, they too might win Nobel Prizes? Here is one who has done it: but without benefit of a blessing from the Kremlin. The implications are so plain that even the Kremlin can see them, and, like the Hungarian Revolution, the spectacle has proved disconcerting.

So much for Russia. But what does Pasternak have to say to the Western intellectual? The first thing, of course, is said by the triumphant artistic achievement of his novel and the poetry which accompanies it. *Dr. Zhivago* itself is greater than any "message" that might be distilled out of it. It is a superb novel which recovers the full creative fecundity that seems to have vanished from our cramped and worried literature; a book with a sense of orientation and meaning in strong contrast with our Western frustration and despair.

Pasternak has become a best seller and a widely read author in the West, but he will always be a writer's writer. His greatest impact has been on the *writers* of the West. He has received letters from all kinds of people, but especially from other writers, in many different countries, not the least being Camus and Mauriac. Pasternak answered all these letters with profound warmth of understanding, and those who were privileged to be in contact with him felt that he had given them much more than they expected — an inspiration and sense of direction which they had ceased to hope for from any other writer!

We have learned from Pasternak that we must never yield to the great temptation offered by Communism to the writer. I do not mean the temptation to be a member of a privileged and respected class, but the far more insidious one of becoming a "writer for the future." Surely there is something apocalyptic about the sinister complacency with which Communism, which has hitherto proved effective only in killing writers or ruining them, proposes itself as Master of the future of literature. "Write for us, you will remembered forever in the Kingdom of the Messiahs who has now come! Refuse our offer, and you will be buried with the world that we are about to bury."

It is against such insinuations of the Beast that Pasternak replies with his doctrine of life and resurrection. This is a doctrine with a strongly Christian basis, using exclusively Christian symbolism. Needless to say, not all of Pasternak's expressions can be fully reconciled with those to be found in a manual of dogma. The Christ of Pasternak is the Christ Who has liberated man from death and Who lives in man, waiting for man's liberty to give Him a chance to transform the world by love. Love is the work not of states, not of organizations, not of institutions, but of persons. Hence:

> Gregariousness is always the refuge of mediocrities. . . .
> Only individuals seek the truth, and they shun those whose
> whole concern is not the truth. How many things in this
> world deserve our loyalty? Very few indeed. I think one
> should be loyal to immortality, which is another word for

life, a stronger word for it. One must be true to immortality — true to Christ (*Dr. Zhivago*, page 9).

Pasternak looks at our world, dismembered by its obsessions
and its factions, each one claiming to be on the side of the angels and calling everyone else a devil. Egged on by journalists,
politicians and propagandists, we cling with mad hope to fanatical creeds whose only function is to foment violence, hatred, and
division. Will we never begin to understand that the "differences"
between these factions are often so superficial as to be illusory
and that all of them are equally stupid? Will we never grow up,
and get down to the business of living productively on this earth,
in unity and peace?

History is not a matter of inexorable scientific laws, it is a
new creation, a work of God in and through man: but this
theandric work is unthinkable not only without man's desire but
also without his *initiative.* Christ has planted in the world the
seeds of something altogether new, but they do not grow by
themselves. Hence history has never yet really had a chance to
become a Christian creation. For the world to be changed, man
himself must begin to change it, he must take the initiative, he
must step forth and make a new kind of history. The change
begins within himself.

You can't advance in this direction without a certain
faith. You can't make such discoveries without a spiritual
equipment. And the basic elements of this equipment
are in the Gospels. What are they? To begin with a certain
love of one's neighbor, which is the supreme form of
vital energy. Once it fills the heart of man it has to overflow
and expend itself. And then the two basic ideals of modern
man — without them he is unthinkable — the idea of
free personality and the idea of life as sacrifice. . . . There
is no history in this sense among the ancients. They
had blood and beastliness and cruelty and pockmarked
Caligulas who had no idea how inferior the system of
slavery is. They had the boastful dead eternity of bronze
monuments and marble columns. It was not until
after the coming of Christ that time and man could breathe
freely. Man does not die in a ditch like a dog — but at

home in history, while the work toward the conquest of death is in full swing; he dies sharing in this work (*Dr. Zhivago*, page 10).

Here is the deep meaning of Pasternak's critique of Communism. It is blindness and sin to seek immortality in the bronze and stone which are already stamped with lifelessness and twice dead when they are frozen into an art without inspiration. "Why seek ye the living among the dead?" Communism, like all characteristically modern political movements, far from opening the door to the future, is only a regression into the past, the ancient past, the time of slavery before Christ. Following these movements, mankind falls backward into an abyss of ancient, magical laws; man comes under the authority of numbers and astrological systems and loses all hope of freedom. But with the coming of Christ the reign of numbers was at an end. The duty, imposed by armed force, to live unanimously as a people, a whole nation, was abolished. Leaders and nations were relegated to the past. They were replaced by the doctrine of individuality and freedom. *Individual human life became the life story of God and its contents filled the vast expanses of the universe.*

These words occur on page 413, far into the book, in an apparently colorless, "unexciting" chapter which is in reality very important to Pasternak's great work — one of the nerve centers where all his meaning is fully experienced.

If we stop to think about what it says, we will realize that if Pasternak is ever fully studied, he is just as likely to be regarded as a dangerous writer in the West as he is in the East. He is saying that political and social structures as we understand them are things of the past, and that the crisis through which we are now passing is nothing but the full and inescapable manifestation of their falsity. For twenty centuries we have called ourselves Christians, without even beginning to understand one tenth of the Gospel. We have been taking Caesar for God and God for Caesar. Now that "charity is growing cold" and we stand facing the smoky dawn of an apocalyptic era, Pasternak reminds us that there is only one source of truth, but that it is not sufficient to know the source is there — we must go and drink from it, as he has done.

Do we have the courage to do so? For obviously, if we consider what Pasternak is saying, doing and undergoing, to read the Gospel with eyes wide open may be a perilous thing!

NOTES

1. "The Pasternak Affair" was originally published in Thomas Merton's *Disputed Questions*.

2. See page 407 [of this volume] for text of his last letter to the author.

3. See "The Young Generation of Soviet Writers," by A. Gaev, in *Bulletin of the Institute for Study of the U.S.S.R.*, Munich, Sept. 1958, pages 38 ff.

Balkan icon of the Archangel Michael.

Monastic saints Dorotheos and Markarios the Roman.
Monastery of Dionysiou, Mount Athos.

THE THOMAS MERTON/BORIS PASTERNAK CORRESPONDENCE[1]

Abbey of Gethsemani
Trappist P.O.
Kentucky, U.S.A.

Aug. 22, 1958.

My Dear Boris Pasternak:

Although we are separated by great distances and even greater barriers it gives me pleasure to speak to you as to one whom I feel to be a kindred mind. We are both poets — you a great one and I a very minor one. We share the same publisher in this country — New Directions. At least for our poetry: for your prose is appearing under the Pantheon imprint and mine appears in another house.

I have not yet had the pleasure of reading your recent autobiography although I am familiar with the earlier one, *Safe Conduct*, by which I was profoundly impressed. It may surprise you when I say, in all sincerity, that I feel much more kinship with you, in your writing, than I do with most of the great modern writers in the west. That is to say that I feel that I can share your experience more deeply and with a greater intimacy and sureness, than that of writers like Joyce whom I nevertheless so well like and understand. But, when you write of your youth in the Urals, in Marburg, in Moscow, I feel as if it were my own experience, as if I were you. With other writers I can share ideas, but you seem to communicate something quite normal and ordinary, and I feel no need to apologize for it. I am convinced that you understand me perfectly. It is true that a person always remains a person and utterly separate and apart from every other person. But it is equally true that each person is destined to reach with others an understanding and a unity which transcend individuality, and Russian tradition describes this with a concept we do not fully possess in the west — *sobornost.*

It gives me pleasure to send you under separate cover a kind of prose poem or meditation on *Prometheus* which had been privately printed near here recently. At least you will like the handsome printing. I hope the book reaches you. I am writing to you in your village home near Moscow — of which I happened to read in an English magazine. If you get this letter, and not the book, I hope you will let me know. I will try again.

It is my intention to begin learning Russian in order to try to get into Russian literature in the original. It is very hard to get much in the way of translations. I would much prefer to read you in Russian, though it will probably be a long time before I am able to do so. What I have read of modern Russian poets in translation is to me very stimulating. I have no difficulty in admitting a certain lassitude and decadence in much western literature. I like Mayakovsky and also I am very much interested in Khlebnikov (is that how you spell it?) What do you think of him? Blok of course I find very interesting. What about the new poets? Are there some good ones? Whom do you recommend? in Latin America? I am particularly fond of a great Negro poet of Brazil, Jorge de Lima. Neruda, of Chile, is probably well known in the U.S.S.R. and I presume you know him.

My dear Pasternak, it is a joy to write to you and to thank you for your fine poetry and your great prose. A voice like yours is of great importance for all mankind in our day — so too is a voice like that of Shostakovitch. The Russian leaders do not perhaps realize to the full how important and how great you are for Russia and for the world. Whatever may lie ahead for the world, I believe that men like yourself and I hope myself also may have the chance to enter upon a dialogue that will really lead to peace and to a fruitful age for man and his world. Such peace and fruitfulness are spiritual realities to which you already have access, though others do not.

These are the realities which are important. In the presence of these deeper things, and in witness of them, I clasp your hand in deep friendship and admiration. You are in my prayers and I beg God to bless you.

Fraternally yours in Christ

27 Sept. (Holy Cross day) 1958

Dear and reverend friend

Thank you from all my heart for your warm congenial letter. It also (like my writings to you) seems to me wonderfully filled with kindred thoughts as having been written half by myself.

It afflicts me only to learn the attention you have paid to *Safe Conduct* and my previous poetry and prose. It does not merit your interest, contrary to the novel in the Pantheon, which will perhaps be more worthy to be read by you.

Your *Prometheus* has not yet reached me. I shall read the poem with pleasure and zeal. But be not impatient for my answer. I often have much letters to reply.

I thank you from the bottom of my soul for your prayers and wish you health and forces enough for your good life and deeds.

I don't sign the letter for the better sureness of its reaching you.

Peredelkino near Moscow
through Bakovka

3 Oct. 1958

Dear Merton, I thank you for *Prometheus* and for the
kind unmerited dedication, which I have received yesterday. I think the strophes IV and VII are the most
succeeded, the last one containing fine individual
Christo-sophical touches.

I take the opportunity to repeat you, that except the Dr.
Zh [*Dr. Zhivago*] which you should read all the rest of my
verses and writings are devoid of any sense and
importance. The most part of my mature years I gave off
to Goethe, Shakespeare and other great and voluminous
translations.

Thankfully yours,
B.P.

Trappist P.O.
Kentucky.

October 23, 1958.

My Dear Pasternak:

What a great joy it was to receive your two letters. It
has given me much food for thought, this bare fact of the
communication between us: at a time when our two countries are unable to communicate with one another seriously and sincerely, but spend millions communicating
with the moon. . . . No, the great business of our time is
this: for one man to find himself in another one who is
on the other side of the world. Only by such contacts
can there be peace, can the sacredness of life be preserved
and developed and the image of God manifest itself in
the world.

Since my first letter to you I have obtained and read the book published by Pantheon, and it has been a great and rewarding experience. First of all it has astounded me with the great number of sentences that I myself might have written, and in fact perhaps have written. Just one example at random: I am bringing out a book on sacred art in which one of the theses is practically this "All genuine art ressembles and continues the Revelation of St John." This is to me so plain and so obvious that as a result I have seriously questioned the claim of the Renaissance to have produced much genuinely religious art. . . . But enough of the small details.

The book is a world in itself, a sophiological world, a paradise and a hell, in which the great mystical figures of Yurii and Lara stand out as Adam and Eve and, though they walk in darkness, walk with their hand in the hand of God. The earth they walk upon is sacred because of them. It is the sacred earth of Russia, with its magnificent destiny which remains hidden for it in the plans of God. To me the most overwhelmingly beautiful and moving passage is the short, tranquil section in the Siberian town where Yurii, lying in the other room, listens through the open door to the religious conversation of Lara and the other woman. This section is as it were the "eye" of a hurricane — that calm center of a whirlwind, the emptiness in which is truth, spoken in all its fulness, in quiet voices, by lamplight. But it is hard to pick out any one passage. All through the book great waves of beauty break over the reader like waves of a newly discovered sea. Through you I have gained a great wondering love for the Urals (here I cannot accept your repudiation of the earlier books, where I first discovered this.) The train journey to the east is magnificent. The exciting and rich part about the partisans is very interesting. Of course, I find in the book too little of Uncle Nikolai and his ideas — this is my only complaint and perhaps it is unjust, for his ideas speak in everything that happens.

Am I right in surmising that the ideas in this book run closely parallel to those in Soloviev's *Meaning of Love?* There is a great similarity. Both works remind us to fight our way out of complacency and realize that all our work remains yet to be done, the work of transformation which is the work of love, and love alone. I need not tell you that I also am one who has tried to learn deeply from Dostoievsky's Grand Inquisitor, and I am passionately convinced that this is the most important of all lessons of our time. It is important here, and there. Equally important everywhere.

Shall I perhaps tell you how I know Lara, where I have met her? It is a simple enough story but obviously I do not tell it to people — you are the fourth who knows it, and there seems to be no point in a false discreteness that might restrain me from telling you since it is clear that we have so very much in common.

One night I dreamt that I was sitting with a very young Jewish girl of fourteen or fifteen, and that she suddenly manifested a very deep and pure affection for me and embraced me so that I was moved to the depths of my soul. I learned that her name was "Proverb," which I thought very simple and beautiful. And I also thought: "She is of the race of St. Anne." I spoke to her of her name, and she did not seem to be proud of it, because it seemed that the other young girls mocked her for it. But I told her that it was a very beautiful name, and there the dream ended. A few days later when I happened to be in a nearby city, which is very rare for us, I was walking along in the crowded street and suddenly saw that everybody was Proverb and that in all of them shone her extraordinary beauty and purity and shyness, even though they did not know who they were and were perhaps ashamed of their names — because they were mocked on account of them. And they did not know their real identity as the Child so dear to God who, from before the beginning, was playing in His sight all days, playing in the world.

Thus you are initiated into the scandalous secret of a monk who is in love with a girl, and a Jew at that! One cannot expect much from monks these days. The heroic aceticism of the past is no more.

I was so happy that you liked the parts of *Prometheus*, and were able to tell me so. The other day I sent you a folder with some poems which I do not recommend as highly spiritual, but perhaps you might like them as poems. Yet I do not insist on this division between spirituality and art, for I think that even things that are not patently spiritual, if they come from the heart of a spiritual person, are spiritual. That is why I do not take you too seriously when you repudiate your earlier writings. True, they have not attained the stature of the latest great work, but they contain many seeds of it. I am deeply moved for instance by the florist's cellar in *Safe Conduct* which, like everything else in life, is symbolic. You yourself have said it.

I shall try to send you a book of mine, the *Sign of Jonas*, which is autobiographical and has things in it about the monastic life which might interest you. Perhaps New Directions can send you one or other book of my verse, but my poems are not very good.

So now I bring this letter to a close. It is a joy to write to you, and to hear from you. I continue to keep you in my prayers, and I remember you every day at Mass. Especially I shall say for you one of my Christmas Masses: on that day we have three Masses and one of them may be applied for our own intention. Usually we have to say the Mass for some stranger. But one of my Christmas Masses will be a special present for you. I was going to say a Mass on All Souls Day (Nov. 2) for all your friends who had died, especially in all the troubles recounted in the book. I was not able to arrange this, but I will do so some other time, I do not know when. I will try to drop you a line and let you know.

Meanwhile, then, with every blessing, I clasp your hand in warm friendship, my dear Pasternak. May the Most Holy Mother of God obtain for your soul light and peace and strength, and may her Holy Child be your joy and your protection at all times.

Faithfully yours in Christ

Gethsemani Abbey
Trappist P.O. Ky.

Dec. 15, 1958.

My Dear Pasternak:

For a long time I have been holding my breath in the midst of the turmoil of incomparable nonsense that has surrounded your name in every part of the world. It has been a tremendous relief to hear from you indirectly and to learn that things are once again beginning to regain some semblance of sanity. You, like Job, have been surrounded not by three or four misguided comforters, but by a whole world of madmen, some of them reproaching you with reproaches that have been compliments, other complimenting you with compliments that have been reproaches, and seemingly very few of them have understood one word of what you have written. For what could be more blind and absurd than to make a political weapon, for one side or another, out of a book that declares clearly the futility and malignity of tendencies on every side which seek to destroy man in his spiritual substance? Perhaps it is the destiny of every free man to bring out, like a poultice, the folly and the putrescence of our world: but such a vocation is not always pleasant.

One of the first things I did when I heard about the Nobel affair was to write a letter to Surkov of the Writers' Union declaring that I spoke for all those who were fully aware that your book was not a political pamphlet and was not intended to be taken as such, and that it was a great work of art of which Soviet Russia should have the sense to be proud. I do not know if it did any good. Incidentally, since we have here no newspapers or radios, it was quite "accidental" or rather providential that I heard so much about the case so soon.

I do not know what the latest developments may be. If the question of making Dr Zh [Dr. Zhivago] into a movie in America should arise and become an issue with you over there, I would strongly advise that you attach no importance to any movie. You should, if the case arises to make a decision, rather oppose yourself to it. The movies here are quite bad, and I have always firmly resisted any attempt to use one of my books in a film. If a refusal on this point, by you, would aid our position with your government, then I would advise making such a refusal. Of course, remember I am perhaps not the wisest judge. But certainly a Hollywood production of Dr Zh would do more harm than good in every respect.

I have indeed been praying for you, and so have my young novices, young and pure souls, who know of you and who have been touched by your wonderful poem on Christ in the Garden of Gethsemani. We shall continue our prayers.

Do not let yourself be disturbed too much by either friends or enemies. I hope you will clear away every obstacle and continue with your writing on the great work that you surely have in store for us. May you find again within yourself the deep lifegiving silence which is genuine truth and the source of truth: for it is the fountain of life and a window into the abyss of eternity and God. It is the wonderful silence of the winter night in which Yurii sat up in the sleeping hours and wrote his poems while the wolves howled outside: but is in an inviolable house of peace, a fortress in the depths of our being, the virgin-

ity of our soul where, like the Blessed Mary, we give our
brave and humble answer to life, the "Yes" which brings
Christ into our world.

I cannot refrain from speaking to you of Abraham, and
his laughter and prostration when he was told by God
that he, a hundred years old, should be the father of a
great nation and that from his body, almost dead, would
come life to the whole world. The peak of liberty is in
this laughter, which is a resurrection and a sacrament of
the resurrection, the sweet and clean folly of the soul who
has been liberated by God from his own nothingness.
Here is what Philo of Alexandria has said about it:

"To convict us, so often proud and stiff-necked at the
smallest cause, Abraham falls down (*Genesis* 17:17) and
straightway laughs with the laughter of the soul: mourn-
fulness in his face but smiles in his mind where joy, vast
and unalloyed, has made its lodging. For the sage who
receives an inheritance of good beyond his hope, these
two things were simultaneous, to fall and to laugh. He
falls as a pledge that the proved nothingness of his mortal being keeps him from boasting. He laughs because
God alone is good and the giver of great gifts that make
strong his piety. Let created being fall with mourning in
its face: it is only what nature demands, so feeble of footing, so sad of heart in itself. Then let it be raised up by
God and laugh, for God alone is its support and joy."

I wish you this laughter in any sorrow that may touch
your life.

Kurt W. has sent the *Essai Autobiographique* and I am
reading it with great pleasure. In my turn I am sending
you a book of mine, also autobiographical in character,
called the *Sign of Jonas*. It may take a little time to get
there. New Directions may also send you a small volume
of my poems, of which I am by no means proud.

I am learning Russian now, a little at a time, and later
on I would be grateful if you would help me to get a few
good simple books in Russian on which to practice — some
good easy prose, and some poems. Is there a Russian

book of saints? Someone has suggested that perhaps the legends of Sts. Evgraf, Lara etc. might throw light on your characters. But anyway, I know nothing of the Russian saints except of course for Seraphim of Sarov. I am very interested in the struggle between St. Nilus and Joseph of Volotsk — you can easily imagine why.

I hope this letter will reach you by Christmas, and it will bring you my blessings and my prayers and my deep affection, for the Holy Feast. My second Christmas Mass is for your intentions and for your family: and I will feast with you spiritually in the light of the Child of God Who comes shyly and silently into the midst of our darkness and transforms the winter night into Paradise for those who, like the Shepherds and the humble Kings, come to find Him where no one thinks of looking: in the obviousness and poverty of man's ordinary everyday life.

Faithfully yours in Christ,

Febr. 7, 1960

My highly dear Merton,

I thank you immensely for giving me such inexhaustible marvellous reading for the next future. I shall regain myself from this long and continuing period of letter writing, boring trouble, endless thrushed rhyme translations, time robbing and useless, and of the perpetual self reproof because of the impossibility to advance the longed for, half begun, many times interrupted, almost inaccessible new manuscript.

I thank you still more for your having pardoned my long silence, the faintheartedness and remissness that are underlying in this sad state of mind, where being mortally overbusy and suffering constantly from lack of leisure and time privation. I am perishing of the forced unproductiveness that is worse than pure idleness.

But I shall rise, you will see it. I finally will snatch myself and suddenly deserve and recover again your wonderful confidence and condescension.

Yours affectionately,
B. Pasternak

Don't write me, don't abash me with your boundless bounty. The next turn to renew the correspondence will be mine.

NOTE

1. The Merton-Pasternak correspondence, archived at the University of Kentucky, Lexington, was originally published in a fine print, limited edition by the King Library Press, University of Kentucky, Lexington.

"*Source of Life,*" *design for an icon. Russia, seventeenth century.*

9

LECTURE NOTES ON
ASCETICAL AND MYSTICAL THEOLOGY
Table of Contents

Thomas Merton

*T*he *Table of Contents below is section one of a three-part presentation highlighting the importance of Merton's lecture notes for a course in Ascetical and Mystical Theology given at Gethsemani in 1961. A.M. Allchin, in section two, writes a fore-word to Chapter VIII of these lectures, "Contemplation of the Cosmos." In section three, this chapter on Maximus the Confessor is transcribed. The entire manuscript of these lecture notes is unpublished and in the collection of The Thomas Merton Center at Bellarmine University in Louisville, Kentucky.*

– Jonathan Montaldo

ASCETICAL AND MYSTICAL THEOLOGY
Table of Contents, Page 1.

I.   Aim of the course — to orient ascetical knowledge and discipline to the mystical life. Page 1.
   1.   By achieving a proper perspective regarding the mystical life:
      a.   Through Church's teaching and tradition;
      b.   Treating mystical tradition as the center of the monastic life, not separate but forming a whole with dogmatic and moral tradition.
   2.   By bringing out the mystical dimensions of our theology:
   3.   By treating some great problems that have arisen regarding mysticism and theology.
      a.   In the ascetical life, and related to mysticism;
      b.   In the mystical life itself, e.g. conflicts, aberrations, heresies, exaggerations and frustrations of true development.

4. The trend of mysticism from the Fathers to the present, outlined;

5. Scriptural foundations, Cistercian and "Western" Mysticisms will not be presented in detail.

II. Various Approaches to Mystical Theology. Page 3.
    1. Asceticism, an ascetic; definitions of those terms.
       In short, "spiritual training," i.e. the methods and principles of spiritual Christian perfection.
       a. Negative side, renunciation of self;
       b. Positive side, following Christ;
       c. Extremes to avoid:
          i. Laxity;
          ii. Palagianism;
          iii. Gnosticism;
          iv. Oversimplification.
    2. Modern separation of asceticism and mysticism. Page 4.
       a. Separation a modern notion;
       b. Fathers saw them as parts of a whole.
    3. Mysticism. Page 5.
       a. False use of word;
       b. Non-Christian, scientific approach;
       c. Catholic approach. Page 6.
          i. 19th century — inactivity in mystical theology;
          ii. 20th century — before World War II, controversy; after World War II, unified approach;
          iii. Characteristic attitudes toward mystical theology.
             1.) Early attitudes, Soudreau to Butler;
             2.) Post-World War II, Gilson, de Guibert, etc.;
          iv. Theology and spirituality. Page 10.
             1.) Modern separation;
             2.) Necessity of treating these two as parts of one whole.

III. Mystical Theology in St. John's Gospel. Page 11.
1. Chapter 1, the Word as object and subject of mysticism;
2. Chapter 3, rebirth in Christ, i.e., sacramental mysticism;
3. Chapter 6, the Eucharist;
4. Chapter 13, charity, as expression of Chapter 6 on Eucharist;
5. Chapter 14, following Christ into a new realm;
6. Capters 15-17, abiding in Christ;
7. Chapter 17, vivifying power of Christ.

IV. The Most Relevant New Testament Texts. Page 13.
1. St. Paul's Epistles;
2. Acts of the Apostles.

V. Martyrs and Gnostics. Page 14.
1. Martyrdom as summit of mystical life.
   a. St. Ignatius, Tertullian and Cyprian — martyrdom as crown of Eucharistic life;
   b. Relation between martyr and monk.
2. Gnosis. Page 18.
   Explanation of Christian gnosis.
   a. Justin, initiator of Christian gnosis;
   b. Irenaeus on gnosis;
   c. Clement of Alexandria, the gnostic.

VI. Divinization and Mysticism. Page 22.
1. Theosis — deificatio — divinization.
   a. Scriptural texts of divinization;
   b. Clement of Alexandria, on divinization;
   c. Origen;
   d. Hypollitus;
   e. St. Athanasius;
   f. St. Basil;
   g. The Cistercian Fathers.

2. Theoria, *mystike*, theognosis: mystical contemplation. Page 27.
   a. Greek classical implications;
   b. Christian use of the term mystic (*mystikos*);
   c. Theognosis and *theoria mystiko*.
      i. According to Origen;
      ii. The Cappadocian Fathers;
      iii. The mysticism of the Cappadocian Fathers. Page 30.
         1.) True greatness of St. Gregory of Nyssa;
         2.) Their influence on Evagrius, Pseudo Dionysius, Pseudo Macarius, St. Maximus, etc.;
         3.) The mysticism of night, or unknowing;
         4.) The Eunomians or Anomean heresy;
         5.) Mystical ascent and the three stages of mystical life.
      iv. The spiritual senses. Page 35.
         1.) St. Gregory of Nyssa;
         2.) Clarification of terms, and scope of the spiritual senses;
         3.) Special problems created by this doctrine in the West;
         4.) The tradition of St. Augustine on the sacred humanity of Christ;
         5.) Dangers in overemphasizing these senses;
         6.) Method of the spiritual senses in Poulain;
         7.) The senses according to Olpho Gaillard;
         8.) The approach of Dom Anselm Stoltz;
         9.) Gregory Palamas, on the spiritual senses;
         10.) Danielou, in St. Gregory of Nyssa's tradition.

VII. Evagrius Ponticus.
   1. The problem of Evagrius. Page 42.
      a. His reputation;

2. Dangers and limitations of *theoria physike*. Page 64.
   a. A relation between the human and the divine:
      i. Involves sense and spirit together;
      ii. Demands man's activity and divine grace.
   b. Alternation and/or delusion of the spiritual by the sensual;
   c. Sense and spirit must be maintained in the right order: i.e. subjugation of sense to spirit.

IX. The Dionysian Tradition. Page 65.
   1. Pseudo-Dionysius as real propagator of Christian mystical theology.
   2. Dionysian writings.
      a. The divine names;
      b. The hierarchies;
      c. Celestial hierarchy;
      d. The ecclesiastical hierarchy.
         i. States of life, and orders within the ecclesiastical hierarchy;
         ii. Sacraments.
      e. The lost book "Symbolic Theology";
      f. Dominant themes in the writings. Page 69.
         i. Symbolism and mysticism;
         ii. Mystical theology;
         iii. The Dionysian tradition in the West. Page 70. Sources of the tradition:
            1.) St. Maximus, in Rome;
            2.) Hilduin's translations of Denys;
            3.) Scotus Erigena's translations;
            4.) Adam the Carthusian;
            5.) Hugh of St. Victor, and the Victorines;
            6.) Richard of St. Victor;
            7.) Cistercians.
               a.) Bernard and William of St. Thierry;
               b.) Isaac and Gilbert.

8.) The thirteenth century.
    a.) Franciscan tradition;
    b.) Albert the Great, Aquinas;
    c.) Bonaventure;
    d.) Gallus and his disciples.

X. Western Mysticism.
Background of Western Mysticism. Page 75.
1. Augustinian element pervades.
    a. All schools have some degree of Augustinianism;
    b. Especially in the "bridal mysticism" of the Rhenish school.
2. Pelagian controversy;
3. Pessimism of Montanists and Manichaeans;
4. St. Augustine. Page 77.
    a. Mysticism based on personal experience, conversion.
        i. Highly reflexive, subjective, personal mysticism;
        ii. Psychological observation;
        iii. Struggle with evil and ascent to happiness in love and ecstasy;
        iv. Summit of mystical experience;
        v. Comparison of Augustine with Gregory of Nyssa;
        vi. Mysticism of the Church in St. Augustine. Page 80.
    b. Western mysticism: Butler's thesis. Page 83.
        i. Pre-Dionysian;
        ii. Pre-scholastic;
        iii. Without visions and revelations.
    c. Further notes on Latin mysticism. Page 85.
        i. The Cistercians.
        1.) Joachim of Flora;
        2.) Joachim's influence on Franciscans.
        ii. St. Francis of Assisi;

iii. The Franciscan crisis — a reaction against the ideal of St. Francis.

    1.) Brother Elias's changes;

    2.) Spiritual Franciscans.

iv. St. Bonaventure and Franciscan mystical synthesis.

    1.) Intellectual contemplation; Page 90.

    2.) Sapiential contemplation.

XI. Fourteenth Century Mysticism. Page 91.

  1. Lay spiritual movements.

    a. "Frauenbewegung";

    b. The Beguines and Beghards.

      i. Influence Cistercian nuns;

      ii. Hadewijch of Antwerp;

      iii. The "second" Hadewijch.

    c. The women saints of late Middle Ages.

      i. Catherine of Siena;

      ii. Other great laywomen saints.

  2. German mystics of the fourteenth century. Page 98.

    a. The German development outlined;

    b. Eckhart (1260-1327).

      i. His doctrine;

      ii. The errors of his teaching;

      iii. Specific errors.

    c. John Tauler (1300-1361).

      i. Psychology of Tauler;

      ii. Two texts from Tauler;

      iii. Tauler and Eckhart, compared;

      iv. Henry Suso: A "minnesinger" of mystical love; Page 107.

      v. Theologian Germanica. Page 107.

        1.) Familiar mystical themes;

        2.) Minimization of personal action in asceticism.

Constantinople, mid-sixth century.

10

THE PRAYER OF THE HEART
AND NATURAL CONTEMPLATION
A Foreword to Thomas Merton's Lecture Notes on St. Maximus

Canon A.M. Allchin

The discovery of God's presence within us, in the depths of the heart, particularly through the use of the Jesus Prayer, the prayer of the name, a prayer which is sometimes spoken of in terms of putting the mind into the heart, is intimately linked with the discovery of God's presence in the world around us, in the whole of God's creation, and specifically with the discovery of God's presence in our fellow men and women, in the whole of the human family made in God's image and likeness. The inner and outer world of prayer and faith are indissolubly bound up together.

These themes are very important in the work of Thomas Merton, both in the sense of his own discovery of God's presence and activity in the world of men and women, in the world that is of human society and human history, and also in the sense of his discovery of God's presence and activity in the whole world of nature both animate and inanimate. In the first case we find Merton called to exercise a prophetic role, to discern God's judgment in the events of the years in which he is living, in the other we find him called to exercise a more poetic and artistic role, to discern and declare God's presence and activity in the very life and being of creation, and in the hidden beauty of the world around us. The second role, the role of the poet and artist, seems to have been with Merton from the beginning; perhaps it came to him from his father. The first role, the role of prophet, he arrives at later and with more difficulty and hesitation. May it perhaps be a gift which came to him in an almost hidden and unacknowledged way, from his mother with her sense of accuracy and judgment?

In both cases the perception of the interpenetration of the inner prayer, the prayer of the hermit, with the outer discernment of God's presence in creation and in human history was of the greatest significance for Merton's life and is one of the things which allowed him to bring together his many-sided capacities into a remarkable unity. Both movements, which formed the two parts of natural contemplation in the understanding of the Greek fathers, come to a certain fulfillment in Merton's life at the end of the Fifties and the beginning of the Sixties. Both are reflected in two of the most remarkable passages in *Conjectures of a Guilty Bystander*, the epiphany of the divine glory in the faces of the passers by in the moment of vision at *Fourth* and *Walnut*, and the epiphany of the divine glory shining out in the silent beauty of the natural world in the less well-known but no less impressive *Prayer to God the Father on the Vigil of Pentecost*. In both cases one can, I believe, sense in and through these moments of vision which Merton describes, the presence of his knowledge of the spiritual theology of Maximus the Confessor, particularly his doctrine of the active presence of the divine *logoi* in and with all the things which God has made.

What I want to do in this foreword is to look at these things in relation to the teaching of Merton contained in the *Lectures on Ascetical and Mystical Theology*, which he gave in the monastery at Gethsemani in the summer of 1961. In particular I want to look at the way in which the chapter on Maximus seems to have developed in the course of the series as a whole and also at the remarkable way in which Merton uses the architecture and craftsmanship of the Shakers not only to illustrate Maximus' teaching on the *logoi* but also to make a more general statement about the nature of sacred art in the light of natural contemplation.

I am conscious that in doing this I am covering ground which I have to some extent already covered in an earlier lecture which was published in the *Merton Annual* Volume 5. Here I look in more detail at Merton's understanding of Maximus. If the material is in some ways similar we are looking at it from rather a different perspective, and in coming back to the subject I myself have seen aspects of it in a way which I had not done before.

I come now to the text of the lectures and I begin with some of Merton's words on Page 1 of the first lecture about the purpose of the course.

The main task will be to *situate* the subject properly in our life. It belongs right in the centre of course.

To give the monastic priest, the future spiritual director and superior, *a proper perspective* first of all.

Then to deepen his knowledge of the Church's tradition and teaching. To make him fully acquainted with the great mystical tradition, which is not separated from the dogmatic and moral tradition, *and forms one whole with it.*

Without mysticism there is no real theology and without theology there is no real mysticism. Hence the emphasis will be on mysticism as theology.

To bring out clearly the mystical dimensions of our theology. Hence to help us to do what we must really do; live our theology.

So at the very beginning we have the insistence that theology and mysticism cannot be separated, and that they cannot be properly studied and taught, unless they are *lived*. We notice already an echo of the formulations of Vladimir Lossky on the relationship between mysticism and theology, an echo, which will become more fully explicit a little further on. This living nexus of theology, spirituality and life is for Merton at the very heart of the Community's monastic calling.

From time to time in this first lecture Merton returns to the question of the definition of terms, so on the relation of mysticism and asceticism he firmly establishes himself on a patristic foundation. "We shall always presuppose that the classic meaning is understood; mysticism and asceticism form an organic whole. No mysticism without asceticism. Asceticism leads normally to mystical life, at least it disposes for it, though of course the mystical life, in its normal fulfillment, remains a pure gift of God."

Only towards the end of this first lecture do we come to some of the principal contemporary guides whom Merton chooses to follow, two of them outstanding figures in the neo-patristic re-

vival in Catholic theology in France and Germany, Jean
Danielou and Hans Urs von Balthasar, and this leads us on to
his first direct citation of Orthodox writers. "After the Second
World War an important manual by Vladimir Lossky has
opened up the forgotten world of Byzantine mysticism, solidly
based in the Greek fathers. Studies of St. Gregory Palamas by
Meyendorff appearing at the end of the fifties and the new works
of Father Paul Evdokimov promise that there will be a very rich
flowering in this field."

Merton concludes this lecture with a section modestly headed
A Few Remarks. It includes some vital pointers to his whole
way of approach to the subject and to the conviction that it is
extremely important for his brethren to enter into its understanding. "This study we are about to undertake is absolutely *vital
to our vocation*. In a sense we will be trying to face THE questions which are at the heart of our spiritual life. We are here
looking at a spiritual movement of which we form a part and
not a negligible part."

"However it is not merely a matter of study and reading. We
must become fully impregnated in our mystical tradition." There
follows a very important paragraph on the nature of tradition
which is worth quoting in full.

The mystical tradition of the Church, a collective
memory and experience of Christ living and present
within her. This tradition *forms and affects the whole man;*
intellect — memory — will — emotions — body — skills
(arts) — all must be under the sway of the Holy Spirit.
Important human dimension given to tradition — its *incarnate* character. Note especially the *memory*.

If we do not cultivate healthy and conscious traditions
we will enter into unhealthy and unconscious traditions,
a kind of collective disposition to neurosis.

For Merton the renewal of tradition was the indispensable
condition for healthy and constructive change and reform, while
willingness to change and reform was an essential part of the
rediscovery of an authentic and living tradition.

Merton goes on to repeat his warning that there must be no
divorce between theology and spirituality. Spirituality without

theology means "the death of contemplation, experience of experience, and not experience of revelation and of God revealing."

The course as a whole begins with a study of the subject in the New Testament and especially in the Pauline and Johannine writings and goes on through the apostolic fathers, through the martyrs into the third and fourth century. But I come forward to the place where the subject of the relationship of mysticism to theology returns in a decisive way in the course of the sixth lecture on *Divinsation and Mysticism*. Here the indebtedness to Lossky's basic position becomes quite evident, as Merton insists again on the close relationship between mysticism and theology.

> In a certain sense the tradition shows them to be one and the same thing. By mysticism we can mean the personal experience of what is revealed to all and realised by all in the mystery of Christ. And by "theology" we mean the common revelation of the mystery which is to be lived by all.

> The two belong together. There is no theology without mysticism (for it would have no relation to the real life of God in us) and there is no mysticism without theology (because it would be at the mercy of individual and subjective fantasy).

In the course of this lecture we come to an important section on the mysticism of the Cappadocian Fathers: "Here we come upon the first great Christian mystics. This applies especially to St. Gregory of Nyssa, in a lesser degree to St. Gregory Nazianden. St. Basil is more an ascetic and dogmatic than a mystical theologian, though himself a mystic. St. Gregory of Nyssa on the other hand is the father of Christian mysticism, much more truly than Clement or Origen."

There follows a long, detailed and highly appreciative account of the teaching of Evagrius on prayer and contemplation, on pure theology, and on union with God. It is as I say highly appreciative, but by no means uncritical. The last sentences of this lecture lead us forward into the following lecture, 8, *Contemplation and the Cosmos*. This is the lecture, which seems to have evolved in Merton's mind as he has been giving the series, since there is no reference to it in his opening account of the subjects he intends to cover. Evagrius he concludes is a brilliant but not always a fully balanced teacher. We need to find someone who can comment on his teaching and show it in a more balanced way. This of course will be Maximus himself.

So we come to the heart of our theme. *Contemplation and the cosmos; theoria physike,* in its various forms.

The topic of *theoria physike* has already been mentioned. Let us now treat it in detail because it is very important. We can in fact say that the lack of *theoria physike* is one of the things which accounts for the stunting of spiritual growth among our monks today. On the contrary, where there is a genuine growth from the serenity of at least relative *apatheia* to the enriched state of *gnosis* by natural contemplation, then we are fully and integrally prepared for *theologia* without forms, beyond all ideas and symbols.

Evagrius calls it the land flowing with milk and honey. It is a contemplation according to nature. It is also a contemplation of God in and through nature, in and through the things he has created, in history. It is the *multiformis sapientia,* the gnosis that apprehends the wisdom and glory of God, especially his wisdom as creator and redeemer.

1. In the Spirit of scripture and not in the letter.
2. In the *logoi* of created things, not in their materiality.
3. In our own inmost spirit and true self, rather than in our ego.
4. In the inner meaning of history and not in its externals (history of salvation, victory of Christ). In the inner sense of the divine judgements and mercies (not in superstitious and pseudo-apocalyptic interpretation of events).

[Allchin:] This is a consideration extremely relevant to our present situation.

After further detailed discussion of the different levels of *theoria physike* Merton sums up. "*Theoria physike,* reception of God's revelation of himself, in creation, in history, in scripture." "We must not believe that sin caused this unique masterpiece which is this visible world in which God manifests himself by a silent revelation." (Maximus.)

We come to a paragraph in which we feel that Merton is speaking partly out of his experience of prayer, partly out of his experience as a writer. He is also certainly reflecting on his reading of the Russian theologians, particularly Bulgakov with his insistence on the theme of the Wisdom of God, and of Berdyaev with his sense of the active cooperation of human freedom in this divinely given activity.

The vision of *theoria physike* is essentially sophianic. Man by *theoria* is able to unite the hidden wisdom of God in things with the hidden light of wisdom in himself. The meeting and marriage of these two brings about a resplendent clarity within man himself, and this clarity is the presence of divine wisdom, fully recognised and active in him. Thus man becomes a mirror of the divine glory, and is resplendent with divine truth, not only in his mind but in his life. He is filled with the light of wisdom which shines forth in him and thus God is glorified in him.

At the same time he exercises a spiritualising influence in the world by the work of his hands which is in accord with the creative wisdom of God, in things and in history. Hence we can see the great importance of a sophianic, contemplative orientation of man's life. No longer are we reduced to a purely negative attitude to the world around us, towards history, towards the judgments of God. The world is no longer seen as merely material, hence as an obstacle that has to be grudgingly put up with. It is spiritual through and through. But grace has to work in and through us to enable us to carry out this real transformation. Things are not fully spiritual in themselves, they have to be spiritualised in our knowledge and love and in our use of them.

Hence it is impossible for one who is not purified to "transfigure" material things. On the contrary, the *logoi* will remain hidden and he himself will be captivated by the sensible attractions of those things. "The Will of God" is no longer a blind force plunging through our lives like a cosmic steamroller and demanding to be accepted willy-nilly. On the contrary, we are able to *understand* the hidden purposes of the creative wisdom and the divine mercy of God and can co-operate with him as sons with a loving father. Not only that but God himself hands over to man, when he is thus purified and enlightened, and united with the divine will, a certain creative initiative of his own, in political life, in art, in spiritual life, in worship: man is then endowed with a *causality* of his own."

Almost every sentence in this paragraph would warrant developed commentary in the light of Merton's own work as a writer, a poet, a photographer, an artist.

In a further section of this lecture Merton begins to take these principles further. "To begin to realise the *logoi* of creatures we must then always be conscious of their mute *appeal* to us to find and rescue the glory of God that has been hidden in them and veiled by sin.

"A special problem of modern time, with its technology; technology with its impersonal, pragmatic, quantitative exploitation and manipulation of things is deliberately indifferent to their *logoi*. Consideration of the symbolic *logos* of a thing would be an obstacle to science and technology, so many seem to think. Hence the *logos* must be excluded. No interest in "what" a thing really is. The chief effort of Teilhard de Chardin in our time has been a noble striving to recover a view of the scientific world, the cosmos of the physicist, the geologist, the engineer, the interest centred on the *logos* of creation and on value, spirit. An effort to reconvert the scientific view of the cosmos into wisdom without sacrificing anything of scientific objectivity or technological utility."

A little further on Merton carries these thoughts further in showing the way in which this way of prayer and understanding demands a total conversion of our ethical life, both personal and social. "*Theoria physike* then demands that we enter into the movement of all things from God and back to God and it implies realisation of the obstacle placed in the way of this movement by *philautia* [self-love] and sin: which makes things created by God serve our own immediate interests. *Theoria physike* implies a sense of *community with things in the work of salvation.*"

Perception of things in their own integrity, a non-possessive and non-manipulative use and enjoyment of them is what is implied. "*Logos* of bread and wine: bread not merely to nourish man physically but to serve the unity of mankind in Christ sacramentally. Of wine: something which points beyond itself to the new wine of the kingdom. The new wine is not something which is purely spiritual and therefore not material wine, on the contrary in the eucharist material wine is transformed not only into spiritual wine but into the mystical wine which is the blood of Christ. The *logos* of a table: realized in the mystical table which is the altar around which the brethren gather for the eternal meal at which the risen Christ will be mystically present and will break bread, Christ himself is the table of the altar."

In subsequent sections of his lecture Merton comes to speak about sacred art:

The sacred artist of all people should be a *logikos*. Hence it is not true that he does not need to be purified. He must in some sense be one who has attained to the summit of *apatheia*. Not of course in the conventional way in which the average pious Catholic might conceive it. He does not necessarily have to be fully respectable in a conventional sense. A kind of unconventionality may be in him a form of humility and folly for Christ and part of his *apatheia*. We must not forbid the artist a necessary element of paradox in his life and conformism will perhaps blind him and enslave his talent. He must at all costs have attained to an inner purity an honesty, a sincerity and integrity of spirit. He must be a *holokleros* who understands the *logoi* of things and is attuned to their *tropoi*. He must be in *communication* with things in their deepest centre, in their most real value. He must be attuned to their voice, he must sense something of their logic, their vocation. He must also sense in what way they are being prevented by man and by society by misuse from attaining to their true spiritual end. The artist at the present time is bound in one way or other to protest against the systematic obscuring and desecration of the *logoi* of things and of their sacred meaning.

For that reason an artist who would serve a completely secular society and put his art at the disposal of propaganda for materialistic illusions would be destroying himself as an artist especially if he served up conventional forms of "beauty." He would be conniving at the desecration and destruction of art. In so doing he would be betraying created things and betraying his vocation as an artist. This by no means condones any illusion of the artist as a "special kind of man," but his technical gifts as a maker demand to be sustained by a spiritual gift as seer.

[Allchin:] Examples of work sensitive to *logoi*:

Shaker handicrafts and furniture, deeply impregnated by the communal mystique of the Shaker community. The simplicity and austerity demanded by their way of life enabled an unconscious spiritual purity to manifest itself in full clarity. Shaker handicrafts are then a real epiphany of *logoi*. Characterized by spiritual light.

Merton was writing this in 1961. The whole flowering of study and appreciation of the Shaker Communities, especially of their art and craftsmanship, had not taken place at that time. Apart from the pioneering work of Edward Deming Andrews, with whom Merton was in touch, very little had been written about them. As often, Merton was way ahead of others. I do not think his intuitions about the Shaker world have been sufficiently appreciated.

See their buildings. Barns especially. Highly mystical quality: capaciousness, dignity, solidity, permanence. *Logos* of a barn? "But my wheat, gather ye into my barn." Note: It is never a question of a "barn" in the abstract and no definite place. Shaker farm building always fits right into its location, manifests the *logos* of the valley or hillside which forms its site. *Logos* of the site. Important in

Cistercian monasteries of the twelfth century. Note absence of this in certain religious settings — pseudo-Gothic, which ignores true *logoi*, substitutes an arbitrary enforced *logos* in the head. Modern architecture with its pretended functionalism is also quite arbitrary. Compare Mumford of U.N. buildings."

Two recent discoveries have helped me to see a little more fully the importance of the Prayer of the Heart — the Jesus Prayer — in Merton's own life.

First I have looked again at the passage in Merton's Journal for September 11th 1960 in which he reflects on the anniversary of Staretz Sylvan, who died on September 11th 1938. I have already quoted from this passage in my article "Our Life a Perpetual Pentecost." Needless to say I have been looking at it afresh in the light of September 11th 2001. Central to Merton's reflection in this meditation on the Staretz are the words of the Lord, "Keep your mind in hell and do not despair." No less pregnant are the words with which Merton concludes his meditation "Jesus, Saviour." Here is the heart of the Jesus Prayer.

Second, I have been sent the recently published tape of Merton's talk on the Jesus Prayer, given to the Community at Gethsemani. This is a wonderful talk overflowing with humour, joy, exuberance. It is marked throughout by the speaker's burning and evident desire to communicate to his hearers something of his own sense of the importance of this prayer, so simple that it can unite itself with all the times and circumstances of our life, so profound that it can bring us into the constant presence of the saving name, showing us through the action of the Holy Spirit that the memory and experience of Christ is indeed living and present within us.

April 2002

Drawing for icon.   Russian, seventeenth century.

11

CONTEMPLATION AND THE COSMOS
*Chapter VIII of Thomas Merton's Lecture Notes
on Theology and Mysticism*[1]

Edited by Jonathan Montaldo

[*Page 41*][2]

The topic of *theoria physike* has already been mentioned. Let us now treat it in detail because it is very important. We can in fact say that the lack of *theoria physike* is one of the things that accounts for the stunting of spiritual growth among our monks today. On the contrary, where there is a genuine growth from the serenity of at least a relative *apatheia* [detachment, not being subject to the passions] to the enriched state of *gnosis* [understanding of God] by "natural contemplation," then we are fully and integrally prepared for *theologia* [contemplation of God] without forms, beyond all ideas and symbols.

Note how the modern controversy about a distinction between "acquired" contemplation that is "dark and without forms" and "infused" contemplation really obscures the issue. There must in reality be a flowering of contemplation in the realm of types [*tropoi*], symbols and *logoi* [rational structure and form], in the *gnosis* of God's mercy in His providence and in His judgments, before there can be a normally mature development in the direction of pure *theologia*.

What is *Theoria Physike*?

Evagrius calls it the "land flowing with milk and honey." (*Keph. Gnost.* III 67.)

It is contemplation according to nature (*physis*).

It is also a contemplation of God in and through nature, in and through things He has created, in history. It is the *multiformis sapientia* [wisdom adhering in all forms and uniting all forms], the *gnosis* that apprehends the wisdom and glory of God, e.g. His wisdom as <u>Creator</u> and <u>Redeemer</u>.[3]

1. In the Spirit of Scripture and not in the letter.

2. In the *logoi* of created things and not in their materiality.
3. In our own inmost spirit and true self, rather than in our ego.
4. In the inner meaning of history and not in its externals (History of salvation, Victory of Christ).
5. In the inner sense of the divine judgments and mercies (not in superstitious and pseudo-apocalyptic interpretations of events).

It is contemplation to which we are led and in which we are illuminated by the angels.

It is a spiritual contemplation, a gift, proceding from love, accessible only to the pure, and essentially distinct from the science of nature which is only intellectual and accessible to the impure as well as to the pure.

It is not only the crown of the active life and the beginning of the contemplative life, but it also is necessary to complete the moral purification effected by the active life.

When the *thumos* [the angry, irascible passions of the heart] and *epithumia* [the desiring, lusting passions of the heart] have been ordered and purified by love and chastity, the *nous* [mind, consciousness] is purified by *theoria*. In this purification there is also a transformation and deepening.

What were merely "simple thoughts" become penetrating intuitions of the *logoi* of things in preparation for a further step — the intuition of pure intelligibles.

Theoria physike gives a supernatural understanding of nature, of history, of revelation, of liturgy, and of man himself. It attains to this understanding in types, symbols and *logoi* which are opened up to us by the divine illumination, but also depends on our own cooperation. Hence *theoria physike* is partly mystical and partly natural. There is a manifest synergy of God and man in its action. Man does not simply receive these illuminations passively.

It is always sustained by faith, or rather by the collaboration between nature and faith: the *logoi* of creatures and the types of Scripture are realities which nurture and preserve faith. Faith feeds on these "words of God." They are a kind of angelic nourishment, without which the intelligence fails and dies.

In effect, the man who is immersed in the
    letter of Scripture
    the materiality of things
    his external self
    the externals of history
is in fact completely blinded, his intelligence starves and shrivels up and, even if he is still alive by "faith," his faith is so languid and weak that it is perpetually on the point of death. His intelligence is deprived of vitally important spiritual nourishment. How can such a one aspire to a life of genuine contemplation? His contemplation will, if it exists at all, be a false illumination by passion and sense stimulation, and by the emotions.

[Page 42]

Theoria Physike, reception of God's revelation of Himself in creatures, in history, in Scripture.

> "We must not believe that sin caused this unique masterpiece which is this visible world in which God manifests Himself by <u>a silent revelation</u>." St. Maximus, *Ambigua*.

Here St. Maximus uses *theoria physike* to protest against the Origenist idea that the world is in itself imperfect being made up of fallen spiritual realities. *Theoria physike* is necessary to correct the deviations of Origenism, including those found in Evagrius.

St. Maximus on whom we rely here is a great theologian of the seventh century, the father of Byzantine mysticism, died 655. He used Evagrius but corrected him and went beyond him. He used Psuedo-Dionysius but also corrected him and went beyond him. One of the greatest of the Greek Fathers. Read *Liturgie Cosmique* by Hans Urs Von Balthasar.

St. Maximus is the great doctor of *theoria physike*. He unites Plato and Aristotle within the Christian framework. He has the broadest and most balanced view of the Christian cosmos of all the Greek Fathers and, therefore, of all the Fathers.

St. Maximus says again: "There is in everything a general and unique mode of the obscure and intelligible Parousia of the unifying cause." *Mystagogia*, quoted in *Liturgie Cosmique*, page 25.

He says again: "The love of Christ hides itself mysteriously in the inner *logoi* of created things . . . totally and with all His plenitude . . . in all that is varied lies hidden He who is One and eternally identical, in all composite things. He who is simple and without parts, in those which have a beginning [is hidden]. He who has no beginning, in all the visible [hides] Him who is invisible," etc. etc. *Ambigua*, 1285. 1288.

Theoria Physike is then:

a) Reception of the mysterious, silent revelation of God in His cosmos and in its *oikonomia* [stewardship of all things, the structure of God's dispensation of the cosmos, God's providence and judgment], as well as in our own lives. [Note this is not a question of <u>epistemology</u> as it was for Augustine. For Augustine (see Guardini, *Conversion of Augustine*, pages 13ff.) it was a matter explaining how we know the essences of created things. This knowledge of essences is not attained by sense, but by *memoria* [remembrance of things], for in his Platonic line of thought the *memoria* is enlightened by God and perceives the reality of things not just in themselves but in the Word. Contemplation of the *logoi* of things is like this, but the perspective is different.]

b) It is the knowledge of God that is natural to man, with God's help (grace). But note it is not "natural" in the modern sense, [that is,] clearly distinct from and opposed to "supernatural." It is natural in the sense that it is what God <u>intended</u> for man in creating him. It is proper to him as a son of God, was his when in paradise, is proper to him as a brother of the angels. We must be restored first of all to this "natural" contemplation of the cosmos before we can rise to perfect *theologia*.

c) This contemplation is demanded by the cosmos itself and by history. If man cannot know creatures by this spiritual *gnosis*, they will be frustrated by their end. If man cannot spiritually penetrate the meaning of the *oikonomia*, it runs the risk of being frustrated and souls will be lost.

d) Hence *theoria physike* is a most important part of man's co-operation in the spiritualization and restoration of the cosmos. It is by *theoria* that man helps Christ to redeem the *logoi* of things and restore them in Himself.

e) This *theoria* is inseparable from love and from a truly spiritual conduct of life.

Man not only must see the inner meaning of things, but he must regulate his entire life and his use of time and of created beings according to the mysterious norms hidden in things by the Creator, or rather uttered by the Creator Himself in the bosom of His Creation.

[*Page 43*]

f) The vision of *theoria physike* is essentially <u>sophianic</u>. Man by *theoria* is able to untie the hidden wisdom of God in things with the hidden light of wisdom in himself. The meeting and marriage of these two brings about a <u>resplendent clarity</u> within man himself, and this clarity is the presence of Divine Wisdom fully recognized and active in him. Thus man becomes a mirror of the divine glory, and is resplendent with divine truth not only in his <u>mind</u> but in his <u>life</u>. He is filled with the light of wisdom which shines forth in him, and thus God is glorified in him. At the same time he exercises a spiritualizing influence in the world by the work of his hands which is in accord with <u>the creative wisdom of God</u> in things and in history.

Hence we can see the great importance of a sophianic, contemplative orientation of man's life. No longer are we reduced to a <u>purely negative</u> attitude toward the world around us, toward history, toward the judgments of God.

The world is no longer seen as merely material, hence as an obstacle that has to be grudgingly put up with. It is spiritual through and through. But grace has to work in and through us to enable us to carry out this real transformation. Things are not fully spiritual in themselves: they have to be spritualized by our knowledge and love in our use of them. Hence it is impossible for one who is not purified to "transfigure" material things. On the contrary, the *logoi* will remain hidden and he himself will be captivated by the sensible attraction of these things.

The "will of God" is no longer a blind force plunging through our lives like a cosmic steamroller and demanding to be accepted willy-nilly. On the contrary, we are able to <u>understand</u> the hidden purposes of the creative wisdom and the divine mercy of God, and can cooperate with Him as sons with a loving Father.

Not only that, but God Himself hands over to man, when he is thus purified and enlightened, and united with the divine will, a certain creative initiative of his own, in political life, in art, in spiritual life, in worship: man is then endowed with a <u>causality</u> of his own.

The Three Laws:

The best approach to the full idea of *theoria physike* is the synthesis of the three laws as described by St. Maximus.

The object of *theoria* is for Maximus something more dynamic and profound than simply the spiritual sense of scripture and the *logoi* of creatures, with providence, etc. (Though Maximus is weak on the importance of <u>history</u> in *theoria physike*.)

The object of *theoria* is not only nature (*phusis*) and Law (*nomos*) but the two together, fused on a higher level of unity in Christ Who is the fulfillment of both nature and the Law.

Hence we have:

Nature (*phusis*) = the Greeks — Elias — Body of wisdom > CHRIST.

Law (*nomos*) = the Jews — Moses — Soul of wisdom > The true law.

Body and soul are united in the higher unity of SPIRIT, which is in Christ, the true Law of the cosmos and its fulfillment, the fullness of wisdom and revelation.

(Moses and Elias are here brought in in reference to their position in the Transfiguration on either side of Christ. *Theoria* is then contemplation of the splendor of divine wisdom in Christ with nature (Elias) on one side and law (Moses) on the other, both looking to Him as to their fulfillment. In the full development of *theoria* they both disappear and we see Christ alone.

[Page 44]

Von Balthasar says: "The meaning of each natural thing and the meaning of every law and commandment is to be an Incarnation of the divine Word; to realize fully its proper nature or its proper law is to cooperate fully in <u>the total</u>

realization of the Word in the world." *Liturgie Cosmique,* page 224.

Note that both *phusis* and *nomos*, without Christ, tend unnaturally and against His intention to separation and not to unity.

Nature: the true *Logos* of man demands unity with Christ in love and in will and in unity with other men. Egoism, however, [as it is] dominated by the action and desire of sense which separates, produces an unnatural state of division. [Such a state of division is] against natural tendency to unity in love.

Law: justice as such tends to unity, as nature does. But the letter of the Law creates multiplicity of cases, distinctions, problems, decisions, and eventual separation between this one and that one, ending with inequality.

Without *theoria physike* which penetrates to the inner *logos* and orientation to unity and simplicity and wholeness, nature and law tend to disintegration, separation and conflict.

With the understanding of the *logoi*, in the love and the light given by God, they fulfill their true purpose and tend to unity, [the] recapitulation [of all things] in Christ.

The LOGOI of Things.

Hence: we now have one important conclusion. The LOGOS of things and the SPIRIT of Law are those inmost and essential elements primarily intended by God, placed in [things] by Him, oriented to unity in love, in Himself.

A. The *logos* of man is therefore something hidden in him, spiritual, simple, profound, unitive, loving, selfless, self-forgetting, oriented to love and to unity with God and other men in Christ.

It is not an abstract essence, "rationality plus animality." It is however the divine image in him. More deeply it is CHRIST in him, either actually or potentially. To love Christ in our brother we must be able to SEE Him in our brother: and this demands really the gift of *theoria physike*.

Christ in us must be liberated, by purification, so that the "image" in us, clothed anew with the light of the divine likeness, is able connaturally to recognize the same likeness in another. [Another's] same tendency to love, to simplicity, to unity.

Without love this is completely impossible.

B. Creatures.

The vision given by *theoria physike* shows us that all creatures are good and pure. This is the first thing, the complement of the active detachment of *apatheia*. Evagrius declares, following the desert tradition (especially St. Anthony), that "nothing created by God is evil," and St. Maximus adds, "nothing created is impure." (He comments on the vision of Peter at Jaffa, the creatures let down in the sheet [*Acts* 10:9-23]. Accommodate sense: all things are seen to be good, made by God and reflecting His goodness.)

This implies not mere negative indifference but a positive awareness, by love, of the value of creatures, divinely given to them, placed in them by the Creator to reflect Him in them. Once again, it becomes clear how and in what sense *theoria* is necessary to complete *apatheia* and gives it positive meaning

The right use of creatures is essential to the proper understanding of them. St. Maximus says we must be attuned not only to the *logoi* of creatures but also to *tropoi* or models of action: we get light from the *logoi*, we get order and love from the *tropoi* [models or examples for moral action]. They not only move us to praise but they guide us in action.

[*Page 45*]

It is very important to realize that *theoria physike* is actually a dynamic unity of contemplation and action, a loving knowledge that comes along with use and work.

Note: the examples given by Maximus are stereotyped and can be improved upon. They do not give the full depth of his conception. For instance, the heavens: it is almost a stoic cliché to say that the *tropos* of the heavens is their stability and their tranquility in order, etc.

Other ones: the eagle, who looks directly at the sun. The Lion whose bones, when clashed together, produce sparks. (Teaches to compare texts in Scripture.) Here we are in the realm of allegory, and very tame allegory. While in reality the intuitions of *theoria physike* penetrate far deeper than this.

To return to the main point made above:

Theoria physike plus *praxis* is proper to man who has attained full maturity and integrity in the spiritual life. The *holokleros* [one whose mind and heart are integrated and illuminated by grace].

This, we repeat, is arrived at through the proper understanding of the logos of things and the natural appreciation of and practical "imitation" of their *tropoi*.

Hence, the completeness conferred by *theoria physike* is not simply a *gnosis* superimposed upon the virtuousness acquired during the practice of virtues in the active life. It is a twofold speculative and practical contemplative gift, a double illumination in the order of action and contemplation, given by God through the *gnostic* evaluation of things and events, particularly of Scripture.

Logos and Mystery

It must be quite clear that the spiritual sense of Scripture, for instance, is something much more than mere allegory. As we said above in connection with Gregory of Nyssa, it is a direct contact with the Word hidden in the words of Scripture.

How do the *logoi* of created things find their expression in relation to the mystery of our salvation?

Certain created material things enter explicitly into the framework of ritual mysteries, the celebration of the mystery of our salvation. In so doing they "represent" all creatures, for all creatures not only "groan with us expecting the Redemption of the Sons of God" [*Romans* 8:18-27] but enter directly or indirectly with us into the great mystery of Christ.

To see the *logoi* of creatures we are going to have to recognize in them this "groaning" and this "eschatological expectation" which depends on us: on our knowledge of them, on our use of them, with a directly sophianic and soteriological reference.

To begin to realize the *logoi* of creatures we must then always be conscious of their mute <u>appeal</u> to us to find and rescue the glory of God that has been hidden in them and veiled by sin.

A special problem of modern times, with its technology: technology, with its impersonal, pragmatic, quantitative exploitation and manipulation of things, is deliberately indifferent to their *logoi*. Consideration of the symbolic *logos* of a thing would be an obstacle to science and technology, so many seem to think. Hence the logos must be excluded. No interest in "what" a thing really is.

A deliberate conversion to the *alogon* [the irrational use of technology], the *meon* [a pragmatism without reference to metaphysical questions]. *Meonic* [concern only for the quantitative, what can work — not what is true] preoccupation, a kind of liberation of the *meon* in order that there may take place a demonic cult of change and "exchange," consumption, production, destruction, for their own sakes.

Centrality of destruction in this process. Technology leads to demonic psuedo-contemplation, mystique of technics and production.

[Page 46]

The chief effort of Teilhard de Chardin in our time has been a noble striving to recover a view of the scientific world, the cosmos of the physicist, the geologist, the engineer, with interest centered on the *logos* of creation, and on value, spirit.

An effort to reconvert the scientific view of the cosmos into a wisdom, without sacrificing anything of scientific objectivity or technological utility.

The *logoi* and the spirit of Scripture are not discovered merely by study. They are not communicated by doctors. They are the Kiss of the Word Himself, not the Kiss of His Mouth.

The Word, *Logos*, teaches us how the *logoi* are oriented to Him.

How they are both in Him and for Him.

The *logoi* of things are in the *Logos*:

They are created in the *Logos*. The *logoi* of things are then the *Logos* in things. "In every being there is a *logos sophos kai technicos* [a principle of wisdom and a principle of technology divorced from metaphysical questions]

beyond our vision." St. Gregory of Nyssa, in *Hexaemeron*, *PG*. 44, 73a.

This is the *theoteles logos*: that in the thing which comes from God and goes to God.

Theoria physike then demands that we enter into the movement of all things from God back to God. And it implies realization of the obstacle in the way of this movement placed in the world by *philautia* [self-love] and sin: which makes the things created by God serve our own immediate interests.

Theoria physike implies a sense of <u>community with things in the work of salvation</u>.

Logos of bread and wine: Not merely to nourish man physically but to serve the unity of mankind in Christ sacramentally.

Wine: is something which points beyond itself to the "new wine" in the Kingdom. The new wine is not something that is purely spiritual and therefore "not material wine." On the contrary, in the Eucharist, material wine is transformed not only into spiritual wine but into the "mystical wine" which is the Blood of Christ.

The *logos* of a table: realized in the mystical table which is the altar around which the brethren gather for the fraternal meal at which the Risen Christ will be mystically present and will break Bread.

Christ Himself is the table of the altar.

Hence, St. Maximus sums it up: "The world is a GAME OF GOD. As one amuses children with flowers and bright-colored clothes and then gets them later used to more serious games, literary studies, so God raises us up first of all by the great game of nature, then by the scriptures (with poetic symbols). Beyond the symbols of Scripture is the Word . . . . "

> The spiritual knowledge of God in things is given to men
> in the desert of this world as manna was given to feed the
> Hebrews in the desert of Sinai. (*Quest. 39 ad Tha.*)

Maximus makes clear that the <u>spiritual senses</u> function in *theoria physike* as in their proper realm. Cf. Gregory of Nyssa.

By the *logoi* of things the Divine Creator draws men who are attuned to *logoi*, the logical men, *logikoi*, to communion with the *Logos*.

When a man has been purified and humbled, when his eye is single, and he is his own real self, then the *logoi* of things jump out at him spontaneously. He is then a *logikos*.

[Page 47]

Art: Logos and Epiphany.

Here we can see the importance of *theoria physike* for sacred art.

The sacred artist of all people should be a *logikos*.

Hence it is not true that he does not need to be purified. He must in some sense be one who has attained to the summit of *apatheia*. Not of course in the conventional way in which the average pious Catholic might conceive it. He does not necessarily have to be fully respectable in a conventional sense. A kind of unconventionality may be in him a form of humility and folly for Christ, a part of his *apatheia*.

We must not forbid the artist a necessary element of paradox in his life.

Conformism will perhaps blind him and enslave his talent.

But he must at all costs have attained to an inner purity and honesty, a sincerity and integrity of spirit. He must be a *holokleros*, who understands the *logoi* of things and is attuned to their *tropoi*.

He must be in communication with things, in their deepest center, in their most real value.

He must be attuned to their voice. He must sense something of their "logic," their vocation.

He must also sense in what way they are being prevented by man, and by society, by misuse, from attaining to their true spiritual end.

The artist at the present time is bound in one way or other to protest against the systematic obscuring and desecration of the *logoi* of things and of their sacred meaning.

For that reason an artist who would serve a completely secular society and put his art at the disposal of propaganda for materialistic illusions would be destroying himself as an artist, especially if he served up conventional forms of "beauty." He would be conniving at the desecration and destruction of art. In so doing he would be betraying created things, and betraying his vocation as artist.

This by no means condones any illusion of the artist as a "special kind of man" but his technical gifts as maker demand to be sustained by a spiritual gift as "seer."

Note that once again this does not imply allegory or explicit symbolism or some special "message." Nor does it imply peculiar forms of "fine art."

The perception of the *logos* of a thing by an artist is manifested by the <u>form</u> which he gives to things.

Examples of work sensitive to *logoi*:

1) Shaker handicrafts, and furniture. Deeply impregnated by the communal mystique of the Shaker community. The simplicity and austerity demanded by their way of life enabled an unconscious spiritual purity to manifest itself in full clarity. Shaker handicrafts are then a real <u>epiphany of *logoi*</u>.

Characterized by <u>spiritual light</u>.

See also their buildings. Barns especially. Highly mystical quality: capaciousness, dignity, solidity, permanence. *Logos* of a barn? "But my wheat, gather ye into my barn."

Note: it is never question of a "barn" in the abstract and in no definite place: the Shaker farm building always fits right into its location, manifests the *logos* of the place where it is built, grasps and expresses the hidden *logos* of the valley, or hillside, etc. which forms its site. <u>Logos of the site</u>. Important in Cistercian monasteries of twelfth century.

Note: absence of this in certain religious settings — psuedo-Gothic, which ignores true *logoi*, substitutes an arbitrary and false *logos*, in the head. Modern architecture with its pretended functionalism also is quite arbitrary. Cf. Mumford on U.N. buildings.

[Page 48]

2) A primitive painter, Le Douanier Rousseau.

Some of his paintings might be discussed as unconscious *theoria physike* on an obscure and not explicitly Christian level: but anyway on a kind of "spiritual" level.

The "spiritual" content of Le Douanier Rousseau. Archetypal symbols.

The Sleeping Gypsy: logos of passion. *Apatheia.* Whether or not Douanier Rousseau ever attained to *apatheia* (in the strict sense highly doubtful! His loves and angers.)

But *The Sleeping Gypsy* represents for him the attainment of balance and a solution of a long inner conflict of which he was perhaps not even aware.

We may see here an analogy of that *theoria* to which primitives are well disposed.

The Dangers and Limitations of Theoria Physike.

a) *Theoria physike* is between the human and the divine.

It involves <u>sense and spirit</u> together.

It demands man's <u>activity and divine grace</u>.
It is not yet pure contemplation, it is only the beginning of the contemplative life. The threshold.

b) It involves alternations, and the possibility of delusion.

A light that is truly spiritual may be seized upon by the senses and diverted to less pure ends.

One may mistake sensible indulgence for spiritual inspiration.

When the senses are refined and spiritualized, and yet not completely purified, there remains a danger that a more exquisite form of sense pleasure on a higher and more refined level may be accepted completely as spiritual and mystical.

c) This problem is explicitly treated by St. Maximus in
 Quest. 58 to Thalassios.

When sense still predominates, natural contemplation is falsified because it <u>seems</u> natural to us to cling to the beauty of things with sense and spirit at the same time, and consequently sense is not subordinated to spirit.

The subordination of sense to spirit *seems to us* unnatural.

Hence the complaints and protests of those who, in demanding that nature be respected, are really asserting illusory "rights" for what is <u>not a natural state</u>, that is, a state in which sense predominates over spirit.

d) The right order: when sense attains to the material object, the spirit attains to the spiritual *logos* of that object and the sense pleasure is forgotten.

There may indeed be a coincidence of <u>contemplation in the spirit and suffering in sense</u>.

Let us be careful not to be misled by legitimate protests against "dolorism" [spiritual masochism, psychological emphasis on suffering] into asserting that the senses have right to more than is naturally due to them: that is to say, to emphasize sense satisfaction as a natural flowering of the spirit, when such satisfaction has to be disciplined and brought into subordination by suffering and sacrifice.

Hence, as Maximus says, that just as Eliakim blocked up the walls around Jerusalem in time of danger, so we should abandon *theoria physike* in time of temptation and return to compunction and simple prayer.

NOTES

1. Thomas Merton, "An Introduction to Christian Mysticism (From the Apostolic Fathers to the Council of Trent)." Unpublished lectures given at the Abbey of Gethsemani, 1961. Thomas Merton Collection, Bellarmine University, Louisville, Kentucky, pages 44-48.

2. These bracketed page numbers refer to the bound manuscript of Merton's lecture notes archived in The Thomas Merton Center.

3. All underlined emphasis is Merton's.

Byzantine fresco fragment, twelfth - early fourteenth century.

12

LOVE FOR GOD AND MUTUAL CHARITY
Thomas Merton's Lectures on Hesychasm
To the Novices at the Abbey of Gethsemani

Transcribed and edited by Bernadette Dieker

Merton studied the prayers and practices of the Eastern Orthodox tradition. His taped lectures from 1962 contain his efforts to teach the monks at Gethsemani ways to develop and deepen their prayer lives from within the Rule of St. Benedict and the Cistercian tradition. Along with providing a thorough history of the Eastern Orthodox tradition, as found both in Greece and in Russia, Merton describes the ascetic lives of the Orthodox monks who followed in the tradition of the Desert Fathers of Sinai. Merton studied extensively the writings of John Cassian, John Climacus and John Chrysostom. In order to explain Russian monasticism, Merton begins with a description of the lives of the Desert Fathers and their practice of pure prayer, and he continues to refer to the Desert Fathers' traditions throughout his description and explanation of the Russian monastic tradition.

Mysticism appeals to Merton because of its contemplative dimension. Though a contemplative and quiet life was possible at Gethsemani, Merton discovered, through his study of *Hesychasm*, a deep connection and wealth of wisdom to be found in the prescribed Eastern Christian ascetic life. From his lectures, a listener learns that Merton advocated a moderate level of asceticism, and that he reminded the monks that the basis of the ascetic life is not a practice of negating the body or the will, but rather, love.

Twenty-two tapes from the Merton collection were reviewed and transcribed (approximately thirty-five hours of taped lectures), selected for their inclusion of Merton's mention of the Desert Fathers, Asceticism, Greek and Russian Orthodoxy, *Hesychasm* and The Prayer of the Heart. Based on the thematic emphasis of this volume, the transcriptions are edited to highlight Merton's descriptions of *Hesychasm* and the role of the staretz in the Russian *Hesychast* tradition. Hesychasm is grounded in "unceasing prayer" and in "*nepsis*," keeping sober in mind and body and "guarding one's thoughts." Merton discusses the diligent self-emptying and self-renunciation required to reach a pure level in prayer through which one may become aware of the Prayer of Jesus permeating the heart, when the mind and heart become one. He explains the necessity of silence and expounds upon its value in the contemplative life.

As in most of his taped lectures, Merton speaks candidly but with authority and ends abruptly when the bell rings, thus sometimes leaving thoughts incomplete and leading to repetition in future lectures. Unlike his formal lectures and essays, Merton's lectures to the novices reveal the more creative, performing aspects of his personality. They reveal Merton, the Teacher.

— *Bernadette Dieker*

CASSIAN ON PRAYER: THE CONFERENCES

Kinds of prayer: meditation[1]

The Holy Name of Jesus is a wonderful ejaculatory prayer that contains a tremendous amount, if you consider the theology of the Holy Name, which exists in the Fathers of the Church. [There is an] immense amount of importance attached to the Holy Name.

"Our Father"; perfect prayer; highest degree of prayer.[2]

The Lord's Prayer leads to perfect prayer, and St. Teresa says that too. [Cassian] starts talking about perfect prayer and fervor in prayer and the graces of prayer and so forth. He says this prayer of the potter leads those who practice it to that higher state, which brings him at last to that prayer of Fire, or *Ignita Oratio*, a burning prayer, which is known and experienced by few but which is an inexpressibly high degree of prayer. This is going to be the prayer of fire this morning.

There's really something going on. It means you're aware of it. That's the basic thing. If you're on fire with this prayer, you should have a vague idea of what it is. Not all high degrees of prayer are like that. There are some high degrees of prayer where you don't know anything. But this is one where you know. And yet, you are aware of something, but you don't understand what it is. He says it's beyond man's senses and understanding. It is beyond grasping and understanding, and then Cassian says another characteristic about it is that it is without words. So it's real sizzling hot and it's without words. No words, no discourse. You don't go from one thing to another. It's all in one.

It's something that can't be expressed. It's got to come out somehow but it can't be expressed. Don't imitate too much of how it comes out, please, when it gets you all in a rush, so to speak. It is without words, without discourse, and it's purely mental, made by the mind, illuminated by the infusion of heavenly light. If you talk about infusion, it means that it is to some extent passive. You receive. You don't produce this — this is something that is given. And then of course, you can tell when a thing like this is given, you get a sort of impression of it being given. Well obviously, how would that make itself felt, how would you realize that?

Instead of being discursive, that is to say successive, one thing to another, Cassian says it's all gathered together at once. All the power is gathered together in unity, and he says it pours itself forth copiously and cries out to God in a manner beyond expression, saying so much in that brief moment that the mind cannot relate it afterwards with ease or even go over it again after returning to itself.

And don't get the idea that our life is geared to produce this all the time, because it isn't. This life is geared to tone down this sort of stuff. Our prayer is definitely toned down. I think it's very important to realize that the character of the Cistercian life is such that it keeps things on a low key. And if we try by one way or another, communal or individual, to keep stepping things up, whether we realize it or not, we go against the life, and we cause a great deal of conflict and confusion. Therefore I think it can be said — and you've got to take it with a grain of salt — any kind of an intensive campaign to make the choir extremely colorful and to give it a lot of zip — our life isn't geared for that. When you spend as much time in choir per day as we do, it's not going to be a prayer with any kind of a zip or any kind of a lift except once in a while. Most of the time, if you're in choir for that long, it's going to be toned down.

And then Cassian comes to the expressions of fervor: how fervor is expressed in the desert. These guys, they're in their cells, about half a mile apart. Apparently, all of a sudden you hear this yelling . . . shouts of intolerable joy. Somebody's un-bearable joy is versed out in order to hear this shouting, "Alle-luia, we made it."

At other times the soul is overwhelmed by grace and reduced to total silence. Well, there's plenty of total silence, but let's just be reduced. Because if we're reduced by the Holy Ghost, the total silence is one thing, but just to be in a state of tongue-tied stupor is another.

The great expression of fervor for all these old traditional documents is what? What's the standard sign of fervor in the tradition?

Tears. Fervor is expressed by tears. And so, now remember this is a conversation between Cassian, Germanus and Abbot Isaac, I think. As soon as Isaac says "tears," immediately Germanus jumps in and says, "How do you get tears?" Now that's what the monks always wanted to know, how do you get tears? That was a great question of these monks. We are much less preoccupied with that nowadays. And that's a good thing, too, as a matter of fact. I think we're better off without everybody sobbing.

Chapter 29 is on the different sources of tears. Which faucet do you turn? And it's a standard traditional material. One of the sources of tears, obviously is the remedy of our sins . . . .

This should be more part of our lives than it actually is, I think. There's no harm in occasionally being moved to com-punction, even if the tears don't run down your cheeks with the thought of Heaven and so forth. That's a good thing. And it has a definite part to play in our life. It should purify our hearts. It really is necessary in a sense because there has to be some feeling somewhere about something, and this is one of the places where it's a little bit legitimate. Then Isaac says that one of the sources of tears is just sheer power. Now don't do that. That's all right for the Desert Fathers, but I don't want any of that around here. Why isn't that good? Of course Isaac qualifies that. He says forcing tears may be necessary for hardened sinners. None of you guys are hardened sinners, so you're all right, so don't force tears.

He says, actually those who have made any little bit of a progress in spiritual matters should not force themselves, because it would be very harmful. So let's assume that applies to everybody here. We shouldn't force ourselves. On the contrary, we should avoid that. Why would that be harmful? There's one very obvious reason why that would be harmful. It would be false. Why does he say a hardened sinner should weep? Well, it isn't false in the case of a hardened sinner. He should weep. We should weep at certain times. We should weep when the Lord wants us to weep, but we shouldn't just weep because we force ourselves.

In the spiritual life, what should be taking place is a real serious, sincere kind of spontaneity. In other words, a man should be more or less the way he feels at the moment. That doesn't mean to say give in to our every feeling, but we should more or less go along with the way we actually feel.

In other words, what he's getting at . . . it would be a very bad thing to tamper with life itself. The Lord gives us our life, and he gives us the sentiments that come from moment to moment. Why doctor them? Why monkey with them? And as he said, that would be pride. It would be a form of self-will in a sense. One of the basic aspects of pride is that it doesn't take life as it comes but forces our own will on life. There are times when we have to force our own will on life — if life comes to us in a bad form, if it presents us with an occasion of evil or something, we have to force it. But we shouldn't tamper with life. We shouldn't just insist on having a preconceived idea, "I'm going to feel this. I'm going to go to church now and today it's going to be a day of weeping."

The penalty of forcing around here is that you leave. People who force emotions or force things to be other than they are . . . you can't make it in the life. It's absolutely necessary in this life to take things as they come, and to be completely in contact with things as they are, as much as you possibly can. In other words, don't suddenly decide, "Well now I'm going to . . . " For me it's the 12th degree of humility [from the Rule of St. Benedict]. "I have arrived, and nobody's going to see my eyes from now until Christmas." That's forcing it — it doesn't work, it doesn't get there. On the contrary, it's very bad.

And then finally he comes out with a quotation from St. Anthony, in which he says, "The perfect prayer." There is no perfect prayer in which the monk understands himself, or the fact that he is praying.

*   *   *

Frequent prayer and constant prayer[3] . . . how do you pray all the time? Of course you've got this sentence from St. Paul. How are you going to learn to pray all the time? What are you going to do? What does it mean to pray all the time, to pray without ceasing? How are you going to do that? What are some of the answers? Just give me some of the traditional answers.

I know you've all got the secret, but what are the traditional answers to that? Offer everything you do as prayer . . . . That means that everything that you do becomes a prayer by reason of the fact that it's offered up to God. That's a standard. But the point is, is that — strictly speaking — a prayer? Well, it is and it isn't. It's perfectly valid. Where did you hear that first?

In the active life, a standard way to make your active life an act of prayer is to offer up everything *en lieu* of prayer so that your work becomes a prayer. That's perfectly valid, and insofar as we have a certain amount of activity here, we've got to do that too. That's necessary for our life. Then . . . what doesn't it mean?

To be constantly conscious of God. You can get a special gift to be perpetually in the presence of God, perpetually uninterruptedly conscious of God, even during sleep. Well, I understand some of the saints had that. [For example,] St. Ambrose. The Blessed Mother — when she was asleep she was going through everything that she had read during the day. Our Lady was never unconscious. Personally, I don't agree with that. The reason why I don't agree with that isn't because I don't think it might be true, but I see no reason for giving a person a grace like that which is useless. Is it a human perfection to be never unconscious? I don't see that it is. It's more perfect to be sometimes unconscious, because conscious rational life on the human level isn't the summit of human existence, and to assume that — just to be constantly in a state of conscious awareness of everything? That's not the perfection of human life. That's taking half of human life, I mean the conscious half, and saying that's the whole thing. Well, you've got both, you've got the conscious and the unconscious, and the perfection of human life isn't to be constantly conscious or to be constantly unconscious, but it's to be alternating between the two. Action and rest. Thinking and not thinking. To think about God twenty-four hours a day is certainly not the idea of a prayer, but why does this have to be mentioned? Because people ordinarily believe, or even if they don't believe it, they sort of keep it in the back of their minds as a distressing possibility, "But maybe that's what it really is. Gee, if I'm not thinking constantly about Him, I'm not praying constantly."

That's not the way to practice the presence of God, by intense concentration. Why isn't it the way? What's concentration? Centering your mind. You're centering your conscious. When you concentrate, you're trying to understand some complicated reasoning, [for example] you're trying to fix a watch. Anything where your attention has to be focused sharply on details. Now it's easy to see that that's got nothing to do with the practice of the presence of God. Why?

No detail. Obviously, on the contrary, if you're thinking about speculative ideas about God, scientific ideas about God, you can concentrate on that, but that's another matter. But the ideas have details, and your thought can have details, but actually this idea of the presence of God considered as something that gives life to your prayer is not something you should concentrate on. Because it isn't like fixing a watch. What is it like, if it isn't like concentrating?

It's like getting under a sun lamp. It's simply opening your-self to receive. The presence of God is like walking out of a door into the fresh air. You don't concentrate on the fresh air, you breathe it. And you don't concentrate on the sunlight, you just enjoy it. It's all around you.

The things in life that correspond somewhat to the presence of God are not things on which you can concentrate, on which you do concentrate. You just simply are in them. When you swim, you don't concentrate on the water. To be in the presence of God is like, in a certain sense, being in water. Not physically . . . .

[At this moment Merton sees a Carolina wren outside the window and takes a moment to look at it . . . he seldom so suddenly leaves his lectures in this way. The wren sings a bit, too.]

So to get back to how Cassian goes at it. I think that Cassian is about as practical as anybody can be about this idea of con-stant prayer. What do they say about it? How do you suppose they handle it?

How are you going to know that you're going to be constantly praying? Of course that doesn't mean uninterrupted in time, but it means constantly renewed. So you're going to have some kind of an act that you renew, and what's it going to be? Ejacu-latory prayer. Simply, it's ejaculatory prayer frequently renewed, so when they talk about constant prayer, that's what they think of. A renewal of an ejaculatory prayer. And an ejaculatory prayer, what is it? It's a short sentence of an exclamation of some sort which sums up what you mean by prayer. There are all kinds of ways of approaching that.

What's important is to get something that means something to you — not just something that comes out mechanically but something that really sums up what's in your heart. An ejacu-latory prayer is meaningless unless it does express something. It isn't just a mechanical utterance of words, even if it's the Holy Name. It should have meaning.

The great thing, then, is to find some repeated formula which sums up everything and which you can just bring into action. As soon as you need it, you just start.

It's very easy. Ejaculatory prayer is absolutely the easiest form of prayer. There is no easier form of prayer than ejaculatory prayer. I can't think of any easier one, except of course some kind of a completely passive prayer. Well that's even easier still. But ejaculatory prayer is absolutely just as easy as it can be and it requires no effort. And it may seem to require an effort. You start thinking, "If I'm saying ejaculations all the time, it's going to require an effort." It actually requires no effort. It's just as easy as breathing, once you get used to it. Don't get the idea that you have to be constantly saying ejaculations and you never stop the ejaculations. Bow down in choir while the other side is saying a verse of the Psalm and you're saying "Jesus, Mary, Joseph" — don't do that. But it is important to get some form of prayer that really just expresses everything. Obviously the classic example of this kind of prayer is what is called the Prayer of Jesus, which the Oriental monks use a great deal. Which is very, simply — what's the formula they repeat in the Prayer of Jesus, quite a long one?

"Lord Jesus Christ, Son of God, have mercy on me a sinner."

Kyrie Jesu Christe, Elaison . . .

Learn it in Russian, learn it in Greek. Say it. Pep up your spiritual life with the Jesus Prayer in the various languages. It's a fine prayer. It's a bit long though. You don't have to say [one] that long. You can just say "Lord Jesus Christ have mercy." You can say "My Jesus, mercy" if you want. That is a Western form. Anything like that.

When the Holy Father the other day gave this three-fold devotion: The Name, The Heart and The Blood — why does he emphasize The Name, apart from he probably has great devotion of the Holy Name? It has an ecumenical import, because, after all, this devotion to the Holy Name and Prayer of Jesus exists in the Oriental Church, and that's an important point. That would be another point of union. St. Bernard says — you read that sermon on the Name of Jesus in St. Bernard, you find that what he says about the Name of Jesus is very much like what some of the Oriental Fathers say. Some of these fathers of Mount Athos say about the Name of Jesus — that it's light, that it's oil, that it's ointment. The different effects and graces that come from repeating the Name of Jesus with faith. This is a little alien from our type of spirituality today, but it's something to remember.

Now what's the main thing that Cassian and company — what's their ejaculation, that the desert fathers thought was the great one that you had to say all the time?

"*Deus in adjutorium nostrum intende.*" [O God, come to our assistance.]

That's the reason why we use that at the beginning of the office. That became popular in monastic prayer due to the fact that the Desert Fathers used it as their constant ejaculation. Now what's the value of that? Why is that a good choice for an ejaculatory prayer? Does that sum anything up? What part of the theological life is summed up by that?

Total dependence — our need of grace. Our total need for grace. So actually when you're saying "*Deus in adjutorium nostrum intende*" — you don't have to say that, but if you are constantly turning to God with the realization of your need for his grace and your total dependence on grace . . . that's the part that he's trying to get across. Any prayer that, for example, sums up our total need for grace — the Jesus Prayer is the same thing — is a prayer for mercy. A prayer for grace, a prayer for mercy — it comes to the same thing. And this is a very good way to learn how to pray, especially if you get a kind of a rhythm in it. If you can't think of anything else to do during the morning meditation, just pick an ejaculation and say it for awhile, then stop for awhile, then say it some more, then stop some more. It's very good when you're distracted — when you're having a dry, hard time, well, bring it in.

One of the early commentaries on the Rule says that it has been and is the custom of monks that in all their works, whether spiritual or temporal, whenever they begin anything, to say this verse three times. It's an ancient monastic custom of the West, taken over from the East, that whenever you start anything, when you begin your work or something, you say "*Deus in adjutorium nostrum intende*" three times. When you go to eat, you say it three times. Well, when do we say it three times?

We used to say it at the beginning of *Matins*. *Chapter*, yeah, in *Chapter* we say it. Of course, what's the *Chapter* the beginning of? It's the beginning of the active day. It's the end of *Prime*, but it's the beginning of [the active day] — and actually you see, according to monastic tradition, work was distributed at or after *Chapter*, and normally we used to go to work after *Chapter*.

CHASTITY: A MARTYRDOM[4]

It has become traditional to associate the torments of the martyrs with the trials of overcoming temptation. One thing that we can remember is that basically [trials] should be regarded as a kind of martyrdom. It can be, I mean, generally accepted, [that] the trials and temptations of a life of chastity are a kind of martyrdom. All the side effects that go with it. Not just that we have to get all sorts of dramatic ideas and get full of self-pity and that sort of stuff, but there are side effects that go with the life of chastity. There's a kind of a nervousness you can get sometimes, these sorts of psychological side effects. They can be a kind of martyrdom. The way the Church wants us to look at it is if this fellow could lie on the gridiron and get roasted, we ought to be able to take a little bit of temptation and try and bring it home to us.

And not just the negative side of the thing, but there's a positive statement made here. The reason why [St. Lawrence, who was martyred by being roasted on a gridiron] overcame that which was outside, was [that] he had a bigger fire burning inside, and he had such a big fire inside that the outside one didn't mean anything. What is important is the positive, the fire of love. If the fire of love is stronger than the fire of temptation, then it doesn't matter so much. But if you've got a strong fire of temptation outside and an iceberg inside, well, it puts it on a different basis. So we should have a lot of love. Generosity is the great idea.

The moral problem of chastity ceases to be a problem when there is real generosity — realism about the thing — and when we're able to accept temptations with generosity and so forth.

You've got to practice chastity not only against your body but to a certain extent using your body as an instrument for chastity. You've got to have your body on your own side if you can. That means to say, while we're going to have to have a lot of asceticism, we also want to have a healthy body. No matter what anybody says, health is not an obstacle. Health is not something bad in a spiritual life. Sometimes you have a sort of a legend [among the Cistercians], which is altogether false, that St. Bernard liked to go to monasteries in marshes where everybody would be sick all the time. Because then if the monks were sick all the time, that would make life tougher and they'd be much more austere. That's not true. There are plenty of instances of places where St. Bernard moved in and found a monastery built in an unhealthy location and made them move it to a more healthy one. It's easier to lead an ascetic life with a healthy body, with a normally healthy body. You don't want to be overanxious about health. Things like diet and rest, they're all important.

The life of people in the world is absolutely ordered to unchastity. It's a life with the normal realm — people outside in the world, I just don't know how they can keep chaste in the life they live. It's just not — everything is against it. That is to say people who drink and smoke and who indulge all their desires and so forth, surrounded as they are by all kinds of things that are more or less a constant stimulation. That's a key word, that word "stimulation." A healthy life is not an overstimulated life.

Incidentally, that's a very important point about the monastic life . . . Let's ask ourselves a question. Is it really a very good thing to be working in the refectory and to have the Office coming to you in the refectory over a loudspeaker? Is this better than if the refectory were purely and simply silent? Personally, I think it'd be a whole lot better. You might say, "Well it's the Office, isn't it?" But the point is this — it's not the Office. By the time it gets to you over the loudspeaker it's a different kind of noise. And it becomes background music. And the Office and background music are two entirely different things. It's very nice to have sort of a background of Psalms coming along and so forth. But you see, what's the difference? Supposing that you got — you're working in the refectory and there are Psalms coming over the loudspeaker, to which you are half listening, and then you're working and you're half listening. This is the principle of background music. Background music is music which doesn't quite engage your attention, it's just there. What's the difference between that and working in the refectory in silence where you either have to pray or be distracted? What's the difference?

A person may want to unite himself with the Psalms. That's fine. The point is he can't hear them, you just hear sound, you don't hear words. You hear singing, you know that there's some singing going on, and the tendency is not to unite yourself with the thing. The tendency is to — if I'm living against a background of background music, my activity is going to be more or less passive and automatic, so that I don't do one thing or the other. I don't pray and I don't not pray. I just sort of automatically put out things, half-listening to something, and it reduces me to a kind of a subhuman level. It's not thoroughly human as the business of making a choice whether you're going to pray or be distracted. At least that's the way I look at it. You can't fully do anything.

Personally I think that a man would be much better off without that kind of a background music thing, because then he could be fully awake, instead of just floating through life in a daze. Background music you're not supposed to listen to.

A lot of corporations today, where you're supposed to . . . more or less, you have to type reports and that sort of thing . . . they've got the stuff going all day long. And it's the worst possible kind of music. I'm not talking about ours. I'm talking about this stuff that they used to call Musak. It's the most indistinct . . . just so you don't have to think. So that your mind won't have to work, keep your mind from working. Get something going so that your mind can be sort of half asleep. There's a kind of anesthesia. Well that's very bad. You go through your life half under an anesthetic, with no resistance to anything, so that any stimulus that presents itself you yield to, and then, having gone through life like that, you get close to death, and they put you out completely. Before you even know that you're going to die, you're out. What chance does a man have? It's awful.

So stop and think of the value of being in a place where you do have to think, and you do have to make decisions and choices and so forth. What is good is not this question of having sounds fed to you and ideas fed to you, it's the question of having to go and get yourself an idea . . . . Supposing you are one of the reasons why we're distracted, and why you may be bombarded by a whole host of impure images and so forth. What's the reason for that? It's because of a lack of interior discipline. How does one develop interior discipline?

It involves the ability to select what you're going to think about. The more disciplined a person is interiorly, the more he can choose his thoughts. How do you learn to do that? You have to learn that by practicing, by making choices. As I say, the fellow who is constantly sort of passively submitting to stimulation that's fed to him, images come and he just accepts them, and everything that comes he accepts. You see that so often. You get real good kids that'll come, nice kids. But they're passive. Nothing happens. Everything that comes they just simply take, without any selectivity at all. It's the TV mentality I guess. You just sort of sit there until the thing goes off. Whereas if you want to have discipline, then you've got to make choices, and then by making choices, to some extent, you can get to the point where you can choose what you're going to think about. And you can prefer to think about good things.

It isn't just a question of pressing a button and saying "I will think about the Crucifixion" or something. Maybe that won't work. It isn't an arbitrary thing. You don't just press a button and change the station . But you do have to learn how to . . . there's a question of developing an interest. And if you are sufficiently interested in some scriptural topic or some theological idea or some spiritual thing, you can be thinking about it, and it'll come along, and it'll occupy your thoughts most of the time. So in other words, you develop a habitual preference for certain types of things. Then in order to do that, you've got to learn how to do that, and that means to say, as I said, you don't just simply insist on one thing. You've got to have a certain variety, which means to say that you also have got to have something light and good. Why? Because your imagination is involved in this, and it's no good simply concentrating on some purely intellectual thing, and not giving your imagination anything to do any time. So you've got to rope the imagination in on this somewhere. And how do you do that? Well, how do you fix your imagination up with something to do?

You've got to have images. The imagination has got to have some part of a balanced diet. Biographies . . . Scripture has great images. One of the things that the Fathers of the Church did, that the early monks did, was to use the Psalms and the Scriptures to fill the mind with other images. As soon as you entered the monastery you started eating up Scripture until your mind was full of the Books of Kings — there's plenty of imagery there. Your mind is filled with all these Scripture stories, and then all this other stuff goes out. And then you're thinking about David and Joseph and Abraham and all these things. And then we could add a little bit on the lives of the Saints. One of the great graces of my life, as far as this question of being imaginative goes, is the fact of having more or less grown up among European cathedrals and monasteries and things like that. I mean to have all that around you when you are a kid is marvelous. And to grow up with that sort of stuff and with that kind of imagery, you see. That's why we put some of this stuff on the board here.

It is good, for example, to have something in your mind like Chartres. Now how are you going to do that? Well, we'll pack up and take you all over to Chartres. Well, I wish I could, but if you can't do that, then why don't you read that book called Mont Saint Michel on Chartres by Henry Adams, in which he talks about these things and talks about the importance and the symbolism and the mentality behind the people who built the Cathedral of Chartres, and who built Mont Saint Michel, and the spirituality of it, which has a great deal to do with the Cistercians. And the reason we got all these picture books in here is, take out that book on the Architecture of Sounds . . .

Your imagination, it doesn't stimulate the imagination, on the contrary is rests the imagination. How? Well, the effect of sun on the stones and light and shadow, these are things that you don't pay too much attention to, but they're healthy and they create a certain atmosphere of silence. They help interior silence. You can't have interior silence just by pressing a button and saying "Got to have interior silence." You have got to live in an atmosphere propitious for interior silence. The irreplaceable thing for that is just simply nature. Woods and so forth. Like you were out there yesterday in among those trees. Nothing is so propitious for interior silence as a bunch of trees. Nice trees. They're quiet, they don't bother anybody, they're not saying anything, and yet they have this beautiful stateliness. There's the wind in trees and there's the sunlight and the birds and all these things. We're made for that sort of thing. God made man for what? For Paradise. Well these things are like Paradise to some extent. Therefore we naturally have a kind of interior silence when we're out in the woods, or just even out in the garden. Or even just sitting out back here looking at the hills. That's the best way to get an interior silence. That's the easiest way.

*   *   *

He (St. Chrysostom)[5] went out in the desert, and after a couple of years, he tried to do total asceticism, extreme asceticism. He almost never slept and he almost never ate, and he learned the whole New Testament by heart. It's an extreme thing, you see. It didn't work, so he had to go back to the world. He returned, and then, having gone back to the world, he tended to have a strong reaction against this, so there is a lot of material on Chrysostom, that these people think that he's against monks. But actually what he's against is this extreme form of monasticism, extreme asceticism. And then he had an influence. He reacted against an extreme form of monasticism — who else did that, another Father of the Church? St. Basil. So Basil and Chrysostom, reacting against extreme monasticism, had a considerable influence in creating a more mild monasticism, and they did this by writing for people in the world, saying, "Now you fellows in the world, you lead a good strict life so you don't have to be like these crazy monks."

Then what happened? More prudent communities were formed, and people led a monastic, ascetic life in the world, and then they gradually got a little further away and gradually they became the standard of monasticism. Then this other big extreme stuff died out and these were left. The people who were reacting against extreme monasticism tended to lay down a program for what actually became monasticism. But they thought they were writing for non-monks.

He considers these basic monastic themes as basic Christian themes, and one of the most basic is renouncing the world. Nowadays, that's become ambiguous. Of course what he means by renouncing the world — he doesn't mean going out into the desert. He means staying in the world but not being of it. And we're more involved — there's the idea of engagement in the world, and so forth, which is absolutely necessary today. The Church has got to realize that Her problems are precisely the problems of the world and no other. The only real problems we've got are the problems of the world. All the other problems are chickenfeed. The problems of how are people going to eat? How are they going to live? What are they going to do? And these are our problems.

Cassian has a big tribute to Chrysostom in one of his books — he praises him as another John the Evangelist and says he was a great man. So obviously with Cassian coming to the West, and you've got this great reputation of Chrysostom in the West, he's going to be very well read in the West as well as in the East.

These [Syrian] hermits lived out in the desert and they had a great effect on the people of the towns. Chrysostom was always in favor of saying "Go out and make a retreat with a hermit." The picture that you almost get is that for Chrysostom, the ordinary Christian should live more or less like people in active religious orders, except that they also may marry — they may or may not. And then the real monk, then he's just way out. He's a complete, total hermit who eats every two or three days maybe once, and who really is an ascetic.

*   *   *

We finished John Climacus last time,[6] and he's got a lot of good stuff later on that you could talk about. Logically from John Climacus you should go right down the line through Oriental monasticism. Sinai is the starting point of a tradition in contemplative prayer. Who knows the name of this tradition in Contemplative prayer?

The *hesychast* tradition. Let's write "*hesychast*" on the board.

What's "*hesychast*" — who's a Greek scholar? You haven't had that much Greek yet — anybody know what a *hesychast* is? He's a man who likes "*hesychia*" — he likes "sweetness," sweetness and rest and quiet and so forth. He loves the rest of contemplation, the sweetness and rest of contemplation. A *hesychast* is one who likes sweetness and rest, preferably off some place in a cave or something like that.

So the story of the Oriental mystical tradition as the *hesychast* tradition — it's a little more than just sweetness and rest. It's built around the so-called Prayer of Jesus. What's the Prayer of Jesus?

"Lord Jesus Christ, Son of God, have mercy on me a Sinner."

You can say it in Greek, and you can say it in the Russian, and you can say it in all sorts of things. And this is repeated over and over again in a special technique — this is very good, you ought to know this. You breathe in a certain way — you say it when you're breathing and so forth. You could do this during the morning meditation. It's the easiest possible way to spend the half hour fruitfully in church, I assure you. Don't go too far with the breathing. The idea is to concentrate on this prayer, "Lord Jesus Christ, Son of God, have mercy on me a sinner," until you follow your breath down to your heart and then BOOM, a big light comes. That's *Hesychasm*. You see, you get the light of Tabor and it shines, and so forth. That's getting a little risqué, but that's this tradition.

Now it started at Sinai, and it worked away from there by means of a man called Gregory of Sinai. It went from there where — where is the great center of eastern monasticism and contemplation? Mount Athos. It goes to Mount Athos, in Greece. So we'll talk about Mount Athos sometime.

This tradition goes to Mount Athos and then it gets from Mount Athos into Romania and Russia, and then we got this Russian tradition. Well, we'll follow that through sometime — it's very interesting. It's good to know about this.

* * *

If you ask people,[7] "Where was the great center of monastic spirituality in the nineteenth century?" What's the answer? Where were they?

Russia. They built up a strong enough nucleus of religion to last through this thing. They had to be pretty rugged to stand this thing. They're holding on, they've still got monasteries, some monasteries.

* * *

[Merton[8] offers a brief history of monasticism in the east, particularly in Russia. He explains, "This is going to be strictly non-expert stuff. I'm going to talk about the Russian mystics . . . " After going through the history of Russian monasteries and monasticism, he brings the novices through the eighteenth century.]

And then, after the end of the eighteenth century, the little father says, "Monasteries are really pretty good." And so the little father says, "Let's have a whole lot of them." So then they open up all over the place. The greatest flowering of Russian mysticism was really in the nineteenth century, and that's most interesting. I think you've got some tremendous people in the nineteenth century in Russia, and I think they're the ones that I would like to concentrate on the most. If you want to get a good picture, a really striking picture, of Russian monasticism in the nineteenth century, think back to the *Brothers Karamozov* . . . remember the Staretz Zossimov . . . he is a very fine example, although he's a bit of Dostoevsky himself. It seems to me a very moving picture of a deeply religious man, of a saint. And a tremendously deep Christian compassion that the man has. This picture of Zossimov is apparently based on a Staretz at one of the monasteries called Optino. A great center of the staretzi people. And perhaps we'll bring him in and talk about this because I don't think there's anything in the West to compare to that. Certainly not in the nineteenth century. This is something really terrific; it really hits you right between the eyes. It is very profound. And we'll get to that . . . .

So let's go back and look at this in a little detail. First of all just a quick look at Sergius. Sergius is the great Russian monastic saint. Sergius — it's a new kind of monasticism, it isn't the old stuff — the old stuff that Anthony and Theodocius began was the big Solovian type. The Russian monasticism of Sergius is exactly like the Cistercian except that it's more eremitical. It's the question of labor, poverty, prayer, solitude — away from the cities. Because the older monasteries tended to be religious centers on the outskirts of a city. And then of course this fellow Fadotov is another type talking about the kenotic spirituality of the Russians and he makes a big emphasis on this — kenotic means "self-emptying" — and he goes into the fact that these Russian saints abase themselves tremendously. All this exaggerated self-abasement, going to great extremes of self-abasement. He emphasizes this very much. One of the great forms of self-abasement in Russian monasticism of course is this idea of being a "fool for Christ." Wanting to be a total outcast from human society, just be regarded as a complete lunatic, you see. And there's something in the Russian character, now you've got to watch your step when you start talking about the Russian character. But there is something about them, I mean they are extreme. They've got a fascination for extremes. I don't know if you've ever been out on a drunk with a Russian . . . . They get into all kinds of fantastic developments.

So that one of the things that they love to do is, apparently, go to the limit of anything. If they want to abase themselves, they go to the total limit of self-abasement. Be a doormat at the front door . . . if you can think of anything worse, they will do that.

Well, he doesn't give any impressive examples of St. Sergius. The only thing that he gives is that St. Sergius used to work for his monks. That is to say, one of the monks wanted an addition put on his cell and St. Sergius did it for him in order to get some moldy bread to eat. And the monk said "Here, moldy bread. . . . " But that's not one of the extreme things. Some of these other people are much more extreme. The thing that you want to get on Sergius, the thing that you need to see with him that I think is characteristic and I think very important is that you've got a mixture of mysticism and maternal charity plus intervention in politics. Very important I think. Because he was, so to speak, the center of resistance to the Mongols. He became pretty much the patron of Russia, as far as I can see. He's sort of the patron of the Muscovite Russia because he was the hard core around which the resistance of the Mongols was concentrated, and he's a national hero.

Sergius, having become a national hero and the leader of the army and all of this, kind of consecrates a union of church and state and a kind of a state monasticism . . . Sergius left a two-fold tradition. On the one hand, novices going towards the hermit life and towards the northern forest where you didn't have to own any land because it was all virgin forest and there wasn't anybody there. He goes off into this "no man's land" where you don't own any land and he starts these small hermit communities which we'll discuss in a minute. They are really beautiful. It's a real good idea. And very loose-knit, very informal, unorganized, emphasis on mystical prayer and complete poverty and manual labor and solitude and he calls it the "*sketic*" life. He calls them "*sketes*," which you've heard of before on Mount Athos. Well his plan for a *skete* — beautiful. One priest, one deacon, twelve monks. And each one with his own cottage in a small group, way up in the Northern forest, and the only time they come together in church is Saturday night, and they're there all night. An all night vigil for Sunday, ending on Sunday Mass early in the morning, and then probably I suppose some kind of a communal reunion and a get-together and getting their supplies and then going back for the week. And what do they do in these cells? Well, the *hesychast* tradition has come in from Greece, you see, and they are really strong on the contemplative prayer and of course on this interior asceticism. We'll talk a little about it and you tell me where it comes from. Tell me what tradition it is. You've got for example a book called *The Tradition and the Skete* — the tradition of *sketic* life. He goes to great pains to explain the nature of the spiritual struggle. At first let me read a little passage of his program here. This is the preface to this book on the *sketic* life:

"By the grace of our Lord and the Savior Jesus Christ and the assistance of Our Lady, I have written a teaching for the profit of both my soul and the soul of my lords [brothers] who are truly related to me in the brotherhood of one spirit. I therefore call you brothers instead of disciples [Merton interjects — "He wouldn't be called Abbot, he didn't want to be called Superior."] We have but one teacher, our Lord Jesus Christ who gave us the Scriptures and sent the holy apostles in the venerable fathers to teach the way of salvation to the human race. These saints began by doing good, only afterwards did they teach. As for me I have done no good whatsoever but I expound the teaching of the Holy Scriptures for those who desire salvation.

"It is my conviction that if it is by God's will that we are gathered together, then we should be faithful to the traditions of the saints and the Holy Fathers and to Our Lord's Commandments instead of seeking to exempt ourselves by saying that nowadays it is impossible to live according to the Scriptures and the precepts of the Fathers. We are weak indeed but we must nevertheless follow according to the measure of our strength, the example of the blessed and venerable Fathers, even though we are unable to become their equals, and that anyone who does not hold this principle must cease to harass me, wretched sinner that I am."

You get this wonderful, this tremendous seriousness that this man had. A great simplicity and great seriousness, and this idea of following the Gospel to the Holy Fathers. In a way it's very evangelical, but they get much more into evangelical later, but it's above all patristic.

Now what he goes into after this is a whole minute discussion of what's called here "mental doing." I don't know what this is. For a term like this you need to know the original Russian term, and the original Greek term that it goes back to, otherwise you don't get the picture, it's not clear. But you can get the picture when you see the whole thing that he says about it.

What he means by this is interior asceticism, I think [this] is about as close as we can come to it. And this consists in very detailed instructions for how to fight thoughts. By thoughts, he means especially thoughts that come from the eight principle vices. And so what he goes into then is a long psychological discussion of these eight principle vices and how these thoughts work and how you can stop them. What it amounts to is how you can stop having thoughts. Because after all, if you want to fight these passionate thoughts, you've got to fight all thoughts. So "Stop!"

And of course you've got to be a little critical about this, please. You've got to sit back now and don't run out into the church and start putting this immediately into practice.

So what does he say?

One of the Holy Fathers has written of the doing of the heart, the guarding of the spirit, mental concentration [Merton interjects, "All of these are bad words, you shouldn't put the term . . . especially, forget 'concentration', because concentration is absolutely the wrong thing"], each using the words which came to him under the inspiration of Divine Grace, but one thing is to be understood by these various expressions . . . from the heart come forth evil thoughts that defile a man, therefore we must purify the inner vessel and worship God in spirit and in truth.

What is this concept of spiritual labor? I think that the essence of the idea is very good. If you latch onto many of the incidentals, you'll have a hard time, but the essence is terrific.

It's the idea of working very seriously at purifying your heart, with rather minute details and distinguishing the different movements of these thoughts. He has a much more precise way of getting you to aim at what you want to hit than we have. We're very confused about this, which may be a good thing, I don't know. We tend to be quite vague about "Well, did I sin or didn't I?" That's about as far as it goes, but with him he's got all sorts of little ramifications there. But first of all, what's the background of this, this idea of purifying your heart by a struggle of interior asceticism and a fight against the eight principle vices? Where do you suppose he got that? Climacus and Cassian. So when he talks about these thoughts, his struggle against the thoughts, an excellent means of struggle. Of course he distinguishes [between] the appearance of the thought. The thought just is there. Or perhaps here [laughter]. Don't anybody get tempted! All right, the very fact that a thought is in your mind, the mere appearance of a thought is nothing, he says, still, that is where you're going to stop it. You've got to hit it as soon as it appears.

The second step where we usually get caught is what he calls dialogue with the thought. So what he's considering there, he's working on this interior business of just simply how to not consent to temptations, to thoughts that come as temptations. Of course what's the basic idea behind this? It's that these things are the devil's way of ruining your life of prayer. This stuff is put in here to get you away from praying. Now of course how are you going to fight it? Obviously what he does not say, what the Russians don't say, and they are very wise in not saying it — what they don't say is "concentrate" on something else. Because if you do that, you're sunk. You become like a handball in a handball game and do this all around the court. Because if you go from one thought to another thought, you're simply in a vicious circle. You've got to get out of the realm of prayer and into the realm of study or something like that — with study it's a different matter. You get down in the books, you get your notebook out, and you go to work on your books, then you can follow the line of thought. But that's another matter, that's reading. That's not prayer, and these fellows didn't read much.

They had the Bible and they had the — they didn't have the *Philokalia* yet, but they had very few books, and the whole thing was this interior struggle, this interior prayer to purify oneself. In a nutshell, what's the idea?

The idea is first finding your heart, getting completely centered inside where the struggle is going on, and then in your heart socking this stuff with the most powerful thing that you've got, which is the Name of Jesus. So you take the Jesus Prayer and you get this in the center of your heart and everything that comes up, WHAM! And you really don't fool around, you hit it. And you hit it out loud to begin with. You're in a cell, you're by yourself, you're not in the Church, and you learn this prayer by saying it with your lips, "Lord Jesus Christ, Son of God, have mercy on me, a sinner." Then you say that about 5,000 times. You keep saying it. And he says if the thoughts get too . . . I will stand up, see, or stretch your arms out, stay there 'til you drop, keep it up. You really work at this thing. It becomes a full time project, and you keep it up until you or the thought gives up. It's "either/or." Now of course this is a bit drastic. I don't think this is what most people need to do, but it's good to recognize that this is a basic approach that some people have. Obviously there are simpler ways of doing it, but this is the way these fellows do it.

Then, after saying it with your lips, you learn that you don't have to say it out loud, you can just whisper it, and then it gets a lot quieter and you begin to calm down quite a bit. Of course this is over a period of time. Then it becomes mental, and you think of it purely in your mind. You don't say any words anymore, and then it gets down into your heart. Mind, Heart, see. And when it gets into your heart, it's a question that the mind and the heart have to be one. This is the key to the whole thing. A very complex idea, it's a very deep idea, actually. A deep psychological idea of uniting your mind and your heart. This is the key to the whole thing. It takes an awful lot of understanding, and a great deal of work, uniting the mind and the heart. What do they mean by that? Well, that requires quite a lot of discussion. The real fruit of the thing is when the prayer becomes completely spiritual — this follows pretty much the old

Greek pattern of words, concepts, and then beyond concepts. That is the way that they go at this thing, and I think that it's very interesting. We'll come across this all the way down — there's the whole tradition, all through Russian spirituality which keeps coming back to this, and this is one of the big things in the nineteenth century. This is one of the sources of nineteenth century Russian mysticism. I think if we keep the idea of serious interior asceticism centered on this idea of a prayer of the heart which is effective in socking these things, but don't try to do it in the wrong way. Just keep in your memory that there is such a method, but that you can't do it just by wanting to. But it's something that is worth considering and you might look into it in the future as something that may have something to it. I'll say at least that much.

NOTES

1. 26 May, 1962, Tape 11, Side A. Not all of the tapes in the collection at the Merton Center, Bellarmine University, Louisville, Kentucky are marked with both contents and date. As available, the subtitles in this chapter are the titles from the cassettes in the collection.

2. Side A, 20 July 1962, Tape 24, Side B.

3. Tape 28, Side A.

4. Tape 29, Side A.

5. Tape 38, Side B.

6. November 1962, Tape 58, Sides A and B.

7. Tape 67, side A.

8. Tape 76B "1st Talk Russian Monks OPG Remarks on Christmas Rituals."

13

ORTHODOXY AND THE WORLD[1]

Thomas Merton

A book review for *Monastic Studies*.
Alexander Schmemann, *Sacraments and Orthodoxy*. New York: Herder and Herder, 1965, 142 pages. $3.50.
Alexander Schmemann, editor. *Ultimate Questions: An Anthology of Modern Russian Thought*. New York: Holt, Rinehart and Winston, 1965, 321 pages. $6.95.

Though the Communist revolution did its best to destroy the institutional fabric of Orthodoxy and though official Soviet atheism still continues to attack the stubbornly surviving Russian Church, the twentieth century has been for Catholicism an age of extraordinary theological renewal. This renewal began in the nineteenth century and gathered momentum in the lively and controversial development of "religious philosophy" in Russia before the Revolution. Names like those of Solovyov, Bulgakov and above all Berdyaev, are fairly well known in the West. They remain of course highly controversial, both within Orthodoxy and outside it. The day when westerners thought Solovyov was "a Catholic" has now set, but he is still not to be seen as simply "Orthodox." Bulgakov, the seminarist who became a Marxist, then returned to the Church, was ordained during the Revolution and expelled from Russia, taught his "sophianism" in Paris and was condemned by Orthodox Synods. Berdyaev, for all his genius, is not by any means representative of Orthodoxy nor is he a theologian. Yet there is today a genuine and powerful renewal of Orthodox theology, emanating chiefly from Paris. There is no question that the theologians trained at the Institute of St. Sergius, are among the most important of our time. It can be said that we do, here, meet with a thought that is fully modern and at the same time in accord with the rich, authentic theological tradition of the Eastern Church. Names like Evdokimov, Meyendorff and

Schmemann are by no means as well known as those of Rahner, Congar and Kung. Yet these men are just as creative, perhaps more so, and may well be, for monks, of much more decisive interest than our western theologians, with the possible exception of Han Urs Von Balthasar.

Fr. Alexander Schmemann, new dean of the Orthodox seminary in New York, still in his forties, has recently published two important books, an anthology and a theological essay, which complement each other in giving us an excellent introduction to modern Orthodox thought. *Ultimate Questions*, the anthology, takes us back before the revolution. It is a more difficult and less rewarding book than *Sacraments and Orthodoxy*, a powerful, articulate and indeed creative essay in sacramental theology which rivals Schillebeeckx and in some ways excels him. Less concerned than Schillebeeckx with some of the technical limitations of Catholic sacramental thought, Schmemann can allow himself to go to the very root of the subject without having to apologize for his forthrightness or for his lack of interest in trivialities.

Let the reader be warned. If he is now predisposed to take a comfortable, perhaps excitingly mysterious, excursion into the realm of a very "mystical" and highly "spiritual" religion, the gold-encrusted cult thick with the smoke of incense and populated with a legion of gleaming icons in the sacred gloom, a "liturgy which to be properly performed requires not less than twenty-seven heavy liturgical books," he may find himself disturbed by Fr. Schmemann's presentation. Certainly, Sacraments and Orthodoxy will repudiate nothing of the deep theological and contemplative sense of Orthodox faith and worship. But the author is intent on dispelling any illusions about the place of "religion" in the world today. In fact, one would not suspect from the title of this book, it is one of the strongest and clearest statements of position upon this topic of the Church and the world.

Where does Orthodoxy stand in relation to the world of the twentieth century? I do not know to what extent we can accept the jacket blurb which describes Fr. Schmemann as "a leading spokesman of Russian Orthodoxy in this generation." The word "leading" can hardly be taken without serious qualification to mean "official." Let us simply say that here is an Orthodox theologian who has a great deal to say with which perhaps some Orthodox bishops might not yet be quite ready to agree. He is not speaking for the kind of conservative and old guard Orthodoxy one remembers from Russian literature of the last century and which perhaps still exists here and there. But he is equally definite in rejecting the more frantic forms of progressivism — the "honest to God" school which, to find itself a place in the modern world, supposes that the most honest thing a Christian can say about God is that he is dead. (This "honesty" at once brings him alive again in the encounter which is then established — one hopes — with the unbeliever. Thus the "resurrection" is reduced to a psychological expression of sincerity of the part of the unbeliever.)

It is characteristic of Fr. Schmemann's approach that the two questions: the nature of the sacraments and the place of the "Church in the world" resolve themselves into being pretty much the same. It is in fact by the sacraments (even more than by preaching or by other forms of activity) that the Church exercises her mission in the world. To make clear what he thinks about the nature of the sacraments, he naturally has to talk about the Church. To make clear what he understands by the Church, he has to talk about the relation of the Church to the World, since the Church is defined precisely by her mission in the world. It is in protesting against the false ideas of the Church, her mission, and her relation to the world, that Fr. Schmemann makes his most valuable and indeed indispensable contribution to current thought on sacramental theology. His book is an indispensable contribution, above all for monks, because he takes a view which is most germane to us and resolves some of the false problems that have been raised in monasteries by an "activist" and indeed "secularist" concept of the Church's role in the world.

First, however, Fr. Schmemann unequivocally rejects the old, short-sighted view which divides the "sacred" from the "secular," the "Church" from the "world," the "spiritual" from the "material," and the "natural" from the "supernatural" in such a way as to make these seem completely irreconcilable both in theory and in practice.

Is the sacramental life (or for that matter the monastic life) simply defined by the fact that it is restricted to a special sacred realm from which all that is "worldly," all that is "natural," all that is "material," is resolutely and forever excluded? Is the realm of God in the world a realm of "pure spirituality" and cult, a kind of mystic enclave in a doomed, unredeemable creation? Is the function of the worshipping Christian, and above all of the monk, to testify, by spirituality and by cult, that the world around him is damned, or at least irrelevant and absurd? Is the function of a monastery to create a little oasis of spiritual life and light in the darkness of fallen and reprobate society given entirely to the love and cult of matter? Must the monks achieve this end by reproving and rejecting every form of interest in the concerns, indeed the tragedies, of their fellow men, and cutting off all contact with them because all that happens in the world is "worldly" and therefore an offense in the sight of an all-pure and infinitely irritated God?

This gnostic perversion of the monastic ideal is surely one of the great offenses against truth in which we are called upon to disavow in our time. It does not affect monks only. Fr. Schmemann incisively describes the ambiguities of a contemporary pseudo-Christianity in which well meaning priests and theologians try to preserve, in principle, this view of the Church's relation to the world, while at the same time selling religion to the world with messages of jollity, methods of self-fulfillment through cult, and all kinds of pseudo-psychiatric help. As if these expedients proved that one can step into the realm of the sacred on Sundays without ceasing to be thoroughly up to date and adapted in modern society!

On the one hand, Schmemann says, "It is difficult to convince the modern Christian that to be the life of the world the Church must not 'keep smiling' at the world, putting the 'all welcome' signs on the Churches and adjusting its language to that of the last best-seller." On the other hand, this very same sales pitch ("religion is lively, up to date, utterly fulfilling, and a lot of fun") has in fact brought Christians unconsciously to the point of accepting "the whole joyless *ethos* of our joyless and business-minded culture."

Do not misunderstand this argument. It is much more devastating than it appears to be. It is not the familiar and well-worn accusation that religion is going to the dogs because it is not religious enough, not spiritual enough, not sacred enough, not liturgical enough, not ascetic enough etc. It is on the contrary a rather sobering indictment of pettifogging "religiosity," "spirituality," "sacredness," perhaps even "liturgy" and certainly "asceticism" for being in large measure to blame for the continued secularizing of Christianity. The principle on which Fr. Schmemann bases this accusation is that to adopt, without qualification, an idea of the sacred, the spiritual, the ascetic, and so on which reduces God's domain to one area — that of official religion — is by that very fact to establish the world as a secular realm in its own right and this leads in fact inevitably to the triumph of a secular mentality, even within the Church.

The heart of Fr. Schmemann's argument is that the Church's vocation to worship and witness in the world is a vocation to a completely eucharistic view of all creation, a view which, far from setting aside worship and confining it to a special limited area of cult, sees and celebrates the world itself as "meaningful because it is the sacrament of God's presence." "Life itself," he continues, in terms that would perhaps disconcert those habituated to the strict logical categories of scholastic thought, "is worship." "We were created as celebrants of the sacrament of life." Man is regarded by Fr. Schmemann as naturally *homo adorans*, the high priest of creation, the "priest of the cosmic sacrament" (the material world).

Even in his most fallen and alienated state, far from the Church and from the vision of God, man remains hungry for the eucharistic life. He longs, unconsciously, to enter into the sacred banquet, the wedding feast, the celebration of the victory of life over death. But his tragedy is that he is caught in a fallen world which is confused and opaque, which is no longer seen as "sacrament" but accepted as an end in itself. That is to say, it is no longer seen as a gift to be received from God in gladness and returned to Him in praise and celebration. It is accepted on its own terms as an area in which the individual ego engages in a desperate struggle against time to attain some measure of happiness and self-fulfillment before death inevitably ends everything. Even when he seeks a "religious" answer to his predicament in the fallen world, man finds himself struggling to produce "good behavior" to make things come out so that he will have happiness in the world — or, failing that, in the next.

Even Christianity sometimes ends up by being a pseudo Christian happiness cult, a judicious combination of ethical tranquilizing and sacramental happy-making, plus a dash of art and a splash of political realism (a crusade!). This of course calls for specialists in counselling, men trained to give the right answers, engineers of uplift! "Adam failed to be the priest of the world and because of this failure the world ceased to be the sacrament of the divine love and presence and became 'nature'. And in this 'natural' world, religion became an organized transaction with the supernatural and the priest was set apart as the transactor." It is precisely from this state of affairs that secularism arises: "Clericalism is the father of secularism."

True to the tradition of the Greek Fathers, Fr. Schmemann sees all life as "cosmic liturgy," and views man as restored by the Incarnation to his place in that liturgy so that, with Christ and in Christ, he resumes his proper office as high priest in a world that is essentially liturgical and eucharistic. The function of the Church (and of the sacraments) is then to lead all mankind back on a sacred journey to reconciliation with the Father. In the liturgy, the Church calls together all men and invites them to join ranks with her and, in answer to the "tidings of great joy," to go out in procession to meet the Lord and enter with Him into the wedding banquet which is His Kingdom of joy and love.

*   *   *

One must doubtless read *Sacraments and Orthodoxy* if one wants to appreciate some of the more difficult pieces in

Ultimate Questions. Among these, for example, is the tantalizing essay on the Holy Spirit by Pavel Florensky, one of the leaders of the pre-revolutionary religious renewal in Russia, who died in a Siberian concentration camp in the early fifties. Here again, the main theme is "the Church and the world," and the right conception of a Christianity which is more than uplift, more than *ethos*, and more that gnostic theosophy: essentially the Gift of the Spirit. Florensky ends his essay by quoting a sublime prayer of St. Symeon the New Theologian. It is long and profound. A few lines must be quoted here (pages 170-171):

> Come, true light. Come, life eternal. Come, hidden mystery. Come, nameless treasure. Come, that which is beyond words. Come, Person Who flees from human comprehension. Come, unceasing courage. Come, true hope of all the saved. Come, resurrection of the dead. Come, O mighty One; thou Who art eternally creating, reforming, and changing all things by a mere sign. Come, thou wholly invisible, sacred, and intangible One. Come, thou Who dwellest eternally immovable even though thou dost bestir thyself hourly to come to us who languish in hell while thou livest above all heavens. Come, Name that is most strictly forbidden to speak about thee and what thou art or to know what thy nature is and who thou art. Come, eternal joy. Come, garland unfading. Come, great God and Lord of our realm.

Almost all the essays in *Ultimate Questions* are in one way or another perplexing if not disconcerting. The Meditations of Fr. Bulgakov on the Joy of the Resurrection are perhaps likely to appeal more immediately to most western readers. We must be grateful to Fr. Schmemann for giving us here, for the first time in English, a text of Fyodorov, one of the most extraordinary religious writers I have ever read. I hasten to add that he has been accused of all kinds of heresy, and that his fantastic conceptions give grounds for the accusation. And yet he remains a figure of unique and most compelling interest, not to say fascination. He is not for the unstable or the untrained, but his message (which one cannot begin to summarize here) is of permanent importance, even though it may in the end seem absurd. (Note that the essay given here does not present a full view of Fyodorov's extremism. Berdyaev fills out the picture in *The Russian Idea*.)

Another disconcerting and very important essay is that of V.V. Rozanov: "Sweet Jesus and the Sour Fruits of the World." This has already appeared in *Cross Currents*, and it demands to be widely read if only because it will shock us into a more objective re-examination of our progressive triumphalism. Here again the theme of the Church and the world is treated, but with the most radical and uncompromising pessimism. Not even Barth and his followers have more ruthlessly and more sweepingly rejected all possible claims for the legitimacy of a Christian humanism. With savage irony, Rozanov declares that the efforts of Russian Christian humanists before the revolution were mere parlor games, seeking to harmonize the love of Christ with the love of art and "sipping it all out of the same pot of tea."

When St. Paul had a day off, says Rozanov, he did not go to the Greek theater to take in one of the tragedies. He did not propose to the Athenians "that they believe in Christ and at the same time go to the Olympic games."

Rozanov is of course frankly one-sided. He does not see the whole picture. He does not procede to reconcile the opposites (which Schmemann does). But his shocking insight is salutary. It is not mere prudery, mere pessimism. It is not even the gnostic or manichaean division which sees the world as irreconcilable with Christ. True, you have to read *Sacraments and Orthodoxy* before you can really grasp what Rozanov is trying to say. But in the end it becomes clear that both for Rozanov and for Schmemann one thing is very clear: Christianity cannot be content to propose a certain amount of cult, a certain degree of good behavior, and then, duty being accomplished, let man live comfortably and prosperously, facing death with equanimity. Christianity is not in the world just to help man find adjustment, happiness and "fulfillment." Since Christ died on the Cross, it is no longer permitted to man to regard the world as a place in which to have fun.

The choice that presents itself to man is not the choice between good clean fun blessed by the Church, earned by the fulfillment of tedious duty, and wicked fun cursed in every pulpit, bought at the price of neglect and rebellion. No: the choice is between the eschatological joy of the Resurrection, and the frustration and despair of the kingdom of death.

There remains one most devastating argument against the Christianity which is content to "offer help," to aid man in accepting suffering, to show him how to live a decent life, to urge him onward up the steep path of duty, while permitting him recreation and entertainment lest he give up. In actual fact, such Christianity (says Fr. Schmemann) no longer celebrates life as a gift, no longer thanks God for the Lord's victory over death. It has merely come to terms with death. Therefore it is thinly disguised paganism. It is well satisfied if people will keep the moral law, fulfill their religious ideas, and live so as to merit a Christian burial. It is concerned to see that everyone finishes his course creditably and is certified as saved. His tombstone is the sign of his justification. It is visible evidence of a righteousness that can no longer be menaced or removed. This kind of Christianity, this reconciliation with death, has altogether ceased to be a revelation of life. If it is, for the modern world, an anachronism or a scandal, this is not the fault of "the world."

"To accept God's world as a cosmic cemetery which is to be abolished and replaced by another world which looks like a cemetery ('eternal rest') and to call this religion, to live in a cosmic cemetery and to 'dispose' every day of thousands of corpses and to get excited about a 'great society' and to be happy — this is the fall of man. It is not the immorality of the crimes of man that reveal him as a fallen being: it is his 'positive ideal' — religious or secular — and his satisfaction with this ideal."

True Christianity, and therefore true sacramental life, is the manifestation of the Living Presence of the Lord, victorious over death leading us all, with Him, though death to life. Death itself then becomes an act of life and an "act of communion with life." To be a true Christian, to die and rise with Christ in the sacramental life of the Church, in faith and in the works

of love, is more than "fulfilling religious duties." It is possession of the Holy Spirit, who teaches us how to live as citizens
of the heavenly Kingdom here and now, and whose fruits in
us bear witness to the eschatological joy of forgiveness and redemption. The Christian's view of the world is not that of a
gnoticism which condemns matter, not of scientism which develops a mystique of matter, but of eschatology which sees the
world as God's gift, fallen and redeemed. Hence, in the words
of Bulgakov, "The life of the age to come is not a simple negation of this age, not its annihilation, but making eternal of everything in it worthy of such a transformation." "While maintaining its own nature, this age passes into the next, is transformed in it, as the body of Our Lord Jesus Christ was transformed in the Resurrection.

The key word is *transformation*, or perhaps even one
might say *transfiguration*. The true Christian does not gloat
over the world's imminent destruction, nor does he expect
its transformation and "spiritualization" though the evolution
of forces implanted in matter. He sees the world already
blessed and redeemed by the resurrection of Christ, wanting
to be transformed by the power of the Holy Spirit. But
the Orthodox theologians see clearly that "the glorification
of creation in the Resurrection is accomplished by the
power of God . . . from within death, by death itself."
(Bulgakov). The Resurrection is "eternal life shining out
of death." To evade or ignore death, or to use the Cross as
a kind of lucky charm that neutralizes the force of death, is
to turn against the Resurrection and therefore to enter into
what is inevitably a cult of the death which one is trying to
escape. Our "death-denying culture" is therefore, precisely
because it is death-denying, a supreme affirmation of death
(extermination camps, the atomic bomb, etc). A Christianity
which is content to accept the categories of such a culture
is, therefore partly responsible for the ideal of the world as
"cosmic cemetery."

This book clearly shows the insufficiency of positions
that are conventional and conservative. But it also demonstrates
the folly of a "progressive" Christianity (and a "progressive

monasticism") which sees no further than the perspectives of a busy, prosperous, actively worshipping Church (monastery of happy citizens — monks — in a comfortable, well-ordered society community).

Our necessary efforts at monastic renewal can hardly have any real meaning unless they procede from a deep and authentic Christian understanding of the monk's place in the world and his relation to it. As these two books show, we run the risk of following one of two misdirected theological orientations. The first of these will continue to assume that the function of the monk is to accentuate the Church's supposed rejection of the world as evil, by huddling together in a tightly enclosed, artificial climate of cult, asceticism and contemplation. The other, sensing the futility and falsity of this exaggerated view, will perhaps go to the other extreme in an equally misguided activism. It will seek to justify the monastic life by a participation in the world dictated by "the world's" own terms. That is to say, it will turn the monastic life, by various active methods, into a cult of self-fulfillment which ignores and evades the reality of death and which therefore remains closed to the mystery of the Resurrection, the mystery of life in death, the mystery of the Holy Spirit.

The true way of the monk is in fact not to be sought in devising some explicit or implicit answer to any special problems which the world may have formulated for itself. The monk is not a man of answers. He need not be concerned with either an optimistic nor a pessimistic attitude toward these questions, however crucial they may seem. His life is an expression of eschatological hope and joy, of the presence of the Lord in His creation which He has redeemed and which, by the power of the Spirit, He will transform. When this is understood, the monastic life will be seen for what it is: complete openness to the Spirit, and hence openness to all that is blessed by God, whether in "the world" or out of it.

It is in this sense that without proposing this or that "answer" to the problems of social injustice, war, racism, technology, automation, etc., the monk will be all the more open, in compassion and love, to his brother in the world, because he is liberated, by his vocation, from the false answers dictated by the world itself. This openness is illusory unless it is explicitly paid for by obedience to the Spirit and to the word of the Cross.

NOTE

1. *Monastic Studies* 4 (Advent 1966: 105-115).

Icon of the Holy Spirit. Crete, sixteenth century.

APPENDIX

THE ROLE OF OUR LADY
IN THE HESYCHASTE PRAYER

Rama Coomaraswamy

*[On the Rosary: The following essay is a talk given at the Confer-
ence on Merton and Hesychasm sponsored by the Thomas Merton
Foundation in 2001. The Hesychaste prayer referred to is "Jesus
Christ, Have Mercy upon me, a sinner." While the conference was
primarily concerned with Thomas Merton's interest in this prayer, it
provided an opportunity for sharing some insights into the nature of
the Rosary.]*

> *Jesus's Name and Person are one and the same.*
> *– St. Bernadine of Sienna*

While *Hesychasm* can refer to the "whole complex of theory
and practice which constitutes the path," the present paper attempts to limit itself to the so-called *Hesychaste* prayer. It
is often thought that this prayer is limited to the classical formula,
"Lord Jesus Christ, have mercy on me a sinner." I think this is
to forget what is central to this prayer, namely the Name of Jesus.
Remove from this prayer the Divine Name, and one voids it
of its essential power. The Name can of course be incorporate
in the West. Whatever the setting, it is the Name which is of
the Essence.

It is often said that the *Hesychaste* prayer in the western church
is manifested within the Rosary. Whether or not this is in fact
the case — my book on The Invocation of the Name of Jesus as
practiced in the western Church clearly shows that the variety of
forms, such as are still familiar in the East were once equally
familiar in the West. The fifteen decade Rosary, so common in
the West from the twelfth century onwards, clearly incorporates
within its formula, the invocation of both the Names of Jesus
and Mary.[1] It would seem, however, that in the West the
Invocation of the Name of Jesus is more closely linked to Mary

than in the East. Why, one might ask, is this close relationship so much insisted upon? This is not to suggest any lack of Marial devotion in the East — one has only to view the icons of Our Lady to realize that such an idea would be false, and indeed, the Greek Rosary or "prayer rope" starts with the following prayer on the red bead: "O great Mother of God Mary Most Holy, Intercede for me and save me." However, not only is the repetition of the Names of Jesus and Mary closely linked in the Rosary; but many Western saints have united them in prayer in the form "*Jesu-Maria,*" and Joan of Arc did so on her banner. Why should this be the case? I would like to share with you a few speculations, using the word *speculation* in its mystical sense, for we see through a mirror darkly, and yet to probe the matter one needs to reflect within by means of the Light of Grace, and at the same time to avoid scrupulously any attempt at being original.

I should like to start out by recalling to you an old fairly tale, the relevance of which will become clearer later, *Snow White and the Seven Dwarfs.* Snow White was persuaded by the wicked stepmother or witch to eat the poisoned apple and fell asleep. She didn't die, and the Dwarfs, the various human faculties, were able to function and keep her alive, but it was only when she was kissed by the Sun-Prince that she recovered. Or again, I would mention the well known story of St. George and the Dragon. It was only after the dragon was slain that the princess was released. Now in point of fact, many of us are like Snow White, asleep to reality, and like the princess, enthralled to the dragon. It is in these paradigms that one begins to get some clues to the problem.

Meister Eckhart said that it was of little import to him if Jesus was born of Mary in history, if He is not born in him, here and now. And he adds elsewhere that, if one would have Jesus born in one, one must become the Virgin Mary. Mystical theologians have spoken of the Spirit blowing on the Waters at the time of the world's creation as a foreshadowing of Jesus being conceived by Mary by the same Holy Spirit. In a sense there are two Marys — though of course there is only one. If there is a temporal and eternal birth of the Son of God, there must also be a temporal and eternal birth of His mother.[2] And indeed, Scripture places these words in the "mouth" of Our Lady:

> "The Lord possessed me in the beginning of his way, before his works of old. I was set up from everlasting, from the beginning, or ever the earth was. . . . When he prepared the heavens I was there. . . . I was by him, as one brought up with him: and I was daily his delight, rejoicing always before him, rejoicing in the habitable parts of his earth and my delights were with the sons of men. When there were no depths, I was brought forth. Before the hills were, I was brought forth."

Protestants frequently complain about the honor Catholics pay to the Blessed Virgin. This is based on their complete misunderstanding of what the Blessed Virgin represents in the divine economy. Now the Blessed Virgin exemplifies for us all the qualities of the perfected soul, and in honoring her we also make her the model of our spiritual life. We must be born of her, and invoking the name of Jesus, which is to ask the Name, that is Jesus Himself, to be present in us, requires that we be conformed to the Blessed Virgin in our souls. Eckhart describes the state of the Virgin's soul at the time of the Annunciation:

> She was sitting in time untimely. She was sitting, a creature uncreaturely. . . . Her soul was deiform. Her spirit was contemplating God. . . . To her nothing at all under God was of any account. Her heart was aflame with the truth. Clear consciousness was her school. Heaven was her cell. Divinity was her reading. . . . She was liberated from creatures and set upon God alone. . . . She was in the land of freedom.[3]

This is the fertile ground in which the Name can strike roots. Apart from this, like seed cast upon rocks or in a dry ground, no germination occurs. To borrow a phrase from Tibetan Buddhism, the Divine Name is the "Jewel in the Lotus" — the Lotus being equivalent to the Rose, the flower which metaphysically represents Our Lady.

What then are the Marial virtues which we should desire to acquire? The answer lies in part in the *Magnificat*, every phrase of which is incidentally drawn from the Old Testament, and which is repeatedly brought to our minds and hearts in the Divine Office. First of all, Mary, when praised by Elizabeth because of her Divine Motherhood, immediately deflected this praise to God who alone is worthy of such praise. And further, as Denis the Carthusian and St. Ambrose state, it is His Image that should be magnified in us. And further, she did not simply say God be magnified, but *magnificat anima mea* – "my soul doth magnify the Lord."

Et exultet spiritus mea in Deo salutari meo. Scripture which never wastes a word makes a distinction between her soul (*anima*) and her Spirit (*spiritus*). Jean Borella comments on this distinction between the soul that magnifies the Lord, and the Spirit that exalts in God. First of all he points out that this speaks to the tripartite nature of man, the fact that all of us are so "constructed" as to have within us the hierarchy of Spirit, *psyche* and body, which is why we must love God with all our heart-Spirit, with all our souls-*psyche*, and with all our strength-body. He then tells us that the soul – *anima, psyche* – glorifies the Lord because it is perfectly pure and virginal because it reflects the Divine Light of the Spirit integrally and the Divine Light is the light of glory. The Spirit exults in God Himself because it is encompassed by the Divine. The soul's perfection is its virginal annihilation, its status of being a pure mirror; the perfection of the Spirit is its exultation, its deifying participation in the eternal dance of Divine Love.

It is clear that Mary is in no way exalting herself – there is no "I" or ego in her response; she is not exalting in herself, but in her Bridegroom – as St. Paul said, "He who glories in God [truly] glorifies." She is clearly, as Dennis the Carthusian states, "illuminated by divine contemplation and fervent love." It is generally understood that in this exchange between herself and Elizabeth, she manifests the virtue of humility. Now humility is often misunderstood as seeking to be lowly in this world. To understand it more clearly, it is good to contrast it with pride which is nothing other than self-love. True humility is the absence of all self-love. It is because of this that she states that "all generations shall call me blessed." Once again, the Blessed Virgin ascribes all this to God "for He who is mighty has made me great." Now all this may seem to be a digression, but what

follows is pertinent to the subject under discussion, for
what follows is *Et sanctum nomen eus* — and Holy is His Name.
If in fact we must become like unto the Virgin, then in acquiring
the various qualities outlined above we, as it were, prepare the
ground in which His Name is Holy in us. The Name apart from
this preparation may have some benefit, may even direct us
towards obtaining these virtues, but it is to a great extent sterile,
for as Christ said, "not everyone who cries Lord Lord, will be
saved. . . . " It is therefore of the greatest importance that the
Name be invoked in a certain setting, a setting of self sacrifice, a
setting in which we, as far as is possible, extrude from ourselves
all self love. *Et miseracordia eius*, for in this setting His mercy
not only will, but *must* flow forth. And indeed, His mercy is
necessary if we are to void in our souls all traces of self-love, for
as He Himself taught, we can do nothing by ourselves.

Mary, preserved from original sin, is the pure creature as God
had willed it to be and just as it came forth from his hands. In
her we contemplate human nature in all of its purity. But what
is this pure nature? The angel of the Annunciation reveals it. It
is "full of grace." In her, God has found the perfect creature
whose will makes itself the receptacle of the Divine Will ("I am
the handmaid of the Lord") to make possible our salvation ("be
it unto me according to thy word"). Here we clearly see how
"the work of creation" and "the work of salvation," the *opus
creationis* and the *opus salutis*, are reunited; it is in Mary that this
joining, this reversal, this conversion of the creative work into
the redemptive work comes about. It is she who offers the Grace
that human nature needed for its work, she who gives to the Divine Word a human nature perfectly obedient to the Father's Will,
which calls for the incarnation of the Son. And it is therefore
within Mary that the key to the supernatural mystery of our
nature abides.

The exemplary perfections of Our Lady are also brought forth
to us by St. Ambrose:

"Virginity is thus proposed to us, as if in a picture, in
Mary's life. From her life, the beauty of her chastity and
her exemplary virtue shine out as from a mirror. Here you
may well receive instruction on how to lead a life in which

virtue, instructed by example, shows you what you must do, correct, or avoid." (*Expositio in Lucam* 2:24.)

This raises the issue of virginity, for few of us are such in the body. While in no way depreciating that sacrifice which perpetual virginity involves — at least for those who do not let their lamps go out for lack of oil, oil being a symbol of wisdom — it is important to understand how her virginity applies to us. As Philo said: "the union of human beings that is made for the procreation of children, turns virgins into women. But when God begins to consort with the soul, He makes what before was a woman into a virgin again." On the feast of St. Agnes the following prayer is incorporated into the liturgy: "When I love him I am chaste; when I touch him I am pure; when I possess him, I am a virgin." Again St. Augustine tells us that "as soon as Naamon had been washed from the stains of the body and mind, he was no longer a leper, but became a spotless virgin without wrinkle." St. Mark the Ascetic in the *Philokalia* tells us: "He who wishes to achieve true, undefiled and complete virginity . . . . struggles to put to death every trace and stirring of passion itself. . . . He prays for the disappearance even of the mere thought of lust, occurring as a momentary disturbance of the intellect. . . . He who hopes to achieve pure spiritual and undefiled virginity crucifies the flesh through ascetic labors and puts to death whatever is earthly in him through intense and persistent self control." Christ Himself said to Margaret of Cortona, a married woman and the mother of several children: "My daughter, your many penances have purified your soul from all the effects of sin to such a degree that your contrition and your sufferings will reintegrate you into the purity of a virgin." No wonder then that St. Therese of Liseaux wrote to her married sister that "we must be virginized."

One final quote on this topic from the English poet John Cordelier:

> Of pure Virgins none
> > Is fairer seen
> Save one
> > Than Mary Magdalene.

And so it is that, if we are to invoke the divine Name, we must take Mary as our *exemplar*. Just as the Spirit "blew" upon the waters at the time of creation, so also the Name which is one with the Spirit must blow upon the well prepared soil. That soil need not be perfect, but it must be sufficiently fertile to allow the Name to grow with us. Marco Pallis, with whom Thomas Merton carried on an extensive correspondence, spoke to this very point: "Mystical experience on the cheap, that is to say, minus any requirement that the would-be disciple should adhere to that religious form where the esoteric teachings he seeks originated . . . . beware of the professing 'master' who offers Sufism without Islam, or a Tibetan Tantric initiation without Buddhism, or the *Jesu* prayer without Christianity. . . . " As the *Book of Privy Counseling* states, "I am presuming, of course, that you have been duly absolved of your sins, general and particular, as Holy Church requires. Otherwise, I should never approve of you or anyone else beginning this work." (Chapter 2.) To invoke the Name apart from Mary and all that Mary represents, runs the risk of self delusion and even self hypnosis such as occurs when any sort of ejaculatory prayer is used outside of the proper context.

But there is yet another aspect of the problem. It is important to understand that when Scripture speaks of "men," it intends to include all mankind, both women and men, and we must recognize — which hardly seems necessary — that women and man are similar in their relationship to God. As Scripture says: "there is neither male nor female: for ye are all one in Christ Jesus" (*Galatians* 3:28). But if in God there is no separation of nature from essence, there is in manifestation such a separation — such being necessary for creation. Hence nature is passive relative to the active or generating force, and this passivity — which is productive — is depicted as feminine. This is why God, who in His essence is neither male nor female, is in manifestation depicted as male. This same relationship of the active to the passive is reflected both in marriage, and in the relationship between the Spirit and the *Psyche*. The traditional view of man, as mentioned above, holds that man consists of the Spirit of God — His Image — which resides in all of us; the *psyche* which includes our thinking processes and opinions; and the Body. Adam was made in the Image and Likeness of God. With the fall, he lost the likeness, or in other words, his *psyche* lost that unity with the Spirit that existed before the fall, before he had partaken of "Snow White's poisoned apple," and it is our task of all of us to regain that likeness. Now in the individual it is the Spirit which must seek out the psyche, and it is the psyche which must desire to be wedded to the Spirit. But the *psyche* must be prepared for the wedding — must be dressed in that pure white wedding garment that symbolizes her purity so that the Word, joined to her, can be fecund. (While we all carry within us this tripartite structure of Spirit, Soul — which includes our thinking processes — and body, the *psyche* and body are frequently considered as a single psycho-physical entity, and hence it is often said that *Duo sunt in homine*, or again that there is a distinction between the Greater Self or Spirit, and the lesser self and that these two, as St. Paul said, can be at war with one another.)

Now relative to the Spirit, the psycho-physical is feminine. Indeed, as one of the Eastern sacred texts states: "all creation is feminine relative to God." He — the Spirit — is the bridegroom to whom we should all aspire to be married. It is in this setting that the kiss of the magic prince allows for the healing of Snow White — a kiss not unlike that which the would be bride in the *Canticle of Canticles* states, "let Him kiss me with the kiss of His lips." Again, the slaying of the dragon by St. George allows for the princess to be wed. *Genesis* tells us that Adam was made in the Image and likeness of God.

The word "soul" can be confusing, and it is oft forgot that, if there is a soul that is to be saved, there is also a soul that is to be utterly rejected. Mediaeval authors distinguished between the *anima* (feminine) and the *animus* or "*intellectus vel Spiritus*" (masculine). Because the concept tends to be unfamiliar, allow me to quote some of the Church Fathers: *Duns Scotus* tells us: "The woman is the rational soul [*anima*], whose husband [literally *vir* or 'man' (with the connotation of 'active power') not *maritus* or *conjunx*] is understood to be the *animus*, which is variously named now intellect [*intellectus*], now mind [*mens*], now *animus* and often even spirit [*spiritus*]. This is the husband of whom the Apostle speaks, 'the head of the woman is the man, the head of the man is Christ, the head of Christ is God.' In other words, the head of the *anima* is the *intellectus*, and the head of the *intellectus* is Christ. Such is the natural order of the human creature. The soul must be submitted to the rule of the mind, the mind to Christ, and thereby the whole being is submitted through Christ to God the Father. . . . Spirit revolves perpetually about God and is therefore well named the husband and guide of the other parts of the soul, since between it and its creator no creature is interposed. Reason in turn revolves around the knowledge and causes of created things, and whatever spirit receives through eternal contemplation it transmits to reason and reason commends to memory. The third part of the soul is interior sense, which is subordinate to reason as the faculty which is superior to it, and by means of reason is also subordinate to spirit. Finally, below the interior sense in the natural order is the exterior sense, through which the whole soul nourishes and rules the fivefold bodily senses and animates the whole body. Since, therefore, reason can receive nothing of the gifts from on high unless through her husband, the spirit, which holds the chief place of all nature, the woman or *anima* is rightly ordered to call her husband or *intellectus* with whom and by whom she may drink spiritual gifts and without whom she may in no wise participate in gifts from on high. For this reason Jesus says to her [the Samaritan woman at the well], 'Call your husband, come hither.' Do not have the presumption to come to me without your husband. For, if the intellect is absent, one may not ascend to the heights of theology, nor participate in spiritual gifts."[4]

Again, Origen teaches "Let us see also allegorically how man, made in the image of God, is male and female. Our inner man consists of spirit and soul. The spirit is said to be male; the soul can be called female. If these have concord and agreement among themselves, they increase and multiply by the very accord among themselves and they produce sons, good inclinations and understandings. . . . The soul united with the spirit and, so to speak, joined in wedlock. . . . " Marriage, as Hugh of St. Victor says, is an external sign representing the *dilectio mutua animorum* of the wedded pair; and this mutual affection symbolizes the love by which God and the soul are bound together when the latter is adorned with supernatural grace. St. Bonaventure likewise de-

scribes the relations existing between Christ and the individual
soul as typical of the relations which should exist between the
bridegroom and the bride, a union "begun here in grace and con-
summated in glory."

We see then the importance of Mary — and why "all generations shall call me blessed." We see also why she is the setting
which allows for the full effectiveness of the invocation of the
Name. Ultimately, of course, it is the Spirit of God who invokes
the Name in us, and its reverberations transform our souls, and
even our bodies, bringing them into unity with the Spirit. With
this in view, let us point out some other aspects of the Rosary as
currently used in the West.

Consider first, some of the symbolism, remembering that a
genuine symbol is not something arbitrarily made up, but is more
properly defined as the representation of reality on a certain level
of reference by a corresponding reality on another level. The
Rosary — the word literally means a "rose garden," and as such
reminds us of Paradise — consists of 153 beads, parallel to the
153 fish caught, according to St. John, when Christ called the
Apostles to become "fishers of men." The Cross is suspended
from the rosary, for in fact all the merits we derive from saying
the Rosary derive from the Cross. We bless ourselves, as we do
at the start of every effort. We follow with the Creed which affirms our faith, a primary condition for the granting of our prayers.
The pendant beads 1-3-1 recall to mind the Trinity. The single
beads, reminding us of the unity or oneness in God who is the
beginning and end of all things. This unity is recalled again with
each decade. The six large beads (*Paters*) represent the six days
of creation. The seventh large bead is replaced by a piece of metal
symbolic of the seventh day and the period of rest at the end of
the Rosary. This piece of metal has three corners, once again
representative of the Trinity. The five decades are like five rose
petals. It is the number of man and also of the five wounds of
Christ. Ten is the symbol of perfection. The Jews did not have
numbers, but used letters to signify number — and 15 is that of
the greatest power. Moses tells us that the flood rose to the height
of a decade and five. The beads are strung on a rope or cord,
which like the golden thread leads us through the labyrinth of

life. One is reminded of Blake's statement: "I give you the end of a golden string. Only wind it into a ball; It will lead you in at heaven's gate; Built in Jerusalem's wall."

There have been many rosaries used in the Church, and even today many of these are still in use such as the Chaplet of St. Michael, or the one described by St. John Eudes which consisted of 33 beads on which one said simply *Jesu-Maria*. However, it would seem that Our Lady has particularly encouraged the use of the 15 decade Rosary as she always has this Rosary in her hands during her recent apparitions — perhaps because it is so pertinent to the days in which we live. Families often say five decades at night with their children, as the full 15 would be hard for them to follow.[5] If we are to adopt the virtues and attitudes of Our Lady, what better way than to join her in our passage through life? The Rosary recapitulates the story of Our Lady on earth and in glory; the story of Christ's manifestation on earth and his glorious ascension, and the story of the Church. It is also the exemplifying story of the individual soul — it is in fact all of these, for if we are Baptized in Christ, Crucified with Christ and are Resurrected with Christ, all these aspects are intimately tied together.

The fifteen decades are divided into three sets — the Joyful, Sorrowful and Glorious Mysteries. These also relate to the purgative, illuminative and unitive stages of the spiritual life, for as is clear from what was said at the beginning, in saying the Rosary, we are traversing the entire spiritual journey of the soul. Every spiritual path includes these three great degrees: "purification," which causes "the world to depart from man"; "expansion," which causes "the Divine to enter into man': and "union," which causes "man to enter into God." One can also describe these three stages as Fear, Love and Union. By following the Rosary, one opens the soul — firstly to the grace which separates from the world, secondly to that which draws one to God, and thirdly to that which, if one may so express it, "reintegrates" one in God.

As every soul must to a certain extent travel its own path, so also no one can give an interpretation of the Rosary which is in any sense complete. As the early Jewish fathers taught, Scripture (from which the Rosary is drawn) is like an anvil. When struck, a thousand sparks fly. However, among the possibilities are those mentioned in what follows:

Consider the first mystery: the angel Gabriel greets the Blessed Virgin — and indeed, each and every soul — offering to the soul the annunciation, for indeed we are all called by grace and hopefully will answer, "be it done to me according to Thy Word." And having made this "*fiat*," immediately charity is manifested in our actions — as with Mary who walked 15 miles barefoot to the home of the elderly Elizabeth, who was six months pregnant — residing with her until she delivered. Now the soul, perfected in charity, gives birth to Jesus — which is our third mystery.

What follows is the presentation to the temple: Our Lady sacrificing, at the age of three — as the Blessed Emmerich tells us — the warmth and love of her home and entering the temple, thus submitting to all the forms of what can be called tradition, which of course involves prayer, study and service — which was her life for many years.[6] We are taught by this that we have great need of the traditional forms which are never accidental. In other words, we must adhere to orthodoxy — which as the Catholic Encyclopedia defines as "true doctrine and sound faith." Lastly we have Christ teaching in the temple, being about His Father's business. We are of course the temple of the Holy Spirit — actually of the Trinity, and indeed, if we but listen, it is Christ who teaches us in the temple of our hearts.

Next we come to the sorrowful mysteries. It may seem a long call to relate this to the illuminative aspect of the spiritual life. However, it is only with purification that the divine light can flow into us. We must crucify in us all that is inimical to Christ. The agony in the garden becomes for us an example in all our sufferings. And, like Christ, we can ask God to remove our anguish and pain — while adding of course, if it be Thy will. What follows is what the soul itself must undergo — all the humiliations and scourges that life so abundantly provides, the willing acceptance and carrying of the Cross — and with a smile reflecting acceptance; and ultimately the Crucifixion — for all that is in us that is not of God must be Crucified so that Christ may live in us.

Finally, the glorious mysteries. We have been Baptized in Christ, Crucified in Christ, and thus will be Resurrected in Christ. The soul then not only is Resurrected in Christ, but ascends to Heaven with Him. The soul is inundated with the Holy Spirit and truly becomes the Bride of Christ — for as St. Bernard says, the Blessed Virgin and the purified soul is the daughter, bride and mother of Christ. It is in this condition that the Blessed Virgin and soul is crowned by Christ in Heaven.

And there is still more! The Rosary also allows us to at the same time invoke the Holy Name of Mary, for this also is a "sacred Name." As St. Ambrose said: "Your name, O Mary, is a precious ointment, which breathes forth the odor of Divine grace. Let this ointment of salvation enter the inmost recesses of our souls." St. Peter Canisius says: "After the most holy and adorable Name of Jesus there is no name more glorious and more powerful than the Name of Mary. At the mention of this Name, the angels rejoice and the devils tremble. Through the invocation of this Name sinners obtain grace and pardon." Again, St. Bernard tells us: "O great, O gentle, O most lovable Mary, thy Holy Name cannot be spoken without inflaming the heart. To those who love Thee, it is unspeakable consolation and joy even to think of Thee; Thou art a sweet memory to those who honor Thee." The Blessed Henry Suso stated: "When I pronounce the name of Mary, I feel myself inflamed with such love and joy, that between tears and happiness with which I pronounce this beautiful name, I feel as though my heart might leave my breast. For this sweet name is like a honeycomb dissolving in the innermost recesses of my soul." No wonder then that St. Ephrem of Syria proclaimed that "The Name of Mary is the key to the gates of heaven." There are saints who have invoked the Name of Mary in isolation, much in the same manner as the Name of Jesus is invoked, thus as it were embracing the gentle "Marial" virtues rather than the adamantine "Christic virtues" though ultimately, of course, they are one and the same.

Every *Ave* carries with it the desire that, in so far as we join ourselves to Our Lady, Christ will be born in us. Thus it is that some have continuously recited just this prayer without the support of the beads.

We have, then, presented the commonest — but not the only — and for many, the most efficacious form of the *Hesychaste* prayer in the Western Church. We have also stressed the importance of doing this within a proper framework, which framework is given us by Our Lady, and by our Holy Mother the Church. It is not just a matter of repeating the Names of Jesus and Mary, though even this can be of great benefit as long as it is done with a modicum of love and respect. But for this method of prayer to be truly efficacious, it is important that it be done in the proper setting, namely within a traditional orthodox framework, and above all with an understanding of the role of the Blessed Mother. It is this which allows the divine seed to fall on fertile soil and not on stony ground. In the Eastern Church the saying of the Rosary is called *Metanoia*, which literally means the changing of one's mind. It is thus that among her many titles, Our Lady is referred to as "the Gate of Heaven," and "the Mediatrix of all graces."

Let us conclude with the prayer of St. Ambrose: "Let the soul of Mary be in each of us to magnify the Lord; Let the spirit of Mary be in each of us to exalt in God."

NOTES

1. From the introduction to Volume 1 of the translation of the *Philokalia*, as translated by Palmer, Sherrard and Kallistos Ware.

2. The recognition of our own sinfulness is fully present in the second part of the *Ave Maria*, "Holy Mary, Mother of God, pray for us sinners now and at the hour of our death, Amen."

3. There have been many different rosaries in the Church. Often called "chaplets," and linked to various saints — such as that of St. Michael — and many of these are still in use today. Cf. *The Rose-garden Game* by Eithne Wilkins. London, Victor Gollancz, 1969. It is pertinent that in Ceylon the word for *Rosary* among the Catholic community is *japamala*, or the garland of the Name.

4. St. Thomas says, "On the part of the child there is but one filiation in reality, although there be two in aspect. (*Summa* III. 35.5 ad 3.)

5. C. de B. Evans, *Meister Eckhart*, Franz Pfeiffer's edition, London, 1947, Vol. II, page 143.

6. Jean Borella, "The Secret of the Christian Way," *SUNI* 2001, page 80.

7. The *Magnificat* tells us later that God *dispersit superbos mente cordis sui*, that God has scattered the proud whose hearts are full of personal thoughts and opinions — a far cry from the heart that exalts in God.

8. Jean Borella, *op. cit.*, page 165.

9. Margaret of Cortona (thirteenth century) had lived in great luxury with a wealthy man, without benefit of marriage, and borne him a son. After his death, she radically changed her manner of life.

10. Marco Pallis, *A Buddhist Spectrum*. New York: Seabury Press, 1981.

11. The quotation marks are taken from William of St. Thierry's *The Golden Epistle*, but the relationship is commonly accepted by theologians of that era.

12. Translation of Christopher Bamford in *The Voice of the Eagle*, Lindisfarne Press, 1992.

13. Sister Emma T. Healy, *Woman According to St. Bonaventure*. Erie, Pennsylvania: Sisters of St. Joseph, 1956.

14. With very young children, one can reduce this to saying only "*Ave Maria.*"

15. Adapted in part from F. Schuon's chapter on *Meditation L'Oeil du Coeur*, Gallimard, Paris, 1950.

16. Those who state that the Church discouraged the education of women should be aware that such is more than false — not only on historical grounds, but also because the greatest model of womanhood was most highly educated.

Eleventh century mosaics in Constantinople.

CONTRIBUTORS

- *Bishop Kallistos Ware* (born Timothy Ware) was educated at Westminster School and Magdalen College, Oxford. He joined the Orthodox Church in 1958 and traveled widely in Greece, staying in particular at the monastery of St. John, Patmos, and he is familiar with the life of other Orthodox centers such as Mount Athos and Jerusalem. In 1966 he was ordained a priest and became a monk, receiving the new name Kallistos. Since 1966 he has been at Oxford University as Spalding Lecturer in Eastern Orthodox Studies; he also has pastoral charge of the Greek parish in Oxford. In 1970 he became a Fellow of Pembroke College, Oxford. In 1982 he was consecrated titular Bishop of Diokleia and appointed assistant bishop in the Orthodox Archdiocese of Thyateira and Great Britain (under the Ecumenical Patriarchate).

- *James S. Cutsinger*, PhD from Harvard University, is a professor of theology and religious thought at the University of South Carolina and secretary for the Foundation of Traditional Studies. His publications include *The Form of Transformed Vision: Coleridge and the Knowledge of God* (1987), *Advice to the Serious Seeker: Meditations on the Teaching of Frithjof Schuon* (1997), and a forthcoming collection of Christian spiritual writings, *Not of This World: A Treasury of Christian Mysticism*.

- *Gray Henry*, director of Fons Vitae and the Quinta Essentia Publishing Houses, lectures in world religions and art history, is a member of the *Parabola* Editorial Board and is the author of several works including *Beads of Faith*. At present she is completing a doctoral dissertation on the final unpublished essays of Ananda K. Coomaraswamy, *Guardians of the Sun-Door* (currently in production for upcoming publication).

- *Canon A.M. Allchin* is Honorary President of the Thomas Merton Society of Great Britain and Ireland. A friend and correspondent of Merton, he is author of several essays on Merton. Canon Allchin is an honorary professor in the Department of Religious Studies at the University of Wales, Bangor. He has published extensively in the field of Celtic spirituality and theology, and lectures in his field all over the world. He was the residentiary canon at Canterbury Cathedral and director of the Centre for Spirituality in Oxford.

- *Abbot John Etudes Bamburger* was Abbot of the Abbey of the Genesee for some thirty years. He lived as of a hermit at the monastery while continuing to teach and work in the community. In 2001, he was appointed temporary superior of Our Lady of the Philippines.

- *M. Basil Pennington* entered the Cistercian Trappists in 1951 and was consecrated as a monk in 1956. After ordination he spent several years studying in Rome, and he assisted at the Second Vatican Council. Pennington is a spiritual father, retreat master, lecturer and author of many books, including *Centering Prayer*, *Vatican II* and *Awake in the Spirit*. His permanent residence is at St. Joseph's Monastery in Spencer, Massachusetts.

- *Patrick F. O'Connell* holds doctoral degrees in both Theology and English Literature. He is on the faculty of Gannon University in Erie, Pennsylvania and has written extensively on Thomas Merton and on Henry David Thoreau. He is a past president of the International Thomas Merton Society and is the Editor of *The Merton Seasonal Quarterly*, and has most recently edited *The Thomas Merton Encyclopedia* with William H. Shannon and Christine M. Bochen.

- *The Most Reverend Archbishop Rowan Williams*, born in 1950 to a Welsh-speaking family, was educated at Christ's College, Cambridge, where he studied Theology. After research in Oxford on Russian Christianity, he spent two years at Mirfield before returning to Cambridge in 1977, where he spent nine years in academic and parochial work. He and Jane Paul were married in 1981, and have two children. From 1986 to 1992, Rowan Williams was Professor of Theology at Oxford. Author of many books on the history of theology and spirituality, Archbishop Williams has published collections of articles and sermons – as well as two books of poetry. He was nominated as Archbishop of Canterbury on July 23, 2002.

- *Jonathan Montaldo* edited Volume Two of Thomas Merton's private journals, published as *Entering the Silence* and edited as *The Intimate Merton* with Brother Patrick Hart. He most recently published his edition of Merton's prayers and drawings, *Dialogues with Silence*. He is the former Director of the Thomas Merton Center at Bellarmine University and is the President of the International Thomas Merton Society for

2001 - 2003. He serves with Gray Henry as a General Editor for the Fons Vitae Thomas Merton Series.

- *Jim Forest* of Holland wrote *The Ladder of the Beatitudes, Praying with Icons, Living With Wisdom* (a biography of Thomas Merton) and *Love is the Measure* (a biography of Dorothy Day). In connection with work on two books about Russian religious life (*Pilgrim to the Russian Church* and *Religion in the New Russia*), Jim traveled widely throughout the former U.S.S.R. — an experience which deepened his long-standing interest in Orthodox Christianity. He is now secretary of the Orthodox Peace Fellowship and edits its publication, *In Communion*.

- *Susan McCaslin* is a poet and Instructor of English at Douglas College in Coquitlam, British Columbia. She is the author of nine volumes of poetry, scholarly articles on Thomas Merton as well as other twentieth-century poets, and editor of two Canadian anthologies of spiritual verse — the most recent of which is *Poetry and Spiritual Practice: Selections from Contemporary Canadian Poets* (The St. Thomas Poetry Series, 2002). Susan lives in Port Moody, British Columbia with her husband and daughter.

- *Bernadette Dieker* is Senior Editor at Fons Vitae Publishing and serves on their Advisory Board. She transcribed and introduced Thomas Merton's lectures on Sufism for *Merton & Sufism: The Untold Story* (Fons Vitae, 2000). With Brother Paul Quenon, O.S.C.O., she edited *Monkscript: Literature, Arts & Spirituality* (Fons Vitae, 2003).

- *Dr. Rama Coomaraswamy* received his early education in India in an orthodox Hindu setting; later, he obtained his Oxford Matriculation and went on to attend Harvard University, graduating from medical school in 1959. After some thirty years as a thoracic and cardiovascular surgeon, Assistant Professor of Surgery at Albert Einstein College of Medicine and Chief of Thoracic and Cardiovascular Surgery at Stamford Hospital, he retired from the practice of surgery and retrained in psychiatry, holding an Assistant Professorship at Albert Einstein College of Medicine. For five years he was Professor of Ecclesiastical History at the St. Thomas Aquinas (Lefebrist) Seminary. Married for fifty years, he was ordained in 1987 by the traditional rites of the Roman Catholic Church. Dr. Coomaraswamy has published extensively in the fields of both medicine and theology, including *Invocation of the Name of Jesus as Practiced in the Western Church* (Fons Vitae, 2000). At present he teaches and maintains a small practice in psychiatry, mainly dealing with problems involving the interface between religion and psychiatry.

The Virgin with Child, ninth century mosaic, in Hagia Sophia.

ACKNOWLEDGMENTS

The editors thank the following persons for their assistance in the preparation of this volume:

- The Contributors, for their generous gifts of time and scholarship to both the Merton and Hesychasm Conference, held March 2002, and to this collection.

- Garrett Graddy, for her thoughtful reflections and advice through the editing process.

- Robert Toth, Director of the Thomas Merton Foundation, and Terry Taylor, his assistant, for organizing the Merton and Hesychasm Conference.

- Gene March, Presbyterian Theological Seminary, for hosting the Merton and Hesychasm Conference.

- Paul Pearson, Director of the Thomas Merton Center at Bellarmine University and Barbara Quigley, his assistant archivist, for assisting with research of the archives.

- Michael Wimsatt and Jennifer Komis of Bellarmine University, who created digital files of archived Merton materials.

- Lourdes Halliday and Rebecca Renzi, for their production work on this manuscript.

- Mark Perry, for his translation from the French of passages by Rowan Williams.

- Mary Hampson Minifie, for her beautifully painted icon of the Archangel Michael.

Additional credits:

- Unpublished material from the collection in the Thomas Merton Center at Bellarmine University in Louisville, Kentucky is included here with the permission of the Trustees of the Merton Legacy Trust. This includes Merton's correspondence with Boris Pasternak, as well as quotes from Merton's reading notebooks and the transcriptions of his lectures to the novices about Hesychasm and the Russian Church.

- Books and articles quoted or cited in the text under the usual fair use allowances are acknowledged with full publication credits in the footnotes of each chapter.
- Longer excerpts from previously published Merton books are reprinted by permission of the following institutions:
  1. "Hagia Sophia" by Thomas Merton, from *The Collected Poems of Thomas Merton*, copyright ©1963 by The Abbey of Gethsemani, Inc. Reprinted by permission of New Directions Publishing Corp.
  2. "The Wisdom of the Desert [Introduction] by Thomas Merton, from *The Wisdom of the Desert*, copyright ©1960 by The Abbey of Gethsemani, Inc. Reprinted by permission of New Directions Publishing Corp.
  3. Permission for reprinting the Preface of Thomas Merton's *The Wisdom of the Desert* (pages 3-24) and "Hagia Sophia," *The Collected Poems of Thomas Merton* (pages 363-371), granted by Pollinger Limited.

In addition, the following chapters originally appeared in some other form:

- Bishop Kallistos Ware's "Silence in Prayer: The Meaning of Hesychia" first appeared in *Cistercian Studies* Number 29, 1976: *One Yet Two: Monastic Tradition East and West*. It is reprinted by permission of Cistercian Publications and by the author.
- Bishop Kallistos Ware's interview, "Image and Likeness," first appeared in *Parabola: The Magazine of Myth and Tradition*, Volume X, No. 1 (Spring 1985).
- Bishop Kallistos Ware's "The Power of the Name: The Jesus Prayer in Orthodox Spirituality" is a pamphlet first published by SLG Press, Convent of the Incarnation, Fairacres, Oxford, 1999. ©1974 The Sisters of the Love of God, reprinted with the permission of SLG Press and the author.
- Donald Allchin's "The Worship of the Whole Creation: Merton and the Eastern Fathers" first appeared in *The Merton Annual*, Volume 5, 1992. "Our Lives, A Powerful Pentecost:

Merton's Meetings with Russian Christianity" first appeared in *The Merton Annual*, Volume 11, 1998. These essays are reprinted with permission by Victor A. Kramer, Emory University, and the by author.

- A.M. Donald Allchin's "Monastic Life and the Unity of Christ" first appeared in *Cistercian Studies* Number 29, 1976: *One Yet Two: Monastic Tradition East and West*. It is reprinted by permission of Cistercian Publications and by the author.

- John Eudes Bamberger's "Thomas Merton and the Christian East" first appeared in Cistercian Studies Number 29, 1976: *One Yet Two: Monastic Tradition East and West*. It is reprinted by permission of Cistercian Publications and by the author.

- M. Basil Pennington's "Thomas Merton and Byzantine Spirituality" first appeared in Cistercian Studies Number 103, 1988: *Toward An Integrated Humanity: Thomas Merton's Journey*. It is reprinted by permission of Cistercian Publications and by the author.

- "Hesychasm" and "Heart," by William H. Shannon, Christine M. Bochen and Patrick F. O' Connell, from *The Thomas Merton Encyclopedia*. Mary Knoll, NY: Orbis Books, 2002.

- Rowan Williams' "Bread in the Wilderness: The Monastic Ideal in Thomas Merton and Paul Evdokimov" first appeared in *Cistercian Studies* Number 29, 1976: *One Yet Two: Monastic Tradition East and West*. It is reprinted by permission of Cistercian Publications and by the author.

- Thomas Merton's "Introduction to The Climate of Monastic Prayer" was published by Cistercian Publications in *Cistercian Studies* Number 1, 1973: "The Climate of Monastic Prayer." It is reprinted by permission of Cistercian Publications.

- Thomas Merton's "The Spiritual Father in the Desert Tradition" first appeared as Chapter IV of his book *Contemplation in a World of Action*, published by Doubleday & Company, Inc. in 1971. Permission for reprinting is given by the Merton Legacy Trust.

Archangel Michael, who combats evil in this world. American, twentieth century.

DEDICATION

In Honor of:

Martin Lings
Read and Virginia Henry
Sophia Maria Majzub
Haajar and Justin Majzub
Mustafa Gouverneur-Henry
Kingsley Van Nagell
Neville Blakemore
Ming Dick
Benjamin Worth Bingham Miller
Eleanor Bingham Miller
Eleanor Hannah Miller
Rowland Antoine Dumesnil Miller
Rowland Dumesnil Miller
Jonathan and Mary Hampson Minifie

"It is simply opening yourself to receive. The presence of God is like walking out of a door into the fresh air. You don't concentrate on the fresh air, you breathe it. And you don't concentrate on the sunlight, you just enjoy it. It is all around."

— From a lecture by Thomas Merton,
to the monks at Gethsemani

Mosaic of Jesus Christ with the soul of his mother.
Chora Monastery, Istanbul, 1315 - 21 C.E.